Advance Acclaim for

Investing in Retail Properties

"This book, which I wholeheartedly recommend, should be 'required reading' for every entrepreneur, developer, investor or finance professional in commercial real estate. In an agile, educational and entertaining style, the author takes us by the hand through all stages of investment in a commercial real estate business, applying the best industry practices. Without false modesty, he makes us partakers of an exemplary business life, built on solid ethical, moral and professional principles."

—Mario Castro F., SCSM, SCMD, SCDP, SCLS
President, Shopping Centers Solutions & Management, SCSM, S.A.
Caracas, Venezuela

"If you want to learn about structuring partnerships for shopping centers, this very personal approach from a 25-year professional in shopping center development is a must-read. I love the more conversational style of writing here rather than a more analytical style. It makes the subject more readable; the author more human in his approach."

—James E. Maurin, SCSM
Chairman, Stirling Properties LLC
Covington, Louisiana, USA

"The author brings an enthusiasm to retail development that comes across in his book."

—Robert G. Gottlieb, Esq.
Partner, Venable LLP
Washington, District of Columbia, USA

"The author has spelled out all of the highlights that a new syndicator-type owner needs to know to get started . . . a great handbook with almost all the answers."

—Norman M. Kranzdorf
Senior Vice President, Urdang Capital Management, Inc.
Plymouth Meeting, Pennsylvania, USA

"It's a soup-to-nuts analysis of the what, why, when and how process, with terrific examples along the way of what has worked as well as what has not. The closing four case studies provide 'in the trenches' actual experiences that are hard to beat . . . a wonderful cross section of selected projects, all representative of our mainline industry. Congratulations to the author on writing such an insightful (and personal) book."

—Gordon T. Greeby Jr., SCDP, PE
President, The Greeby Companies, Inc.
Lake Bluff, Illinois, USA

"It is a very good book . . . a legacy to our industry."

—Marcelo Carvalho, SCSM, SCMD
Co-President, Ancar Ivanhoe Shopping Centers
Rio de Janeiro, Brazil

To my dad, who taught me to care for my fellow man
as I would want my fellow man to care for me.

INVESTING IN RETAIL PROPERTIES

A Guide to Structuring Partnerships for Sharing Capital Appreciation and Cash Flow

INVESTING IN RETAIL PROPERTIES

A Guide to Structuring Partnerships for Sharing Capital Appreciation and Cash Flow

Gary D. Rappaport

SCSM, SCMD, SCLS, SCDP

International Council of Shopping Centers
New York

About the International Council of Shopping Centers

The International Council of Shopping Centers (ICSC) is the trade association of the shopping center industry. Serving the industry since 1957, ICSC is a not-for-profit organization with more than 55,000 members in 100 countries worldwide. ICSC members include shopping center

- owners
- developers
- managers
- marketing specialists
- leasing agents

- retailers
- researchers
- attorneys
- academics
- public officials

- architects
- contractors
- consultants
- investors
- lenders and brokers

ICSC holds nearly 300 meetings, conferences and educational events a year and provides a wide array of services and products for shopping center professionals, including publications and research data.

For more information about ICSC, please contact:

International Council of Shopping Centers
1221 Avenue of the Americas
New York, NY 10020–1099
Telephone +1 646 728 3800
info@icsc.org (for general ICSC information)
publications@icsc.org (for information about ICSC publications)
Fax: +1 732 694 1755
www.icsc.org

> This publication is designed to provide accurate and authoritative information in regard to the subject matter covered. It is sold with the understanding that the publisher is not engaged in rendering legal, accounting or other professional services. If legal advice or other expert assistance is required, the services of a competent professional person should be sought.
> —From a Declaration of Principles jointly adopted by a Committee of the American Bar Association and a Committee of Publishers

Companies, professional groups, clubs and other organizations may qualify for special terms when ordering quantities of more than 20 of this title.

Published by
International Council of Shopping Centers
1221 Avenue of the Americas
New York, NY 10020–1099

ICSC Catalog Number: 264

International Standard Book Number: 978-1-58268-093-4

SUSTAINABLE FORESTRY INITIATIVE
Certified Fiber Sourcing
www.sfiprogram.org

Cover: Photo illustration of Gary D. Rappaport at Central Park Marketplace, a 215,500-square-foot shopping center owned by institutional investor ING Real Estate and managed by The Rappaport Companies. The Fredericksburg, Virginia, project is part of the 2.5-million-square-foot Central Park Power Center, in which Mr. Rappaport also personally owns 700,000 square feet, and is located at the entrance of Celebrate Virginia, a massive mixed-use development that includes the Fredericksburg Expo Center, three hotels, 3 million square feet of office space and residential units under development.

Cover design by Design Plus
Book design by SD Designs

Contents

Preface

I LOVE RETAIL REAL ESTATE. To me, the retail sector is much more exciting than office, residential, hotel or industrial, because retail is so fast-moving, so entrepreneurial, so innovative, and constantly reinventing itself, and because every tenant's success is attributable to synergies it shares with the other tenants within the shopping center.

Most of us patronize retail businesses as we grow up, so we relate to retail by instinct. Growing up in the New York metropolitan area, I was exposed to both urban street retail and suburban shopping in stores located in shopping centers, the latter being the most prevalent form of retail in the United States today. My family moved out to West Hempstead in suburban Long Island (Nassau County, New York) from the very densely populated New York City borough of Brooklyn when I was only two years old.

My mother, Phyllis Rappaport, would take me shopping for clothes in Hempstead, New York, at Abraham and Straus (A&S), a full-line department store that has been out of business for many years. Hempstead was then the marketplace for the eastern outlying rural farming communities as well as for suburban living as New Yorkers moved out of Manhattan and nearby urban boroughs into Nassau County.

There was so much retail activity surrounding my childhood that the Hempstead A&S store had the highest volume of any suburban department store in the country during the late 1960s as I was transforming into a fashion-conscious teenager shopping for button-down-collar Gant shirts and hand-stitched Weejuns penny loafers.

The Hempstead Village became Nassau's retail mecca during my childhood. Yet, during my years at West Hempstead High School, I do not remember ever thinking of hanging out at strip malls with ample parking lots and I infrequently visited the sprawling Roosevelt Field shopping mall, then open-air and anchored by archrivals Macy's and Gimbels, which was less than 5 miles from my home. Like most other kids growing up in the early 1960s, I never thought about what I wanted to do professionally. When I was not attending school, I played football, baseball and basketball. I visited the Malverne Theatre (now the multiplex Malverne Cinema) for double-feature movies during Saturday matinees and watched TV at home, things all baby boomer kids used to do.

Oddly enough, I would get up very early on Saturday mornings to watch *The Modern Farmer* on the ABC television network. It was a show mostly about tractors, milking machines, strip-till rigs and a life of farming in the Midwest. I was fascinated by the large machinery harvesting the different crops, something now alien to my career as a shopping center developer.

I also watched TV shows about baby boomer family influences such as *Leave It to Beaver*, *Father Knows Best* and *The Donna Reed Show*. The fatherly figures who dominated these shows reminded me of my own father. Jeff Stone, one of the boyhood characters in *The Donna Reed Show*, played by Paul Petersen, even recorded a 1962 hit single called "My Dad" for an episode of the show, dedicating it to his costar Carl Betz, who portrayed Dr. Alex Stone, the boy's father in the series. To this day, I think of my father and how he influenced me when I hear Petersen's recording, singing, "My dad, now here is a man. To me he is everything strong. No, he can't do wrong, my dad."

My father, Mannie Rappaport, was a neckwear manufacturer who, in running his business with his older brother, purchased fabric, designed patterns, colored every design, oversaw production and then sold the finished product, the ties, to retailers. My uncle oversaw the production of the shirts and sweaters they also manufactured. My father's first love was his family—my mom, my three sisters and me—but his second love was his business in the budding New York garment district of the 20th century.

Dad was an honest man who would never take advantage of any situation that could hurt another person. He was optimistic and good-natured. Dad believed that in his life, the glass was always half full rather than half empty.

He felt very fortunate, even though he grew up quite poor living in New York, first in the Bronx and then in Brooklyn.

My dad started working in 1936 when he was 15 years old, every day after school and then full-time when he graduated from high school. While attending high school my father sold ice cream on the beach at Coney Island and then would share his wages with his mother and father to help his family make ends meet. He could talk to anyone from any socio-economic level and make the person feel comfortable in their conversation. I learned from Dad about these important American values and how he applied them to his business.

By the time I attended high school, my father ran a business on the sixth floor of an old building in the Queens borough of New York where row after row of middle-aged and older Jewish men used cutting and sewing machines to make thin neckties from brightly colored fabrics. He would walk me around the floor teaching me the garment business, talking about how fortunate he was, and how he felt responsible in a way for all the people who worked for him. He taught me that they too were part of his family. These people depended on him for a living, and he depended on retailers to purchase his ties to sell to the general public.

Working with my father as a teenager, I learned about fabrics, fashion design, manufacturing and selling—necessities to operate a successful business. My education took me on the road, and I remember traveling with a salesman during one of my summer school breaks selling my father's ties wholesale to small independent retail clothing stores located in various small towns in the Midwest.

Retail was exciting to me, but it was real estate where I felt I could build substantial assets and personal net worth over my career. Retail real estate was a natural melding of both retailing *and* real estate.

Early in my career, from 1973 to 1981, I became a residential single-family homebuilder. My company was called Par Construction, and with a partner, I built a few hundred homes in the Washington, D.C., metropolitan area.

When I decided to transition into retail real estate, I worked for several years for a shopping center company where I was able to learn property management, leasing, construction, finance and marketing. More importantly, however, I learned how one could create substantial value/net worth in new construction as well as acquisition, renovation, remerchandising and re-leasing of existing retail properties.

Throughout this book, I will often refer to *my model* and *my goals*. While my model and my goals have changed often throughout my career, there is always a *model* and there are always *goals*. In fact, I always have an annual goal, a five-year goal and an end-of-career goal.

I believe this discipline has given me the structure to survive and prosper as an entrepreneur in good and bad times in this very risky but very lucrative business of retail real estate.

While I enjoyed designing, building and selling homes, I shifted course from residential development to commercial ownership because I felt that there was tremendous value to be created by the long-term ownership of real estate, as opposed to the building and selling of residential single-family properties. Commercial real estate gave me the opportunity to own property for the long term and create value with the real estate I owned while continuing to add to my portfolio by building or buying additional properties. I have never yet sold a property and do not expect that I will sell many, if any, in my lifetime. My model is surely not the only proven method of success for the entrepreneurial real estate developer. I even admit it is a very risky model.

Some of my retail real estate developer friends are known as *merchant builders.* They have been very successful simply building and flipping. They find a property—whether a new development or existing—they purchase the property, create added value, sell the property, divide the added value between their partners/investors and themselves, take part of the proceeds to live on and invest the rest in the next opportunity that comes along. There is nothing wrong with that model as long as it works for them. But it is not for me.

My model is much riskier. In my model, I also find a property—an opportunity—in the same way the merchant builder does. I create value for my partners/investors and for myself as well, but I do not sell.

While I might have some initial cash flow from the investment, which is expected to increase over the years, the creation of significant value cannot be leveraged unless the investment property is sold or borrowed against.

That is exactly what I have done repeatedly—borrowed against this illiquid value that I have created—most often with great success but sometimes

Here at the Sully Station Shopping Center groundbreaking in 1986 with James Wheeler, vice president of leasing (now deceased), and Kristin Bidstrup, then office manager and now director of executive offices for The Rappaport Companies. Sully Station, which opened in 1988, was the second shopping center I built from the ground up. It is no longer part of my portfolio. I had signed a personal guarantee for the loan with First American Bank of Virginia, and the lender foreclosed during the real estate down cycle of 1990–1991. That financial crisis did not spare the banking industry either. The lender, which was then part of First American Metro Corp., was acquired by First Union National Bank in 1993, and First Union later merged with Wachovia (now part of Wells Fargo Bank).

with regrettable failure. I typically borrow against the value I have created using my personal guarantee. Not to be taken lightly, a personal guarantee is a promise I make to use my own money to repay the shopping center's debt in the event it defaults on the mortgage loan.

My personal guarantee assures the bank that I will vouch to repay the property's debt even if unforeseen events, such as the bankruptcy of a major tenant, prevent the property ownership from making the loan payment. In that event, I am fully aware that if I were unable to cover the debt personally, the bank would seize my personal assets. In my early years as well as now, I have taken that risk on behalf of my investor group, and while that is never comforting to members of my family, they recognize and support me in the risk and stress I live with under this model.

I started my company, The Rappaport Companies, on May 31, 1984, in shared office suites with one small office, and I paid the office suite management for administrative help as needed by the quarter hour.

I bought my first shopping center also in 1984 with 14 partners. The 15 of us each invested $35,000. Then undercapitalized, I had to borrow part of my $35,000 investment from a friend. Today, after 25 years, while some of the original partners are no longer involved, many of them are still partners. Every time I visit this shopping center, and each time I have an opportunity to speak to one of the original investors, I feel very proud of what I have accomplished for all of us.

Today, I am president, chief executive officer and 100 percent owner of The Rappaport Companies (TRC). TRC, which is based in the Washington, D.C., metropolitan area, receives fees such as management fees; leasing commissions; construction management fees; and sometimes acquisition, refinancing or disposition fees from all of the shopping center partnerships we oversee, whether they are shopping centers I have an ownership interest in or simply manage for others.

We advertise ourselves as a full-service retail company—offering all or any part of our services where needed. About 20 years ago, our company had 40 employees, but we had to downsize to 25 due to an economic downturn. It concerned me deeply to have to let go of good people when there was no job otherwise available for them. This led me to change my model so that in addition to development and acquisition, I was determined to offer services to other shopping center owners, high-rise office and residential owners who operated retail on the first level and retail tenants who needed our services for leasing and representation.

This fee-based business is unquestionably not where I have created substantial net worth, but it has allowed me to sustain my organization during difficult economic times such as the 2008–2010 financial crisis, when there was very little, if any, development, and certainly no large construction management and leasing fees to be earned.

In addition to bringing stability to survive weak economic periods, this multiservices model conveys credibility with all stakeholders for building long-term successful properties, capital preservation and value appreciation. Besides, why pay other companies to do what we have the expertise to do for ourselves?

This business model has enabled my company to grow and has provided comfort for the employees who decide to devote their careers to TRC. It has provided them assurance that there is a good chance the company—and their jobs—will be secure in bad times as well as in good times.

Today, The Rappaport Companies' portfolio includes more than 50 shopping centers and ground-floor retail in some 100 mixed-use properties, both residential and office, located primarily throughout the mid-Atlantic region. Of this roughly 13 million square feet, I have an ownership interest in slightly less than 4 million square feet.

For more than a decade, I have been teaching a course on real estate partnerships for the International Council of Shopping Centers (ICSC) at its University of Shopping Centers held annually at the Wharton School of the University of Pennsylvania in Philadelphia.

This course helps me share my experiences in shopping center development with many students who are already professionals and who either want to sharpen their skills in shopping center ownership and development or are working for others and have a dream of someday starting their own business in this field.

In this class, I talk about structuring partnerships, but quite honestly, I talk about my life. I talk about my experiences. I talk about the great risks I have taken over the past 25 years as an entrepreneurial developer.

I discuss the successful projects and my unsuccessful projects. I tell

Here teaching the ICSC Executive Learning Series course at my company's headquarters in McLean, Virginia, in January 2010.

PHOTO: R. E. MILIAN

them about the stress that comes with real estate ownership and the highs and the lows. I explain that my model is not a model for everyone. Finding that right place is different for each person, and if what I do every day is what you want to do, then anything I can do to help you reach your goals becomes my goal.

At the time of this writing, our industry has been experiencing difficult times. However, it was not that much different 20 years before and similarly, 30 years before, when we experienced downturns and bad cycles in real estate ownership. Actually I started my business during similarly difficult conditions in the early 1970s. Therefore, I have been through three down cycles, and in some ways, the 2008–2010 real estate crisis is a good time because this time, I believe, I am best prepared to be an opportunistic buyer for some of these troubled assets.

These are called "distressed assets" because compared to the time when these properties were financed, the rents are now lower, the vacancies are higher and the cap rates are higher; thus, the property values used to determine loan-to-value (LTV) ratios during financing are now lower, making LTVs out of whack.

Many of the properties—even if their owners are able to afford the monthly debt service—have been assigned appraised values lower than the debt, an unsatisfactory situation to the lender and banking regulators. These *distressed owners* have to decide if it is prudent to invest additional funds to lease vacant space in order to re-create value greater than the debt or put in additional equity to satisfy the lender's LTV requirements upon loan maturity.

The most distressed properties are the ones where cash flow is insufficient to service the monthly mortgage payments. These are the properties that are truly distressed, where often the lender cannot re-create the value in a foreclosure scenario. These are the types of properties that the lender seeks to take back to sell below the present debt amount to a new purchaser, if feasible.

I was a *distressed owner* 30 years ago, and I was a *distressed owner* 20 years ago. In the real estate downturn of 2008–2010, I expect to be an *opportunity buyer* when these properties are resold by the lenders during the early years of the 2010s.

In teaching for many years, I recognize how many of my students have a very strong desire to own real estate and to own their real estate companies but just do not know where to start. The focus of this book is to teach young entrepreneurs how to structure partnerships in creating their own development and operating real estate companies. Based on the added risks the managing partner incurs in structuring and overseeing the partnership, I am teaching my students how cash flow and appreciation are shared between the managing partner and the other investors.

Many of the principles and fundamentals of successful retail real estate that I am outlining in this book work for all types of income-producing real estate, not just for shopping centers. Whether you are interested in being a successful real estate entrepreneur or learning more about real estate investing, I hope this book will help you to understand the partnership structure, and how you can evaluate risk and create added value in a property so that both the managing partner and the investment partners can be fairly compensated.

It's that simple. To be successful in the risky business of retail real estate you have to be able to add value. That takes perseverance, time, skills and investment capital. However, do not discount the qualities of good, successful businesses that fall outside strategies, tactics and the fundamentals of the business. They stem back to what my dad taught me when I was still a teenager: to be a good businessman, you must first—absolutely first—be a good person.

If you strive to run your business in an honest, fair and trustworthy fashion, people will tend to do business with you rather than with a company that does not exude these qualities. That goes for partners, tenants, vendors, customers and employees. It is called *business ethics* and relates to distinguishing between what is right and wrong in your business dealings, and always doing what is right—never compromising your standards for short-term benefits.

This principle is ingrained in the content of my character, and I have my father to thank for it. My dad passed away on March 6, 2006, and I think of him every day.

My business has grown bigger than any enterprise my father ever dreamed of building. But it is the values he handed down to me, coupled with my formal and continuing education that I attribute to the success of my career.

I still strive to live my life as my father did, with the same priorities, the same caring and the same giving to others. My glass is also always at least half full and I am grateful that my father showed me the happiness of what life can be for all of us if we are fortunate enough to appreciate and practice these values. This is the reason I dedicated this book to Mannie Rappaport, my dad.

Here with my dad, Mannie Rappaport (b. February 22, 1921–d. March 6, 2006), a manufacturer of neckties who taught me the principles of being a successful businessman.

Acknowledgments

WITH APPRECIATION AND GRATITUDE to my wife, Daphne, for her patience as I wrote and rewrote this book sitting at home on the family-room sofa as well as sitting in bed after the kids went to sleep. I also wish to acknowledge ICSC's Rudy Milian, who convinced me to write this book and acted as executive editor, continually pushing me and never allowing me to stop, and also Saira Ali, who under my direction prepared all of the financial reports I used in this book and in all the classes I taught over the years, which helped prepare me to write this book and tell my story. Special mentions go to Robert Gottlieb of Venable LLP, my attorney, whom I speak to several times a day and who helped me organize my thoughts, to Sam Lehrman, my good friend and partner who showed me compassion and understanding, and to Geoff Smith, managing director of NATIXIS Real Estate Capital Inc., for his continued support and encouragement.

ICSC and the author of this book express appreciation to the following professionals for reviewing this work and making suggestions or comments:

Marcelo Carvalho, SCSM, SCMD
Co-President
Ancar Ivanhoe Shopping Centers
Rio de Janeiro, Brazil

Robert G. Gottlieb, Esq.
Partner
Venable LLP
Washington, District of Columbia, USA

Mario Castro F., SCSM, SCMD, SCDP, SCLS
President
Shopping Centers Solutions & Management, SCSM, S.A.
Caracas, Venezuela

Nicholas R. Guild
Portfolio Management Senior Associate
The Rappaport Companies
McLean, Virginia, USA

Gordon T. Greeby Jr., SCDP, PE
President
The Greeby Companies, Inc.
Lake Bluff, Illinois, USA

Norman M. Kranzdorf
Senior Vice President
Urdang Capital Management, Inc.
Plymouth Meeting, Pennsylvania, USA

James E. Maurin, SCSM
Chairman
Stirling Properties LLC
Covington, Louisiana, USA

Rudolph E. Milian, SCMD, SCSM
Senior Staff Vice President
International Council of Shopping Centers
New York, New York, USA

Marlon D. Pilgrim
Senior Financial Analyst
The Rappaport Companies
McLean, Virginia, USA

Stephen R. Pugh, CPA/CITP
Chief Operating Officer
The Rappaport Companies
McLean, Virginia, USA

Larry M. Spott, SCDP
Executive Vice President of
    Development
The Rappaport Companies
McLean, Virginia, USA

Investing in Retail Properties

A Guide to Structuring Partnerships
for Sharing Capital Appreciation
and Cash Flow

CHAPTER I

Introduction to Ownership and Investing in Shopping Centers

Retail Real Estate as an Investment

IT SEEMS AS IF every time you turn around, there is a new recommended way to invest—from buying stock in the hottest new industry to sinking funds into a bank's latest type of interest-bearing account.

One type of investment, however, usually appears in an investor's asset allocation because it seems to yield satisfying results over the long term: income-producing commercial real estate. While there might be volatility over short periods, over the long term, real estate has proven to be a good, secure investment that can protect the investor against inflation.

The Practice of Asset Allocation

A wise investor will divide his or her resources set aside for investment among different categories such as stocks, bonds, mutual funds, private equity, cash equivalents and real estate. This way the investor can lessen risk because each asset class has a different correlation to the others.

History has shown that often when stocks rise, bonds tend to fall. When the stock market starts a downward trend, investments in commercial real estate may begin generating above-average returns because income-producing real estate has a guaranteed stream of income secured by leases.

Why Real Estate Is an Important Part of Diversification

Income-producing real estate can be classified by sector; for example, residential (single-family or multifamily rental), office, hotel, industrial and retail. While diversifying one's portfolio is a hedge to the ups and downs of real estate investing, this book is about retail real estate, as that is the road I took earlier in my career and that is the only sector I have worked in for more than 30 years.

What makes retail different from other forms of real estate investments? Retail has proven to be one of the wisest as well as among the most complex forms of real estate investment for a number of reasons. The main reason is that there is significantly less speculative building in the retail sector than in other commercial sectors such as office buildings or residential developments.

Builders of office complexes can construct an office building on spec and lure tenants away from other office buildings with promises of lower rents and higher-quality (tenant improvement) buildout of their new offices. There is no need, in most cases, to remain in an office location because of the office tenant's customers or because of the office's tenant mix. Loyalty to a location is not an important factor in an office tenant's decision to relocate. Accordingly, there is much more brand value in retail locations than office locations.

Residential developers have a different level of risk. Whether they are planning to rent or sell condominium units, they have to build the entire complex before they have any material guarantee of income from the rentals or sales. Of course, they can have some rental units leased or a certain number of condominium units sold before they begin construction, but as it has been shown during difficult times in the most recent 2008–2009 recession, many of these rentals and/or sales have evaporated when the market falls.

The developer might be able to file a lawsuit against a residential tenant or prospective residential buyer to keep their deposit if the deal falls through, but the laws protecting residential renters and homebuyers do not give the developer sufficient rights such as enforcing (and eventually receiving) the rents over the term of a lease. The same holds true about the property owner's loss if the renter does not move in and rent or if the buyer does not perform and buy a condominium unit after making the commitment.

However, a 125,000-square-foot neighborhood shopping center cannot be built without tenants, at least not without an anchor tenant, and in the case of a neighborhood center, not without the grocery tenant. With the 125,000-square-foot grocery-anchored neighborhood shopping center, the grocery store must be built out from the start following the detailed plans of that specific grocery-food operator.

That grocery-food anchor space, which at the beginning of the 2010s was usually around 55,000 square feet, has mechanical, plumbing, electrical and technology-specific requirements that must be part of the initial construction. In order for the developer to agree to build such a distinct building, the grocery tenant will typically sign a minimum of a 20-year, and in many cases, a 25-year lease. This gives the developer assurances that it has at least a minimum amount of income as soon as the center opens to the public.

It is then less likely that the grocery tenant will vacate the center in preference of another competing location during the lease term. This is not only because the grocer has guaranteed to pay rent for 20 or 25 years but because the grocery store stands to lose its customer base, which looks to shop at that store located in that specific shopping center. Having this main tenant in place lowers your level of risk. Since there is some security from this anchor, financing is easier, and there is a precommitment for some of the rent.

As for the competition, it would be difficult for another developer to build a speculative shopping center across the street and ask your tenants to move. In most cases, retail tenants have loyalty, and their customers are loyal to their location. A retailer cannot easily move across the street or down the block, because they have established customers who know where to find them.

In addition, a retail development depends on a mix of retailers to drive shoppers to the shopping center. This appeal—known as *tenant mix*—forms a critical mass of retailers. It acts as a magnet to benefit all the retailers in the center and helps with cross-shopping that makes a shopping center successful. In developing a shopping center, you are hopefully creating the better mousetrap that allows your tenants to optimize their revenue and thus ensure their success.

This is unlike other forms of real estate, such as an office building, whereby you would be creating a place to conduct business without affecting the tenants' ability to enhance their revenue. In retail, it is all about retail sales and every location is unique because of its tenant mix.

Because of these reasons, a shopping center should prove to be a safe and secure investment over time if properly developed, leased and managed. Retail real estate is a long-term investment. You must consider location, demographics, psychographics, specific retailers and the overall tenant mix, and then package it all together for long-term success.

Even within the sector of retail real estate, there are several subcategories—small nonanchored strip center, neighborhood grocery-anchored center, community center, power center (big-box), town center, lifestyle center, mixed-use property, off-price/outlet center and the perennially dominant enclosed mall. I often hear in this business, "It's in the *details*." I am a very detailed-oriented individual, and it has proven to be the backbone of my success.

As one looks for the right opportunity, whether it is to find the right property, the right location, the right accessibility to the project, the right layout of the property, the right anchor tenant, the right tenant mix or the right demographic profile of the surrounding customer base, it is the details that make it all happen.

Retail real estate is a local business, and we list, map and track every retail property over 50,000 square feet in our market. We might not know who owns each property or if the property is for sale, but we know each property. In every county, city and town in the Washington, D.C., metropolitan area, we track every planned retail project from the time a comprehensive plan is introduced for entitlement, to a rezoning, to permits, to construction. We know every major road that is planned, where every major intersection lies and where growth is occurring—and projected to occur. When an opportunity presents itself, we can react quickly, as we know our market and the existing competition and future competition.

We are often asked, "How did you find that property? How were you able to purchase that property?" It was because of our relentless diligence. My philosophy has been that while we might be working on several opportunities concurrently, if we can purchase an existing property or build one new development a year, as we do not sell, then after 25 years we will own 25 properties. That is exactly where TRC is today. We have been in business 25 years, and today we own 25 properties comprising about 4 million square feet combined.

Of the 25 properties in which I have an ownership interest, 22 of them have been existing properties that I have acquired and 3 have been new ground-up developments. I very much wish to continue acquiring and developing ground-up projects. However, it is much easier and less risky to purchase existing shopping centers than to develop vacant land into new shopping centers.

My recommendation to anyone looking to own real estate is to first look to purchase an existing shopping center rather than to develop from the ground up. It is far less risky, as one does not have the uncertainty of properly understanding the land development issues. I have witnessed some very astute developers encounter major problems due to adverse soil conditions, whether unexpected rock or poor soil conditions, that have made an otherwise successful project fail due to extensive added costs of land development.

Learning development techniques by trial and error is too costly. It underscores the importance of obtaining a proper soil test prior to signing the purchase contract or at least making the contract contingent on securing a satisfactory soil test.

However, the main reason I strongly suggest acquiring instead of developing new for your first several projects relates to the ease or difficulty of raising equity capital. For example, say you are preparing a package to present to an investor and you are going to show them what they should be expecting in terms of cash distributions for the first few years of the project. If it is new development, you will need to explain to them that during the first year after land acquisition, you will be obtaining all your entitlements and signing a lease with, at least, your anchor tenant and thus, of course, no distributions of cash as a return on the investor's investment are being planned. In Year Two, you will be drawing plans, obtaining permits and securing debt financing to build the project.

Again, no distributions are possible. In Year Three, you will build the project. No distributions are planned either. In Year Four, you will fully lease the property, stabilize the income, understand the sales of your tenants and build a reasonable reserve of funds. You might have some minimal distributions to your investment partners but probably not. By Year Five, you should start distributions. It is a hard story to sell to your investors unless you have built up a strong track record by previously having several successful partnerships in which you are making adequate annual returns on their investments.

If you are buying a property to add value through upgrading of the property—maybe through a renovation, an expansion or a remerchandising of the tenant mix—and thus an increase in the rents, this should result in an increase in the net operating income of the property.

Probably in Year One, you cannot distribute an 8 percent return on the partners/investors investment, but you can certainly distribute at least a 4 percent return. In Year Two, you would have completed some of your upgrades, maybe re-leased a space or two at higher rents, and you can distribute about a 6 percent return. In Year Three, you could have completed your upgrades, re-leased a few more spaces and could give your investors an 8 percent return. As the years go by, you can look forward to rewarding them with an increasing return exceeding 8 percent.

Another challenge to securing equity capital is that it is difficult to raise money on a new development until you have a property with "enough of a story," meaning enough of the early diligence already complete, so that your investors believe that the risk and future return for them is worth their investment. The amount of cash needed for a new development for preliminary due diligence, deposits, lease negotiations, and preliminary work with one's consultants—whether for civil engineering, traffic studies, architectural drawings, geotechnical studies, environmental consulting, marketing brochures, etc.—requires a very large cash outlay.

Of course, if you are able to acquire the land and raise the equity, these costs become partnership costs and will be reimbursed to you or owed to you by the partnership. However, you are likely to be fronting all these costs initially. This would result in much higher upfront investment by you than by acquiring an existing property.

It is easier to raise equity capital from partners/investors who from the outset can visit the property ("kick the tires," so to speak), see what they are investing in and immediately start to receive a distribution rather than having to wait several years to ascertain the extent of payback they will get on their initial investment. That is why after 25 years, TRC has many more properties that we have acquired than we have developed from the ground up. Now that we have built a strong track record after many years, we have more cash available, more expertise and experience, and are accepting more risk in new developments in anticipation of superior returns.

The first year's anticipated net operating income (NOI) divided by the capitalization rate (cap rate) established by market forces equals the value of the asset. This simple concept can be applied to determine the value of your investment at any point in time from the initial purchase to the final disposition of the investment.

However, the annual return on your initial investment is more closely related to the net cash flow that an income property produces annually. A sound investment in a well-located retail property that has been properly managed and optimized can produce both an above-market yearly cash return on the initial investment and considerable appreciation upon exiting or refinancing the investment.

Risk and Reward

In deciding where to invest, an investor must always evaluate risk against expected return. If an investor chose one of the safest investments, the investor would invest in U.S. government securities, such as a Treasury bill, Treasury bond or Treasury note, and would receive in exchange a small but guaranteed return backed by the U.S. government.

Buying shares in a publicly traded real estate investment trust (REIT), simply by its formation and underlying fundamentals, offers a better return than buying Treasurys, and is in most cases a safer investment than you can give an investor investing with you. Some of the reasons investors invest in a REIT stock are:

1. Buying stock in a real estate company allows an investor to buy shares in small dollar increments.
2. Liquidity, in that the shares are easily traded if the investor wishes to sell his or her stock.
3. The investment is a relatively small investment spread over a large number of properties, generally in wide geographic zones.

Therefore, REIT stocks cannot create high returns commensurate with an investment in a successful individual property.

For an investor to decide to invest with you in direct ownership of any given property with the risks associated with such investment, the investor expects a greater return in reward for the increased risk. As a result, you need to find the right opportunity that will offer the investor a return that is commensurate with the risk as well as provide you a handsome return for the risks you take as the managing partner in structuring the deal.

How the Game Is Played

There are different roles that partners play in an investment group. There are passive partners and active partners. An active partner is the managing partner—the decision-making partner or sponsor of the partnership. Depending on the legal requirements of different states, when I sign documents on behalf of the partnership my title is usually *managing member* or *managing partner*. (However, for clarity, I will usually refer to the developer and sponsor of the partnership as the managing partner in this book.)

The passive partner is the individual investor who is only a participant in an investor group by virtue of the investment funds the passive partner gives to the managing partner to share in the returns of the deal.

The managing partner is the decision-making member of the partnership from the inception of the partnership until the property is sold and the partnership is dissolved. Of course, in my model, no partnership is ever dissolved, because, to date, I have never sold a property.

As the managing partner, you have the responsibility to assemble the deal and take on the initial risk. This happens prior to raising the equity at your cost (to be reimbursed to you as a partnership expense but only if the deal proceeds to fruition). If you find the right opportunity, you will likely take 10 major steps:

1. Pay the legal costs of negotiating the purchase agreement
2. Put the property under contract
3. Put up the deposit
4. Complete the due diligence
5. Devise a plan for the property to create value
6. Prepare the financial projections
7. Prepare the debt-financing package and obtain the debt financing

8. Personally guarantee the debt financing, if necessary, which might include signing on to the nonrecourse liability carve-outs even if you are not personally signing on the debt financing
9. Determine the sharing arrangements between you and your partners/investors pertaining to the cash flow and appreciation
10. Create the investment package for your presentations to your investors to entice them to invest with you

Once you have put together the initial deal and raised the equity, borrowed the debt financing and closed on the property, it becomes your responsibility to accomplish all that you have promised. The passive investor can just sit and wait for you to make money. Assuming you have purchased an existing center, you must complete the upgrade, renovation or expansion of the center, if that was part of your plan. You must establish the new tenant mix and oversee the new leasing and marketing plan. You are the decision maker on all the terms and conditions, economic and noneconomic provisions, of every new lease and lease renewal.

You are the signer of all documents including all the leases. You are obligated to pay the expenses and taxes on behalf of the partnership. As such, you would prepare the monthly financial reports to send to your partners. You would update your partners on what is happening with their investment as well. You would always make yourself available to discuss with them any questions they might have regarding the investment.

The investor/partner (unless it is an institutional partner, which will be covered later) has very limited rights. These partners will be investing as much in their confidence in your reputation and your expertise as they will be in the assets of the individual property.

I have had partners, while rare, who have never visited their investment property. These investors/partners were once called *limited partners* when the sponsor was referred to as the *general partner*, and when the deals were structured as limited partnerships.

However, in the late 1980s and early 1990s, the preference for the structure of these partnerships changed in most states to what today are called Limited Liability Corporations (LLCs). The tax structure is generally similar through various rulings and regulations adopted by the Internal Revenue Service (IRS) over the years, but the liability issues were strengthened to protect the partners. Each LLC document is slightly different, but in most of my partnerships, the investor/partner has no approval rights except the right to sell their interest at certain times in the life of the LLC.

As you can see, the responsibilities, the time commitment and the risk are quite daunting, especially if you, as the managing partner, are personally signing on the debt financing. That is why you deserve a greater share in the cash flow and the appreciation, particularly if the investment performs as you projected.

Yet nothing is more important than your reputation and your track record. Considering that I have had a few partnerships that have not paid out the returns I initially projected, I have never had a legal issue with any of my partners—and I have had a couple of hundred partners over the past 25 years. This includes one deal where I, as well as all my investors, lost our entire investment.

As the managing partner of a retail property, you have many responsibilities, many of them overlapping. You have investors who do not get involved in the day-to-day running of the property. They do not know the individual tenants, the loan officers at the lending institution or the leasing agents who might represent some of the tenants in the shopping center or who are seeking to lease space in the center. Some of these investors may not even know the other partners in their investment.

You, however, must know all these individuals. In many cases, you oversee—almost control—the livelihood of individuals who are your tenants. An accounts receivable problem with a tenant becomes your problem to solve. You will have to accept the fact that once you renovate a property, maybe one of your long-term tenants will never be able to afford the new and justified higher market rent and will have to find another location to conduct business.

There is no proper venue to talk in depth about your reputation. This is something you earn over the years, but how you handle these difficult issues sometimes sets your reputation. There is no better compliment to me than when my peers have told me that I am a good businessman, who with humility and caring for his fellow man balances fairly the day-to-day decisions a managing partner has to make.

Maintaining a reputable record of accomplishment is truly a balancing act. Just think about how many assumptions you have to make in preparing your financial projections. You have to be honest in doing so. How much will it cost to upgrade/renovate and expand? What will the new rents be on every tenant space coming up for renewal or for replacement with a new tenant? How much will the partnership have to contribute in tenant allowance required to lease a space? What will the interest rates be over the term of the project if they are not fixed initially? What will be the expenses to run the center, the vacancy rate, the accounts receivable issues and more?

Prepare your projections too aggressively and the investment will not perform. Prepare your projections too conservatively and no project will show acceptable returns or allow you to purchase a property at the price the market deems to be the current market value.

There is no easy answer, but you have to recognize that our reputation is derived from our track record. Our deal size grows over the years and, accordingly, we grow as our investor base expands through our previous successes. In summary, I have several partners who have never seen their investment but who believe strongly in my reputation and track record, and because of it, they continue to invest with me.

Getting Into the Game

The road to starting your own shopping center development company is not mapped on Google or paved with 6 inches of asphalt for easy cruising. It is not level and it is not without curves. You have to make your own path, set your own course and maneuver carefully.

In fact, most of the developers I know did not travel through my system for entering into real estate and growing their business. Each did it in his or her own inimitably different way, although we shared similar motives.

I started my business because I wanted to build something where I could use my knowledge, experience and skills, and then later realized how much more there is to know, do and practice.

I had in me what it takes to move from employee to owner of a startup business in the world of retail properties. I had the knowledge, skills and drive, but most important, I was willing to take the risk.

If you have similar qualities and goals, and desire to make a move in this direction, you might wonder what it takes to be a good developer or managing partner.

If you are setting out to develop and own shopping centers, it is best if you already have experience in the retail real estate industry, as that experience will give you credibility when approaching potential investors.

The managing partner is like the captain running the ship, overseeing all aspects of the business from renovating to managing leases to marketing the center to potential retailers and consumers—not to mention the financial aspects of dealing with investors and the lender.

Characteristics of a Successful Developer/Managing Partner—Five Areas of Expertise

Expertise should lie in five main realms. Do not lose heart if you lack knowledge in one or more of these areas. The most important thing is to know exactly where, how or from whom to get the necessary expertise. Do you have the ability to hire attorneys, civil engineers, architects, geotechnical consultants or any other experts that you might need?

1. Construction: Know how to oversee a construction project, whether it involves building a new structure or renovating and expanding an existing structure.

This knowledge should extend to fixing up a center's interior and exterior space, either by painting, installing a new facade, replacing the roof, upgrading the lighting indoors or out, repaving and restriping the parking lot, adding curb cuts, reconfiguring entrances and drive lanes, replacing landscaping or putting up new signage.

2. Leasing and Tenant Analysis: The practice of leasing and re-leasing—often called remerchandising—is often a key factor that determines the success of a shopping center. Proper anchors that help attract customers for other retail uses that satisfy market needs and demographics are key.

Additionally, it is necessary to understand what makes a good tenant mix, how to differentiate good tenants from bad tenants and how to evaluate the financial strength and desirability of a potential tenant. You can employ different methods for evaluating a potential tenant. One technique is to review its financial statements, including the balance sheet, operating statement and statement of cash flow. You can examine the prospective tenant's sales, expenses (including its occupancy expenses) and its ability to service its debt without conflicting with its capability to pay its ongoing operational expenses.

Another method is to make a site visit to one of the retailer's locations. Yet another is to visit its competition. It is also necessary to be able to comprehend a variety of different retail leases in order to collect all types of rents and extra charges when due. Understanding restrictions, rents and the economic and noneconomic terms that relate to everything from rights of assignment to use clauses is essential.

3. Property Management: This area of expertise is about managing your tenants, maintaining the physical plant of the property and knowing what it takes to run the day-to-day operations of a shopping center. This might entail keeping the property clean and in good repair, putting together budgets of expected expenses and revenues, and dealing with tenants and helping them solve any problems that might arise.

Once the tenant occupies the premises, the property owner's presence shifts from the leasing agent to the property manager. This manager becomes the face of the landlord to the tenants and of the property owner to the community and local government.

4. Marketing: Another aspect to property management is marketing the property to consumers and potential tenants. A community center will be successful if you understand the best ways of getting customers into stores.

Deciding how best to put together mailings or advertisements, creating buzzworthy events and activities within the center and weighing the best way to contribute donations or services to the community, in order to be seen as a good member of the community, are all aspects of consumer marketing.

Marketing, in short, is all about making sure that the center is as successful as possible for tenants by persuading existing and potential customers to visit the center frequently to shop for their daily needs and wants.

5. Financial: Having financial acumen and knowledge is a big part of being a successful managing partner of a shopping center asset. You will be dealing with lenders to procure loans, working with your investors to make sure that they are satisfied with their participation in the program and making sure that the returns you promised are as close as possible to what you are actually distributing. You need to know how to create and maintain master cash-flow projections and distributions.

You must determine the best way to inform and update investors with information they understand, and with which they are comfortable. It is important to be able to oversee every financial aspect of the business so that neither the lenders nor the investors are questioning whether they are getting what you initially promised them.

Some of these five areas of expertise might seem daunting. However, you should make sure that if you do not understand or excel in one of these areas, you know how to get answers and services from someone who does.

One way to make sure that the business runs well if you are missing an important component of these five attributes is to find a business partner who possesses the areas of expertise that you lack or hire someone whose skills complement yours. Together, you will make a team that is knowledgeable and proficient in all aspects of communicating with your investment group and running an efficient shopping center.

Characteristics of a Good Real Estate Investment Partner

Selecting the right investment partners is as important as selecting the right property. No one wants a legal challenge from a partner in the event you are unable to meet your projections. Your partners need to recognize that you are making assumptions to the best of your ability based on information available at the time. The timing of the returns you projected might require a deferral of distributions from cash flow to achieve better long-term appreciation.

Deciding who can invest with you is not exactly like finding a marriage partner or hiring an employee, but in some ways it is similar. You need to ask yourself constantly, "If the project is not meeting projections, will this partner understand and patiently support me even if they are not happy with short-term results?"

I have never had a dispute with an investor even though, as previously mentioned, I have had partnerships that have not met expectations and some investments have even failed.

However, through detailed monthly financial statements, letters, personal phone calls and meetings, every partner is informed regularly about the progress of his investment. I have learned through experience that an investor prefers to know what is happening, whether it is good news or bad, than not to know at all. Openness and honesty will always lead to the best outcome.

Cash Flow

Some of my most sophisticated investors do not consider cash flow as important as long-term appreciation. Typically, these investors are not relying on the yearly cash flow. They evaluate the risk of the investment, look at the overall return of their investment, determine the time value of when they will be receiving their distributions and decide if they wish to invest.

The primary objective of these investors is maximum long-term capital appreciation. They are willing to tolerate fluctuations in cash flow distributions and can withstand several years of no distribution from cash flow to secure a large distribution at a later date that reflects a sizable appreciation of the investment asset.

However, these investors are the exception, not the rule. As most of my investors are individuals (compared to institutional investors), distribution from cash flow is an integral part of the return they expect.

While they can usually understand and accept a smaller yearly distribution initially, they expect the cash return will increase each year. In preparing your financial projections, if possible, I recommend that you plan to increase the cash distributions to your investors, even if slightly, each year.

Long-Term Capital Appreciation

However, it is the long-term capital appreciation, whether disbursed to you and your investors upon a refinance or upon a sale, where you and your investors, especially on a successful project, will receive the largest portion of return on initial investment. Long-term capital appreciation will depend on how much you are able to increase net operating income (NOI) as a result of what you have done with the property less the monies you have invested to create this additional NOI. This is, of course, assuming the capitalization rate (cap rate) remains the same (or better yet, compresses) upon a refinance or sale as it was at the time you purchased the property.

The cap rate is a key measure of investors' expectations of property income and value of income-producing properties. A low cap rate is an indication that investors perceive less risk in the property and is comparable to other properties with similar risks. The higher the cap rate, the lower the property is valued.

While the increased NOI gives you the means to increase cash distributions to your investors throughout the life of the investment, by "capping" this additional NOI upon a sale or refinancing, you can substantially increase the value that you create for the partnership simply by increasing the NOI.

For example, if you are able to increase the NOI by $100,000 and the cap rate is 10 percent, then you have increased the value of the property by $1,000,000. If the cap rate falls to 8 percent (due to market forces or because you have strengthened the reliability of the income through bringing tenants that have market dominance), you would have increased the value of the property by $1,250,000 using the same NOI increase of $100,000. On a cap rate of 6 percent, you would increase the value of the property by $1,666,667 with the same additional $100,000 in increased NOI.

Of course, the reverse holds true: Value can also decrease if NOI slips. However, generally, in a successful project when NOI increases, a substantial increase in value occurs, a concept known in real estate investing as long-term capital appreciation.

Liquidity

Real estate investments are inherently risky. Some of these risks pertain directly to your investment while others do not and are beyond your ability to control. When they are property-specific risks, you must always reevaluate these risks. Nothing is more critical to the survival of a real estate investment than the lack of liquidity. Liquidity is the cash that is needed to pay the debt service, tenant improvements, leasing commissions, repair and maintenance to operate the property, and to invest new capital in the property.

It is only after there is liquidity for all these items that there is liquidity for cash disbursements to your investors. Always make sure you have the safety of enough liquidity to withstand a large tenant bankruptcy or having to possibly reduce rents for a brief period in order to stop a tenant from relocating to a competing property.

If you feel you need to build greater reserves than originally planned or you just need to hold on to reserves that you have, do so with confidence. I have never had an investor demand his or her expected cash disbursement upon notification that cash needs to remain on reserve. It is better to be safe than sorry.

No investor wants the project to lack the liquidity available to increase long-term value. Always make sure the property has the needed available funds; then you can distribute—and never before.

A Typical Investment

Some developers feel that their contribution to increasing the value of a property (over and above its purchase price), created by their hard work in enhancing its income potential, is sufficient. That is known as *sweat equity*. Not me. In all of my partnerships, I always invest real cash just as my investors do.

In several of my early partnerships, the amount of money I could afford to invest defined the amount of money I asked each of my investors to put up as their share. In my first partnership, in 1984, I had 14 partners. Each of us invested $35,000. I told each of my investors that we were all investing the same amount of money. All of us shared equally until we all reached a specified return on our investment, in this case, 8 percent, and then, and only then, as the returns increased above 8 percent did my percentage increase.

After I had put together a few successful partnerships, I gained more credibility. I began to attract investors who wished to invest much more than I could afford to invest. But in every partnership, I have invested real cash of a meaningful amount—usually somewhere between 10 percent and 20 percent of the total initial equity investment.

In some of the partnerships, a 10 percent investment was more cash than I had available. In these cases, I went to a bank and personally borrowed against the illiquid asset of an earlier deal where I had created value for myself. I have used this high-risk model for twenty-five years.

How Much Money Can You Raise?

I am often asked, "What size project should I try to purchase?" I always return the question with another question: How much money can you raise?

For example, suppose you are able to attract nine investors to invest $100,000 each with you and you are also able to invest $100,000, building a total equity investment into the newly formed partnership of $1 million. And, you are able to borrow 75 percent of the acquisition cost of the property, as well as 75 percent of the due diligence, settlement costs and costs of the upgrading and/or renovation you are planning. Thus, your $1 million equity investment equals the remaining 25 percent. Accordingly, the 75 percent equals $3 million. The total initial cash required for the purchase is $4 million: $3 million in debt (75%) and $1 million in equity (25%).

If, on the other hand, the debt lender will only lend you 70 percent of the total costs, you must raise more equity. If $4 million is what you need, then you are able to borrow $2.8 million ($4 million x 70%). As a result, you need equity of $1.2 million ($4 million x 30%). If you cannot raise $1.2 million in equity then *a $4 million deal* is too large for you to undertake and you would need to start with a smaller acquisition.

On the debt side, there might be two different reasons besides market forces why the lender will only lend you 70 percent instead of 75 percent or even 60 percent instead of 75 percent, which was more typical of the deals of the 2000s decade.

One reason is that the underwriting of what you are acquiring and proposing to upgrade lends itself to a lesser percentage of debt. The other reason is that your financial statement and track record will only allow a lesser amount of debt than your lender is willing to risk with you until you have completed a deal or two and have gained more credibility.

Whatever the reason, you need to understand what is probable as to how much debt you can and wish to borrow, and then determine how much equity you can probably raise to back into the size deal that is possible. Then you must do the projections to see if the returns compensate you and your future investors for the risk you are assuming.

Summary

This chapter examines the fundamentals that play a critical role in the success of real estate property investments. The most important among these fundamentals is the concept that increasing NOI most often results in increased cash flow distributions to investors as well as an increase in the value of the investment that is realized upon refinancing or upon the disposition of the asset when the NOI is capitalized to arrive at the value.

Single-property investing is a high-risk proposition compared to investing in shares of a large portfolio of properties. However, the high risk often results in the highest rewards but only if the investment receives the attention that comes from expert knowledge and skill.

This overview serves as the foundation for retail real estate investing and development. Now we will drill down on the details that make it fail or succeed.

Long-term capital appreciation relies on your ability to increase net operating income by bringing in highly productive retail tenants, as in the case of our Penn Mar Shopping Center, a 387,028-square-foot community center in Forestville, Maryland. Our leasing team worked to bring a strong retail line-up that includes Marshalls, Shoppers Food and Pharmacy, Staples, Burlington Coat Factory and Starbucks Coffee.

CHAPTER II

Getting Started as a Developer and General Partner

Your First Investment Property

ONE OF THE FIRST DECISIONS to make when choosing an investment property is whether to buy an existing center or to build a new development. While building a project from the ground up may seem exciting, it is most likely a safer choice to invest in an existing shopping center that shows potential for boosting the income stream.

There is a greater risk in building something new, since there are many unknowns that go along with land development, construction costs and details, market forces, and whether the available location can attract retailers.

Buying an existing center is far safer because it has already been built. It probably has some stable tenants, and it has already become part of the customers' shopping habits. This allows you to focus on ways you can create added value to the center through renovation, expansion or remerchandising.

Moreover, it is easier to raise equity from partners when there is something already there to show them. When buying an existing shopping center, there is already an established cash flow right from the start, although it might not be until renovations are done that improving the value and building equity can begin. A potential investor is more likely to invest if they can see and visit the property and if there is some amount of cash projected to be distributed to the investor in the first year of operation.

Buying an undeveloped piece of land on which to build a brand-new shopping center might preclude investors from receiving any money for the first year, as obtaining building permits, leasing space, building the structure, moving in tenants and stabilizing the business must first take place. In fact, it might be two to four years before any cash flows from the business.

You could arrange a deal for ground-up development with investors who you have worked with on redevelopments after you have already built up your credibility with them. It is unlikely that you will be able to convince potential investors to part with their hard-earned money so you can buy a vacant plot of land with only the vision that a shopping center will one day stand on it.

In hunting for the ideal shopping center in which to invest, the following are some key factors to keep in mind.

Market: Choose a specific area within your target market. When starting your own shopping center business it is always better to invest in properties that are in or near where you and your investors live because you are already familiar with the area and its demographics. You can easily visit the center to see how it and its stores are faring. Additionally, if you are familiar with the market, you will know the community and its growth potential.

You might even be aware of the municipal master plans in terms of road building and maintenance, new developments and other factors that could affect local businesses. You will also be aware of shopping habits and understand firsthand what key stores are missing.

The local market is also a source for potential investors. We call them "drive-by investors." If you pursue investors who live near the property, they will likewise be able to visit the property and feel they really own a piece of real estate and, as a result, you will have an easier time convincing them to commit to invest with you.

Layout, Location and Accessibility: If you are buying a property for its hidden potential, you will most likely be buying a center that is 20 years or older. These older centers are often laid out very inefficiently, primarily because they were built on cheap land and may have excessive parking ratios. In redesigning the center's layout, you can usually yield more GLA without expanding the site.

You should ascertain if the basic layout of the center you are considering is suitable in other ways. Shopping centers, for example, that run parallel rather than perpendicular to the main road are much more valuable, as they give your tenants more visibility to drive-by traffic and thus more customers, more sales, and therefore the ability to pay a higher rent.

Have you noticed that one side of the road seems to have more retail than the other side? This occurs often but most people do not even notice it. However, to a knowledgeable retailer it is an important consideration when deciding where to locate a store. This is known as locating on the *going-home side of the road*. Most shoppers who do not do their shopping on the weekends do their shopping on the way home from work, especially if they are shopping for food where they might be picking up perishables such as fruits, meats or frozen food.

Time-starved consumers are looking for quick access in and out of shopping centers. Think about it, because retailers often do so in planning their store locations. As a consumer, if you had a choice of making a right turn into a shopping center on the way home from work, quickly running into the store to buy what you need, then quickly jumping back into your car and making an easy right turn out of the parking lot to continue your trip home, then that is what you would want.

When heading home, the alternative would be much more time consuming. You would have to get into the left lane, wait for the green traffic signal, turn into the center and then buy what you need. You'd then have to wait again for the green light to make a left turn to then continue your drive home. Given another choice, this scenario is not acceptable to most consumers.

However, there are certain tenants and certain types of shopping centers that can be successful for other reasons. Small nonanchored strip centers located on the *going-to-work side of the road* as opposed to being on the going-home side of the road is exactly where Starbucks Coffee Company seeks their store locations. Starbucks is not going after the commuter who is heading home after a long day of work. Starbucks's customer is the commuter who wants to make that right turn in, quickly buy that cup of coffee, quickly make that right turn out and then drive on to work.

However, a retailer like Starbucks seeking morning customers is not the norm. Most retailers want to attract the customer more often on the way home from work rather than on the way to work.

Accordingly, accessibility in many respects is critical to the success of a shopping center. When considering a site to purchase, ask yourself the key questions that your potential retail tenants will ask themselves. Can customers easily get into or out of the center? Is the center at a traffic light, especially if the center is on a divided highway?

A center that only has access or egress from one direction—what we call a right-in/right-out situation—is a very detrimental issue for the long-term success of a shopping center. Only in heavily trafficked and heavily populated areas where there are no alternatives can this situation be acceptable. However, it will always make the shopping center with this access/egress issue the second choice to other shopping centers with access/egress from both directions for tenants and their customers.

You should ask yourself: If some of these basic issues are not conducive to getting customers easily in and out of the center, is it possible to correct the situation? If not, this might not be a desirable property.

Size of Project: How big a project can you afford to buy? Think about how much money you could raise, how many investors you could line up and how many dollars would each of these investors be willing to put up.

It is important to think about your own share if you are planning to buy a share in the project. How much cash can you yourself come up with to invest? Generally, centers that are 10,000 to 20,000 square feet are good starting points for first-time investment projects. Stay away from the 100,000-plus-square-foot projects until you are more established.

Determine what sort of plan is realistic based on the amount of equity you are going to need and how much debt will need to be borrowed from a bank or other lending institution in order to purchase this property. Do not forget to factor in how much money you would need for acquisition costs such as due diligence, settlement costs and legal expenses as well as the costs to make the necessary renovations, improvements or expansions you expect to incur to enhance the asset.

Existing Leases: Read carefully and completely all tenant leases and all correspondence in all tenant files to make sure that you will be able to create value in the center. If every tenant has relatively new 20-year leases, there is little that you can do to raise revenue and show an added return on the investment if you make improvements or upgrades to the center.

However, leases that will be expiring soon give you the opportunity to remerchandise the center if need be. Vacancies and expirations let you add prestigious high-volume tenants and do away with less desirable tenants. Because of your investment in upgrading the property, the existing tenants will benefit from an increase in their sales, which will enable them to pay a higher rent. It also allows you to raise rents on vacant spaces and expiring leases to market rent.

Some leases might have a percentage rent clause—giving the partnership a percentage of the store's income—in which case a long lease might not be a deterrent to increasing rental income due to renovations.

The reason your due diligence team must read all correspondence and tenant files is because a few times I have found letters of agreement between landlord and tenant that were not properly documented in an amendment to a lease but would still constitute a legal modification of the lease between landlord and tenant, that is not reflected in the rent roll.

Potential for Improvement and Expansion: You are not looking to buy a stable, successful property where you can collect the rents and keep the property clean simply to preserve your investors' asset, like "clipping coupons on a bond," as we used to say. After all, a property like that probably would not offer you the opportunity to purchase the property *and* add enough value to give your investors and you the type of return commensurate with how your investors would evaluate the risk of investing with you.

Instead, look for a property that needs some work. What kind of cosmetic and/or structural improvements can you make to the center, and how much will this cost? Could you add value by upgrading the landscaping, changing the signage, repairing and resealing the parking lot, upgrading the lighting, painting the center, replacing the pylon sign or renovating the facade?

In addition, is it possible to expand the shopping center? Check with the local zoning codes, as it might be possible to add on to the center or to build another small building within the parking lot or adjacent undeveloped land, for example.

Expanding the shopping center is one of the methods I have used to achieve some of my greatest increases in cash flow and asset appreciation. An expansion does not have to be a massive addition to the structure. It can simply be erecting a freestanding store on a vacant outparcel pad on the periphery of the center, adding new retail square footage by increasing the size of existing stores or expanding the gross leasable area (GLA) of the property by building additional in-line retail space that brings rental income.

Why is expanding the center a huge opportunity to create more cash flow and appreciation?

1. There is no added land cost.
2. The additional leasable retail space is usually being carved out from the suburban shopping center parking lot, which produces no income.
3. There are generally no additional offsite road or other improvements required to be built.
4. You already are probably receiving the lowest rent from your anchor tenants, and the tenants that will be locating in these new spaces will be likely paying the highest rents.
5. The cost of constructing this additional space is relatively low compared to the other buildings on the site, and certainly less costly to build than the grocery store, if that is your anchor tenant.

For these reasons, I do not look to buy an A-plus property. Shopping centers that need some fixing come with a level of risk, but that is okay. I am the ultimate risk taker.

However, pension funds are one of the types of buyers for A-plus properties. A pension fund advisor, who buys these types of properties for pension funds, once told me that his model is to buy safe, secure investments because his clients are investing for the future retirement needs of their beneficiaries. While he might like to hit a home run on an investment, he does not ever expect such—but he'd better never strike out. His model is to always hit singles and doubles, to put it in baseball terms.

As he is expecting lesser returns than I am looking for, he can purchase a property at a higher price than I can. But his risk profile usually does not allow him to purchase the property that I wish to purchase. If he does wish to make such a purchase, it is usually only with a partner like me who can help him to create that greater return and mitigate the risk.

For the first center I purchased, in 1984, which was originally only 40,000 square feet, I was able to reconfigure the parking spaces and build onto the center 8,000 square feet—5,000 square feet on the right side and 3,000 square feet onto the left side of the center. That means that with a little creativity, effort and investment, I expanded the gross leasable area (GLA) by one-fifth.

The total hard and soft costs of building the 8,000 square feet was $100 per square foot, and the initial triple-net rent I received on the new space was $15 per square foot (both in 1984 dollars). Thus, the total cost was 8,000 square feet times $100 per square foot, or $800,000. The total initial annual rent for the 8,000 square feet multiplied times $15 per square foot equals $120,000. Applying a cap rate of 8 percent to $120,000 in income that flowed directly to the NOI results in $1.5 million. In essence, I created value of $1.5 million, which after subtracting $800,000 in one-time costs, brings the first year's appreciation to $700,000 simply by building this 8,000-square-foot addition.

As the total equity investment on my first deal was $495,000, I was able to return the total equity investment to all the investors upon the completion of this addition and share in future cash flow and appreciation in a much greater way, as I will explain in detail later.

How Do You Find a Property With Potential for Growth?

Before you start looking at available property for sale, you should define what you wish to acquire. Perhaps it is a shopping center within 30 miles of your home or office. Maybe it is between 20,000 and 50,000 square feet. The center may be 10 to 30 years old, needing some major work or at least some tender loving care. You will want it to have enough leases expiring in the near term so that you can add value. The center should offer good visibility to the major roads, good ingress and egress access, and be well located, of course.

Once you have defined the qualities of the center you are looking for, you can convey your preferences to sales agents who have shopping centers listed for sale. Call every real estate broker that sells—not leases—commercial properties in your target area and give your basic criteria. For example, you might tell them, "I'm looking for a shopping center that's between ten thousand and fifty thousand square feet in the Washington, D.C., area, preferably in northern Virginia. I'm looking to buy a property that has some vacancies, needs a little renovation and has the ability to be expanded."

These listing agents will start sending you sales packages on properties they are trying to sell. Initially most of the proposed properties will not be ones you will have interest in purchasing. As you receive the sales packages, do not immediately dispose of the ones that you think would not work. Instead, use each of the shopping center sales packages as an example to practice putting together an investor package in order for an investor to decide to invest with you.

For each shopping center offered for sale, prepare all the sections of an investor prospectus package. Do it as if this were the real-deal package you would use to solicit investors to invest with you. Put together the table of contents, which includes sections that I call a project overview, location, financial analysis, leasing analysis, ARGUS backup schedules, sponsor information, partnership documents and major tenant profiles. Key elements:

- The *Project Overview* section includes subsections called Executive Summary, Term Sheet, Sources and Uses of Funds, 11-Year Cash Flow Projections and Return on Investment.
- The *Location* section includes subsections called County Map, Aerial Photograph, Competition Report, Leasing Prospects and Demographic Report.
- The *Financial Analysis* section includes subsections called 11-Year Cash Flow Projection, Rent Roll, Assumptions, Estimated Settlement Costs, Prior Operating Statements (for the past year or two) and Operating Statement (for the present calendar year, with current year-to-date performance leading up to the date of the package).
- The *Leasing Analysis* section includes subsections called Vacancies, Expirations—Current Terms, Expirations—All Terms, Rents per Square Foot and Market Rents. These exhibits are all color-coded, and the site plans depict the information in color for each leasable space in the shopping center.

You can use property management software for calculating costs and income and other financial projections. I prefer ARGUS Software, which is a financial software program we use to input all the assumptions and acts as the backup information to the other financial projections. The ARGUS Asset Management software package allows me to create financial models for the acquisition process and can be used in conjunction with ARGUS Valuation–DCF, which appraisers use for asset valuation purposes.

ARGUS Valuation-DCF can be used to document your assumptions and support your financial conclusions with its standard reporting of all input data, property- and portfolio-level summary reports and detailed tenant-by-tenant supporting schedules. It is also flexible in that it supports various data transfer tools and utilities that you might access during the due diligence phase from the seller to incorporate into your valuation model. These include an Excel Import Wizard, native reXML support for downloads from MRI and Yardi, RealmX for ARGUS Property Management integration, Open-ARGUS integration with MS Access or SQL and an Excel export tool and embedded Excel Report Writer.

Some developers still use the more rudimentary Microsoft Excel spreadsheet to back up schedules to present the financial projections in Excel format, but while Excel works fine for projections, the data you input does not tie directly to each leasable space and the income you can derive from it. You would need to insert manually any changes on assumptions you make regarding a particular space. However, Excel is fine if you are just starting, because ARGUS is relatively expensive.

When I started my business, there were no programs like Excel. I used programs that are no longer around today like VisiCalc, developed by Software Arts, which was the first spreadsheet program available for personal computers. Later I began using SuperCalc, a spreadsheet application published by Sorcim, which was an improvement over VisiCalc. Microsoft was then marketing a spreadsheet program called Multiplan, which worked on CP/M systems, but Lotus 1-2-3 quickly became the leading spreadsheet for the then-popular DOS operating system in the mid 1980s. Microsoft released the first version of Excel for the Mac in 1985, and the first Windows version late in 1987.

ARGUS Software (formerly Realm Business Solutions) has taken over the financial software market for the commercial real estate industry with products like ARGUS Valuation-DCF, a discounted cash flow (DCF) financial analysis program to forecast cash flows and value for real estate properties.

Compared to the earlier spreadsheets, ARGUS Software is relatively new. ARGUS Valuation-DCF was originally released in 1987 for DOS and in 1994 for Microsoft Windows. ARGUS surely makes it easier today but it is not essential.

Now that you understand the methods for creating cash flow projection models, let us review other sections of the investor package. Under the Sponsor Information section, you have the opportunity to sell yourself, your expertise and your credibility.

In this section, you need to shine. Talk about all the experiences and expertise that anyone in your company has that can help you sell your ability to be the managing partner of the investment. Show prior projects you have worked on, whether you owned the projects or they were projects you have been involved with in other companies where you have worked.

Under the Partnership Documents section of the investor package, include the proposed LLC agreement and the property management and leasing agreement.

All of this preparation will allow you to back into a purchase price for the property that works for you. The asking price does not matter at this stage. The final purchase price has to be the purchase price that works for you and your investors.

By creating the full investor presentation for each property scenario that comes your way, you will be preparing yourself for the real deal. At a minimum, it will highlight the areas where you need help. It will bring out questions that you will need to answer and might indicate areas where you would need to seek outside help. Working through this discipline will allow you to recognize the right opportunity when it comes along. Then you can react quickly to determine the proper purchase price and present such an opportunity to your investors.

Set Your Model: How Much Equity? How Much Debt?

The lender will typically set a maximum percentage of debt they will lend according to internal policy, which varies depending on many factors. While during the 2008–2010 financial crisis many lenders were willing to underwrite loans of no more than 60 percent of the property's value, historically a lender has been typically willing to lend up to 75 percent debt, and even at times up to 80 percent.

It also has been possible to borrow up to 90 percent of the purchase price using additional mezzanine financing. The more debt or leverage you put on the property, the easier it is for you to show higher returns for your investors and you. However, I have never leveraged the deal with over

Expanding the shopping center is one of the best methods to achieve increases in cash flow and asset appreciation. Pictured is Warrenton Center in Warrenton, Virginia, a community center we renovated and expanded to 215,609 square feet of GLA by adding a Borders and a Panera Bread. Peebles department store, PETCO, Staples and Rankin's True Value Hardware anchor this center.

75 percent debt. Most of my deals have been at 75 percent debt, and some deals have been as low as 65 percent to 70 percent debt. Accordingly, most of my deals have brought in about 25 percent of equity and at times between 30 percent and 35 percent of equity.

Set Five- and Ten-Year Goals

Where do you want to be as a developer in 5 years and 10 years? This is not for fate to decide. You will need to ask yourself this question in order to create a business plan to take you there.

I have always had goals. Some are short term. Others are long term. As I have reached some of my goals, I have reset my goals. I always know where I want, or at least hope, to be at different stages of my career. I have always had a goal for where I wanted to be in 5 years, in 10 years and at the end of my career. I have never accepted the cliché "I will get it done as soon as possible." If someone says to me, "I will get you something as soon as possible," I always ask for a specific day and time.

If I need something at a specific time, I set that time. If I do not need it at a specific time, I ask the person promising something what day and time it will be accomplished. Everybody performs better and more efficiently when there is a deadline. I like to cite the example of the greyhound racing after a rabbit on the racetrack. The greyhound never catches the rabbit, but the dog surely runs faster than if there were no rabbit to chase after.

Likewise, I believe that I am more efficient and productive with timelines whether it is something that has to be done, for example, by tomorrow at 2 in the afternoon or something I want to accomplish in 5 years, 10 years or by the end of my career. Set goals and you will be more successful than you ever imagined was possible.

Unlike the merchant builder who buys and flips, my model calls for buying and holding, all the while taking the returns derived from the cash flow and from the appreciation of the asset upon refinancing. Therefore, my goals have to be precise and monitored in order for my investors and me to profit along the way. By focusing on my goals and not straying from my model, I am able to concentrate on a formula that has stood the test of time. Especially, at this time in my career, you can imagine how many e-mails, letters and calls I receive about so-called opportunities. I receive information on existing properties for sale and land for development from all over the United States. I get information about nonanchored retail strip centers, grocery-anchored centers, community centers, power centers, enclosed malls, urban village types of town centers, lifestyle centers and properties that have no retail component.

At this point in my career, the conundrum I face is not that I cannot raise enough equity for a property I want to buy. It is the opposite: I am at times frustrated that I frequently have insufficient properties for capital available from investors who wish to invest with me. Nevertheless, I stick to my model.

Although the expertise and experience I have gained through the years allow me to stray from my model, it has not materially changed it. I am still an acquirer of grocery-anchored neighborhood shopping centers located within 50 miles of my office.

I love to visit the very exciting new mixed-use projects that have been developed all over the country. I love to shop there as well, but I am not interested in developing or acquiring such projects.

I consider these types of real estate to be a high-risk business compared to the staple shopping center that acts as the fabric of America's marketplace for purchasing basic goods and services. I always evaluate the risk against the return, and the reason I have survived over 35 years in real estate investing—even through the financial calamities of the early 1990s and late 2000s—is that I have set a model that works for me.

Grocery-anchored shopping centers—like Springfield Plaza in Springfield, Virginia, a 260,974-square-foot community shopping center anchored by Giant Food, CVS/pharmacy, Trader Joe's, buybuy BABY and David's Bridal—have proven to be the least risky of all retail property types because people will always need food whether in good or bad times. Springfield Plaza is highly desirable to national retailers because it is surrounded by well-established neighborhoods and provides great visibility from Old Keene Mill Road in Springfield.

Why Grocery-Anchored Neighborhood Shopping Centers?

Historically, grocery-anchored shopping centers have proven to be the least risky of all retail property types. They are essential to the communities they serve. More important, the merchants operating in these neighborhood shopping centers largely carry consumables rather than durable or discretionary merchandise. Consumables are goods used by individuals who must replace them regularly because they consume them, such as food and prescription drugs, or use them up, such as toothpaste and computer printer ink, or even wear them out, such as clothing and razor blades.

Stores that sell consumables are considered to be relatively safe harbors for neighborhood center investors when the economy slows down because people always need to buy groceries, clothes and gasoline regardless of what happens to the economy. In fact, the U.S. government tracks a basket of consumables to calculate the Consumer Price Index (CPI) in monitoring inflation. Economists monitor this inflation in consumables because higher prices of these necessities lower the discretionary income people have left over to spend on discretionary items.

Discretionary spending consists of luxury items such as perfume, jewelry and expensive clothing, as well as durables like washing machines, television sets, personal computers and cars. Entertainment expenditures such as dining out, going to the movies and taking vacations are also considered discretionary.

Upscale shopping centers that offer a wide array of discretionary merchandise, entertainment venues and services can perform quite well in a strong economy, but neighborhood centers with tenants that lead their competitors in offering consumables and necessities do well in good as well as bad times.

Because of this philosophy, my investment properties tend to focus on retail tenants that sell consumer staples, because many of their products are household- and food-related. These properties also seek out service-oriented tenants that cater to the convenience of their surrounding neighborhood households. These service-oriented tenants include a laundry, a bank, a dry cleaner, an insurance agency, a residential real estate office and other consumer-oriented services. Because neighborhood centers lease to tenants that cater to the local customer, some of the tenants will be mom-and-pop stores, which help to complement the draw of regional and national credit tenants like the well-capitalized Safeway supermarket chain and Walgreen's pharmacy chain.

Mitigating Risk in the Leasing Process

Mom-and-pop stores are independent retailers that own and operate one or two locations, rather than creditworthy regional, national and global chains. While mom-and-pop stores have virtually disappeared from the regional mall scene, many of these independent retailers thrive in neighborhood centers because they offer a shopping alternative to consumers. They typically operate pizza parlors, Chinese restaurants, dry cleaning stores, hairstyling salons, jewelry and repair shops, and gift as well as apparel stores.

As the managing partner of the property investment, you should be constantly trying to balance the reliability of the rental income stream with the objective of maximizing the property's income. As a result, creditworthiness of your tenants is an important consideration but not the only one when you are creating a tenant mix that attracts the most customers and results in the highest possible average rent per square foot.

For example, which would you rather lease to in your center—Master-Cuts hairstyling salon, run by the publicly owned Regis Corporation, which is the industry's leader in beauty salons, operating company-owned and franchised stores in almost 13,000 worldwide locations, or a mom-and-pop beauty salon? The answer is, "It depends if the locally owned salon is in a shopping center across the street from yours performing at $900 per square foot with a steady clientele and is considering moving into your center."

Simply put, you need these moms-and-pops, and you are going to factor the inherent risk. Even with the developer's personal guarantee secured by the equity of their home, the added security does not match the assurance that a global chain like Regis Corporation offers in guaranteeing their lease obligation for the full term of the lease. Hence, a risk premium for noncredit tenant leases is usually priced into the deal.

For all my grocery-anchored shopping centers, my finance and leasing teams monitor the ratio of credit to noncredit tenants to maintain the risk of the investment in check.

For example, in a 125,000-square-foot grocery-anchored shopping center, the grocery store anchor comprises 55,000 square feet on average, depending on the operator. With possibly a pharmacy (which the grocery tenant does not always allow if it has an exclusive provision in the lease), a bank or two, and a few other regional and national credit tenants, the tenancy of my typical neighborhood center generally consists of 60 percent credit and 40 percent noncredit. This enables the shopping center to attain a highly productive rental income stream. While some of the individual tenant's rents are high and some low, the average rents provide a good mix and spread the risk among credit and noncredit tenants of all types and sizes.

Something to keep in mind in retail real estate is that risk is always a factor whether you are dealing with moms-and-pops or large chains because retail is a very competitive arena where retailers are constantly changing to keep up with ever-changing consumer demands. While the pool of retailers to choose from when leasing a neighborhood shopping center is staggering, your choice of retailers leading in particular sales classifications are few, primarily for big-box specialty stores to anchor the center.

Retail consolidation in the 2000s has lowered the number of available big-box credit tenants in categories other than grocery. At the outset of the 2010s, we have two major players in value-oriented general merchandise. Those are Wal-Mart Stores Inc. (Walmart), the world's largest retailer, and Target Corporation (Target), widely recognized by its red trademark bull's-eye logo. Sears Holdings Corp.'s Kmart and Kohl's Department Stores Inc. also operate stores widely in neighborhood and community centers.

In building material and home improvement, only two major players remain. Those are The Lowe's Companies (Lowes), with the blue and white logo, and The Home Depot, the global do-it-yourself store where all associates sport a familiar orange apron.

Only two major booksellers reign in bricks-and-mortar superstores averaging 25,000 square feet: Barnes & Noble Inc. and Borders Group Inc. (Borders). A distant third, Books-A-Million, operates more than 200 stores, including Books-A-Million and Books & Co. superstores and traditional bookstores like Bookland.

According to Dun & Bradstreet's Hoovers Inc., U.S. bookstores ring in $15 billion in annual sales and operate more than 11,000 stores, most of them also selling on the Internet. National booksellers like Borders have been closing its smaller Waldenbooks stores, and Barnes & Noble revised its business model to shutter all its B. Dalton Bookseller stores in 2010. Both chains currently prefer to focus on their larger store format and selling through their popular Web sites, which includes book downloads.

Fortunately, there are more tenant choices in other retail categories, although not all operate in big boxes. In pet and pet supplies, you can select from PetSmart Inc., PETCO Animal Supply Stores Inc., Pet Supplies "Plus"/USA Inc. and the small-format Petland Inc. This category in the United States alone accounts for $8 billion in annual sales from 7,500 stores.

The office supply category offers adequate choices for large-box operators from the likes of Office Depot Inc., Staples Inc. and OfficeMax Incorporated.

In footwear, there are more choices for big-box anchor stores including Shoe Carnival Inc., Marty Shoes Inc. (Marty's Shoes), DSW Shoe Warehouse, Brown Shoe Company (Famous Footwear), SHOE SHOW Inc. (SHOE SHOW, SHOE DEPT. and Burlington Shoes) and others. The sporting goods and sports apparel category offers yet more retailers that anchor neighborhood and community centers, such as Henry Modell & Company Inc. (Modell's Sporting Goods), The Sports Authority Inc., Eastern Mountain Sports, Dick's Sporting Goods Inc., Recreational Equipment Inc. (REI), Academy Sports + Outdoors, Dunham's Sports, Gander Mountain Company (Gander Mtn), Cabela's Inc., and several other national and regional chains.

Actually, there are hundreds of retailers that operate big-box stores that you can choose to anchor your community and neighborhood centers in a myriad of categories from craft stores like Michael's Stores Inc., Jo-Ann Fabric & Craft Stores and A.C. Moore Arts & Crafts to apparel stores including TJX Companies (TJ Maxx, Marshall's, HomeGoods and AJWright), Gap Inc. (Gap, Banana Republic, Old Navy), Bob's Stores, Ross Stores Inc. (Ross Dress for Less) and Dress Barn Inc., to name just a few.

An exhaustive list of retailers by sales volume, retail classifications, etc., can be searched on *www.findouter.com* worldwide and more specifically in *www.findouter.com/USA* for U.S.–based retailers.

However, the stiff competition of the mid-2000s followed by the downturn of the late 2000s took its toll in other important categories anchoring community centers, neighborhood centers and power centers. Best Buy Co. Inc. (Best Buy) is the only major national player in large-format consumer electronics still standing after challenging its fierce competitors with its low-priced model for decades.

Bankrupt electronics retailer Circuit City liquidated its remaining 567 stores in 2009, turning several hundred otherwise successful neighborhood and community centers into distressed real estate. Similarly, Bed Bath & Beyond Inc. (operating stores under the names Bed Bath & Beyond, Christmas Tree Shops, Harmon, Harmon Face Values and buybuy BABY) beat out its competitor, Linens 'N Things, in the linens and home goods category, when the latter closed its remaining 371 stores in 2008.

Even though there are regional players in these and other big-box categories, it puts a different level of risk on the investment when instead of leasing to a specialty retailer, you can lease to a strong grocer to anchor your shopping center.

There are hundreds of retailers operating big-box stores you can choose to anchor your community and neighborhood centers, such as the young family magnet buybuy BABY, a unit of Bed Bath & Beyond Inc., seen here at Springfield Plaza, in Springfield, Virginia.

During the 2008–2009 recession, I witnessed several very successful owners of shopping centers being forced to give back their properties to their lenders in foreclosure. Everything seemed to be going well for them until one of these big-box tenants went out of business, a situation that caused an immediate drain in cash flow from the loss in rent of these tenants, as well as a trickle-down effect on the smaller tenants.

At least in the Washington, D.C., market where I operate, as in most markets, the grocery category still has many competitors, but even that category has its threats. At the start of the 2000s, industry observers said that the Walmart Supercenter and SuperTarget—with their wide array of low-priced groceries and general merchandise—were going to put all the grocery stores out of business.

Winn-Dixie Supermarket Grocery Stores, Bruno's Supermarkets, Bashas' Supermarkets Inc., BI-LO LLC and other grocery store chains had to file for bankruptcy protection while they reorganized, but for the most part, the grocery business retrenched and became stronger.

Walmart Supercenter, SuperTarget, Costco Wholesale Corporation, Sam's Club, BJ's Wholesale Club and other low-cost food-for-home providers have unquestionably snatched a large share of the grocery business, but it is such a vast category catering to every American family year-round that there are millions of people who still prefer choices beyond these hypermarkets and wholesale club formats.

U.S. retail grocery annual sales hover around $500 billion, according to Hoover's, and 70,000 stores nationwide generate these staggering sales. The 50 largest grocers, which among them are Ahold, Kroger, Safeway and SUPERVALU, account for 70 percent of the grocery volume.

In our market, we have Giant Food LLC owned by Royal Ahold (operators of Giant and Stop & Shop), Safeway Inc. (operators of Safeway, Eastern, Genuardi's Family Markets, Dominick's, Vons, Tom Thumb and many others), Save-A-Lot, SUPERVALU Inc (operators of Shoppers Food Warehouse, Acme, Albertsons, Bigg's, Bristol Farms, Cub, Farm Fresh, Hornbacher's, Jewel-Osco, Shaw's/Star Market, and Shop 'n Save), Harris Teeter, Wegmans Food Markets Inc. (Wegmans), Whole Foods Market Inc. (Whole Foods), Food Lion LCC owned by Delhaize Group (operators of Food Lion, Harveys Supermarket, Bloom, Bottom Dollar Food, and Reid's), Trader Joe's and several regional ethnic grocery store operators.

My business model takes into consideration the strength of this phenomenal retail category in the stable Washington, D.C., metropolitan area, where so many strong players serve as anchors to hundreds of neighborhood centers. If a grocery tenant were to vacate a space in one of my shopping centers, it is comforting to know that I have several possibilities to re-lease that space to another—hopefully more resilient—grocery tenant.

The stability of the federal government helps to maintain the Washington, D.C., metropolitan area relatively robust during U.S. recessions, and for that reason historically draws a large pool of national retailers. Although not exactly recession-proof, the Washington metro area ranked the lowest in retail vacancy rates in the nation in the third quarter of 2009 as the severe downturn in the economy was ending. In that period, the average vacancy rate in this market was the lowest for nongrocery and grocery-anchored shopping centers combined among large U.S. metros, according to an independent year-end retail report by Delta Associates, which TRC sponsored.

The report cited an overall vacancy for all types of shopping centers in the Washington metro at 5.6 percent, compared to the national average of

9.4 percent. The metro area includes D.C., Arlington and Alexandria as well as the Maryland counties of Montgomery and Prince George's and the Virginia counties of Fairfax, Loudoun and Prince William. For comparison, the second-lowest retail vacancies occurred in the San Francisco metro area, at 5.9 percent, and the New York metro area, which ranked third lowest in retail vacancy in the United States, at 6.3 percent.

The Delta report cites grocery-anchored centers as having the most stability compared to other retail property types. According to Delta, 319 grocery-anchored shopping centers account for 55.9 million square feet in the Washington, D.C., metro area, which is nearly half of the 118 million square feet of retail space in the area comprising more than 1,000 shopping centers. More than half of the total metro retail space is in northern Virginia.

Delta estimates that the Washington metro area accounts for 25 square feet of retail space per capita, compared to the national average of 23.4, but the inner core comprising the District of Columbia remains underserved at just 8.5 square feet of retail space per capita.

Grocery stores in the D.C. metro area averaged $24.4 million in sales volume per store during 2009, according to Delta, with Wegmans producing the highest per store volume at $62.2 million per store.

In the third quarter of 2009 as the 2008–2009 recession was ending, inner-core D.C.–area rental rates at grocery-anchored centers had decreased by 5.8 percent from 2008 to $31.77 per square foot for in-line tenant rents while rents in the outer ring of the Washington metro area had dropped by 7.4 percent to $27.02 per square foot.

Considering the negative impact that recessionary forces can have on retail vacancy and rental rates, this relatively mild drop in occupancy and rental rates in the Washington market gives me confidence in my long-held belief not to venture too far from Washington in expanding my retail real estate enterprise.

A 50-Mile Radius

My team is well aware of my 50-mile rule. A 50-mile radius—certainly no more than a two-hour drive—from my office allows the senior executives in my company and me to visit our properties more frequently than we could otherwise if we operated properties spread out over hundreds or thousands of miles.

I am not the only developer who sticks to a two-hour drive for owning and managing retail properties. In rural areas, an equivalent measurement of a two-hour drive might be 100 miles but it is the same concept. Whether it is the vice president of property management inspecting the properties and visiting with his property managers or the quarterly and yearly onsite inspections that our senior executives make or the number of times I can visit any of my properties, 50 miles works well for us.

It also helps us to become intrinsically familiar with the market. Real estate is a local business. This factor alone gives regional developers like me a competitive edge over national developers. It underscores why a smaller developer can compete with a bigger, better capitalized developer that does business over a wide geographic area, sometimes from coast to coast.

The regional developer concentrates on knowing everything there is to know about the market. Knowing every street; knowing the competition today and what is planned for the future; understanding the different submarkets in a way that demographic reports cannot always reveal; knowing where the growth is planned and building up a reputation with community groups are essential to be successful in retail real estate.

Moreover, knowing public officials personally and through reputation helps in the entitlement process. These firsthand contacts are another advantage, whether it is obtaining a rezoning, a building permit, a special exemption, or approvals for a zoning variance to expand your property. Conversely, these public officials prefer developers who reside in the community and are considering their investment as an investment in their community rather than just a financial investment.

Proximity also gives drive-by investors a comfort level to invest with you when they know you can readily watch over their investment. An additional benefit to the investor is that they *too* can more easily visit their investment property.

Knowing the market intrinsically, recognizing which tenants are expanding in the market and understanding the market needs for retail often reveals the market-driven justifications for developing, managing, leasing and investing in specific retail projects.

When anchors disclose to you their expansion desires, you can use your market expertise to accommodate those anchors in your shopping center as well as at other noncompetitive centers.

In a best-case scenario, you can utilize this knowledge to approach other owners to convince them to sell you a property that has not been listed for sale. Or as an alternative, you might work out a joint venture where their center and your organization can benefit together from anchors' expansion plans you bring to the table.

CHAPTER III

Raising Capital: Debt and Equity

Assessing Capital Needs

AFTER YOU FIND the right investment, one of your main responsibilities as the sponsor of the partnership is to assemble the capital needed to acquire and fund the investment. You will be raising capital from a combination of sources that will result in putting new debt on the property and giving up ownership interest to other stakeholders, your partners.

If you are starting an entrepreneurial partnership to develop retail and are not familiar with raising equity or assembling debt as more sophisticated real estate developers would, you may feel somewhat intimidated at first. Do not allow this to hold you back. It is not that complicated.

Deciding the appropriate balance between equity capital and debt financing is going to be your first step.

Understanding Your Lender (the Debt)

Banks do not usually lend money to a homeowner to buy a residential property unless the homeowner puts a down payment deposit of at least 20 percent of the purchase price. That down payment becomes the homeowner's equity that the bank would assume as collateral in repossession if the homeowner defaults on his loan. This allows the bank some leeway to remain whole if it has to sell on foreclosure.

Commercial real estate functions in a similar manner. The owner needs to put up equity to obtain a commercial mortgage. You can raise that equity by selling a portion of ownership interest to investors that will enable you to acquire the piece of real estate.

Conversely, raising capital through debt financing does not involve selling the equity at all. The process involves borrowing the debt along with raising the equity that you and your partners will invest. Usually, when you first purchase a retail property, the debt is going to be with a commercial bank. You are very likely going to have to give the lender your personal guarantee and as such, you will need to establish a personal relationship with the loan officer.

Years later, when the property is stabilized, you can replace the commercial debt with a nonrecourse permanent loan (except for nonrecourse carveouts) where you will have few dealings with a master servicer who processes your loan payments. (*See Chapter VI, Setting Up the Deal, "Lender Requirement," on pages 94–100*).

At that stage, you would not have a personal relationship with the master servicer because he or she acts as an agent to service thousands of loans for banks and other institutional investors.

Servicers do not lend money. They simply collect from borrowers and deposit the funds in the lenders' accounts. As long as you are making adequate loan payments on time, you will have little dealings with the complacent master servicer assigned to your account. That is all they care about when it comes to you as a client.

If you miss making several timely payments, the holder of your note will take your account away from the master servicer and assign it to a special servicer who will delve into your business to make sure the lender is protected. That special servicer would be involved in loan workouts and alternatively, worse, foreclosure recommendations to the lender.

Loans held by commercial banks in their portfolio (portfolio loans) are serviced differently than conduit loans (CMBS loans), which are securitized. These two types of debt represent the principal categories of commercial real estate first mortgage debt.

Lenders typically originate and hold portfolio loans on their balance sheet through maturity. The commercial mortgage-backed securities (CMBS) model involves many single mortgage loans of varying sizes, property types and locations, pooled and transferred into one trust. The trust issues a series of bonds that may vary in yield, duration and payment priority. National rating agencies assign credit ratings to the various bond classes for investors to buy according to the level of credit risk, yield and duration that they seek.

The typical structure for the securitization of commercial real estate loans is a real estate mortgage investment conduit (REMIC), which relates to tax law that allows the trust to pass through tax obligation, thereby not being taxed at the trust level. CMBS transactions comply with REMIC regulations.

If you are not familiar with how to place debt on your soon-to-acquire asset, enlist the services of a knowledgeable consultant who can guide you through the process. Keep in mind that the focus in raising debt capital will be on the initial debt you place on the property. Therefore, select your initial lender carefully, but be mindful that although selecting a lender is important, it is by far easier than selecting an investor partner.

Your lender is truly *not* your partner. Your lender is not interested in taking risks as your partner ordinarily would. Your lender is in the business of making money from you by letting you use its money for a specific period. The details of that business relationship will be spelled out in the loan documents, as commercial real estate mortgages are usually lengthier than home mortgages. On the other hand, your partners will likely be with you as long as you own the investment and that can mean decades after you have repaid your initial mortgage.

Lining Up Potential Investors (the Equity)

Lining up investors—the equity—for your investment property will probably be where you will spend most of your time, energy and resources. Unlike obtaining permanent financing involving a mortgage governed by a mortgage agreement (which the underwriter often sells to investors represented by a master servicer who collects your monthly debt service), the equity piece will typically demand more of your attention.

A group of private investors usually funds the equity portion. These investors have one thing in common. They are expecting a high rate of return on their investment for the risk they are assuming. These investors will be watching what is occurring monthly and comparing the progress to your initial business plan.

An equity investor, who would be interested in investing with me, is interested in a shopping center that shows great potential for an increase in cash flow and appreciation. The investor understands that if you grow the asset, his share of cash flow and appreciation will increase as well. The investor recognizes that his investment lacks liquidity and carries great risk, for which he expects to be properly compensated.

Otherwise, the investor would keep his money invested in a well-balanced portfolio containing stocks, bonds and money market instruments that he could liquidate at a moment's notice. That type of investment caters to investors who are satisfied with the safety, cash flow and modest capital appreciation they derive from these safer investments.

However, the type of investor you are seeking has much different traits. Among these traits is the investor's expectation that you will acquire under-performing real estate that with your expertise and hard work will produce substantial cash flow and appreciation from the rental income to deliver solid returns for the long term.

Some developers do not sell shares in their investment themselves and prefer using a fund-raiser to attract equity capital. I have used a broker dealer to raise capital on only two occasions. However, in most instances, I like to reach out to potential investors directly and build a relationship with them from the outset.

Relationship-building and frequent communication thus become the cornerstone of an enduring investor partnership. In your first several deals—perhaps every deal you ever do—you will want to establish a personal rapport with all your investors. Personal meetings provide the opportunity to more fully discuss your objectives, the merits of the investment and potential risks. They also provide investors a one-on-one opportunity to address his or her specific concerns or questions in connection with his or her own independent due diligence.

As such, I think dealing with informed investors who personally know you is an important part of avoiding future litigation with your investors in case the investment property is not successful or, even if successful, not as successful as you initially projected.

In every one of my partnerships, I have personally met every investor before accepting their offer to invest with me. That does not mean every investor was a personal friend prior to investing with me. My other investors recommended some of these investors to me. This process has an inherently lower risk of litigation resulting from disputes between the sponsor and his investors.

The interests you will be making available to equity investors will be "securities" under the U.S. Securities Act of 1933 (the Act). Absent an exemption, a sponsor of a real estate partnership would be required to register the offering of such securities with the Securities and Exchange Commission (SEC).

To avoid registration and other substantive regulation, most real estate investment partnerships are structured to rely on one or more exemptions from registration under the Act, and most often the private placement exemption available for "transactions not involving any public offering."

Often referred to as the *Truth in Securities* law, the Act has two basic objectives:

1. Require that investors receive financial and other significant information concerning securities being offered for public sale
2. Prohibit deceit, misrepresentations and other fraud in the sale of securities

The ability to rely upon the private placement exemption depends upon several factors, including:

1. The manner of the offering (An issuer may not engage in a general solicitation or publicly advertise.)
2. The nature of the offerees (The exemption is intended where prospective investors are believed to be sufficiently knowledgeable and sophisticated to understand the merits and risks of the offering and, therefore, able to fend for themselves.)
3. The number and quality of offerees (not just the number of purchasers) and their relationship to each other and the issuer

A fund sponsor generally is not considered to be engaging in a general solicitation where they have had a prior substantive relationship with the prospective investor prior to making any offer to invest. A "substantive" relationship is one where the issuer has sufficient information to evaluate the prospective investor's sophistication and financial circumstances. In other words, do they have the financial acumen to understand the merits and risks of the offering, and can they bear the financial risk of loss with respect to the investment?

At the risk of stating the obvious, wealth does not necessarily correlate to financial sophistication. As part of the getting-to-know-you process when raising equity capital, you should seek information to help you evaluate the prospective investor's financial acumen and investment experience. Such information typically includes information related to a person's employment history, business experience, investment experience, income and net worth. Income and net worth considerations are important for other reasons, as I will relate later.

When dealing in small circles and with close business associates, much of this information is often gleaned naturally and more informally over time. When relationships are less developed, issuers often ask prospective investors to complete a written questionnaire or other form that solicits such information.

All of my partnerships have been offered through a private placement, so I have not had to endure the registration process. Though interests offered in a private placement may be exempt from registration, you must still provide your prospective investors with information about the investment offering, yourself as the issuer and your underlying objectives for the offering.

The level of disclosure may be driven explicitly by the Act and, more specifically, by Regulation D under the Act, to the extent an issuer seeks to rely upon Regulation D. Regulation D is a nonexclusive safe harbor that, if followed, ensures that an offering will be exempt from registration. By its terms, a safe harbor cannot be violated. If the safe harbor's requirements cannot be met, an issuer can seek to rely upon other exemptions from registration.

The level of disclosure required by Regulation D depends upon the size of the offering and the types of investors to whom an offer is made. Rules 504 and 505 of Regulation D deal with offers and sales of securities not exceeding $1 million and $5 million, respectively. Offers and sales without regard to dollar amount are addressed in Rule 506.

The level of disclosure also will depend upon whether offers are made exclusively to accredited investors or whether they are extended to nonaccredited investors. An individual is defined to be an accredited investor under the Act if the individual's net worth or joint net worth with that person's spouse equals or exceeds $1 million at the time of purchase.

Alternatively, an individual is an accredited investor if such person's gross income exceeds $200,000 per year (or $300,000 collectively with such person's spouse) for the most recent two years and such person has a reasonable expectation of reaching such income level in the current year (the year of investment).

Entities and other institutional investors generally must have assets in excess of $5 million in order to fall within the definition of accredited investor. Larger offerings under Rules 505 and 506 limit the number of nonaccredited investors to 35.

The level of disclosure is also driven implicitly by the Act's antifraud rules set forth in Section 10(b) and Rule 10(b-5). These prohibit an issuer from making any untrue statement of a material fact and omitting a material fact necessary to avoid misleading the prospective investors.

In essence, when you are raising equity, you are subject to the Act's antifraud rules regardless of whether or not the offering is exempt from registration. The antifraud rules apply to material omissions and misrepresentations. What is material to one investor may not be material to another. The standard is generally whether it would be substantially likely that a "reasonable" investor would consider a fact important.

Determining what constitutes the "reasonable" investor is inherently difficult. Thus, to better protect yourself from potential liability under the antifraud rules, you should make available to prospective investors the same kind of information that the Act would require to be made available in the form of a registration statement. You should then deliver the information so that the potential investor has an understanding about the issuer, its business and the securities being offered.

Given the uncertainties and the potential liability resulting from inaccurate disclosures or material omissions, many issuers seek to include the information identified by the SEC in Form S-1 (the form registration statement under the Act that is used in registering securities under the Act) and Form N-1A (the form registration statement used to register a publicly offered mutual fund under the Investment Company Act of 1940).

In such instances, the SEC arguably has indicated the type of information that it believes is important enough to require to be disclosed to public investors. The SEC Web site provides the Commission's forms as well as instructions: visit *www.sec.gov.*

Anyone forming a partnership to pursue equity investments should seek legal advice as to the requirements of the Act, as some sections pertain to the type of partnership you will be forming, and you must adhere to what the Act requires you to disclose to potential investors. As part of the first three deals I completed, my attorneys suggested I convey the offering in a Private Placement Memorandum (PPM). The law firm that represented me specialized in securities trading and thus assisted me in preparing the PPM at a substantial cost for legal, accounting and consultant fees. Even though the partnership incurred the cost of preparing this package, it was nevertheless expensive relative to my typical investor package.

I surmise that my attorneys wanted to limit my exposure in the deal back then. By preparing the PPM, I could control the information provided to investors and seek to ensure that the scope of information provided and the level of detail were consistent with the registration statement required to be filed with the SEC and made available to public (less sophisticated) investors.

By delivering the PPM, I could ensure that investors received such information. And through the fund's subscription agreement, which I required prior to permitting an investment, I was able to secure documentation that the investor had read and understood the offering memorandum and had the opportunity to ask me questions about the proposed investment.

Today, preparing a PPM to raise equity for a typical property investment can cost between $35,000 to $50,000, while my typical investor package, which is mostly done in our office, costs less than $100.

As in my case, knowledgeable counsel—attorneys and accountants—will need to guide you in this regard. No single investment prospectus package fits all situations. Keep in mind that your investment package needs to comply with all applicable laws and regulations that may cross over various jurisdictions.

Each state has different securities requirements to protect investors. Even federal regulations may change because of the highly publicized conviction of Ponzi-scheme operator Bernard L. Madoff, who bilked investors in a multibillion-dollar fraud, and because of the trillions of dollars in net worth lost by millions of investors during the financial crisis of the late 2000s.

Members of your investment group should be made cognizant that you as the sponsor also have your money at risk in the investment and that your decisions will be aligned with the interests of the investment group.

As the sponsor, you would share in the loss with all members of the investment group if the investment fails. On the other hand, if the investment is profitable, you would gain in proportion with the rest of the group and then receive a carried interest or back-end promote provision as an incentive for enhancing the investment. I will explain this in more detail in Chapter VI.

The question that students most often ask me in the class I teach for ICSC on this subject is, "How do you find investors?" Unfortunately, there is no shortcut or magic answer. It is a matter of talking to others about your project, approaching people that you think might be looking for an investment opportunity and, most important, being credible and having a proposal that is straightforward and that seems like a promising opportunity.

There is no doubt about it: Your first deal will be the hardest for which to find investors. However, as your track record is established and you assemble a group of satisfied investors, you will have a growing pool of individuals who are willing to invest with you based on your credibility and your previous successes.

Institutional investors, such as insurance companies and investment institutions, might also serve as potential partners. There are advantages and disadvantages to both types of investors. I will cover the two types of investors and how to structure the deals in greater detail in Chapter IV.

Your Investor Book

As the sponsor or managing partner, you will need to select the investment property, create a business plan for that property, seek out investors and borrow funds to acquire the property.

One key tool to find investors and borrow money is creating a package that describes the property and the plan you have for the property.

Preparing "the Book"

What I call "the book" is a property investment package or investor prospectus. Whether the book is a PPM or is your own presentation of information about the deal, certain information on the deal must be presented. Investors will use this prospectus to consider the merits of your offering and make educated investment decisions.

When you start planning your first investment, you will find yourself spending dozens of hours preparing a mammoth, comprehensive package that will act as a road map for you and as a business plan for the property. Your potential investors will read this important plan to see if they trust your skills and abilities enough to part with their money.

The investor prospectus I create contains details on the property, investment strategy, redevelopment opportunities and how cash flow and appreci-

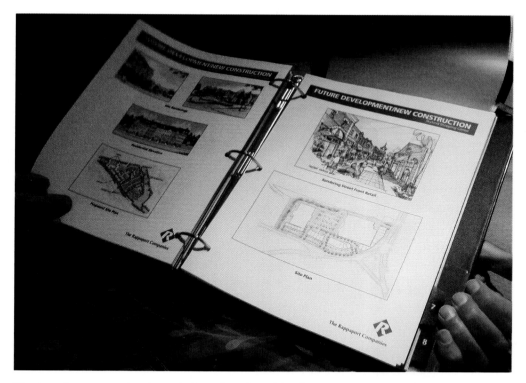

The investor prospectus I create to sell partnership shares to my prospective investors contains details on the property, investment strategy, redevelopment opportunities and how cash flow and appreciation will be shared during the property's operation and upon refinancing or disposition.

PHOTO: R. E. MILIAN

ation will be shared during the property's operation and upon refinancing or disposition.

The book gives your qualified investors an in-depth look at the investment, its risks and projected returns for the investment partners. The book also serves as a model for obtaining financing with some modifications pertinent to a potential lender.

"The Book" for Investors (the Equity)

At a minimum, the investor package should contain:

- Purchase price of the project (along with costs of any immediate repairs or other work that needs to be done)
- Photographs and information about the shopping center, including location, demographics and retail mix
- Suggestions for expansions, renovations and remerchandising projects that can be undertaken, and the costs involved in each
- Sources and use of initial funds for purchase
- Overall cash flow projections over an 11-year period
- Overall return on investment, based on expected sale or refinancing upon stabilization of income stream
- Estimated timing on the return of investment
- Details of net cash flow and return to investors

The more times you create such a package, the easier and more efficient it will become, and you will be prepared when the ideal property comes along. Being able to look at the finished packages also can help you see what might not work in each shopping center. For example, you will easily recognize if a list price is too high or if the center is in a bad location or if it has undesirable key tenants that are not easily replaceable.

The ideal property will be well located with steady traffic, easy access and exit onto the road or highway, and plenty of opportunities for remerchandising, renovation and expansion. The ultimate goal should be to make the more significant changes over a three- to five-year period at most.

Upon completing the book, your next step will set the course for assuming control of the property. That step is securing the equity. Make an appointment with each potential investor as soon as you are ready to present the deal in the most professional manner (even before you have the property under contract). Be prepared to make your face-to-face presentation. Create a PowerPoint presentation and practice delivering it in front of a mirror, if necessary. You will frequently be presenting to an investor who will be accompanied by a spouse. Both are just as important to convince.

Be passionate about what you will be able to do to grow the investment. Believe in your plan. Your words and expressions will convey your confidence. If you use slides, they should also be included in the investor package that the potential investor will read to refresh himself or herself about what you say during your presentation.

Make sure you state clearly and eloquently the issues and problems with the property (why you are acquiring below the underlying value) and your solution (how you will realize that value). Show several slides of the property as it is today, including slides of the plot plan and lease plan. Follow with slides depicting the expansion or renovation scenarios you are planning for the same plot and lease plans.

Discuss the current tenant mix and market highlights as well as point out how you plan to enhance the tenant mix. Be thorough in explaining the market. Describe the competition in an honest and candid manner. Explain the competition's strengths and weaknesses, and most important, discuss the property's competitive advantage and what you plan to do to make it even stronger.

If you follow my model, your potential investor will be local to the area and may know the market as well as you. Refrain from hesitating or wavering from your message. You cannot afford to falter. Your potential investor's knowledge of the market serves to reinforce your expertise. Remember, *you* are the retail expert. You are the authority who knows what tenants are interested in entering the market and why this investment property suits their needs.

Show slides with figures that depict income and expenses as the property stands today and how the property would perform after an expansion up to the stabilization of the incremental income. Carefully select your financial data in order to clarify the capital expenditures needed and how you plan to finance those expenses. Depict how the debt service you are planning will impact the property's funds from operations.

Review the investment property's anticipated returns from cash flow and how cash will be divided upon a refinancing or disposition. Show the effects of the potential appreciation of the property coupled with cash distributed for a projected total compounded investment return.

Lastly, sell your management team and your development skills. Sell yourself and your expertise. Tell the potential investor how you have accomplished similar challenges whether or not you executed these types of enhancements for yourself or a past employer.

Leave plenty of time for questions. Your potential investor will not remember everything you said. Be patient and not condescending in answering all questions in a conversational manner.

"The Book" for the Lender (the Debt)

The book for lenders is very similar to the investor package. For the most part, the same information that is used for the investor package can also be used for the lender package. Information that is pertinent only to the investors should be excluded from the lender package, such as how the cash flow and the appreciation are shared between the investor group and yourself, or the return on investment you are projecting to your investors.

In your package, the lender will pay close attention to your cash flow before and after debt service, as well as the projected value of the property upon maturity of the mortgage, to make sure you have a financially sound exit strategy that will enable the loan to be repaid.

Unlike the investor, the lender will not be reviewing the book to measure how steep the yield curb is because the lender will not be sharing in your distributions of cash flow and appreciation. The lender only wants to be assured that at any point in time, you will have the ability to repay the loan and that if not, it will at least be able to foreclose on your mortgage to recover the debt still owed from the proceeds of a sale.

The lender package should include a term sheet that outlines what you expect to receive regarding the interest rate, guaranty and term of the loan. It also may be beneficial to show loan-to-cost (LTC), loan-to-value (LTV) and debt coverage ratios.

The LTC ratio refers to the price paid for the asset compared to the value of the loan that is obtained to finance the purchase. Lenders use the LTV ratio to compare how much the property is worth in relation to the loan. By comparing these two numbers against each other, they can accurately gauge the amount of risk that will be involved with the loan. The lower the LTV ratio, the more the lender is going to be willing to lend. This means that if you need to borrow significantly less money than what a property is worth, your odds of getting approved increase dramatically. The debt service coverage ratio (DSCR) is the ratio of cash available every month for servicing the debt to pay the monthly interest and principal owed.

Making the Presentation to Your Investors

Present the investment opportunity to possible investment partners as soon as you are ready to present the deal. Do this before you have the deal under contract or have an understanding with the seller. When I come across an opportunity to purchase a property that I wish to pursue, I recognize that this opportunity is probably evident to many other developers as well. Therefore, a timely presentation to potential investors might be the difference between a commitment to invest or a refusal of one.

For example, most purchases that I am involved with have at most a 30-day time frame to conduct the feasibility study with perhaps another 30-day period to close. I have a narrow window before my deposit is at risk and a limited period of time to raise the equity and obtain the debt. If you can buy more time from the seller, you can try negotiating a deal where instead of putting up a large deposit at risk, you can try to get a long study period at no cost or risk to you or with only a small cost (option) that you would forfeit if you decide not to proceed with the deal. This is not easy to accomplish in a hot market, but can be done if the seller is willing.

Whenever you have the opportunity, you should always make your presentation at the subject property. Investors feel closer to the opportunity presented when they can see the investment firsthand. It is also easier to explain how you are going to add value to the investment when doing so in person, walking through some of the stores or even standing on a vacant piece of land. In this case, no PowerPoint presentation is necessary.

My presentation begins in the parking lot, discussing the landscaping, asphalt, roofing, lighting, signage, painting or renovation I am proposing to do. I then walk my investor through some of the stores, especially those that I am planning to remerchandise with better tenants or subdivide in order to create a higher rent and a better mix. We will then visit one of the food establishments, if there is one, such as a coffee shop or sandwich shop, order something to eat or drink and take out the investment book.

I always have a complete book for each of the investors with me, as well as one for myself and anyone else from my company who might be accompanying me for the presentation. If the potential investor is visiting the property, for example, with his wife, one of his children and a friend, then you should have four complete investment books for the four of them, and when they leave each should be taking with them one of the books.

It can take anywhere from 30 to 90 minutes to go through the book depending on how many questions you are asked. You might have someone say right there and then that they would like to invest with you, but more often they will thank you, take the books with them and leave to review the material later.

If they have not committed, I always ask them if it is okay to call them in two days to further discuss their thoughts of investing. I always try to set a specific time they will be expecting a call from me. Bear in mind, it is your responsibility as the managing partner to close the deal.

In a way, we are all salespersons and we are always selling ahead of performing. We live on our past performance and our reputation, but we are also always selling what we can accomplish as well. As retail developers, we do this in our leasing as well as our raising debt and equity capital to enhance the investment.

We tell the retailer to lease space at our property. There is no better location to be successful because we understand tenant mix and how to manage the property. We tell the banker to lend us the money because we are a reliable borrower. And we tell the potential investor to invest with us because together we make the best investment partnership.

In your investment package and in your personal presentations you have to sell your attributes and skills as well as your company's virtues and the expertise of your senior management. The section in my investment book where I boast about my previous successes, my experience, my company and all my employees might be the largest section in the book. Do not be shy on selling everything positive about you, your company and your senior management team.

Prior to meeting with potential investors at the property, I fully review the investor book in my office and I prepare to describe the contents as well as the attributes of the shopping center and my company's experience in adding value to the investment.

Many developers have no cash to invest alongside their partners and instead put up their sweat equity on the deal, which is the personal time they invest in the property to create value for all partners. I always invest real cash in the partnership at an equal rate, *pari passu*, with my investors, and I always make sure they understand that. However, I never talk about contributing sweat equity. I contribute plenty of sweat equity, but I also put up my own money at risk with my investors.

I do not like the concept of sweat equity, and I think many sophisticated investors see it as a partner not willing or able to invest real cash in the deal. I do talk about a disproportionate sharing of cash flow and appreciation but only if I achieve substantial financial hurdles for all the partners to benefit. But whether I meet those projections or not, I am investing real cash with them from the first day of the partnership.

In my first several partnerships, the amount of my cash investment equaled the amount of the investment unit I was trying to sell—that way I could tell each possible investor I was investing the same amount of money as I was asking them to invest.

As my success and the success of my deals grew, so did the amount of equity I needed to raise, the size of my investor pool and the financial ability of some of my investors to invest larger amounts of money than I was able or wished to invest. As the deal size grew, my investment no longer equaled the investment unit I was trying to sell. However, in all cases I made sure every investor knew, right from the beginning, how much as a minimum I was going to be investing.

I also make sure every investor knows if I am personally guaranteeing the bank loan, or even if it is a nonrecourse loan and that I am personally guaranteeing the nonrecourse carve-outs.

Investors of real estate tend to have one thing in common. They want to see the value of their investment grow substantially over time. They are hiring you to create value. Creating value is your main role as the developer. Keep in mind that to attract investors you will need to convince them that the property has potential for substantial asset appreciation.

If that property is a vacant piece of land, it is building a shopping center that will create the value. If it is an existing operating property, it will be a property that needs a capital infusion. In return, you are going to be able to increase rents. In residential properties, they call this a *fixer-upper.* You really need a bargain-priced fixer-upper to create value in retail as well.

Asset Appreciation

Managing an investment shopping center property is not just about maintaining the status quo, keeping it clean and collecting the rents. You will want to make sure that there is plenty of opportunity to make positive changes to the property. This is not only to drive more traffic, but also to create better value for the tenants and require higher rent rates based on substantial improvements made to the property.

There are three ways to significantly transform a shopping center:

1. Renovation: This might be nonstructural upgrading such as increasing light levels in the parking lot and under the canopy, changing signage, adding landscaping, restriping the parking lot, making minor repairs or maybe even painting the shopping center. Renovating the property can also consist of major facade renovations that totally change the look of the center, which would include major structural changes to the building, such as replacing roofs, overlaying the entire parking lot after all structural repairs in the asphalt have been repaired or even replacing storefronts. Any or all of these items create the look that enables you to be able to set higher asking rents on vacant spaces and increase rents on spaces where lease terms are coming up for renewal.

2. Remerchandising: This involves taking a hard look at the current tenants, the present vacancies and each and every space, and seeing how you can maximize rental income while creating a tenant mix where tenants complement one another—in effect increasing the appeal of the property to the customer.

Can an existing tenant be replaced with a tenant that can pay more rent, have stronger financials, generate higher sales, or just fit into your overall plan for making your property more valuable? Can two spaces be combined to accommodate a larger, more productive retailer? Or can a large space be divided in two that can generate higher total rents?

Evaluate the existing tenant mix, the terms of the existing tenants' leases and the increases in their rent over the remaining terms of their leases. Figure out, based on when each lease ends, how and when you can increase rental income while also improving the tenant mix based on your plan for the property. Just remember, you must have a plan. The details of your plan provide the foundation you need to substantiate the financial projections that you are presenting to your partners.

For example, you have a shopping center that has less desirable tenants, such as a tattoo parlor or a check-cashing store. Improvements to the center, major or even just cosmetic, can entice chain stores and franchises such as Starbucks, Panera Bread Company and other successful regional or national chains to lease space at your center where before your improvements these types of tenants would not locate at the property even if you offered free rent.

While such tenants are more stable and have the ability to pay a higher rent than you are probably presently receiving from tenants that signed leases before you completed your improvements, they will most likely help you set a tone to attract better tenants to the center.

Some say retailers have a herd mentality. They locate alongside other lending retailers. There is some truth to that saying because good retailers attract more customers, and these customers visit and shop at other stores in the shopping center. The tone you set with your leasing strategy will allow you to obtain higher rents from some of the local tenants and chain stores that very much want to be cotenants with these strong regional and national tenants.

3. Expansion: More involved and complicated than renovation or re-merchandising is expanding the shopping center. Be creative about maximizing the GLA of the property. For instance, maybe a gas station or fast-food restaurant could be built on a pad in the parking lot or some new stores could be built out to either side of the shopping center. Perhaps several existing stores can be consolidated into a larger store that would be deeper than the existing stores and thus square footage would be increased.

These new additions often can command a high rent because they are the newest of stores within the center. New tenants moving into an already established center with anchor tenants in place are likely to pay higher rents per square foot than existing tenants, including the anchors.

What's more, if you are adding onto the side of the existing center, you have an opportunity to not only obtain the highest rents on the center but to build stores at a relatively very inexpensive cost. As for these additional stores, you usually have no added off-site costs, no added stormwater management facilities, no more major underground pipes to install and no additional parking lot to build. Furthermore, the utilities for the building, such as gas, electric and water, are adjoining and thus close by in the existing stores to hook up at minimal costs.

Expansion opportunities are frequently found in the parking fields of many sprawling community centers. This is because acceptable parking levels have gone down over the past 30 years from five to six cars per thousand square feet of GLA to as low as four to 4.5 cars in suburban areas, and even lower in densely populated areas. Today, developers can usually obtain permission to reduce parking ratios from anchor stores and seek zoning ordinance variances from communities to reduce excessive parking ratio requirements.

Before getting too involved in planning an expansion, make sure that the leases of existing stores do not prohibit certain new construction, that there will be adequate parking with the new businesses in place and that local zoning laws will allow for the expansion.

Getting the Investor to Sign on the Dotted Line

After the investor agrees to make his investment, he will be required to sign the limited liability corporation, or partnership agreement, a form confirming he is or is not an accredited investor, and submit his funds to you to proceed with acquiring the property and obtaining financing.

Be ready when the time comes. You may ask, "How do I learn and practice before I am ready to plunge in as a developer and sponsor of retail property?" As the sponsor, you will start by sorting through many investment properties that you will have no interest in purchasing before choosing the right opportunity for yourself and your investors.

At the ICSC University of Shopping Centers, I tell my students who are considering starting their own investment and development companies to practice the process even before they are ready to undertake their first investment partnership. Choose a property that meets your criteria and begin the due diligence process. Selecting the right property is essential to your success. Study the prospectus; analyze the lease rent roll and lease expirations; visit the property; and look for expansion opportunity.

Try to determine market rents and compare with actual rents. Visit the competition. Identify retail prospects for the shopping center that can satisfy the market it serves and that can perform the highest sales in order to compensate the partnership by paying the highest rents. Determine cost, value and ability to finance and raise capital for the investment that meets your prescribed investment model.

Times dictate how much equity needs to be raised in proportion to financing available. Most important, project the potential for asset appreciation the property can offer upon refinancing or disposition some years later. Unlike other forms of investments, income property offers its big payoff many years later while rewarding your investors and you with returns on your initial investment along the way.

Create a plan you feel comfortable with because it is confirmed by your financial projections and has been designed to provide increasing cash flow as well as appreciation over the expected holding period of the investment. This will require balancing the amount of money you believe needs to be invested in the property, along with the new rents you are going to be able to obtain and a realistic time frame to reach a level of stability for a disposition of the asset, or at least an assumed sale that depicts the benefits of an appreciated asset. The pro forma must be realistic and depict costs and income projected over time.

At the time of the initial acquisition, I often show statements that describe my sources of funds and how I intend to use those funds. (Refer to tables in the case studies presented later in this book.) The Uses of Funds statement depicts monies projected to be used for tenant improvements or tenant allowances as well as leasing commissions so that the bank will approve and fund these costs as needed—or at least 65 or 75 percent of these costs—over the term of the loan . This allows me to raise the equity in my initial offering for the additional sums the bank is not willing to fund after the initial acquisition.

Your investors should not be obligated to contribute any more money to the partnership after their initial investment. This is why you need to make sure you have money for these items and are not materially limiting cash flow from operations in order to fund these costs.

Crafting the Splits and Returns to Investors

In crafting how cash distributions and appreciation are shared upon a sale (or refinance) between your investors and yourself, you will need to determine the overall return you will allocate to the investor as well as the overall return you will receive as the managing member of the investment property. This is always a gray area, as you need to give your investors a market return, based on the risk of investing with you, and then you receive a distribution as well, if available.

Later in this book, I will cover how I set up the sharing of cash flow and appreciation and how these sharing arrangements are flexible. You always need to recognize the overall return you must give your partners if you wish them to continue to invest with you in future deals.

It is that simple. Once you feel you are skilled with years of experience in developing, leasing and managing retail properties for a past employer, you are ready to begin the process for yourself in real life with you in sole command.

CHAPTER IV

Your Investment Partners

How to Choose Investment Partners

THE SHOPPING CENTER BUSINESS has many stakeholders who have interests in shopping centers. If the shopping center does well, they stand to benefit. If it does not, they have something to lose. Their interest might be similar to the interest of an owner or investor, but it can also mean other things. These stakeholders are either internal or external.

External stakeholders are tenants, employees of the stores or shopping center, suppliers of the stores or shopping center, the local government and the community at large. You will need to give these external stakeholders the ability to have a voice and an influence upon you as a managing partner but with one caveat: you are in control and must do what is right for the owner, the investor and the asset itself.

Retail tenants, particularly anchors—whether they lease space from the shopping center or are adjacent property owners bound by a reciprocal easement agreement—take great interest in the affairs of the shopping center. They have a great deal at stake if you do not lease and manage the property according to their expectations. They have a voice with the landlord and will not hesitate to exercise their privilege to convey recommendations—even make demands—to you.

Internal stakeholders control the asset. These can be the managing partner, the investment partners and the lender, and each plays a different role.

65

In this chapter, I am going to concentrate on the two most important stakeholders that will share ownership of a real estate asset with you as the developer and managing partner. I am referring to the individual investor and the institutional investor.

As the managing or general partner, you wear many hats. Recognizing that each stakeholder needs some attention, the owners or partners whose money is invested in the asset become the most important clients for the managing partner to nurture.

Institutional Investors Versus Individual Investors

Working with a group of individuals allows you as the partnership sponsor to put together a deal that is more favorable to you, since individual investors typically require less of a cut than an institutional investor would. On the other hand, working with individuals means that you need to communicate with each investor individually, answering questions, reassuring them, and listening to their input. This can be a time-consuming endeavor.

Institutions are advantageous because you are only working with one entity, not a number of smaller ones. This automatically cuts down on the amount of communication that you will need to do. However, as mentioned, institutions will want a deal that is more favorable for themselves. If you are established and proven, you will probably be able to secure a larger amount of equity investment from working with an institution than you would from a handful of individual investors collectively.

Most of my institutional deals are shorter-termed, with a three- to five-year time horizon, especially the ones that need my expertise and thus need me as managing partner. The institutions are expecting you to create value for them, and then to sell their share to realize the gain for their investors.

If you have built up sufficient equity by the time the institution wants to sell out, you can consider buying the institution's interest in the partnership or increasing your share, and along with additional investors buy out the institution's interest.

Real estate is for me a long-term hold, and in the case of individual investors, although you might set a time frame in your projections in which you would pay back their initial investment, they will most likely want to hold the investment over a longer period.

Individual Investors

As the sponsor, you have the duty to seek the proper members of the investor group, which gives you the option to qualify investors. You will need to screen investors who may not be suitable for a particular investment or be unable to work as a cohesive investor group willing to make decisions for the benefit of the group.

As you qualify investors for your new investment property, think about their planned investment horizon. Individual investors' personal situations can affect others who are part of an investment group. Even with careful planning, there can be unforeseen circumstances such as succession estate planning and catastrophic changes like major illness and divorce that can motivate an individual investor to cash out early from an investment property whose net operating income is not yet stabilized.

Assembling the investor partnership is a two-way street. It is as much about proving the investor is right for you as it is for you to prove to the investor that you can achieve the returns he or she is seeking.

Starting any business is difficult because you have no track record to show. For your first real estate deal, it is unlikely that a large institution would consider investing with you. Instead, you will have to focus on putting together a group of individual investors. Consider the people you know, whether they are relatives, friends, business associates or acquaintances. My first group of investors included a family member, principals from a law firm and an accounting firm that I worked with, friends and business people that I had met throughout my career. I approached anybody that I thought could afford investing in my project while focusing mainly on people who were actively involved in the community, so they could see the project and feel comfortable about where it was located.

You may qualify the investor by the amount of money he probably would invest with you—$50,000, $100,000, $500,000—and place the investor on a list for future offerings when the right property comes along. Some properties will require equity of $1 million (ten investors at $100,000 each) while others may only require $500,000 (ten investors at $50,000 each). If possible, you should plan to buy one share of the equity as well. This allows you to show potential investors that you are putting your money where your mouth is, and investing real money yourself, as was discussed in Chapter III.

One way to determine the amount that each share will price per invest-ment unit is to consider how much you can comfortably invest. Use that amount as your guide, and determine from there how many investors you need, each contributing that set amount, to come up with the amount of equity you are going to put in.

A good rule is to assume you will need to raise 25 percent in equity, and then obtain a loan for the remaining 75 percent of the total dollars you will need, hard and soft costs, to purchase the property and complete your plan to add value. However, in tight credit markets such as the one we experi-enced in 2008 through 2010, the equity required by lenders were far more, and often the loan was nearly impossible to obtain. This is another reason to shop for your loan before you get too far into your due diligence process involving a costly acquisition.

The amount of investment shares will likely grow as your business pros-pers. My first deal involved 15 investors contributing $35,000 each. At this writing, my usual investor generally invests $500,000 in one of my deals.

Investors that have not been able or do not wish to increase the amount they invest, in most cases, are no longer investing with me. While always try-ing to be loyal to your earlier investors, consider the best ways to use your time and energy: is it easier to take on one investor at $500,000 or 50 in-vestors at $10,000?

Bringing in investors is like hiring employees. It is essential to be able to trust the individual. For example, I never work with investors that I do not know. You also want to keep in mind a person's temperament and anticipate how they might react if the deal goes sour. Obviously, you want and hope that the project will be successful. But if it is not as successful as planned, you do not want to be faced with disputes from investors that cannot stom-ach losing part of the principal they put up.

The best approach is to have an honest conversation about the invest-ment. This is particularly beneficial if the investor has never invested with you or has never invested in direct ownership of commercial real estate. Asking questions like "Do you need your initial investment capital by a certain date, such as to send a son or daughter to college?" can help define their appetite for investment risk and reward as well as timing.

You should discuss your investment objectives for the properties you are planning to develop and determine if the types of projects you offer are in accord with their investment goals. Be sure to disclose to potential investors the risks associated with retail real estate investments. This includes but is not limited to lack of liquidity, the time horizon an asset requires to appreciate in value, market forces particular to the retail business, economic conditions, retail tenant competitive forces, unforeseen costs and liabilities.

A potential red flag is an investor partner who hopes to live off the expected return on the investment, at least initially. Far better would be a financially secure investor who is considering this investment as a way to grow his or her nest egg. You do not want to find out years before a property's NOI is stabilized that one of your investors was in dire need of the returns that you had planned, but had not necessarily guaranteed to give him or her.

Putting together an investment deal is like juggling. You need to be simultaneously looking for the perfect investment property, while looking for potential investors and alerting them to what you are doing. Before you find a specific property that you are interested in bidding on, you can quietly contact potential investors and notify them of your business plan. Tell them that you are working on some opportunities in the retail real estate sector. Give them an idea of how you intend to add value to a property and what sort of returns you believe you can achieve for them.

Because you have been practicing putting together investor booklets with some of the real estate offerings that have been coming your way, you should already have a pretty good idea of the costs involved for the investment and the returns you hope it will yield.

You might say to them, "I'm looking to buy a shopping center. I will be creating value by remerchandising or renovating it and fixing it up through landscaping and cosmetic repairs. I'm going to create some value, and I believe I've got the expertise to do this based on where I am now in my career. I would like you to be an investor with me. The investment shares will be around fifty thousand dollars. I'd like to know if you have an interest in taking a look at my investor package when I put it together."

It is imperative to round up a group of potential investors before you actually have a property you want to act on because when the perfect opportunity comes along, you will need the flexibility to move quickly on acquiring the real estate. Having investors ready and prepared to buy shares because

Risk-averse individual investors and institutional investors are attracted to stable assets with a growing residential population and strong anchors such as Bristow Center, a 200,000-square-foot neighborhood center we own and operate in Bristow (western Prince William County), Virginia, anchored by Harris Teeter. The Southeastern neighborhood supermarket chain is among the most family-friendly stores, often using the store's mascot, Harry the Dragon, to greet children with a balloon, a coloring page and a cookie.

they are excited and intrigued about your investment opportunity will make the process smooth and efficient.

Institutional Investors

Institutional investors typically represent banks, insurance companies, retirement and pension funds, endowment funds, hedge funds and mutual funds that pool large sums of money from many investment sources to invest on behalf of their investors. After you have a few successful real estate investment projects under your belt with individual investors, you will have the track record for an institution to consider investing with you. However, be aware that working with an insurance company or some other institutional investor has a completely different set of challenges and rules than you would encounter in working with individuals.

It is also important to keep in mind that institutional partners inevitably require sharing arrangements that are more beneficial to them than the type of return-on-investment arrangements you might set up with individuals.

Many institutions also have internal limitations in asset allocation. When they are overinvested in real estate according to their own internal allocations, the institution can accelerate an exit strategy unrelated to the fundamentals of the property. This would, of course, be governed by the partnership agreement you set up with your institutional partner.

However, institutional investors do bring stability to ownership. They will invest a large portion of the equity, usually 90 percent, and generally require you to invest the remaining 10 percent. These percentages, however, are flexible. In my first institutional partnership, the institution was willing to invest only 80 percent of the equity and required that I invest 20 percent.

I have also had partnerships with institutions where I have invested only 5 percent of the equity, and even have had potential institutional partners tell me that I did not have to invest any equity if I did not want to and could still share in the cash flow and appreciation. However, in most of my institutional partnerships I have invested 10 percent of the equity.

A good way to get your foot in the door with an institution is by hiring a specialized broker. He or she is knowledgeable of many institutions seeking investment opportunities and will know about their always-changing criteria and available allocation of dollars for partnering with a real estate developer. And institutional investors' criteria are constantly changing. One month they might be looking for retail real estate; the next month they might be in the hunt for other types of projects.

The size of the project, location and type of profile in terms of risk and return change constantly for institutional investors whether in good times or bad times. It would be a full-time job for you as a developer and managing partner to keep abreast of these changes and would not be the best use of your time. Far better is to hire a broker who can make it his or her business to help you find the right institutional partner and to help prepare and present your project so that it can be given proper consideration by the right type of institution.

The amount and the manner in which brokers' fees are calculated vary from company to company. Fees might also depend on your individual arrangement or the region of the country. You might pay the broker a commission based on equity alone, such as 1 to 3 percent of the equity. Alternatively, if the broker is also helping you obtain the debt, in addition to the equity, you might pay him or her 1 percent of the total debt and equity.

For example, if you have a deal for a real estate purchase of $10 million planned as $7.5 million in debt and $2.5 million in equity, the broker coordinating the equity investment might receive a commission of 3 percent of the equity, or $75,000. On the other hand, if the broker were also arranging for your debt, the broker would receive 1 percent of the entire $10 million deal, or around $100,000.

The investment package you prepare for an institutional investor is similar to what you might present to individual investors. You would still outline the profile of the property, present your ideas for increasing value through renovation or remerchandising and make your projections on the cash flow investment and the return on investment.

The difference in the deals between individual and institutional investors is the sharing arrangement that you are proposing to the investment partner.

Occasionally, you will have to change your fee structure according to the institutional investors' requirements. Because they require a higher amount of return on their investment, the sharing structure would be the main difference in your investment book, compared to the book you would create for individual investors.

Keep in mind that when working with an institution, the documentation of your work on their investment is much more onerous than it is in a partnership agreement with an individual investor. This is because institutions demand more rights to protect their investment than does an individual investor. Institutions might also require a greater role in approving certain decisions you make in your overall management of the property because their rights to protect their investment are greater.

Generally, with individuals, their only rights (as a majority) are to approve the sale of the property. When it comes to things like entering into leases or remerchandising, an individual investor would typically not have a voice in your decision as managing partner.

However, institutions often negotiate certain rights, such as approving tenants over a certain size or approving leases of a certain length of duration.

Some institutional investors also expect to have a say in renovations and expansions, even to the point of approving plans or choosing contractors.

Some institutions, for example, operate under a policy that requires minority contractor participation because the institution also functions as a contractor to the federal or state government. In this case, when they take a position of ownership in your property, you might inherit their operating policies in certain cases. After all, you are dealing with a more sophisticated partner that has substantial funds at its disposal and is able to negotiate a better deal for itself than multiple individual investors can.

So what is the benefit to working with an institution? It is "one-stop shopping" for your equity, so to speak. If you were looking for $5 million in equity, it would take far more time and effort to find 10 investors who can invest $500,000 each as opposed to approaching an institution that can put up all $5 million.

Even though an institutional investor will likely be contributing a vast sum of money to the equity, it is also a good idea, and usually a requirement, for you to put in your own money as an investor partner. This is because institutions prefer to have a partner who shares risks, especially if you expect to share rewards of participating in cash flow distributions and appreciation.

CHAPTER V

Structuring the Partnership

Setting Up the Corporate Entity

STARTING YOUR OWN COMPANY to acquire commercial real estate is probably one of the most important decisions you will make in your lifetime. When, how and what are questions you will need to answer. External factors such as the state of the economy, opportunities in the retail real estate industry and others are crucial, just as internal factors about your career and family should influence your decision.

When I started my company, I set up a corporation and I was the sole owner. Those were the days when Ronald Reagan was running for a second term as president. Tina Turner was making her comeback, Sir Paul McCartney teamed up with Michael Jackson for making hit music, and Prince was the artist still known back then as Prince. It was a good time to start a real estate company. Federal Reserve Chairman Paul Volcker had declared that in the past year the recovery from the recession was well under way. This gave investors confidence. Business credit, consumer credit and mortgage credit were increasing at a rapid pace quarter after quarter.

It became evident in 1984—the year I started my business—that none of the predictions of a totalitarianism society that George Orwell had written about in his dystopian novel *1984* would come true. There was a sense of optimism, which is necessary in the world of real estate for investment capital inflow.

I was determined to succeed in my new business. My outlook was optimistic, but cautious, after experiencing the decade of 1970s hyperinflation when the prime lending rate increased from 5.5 percent to 21.5 percent. I controlled my expenses vigilantly. I did not have employees, only a part-time secretary to answer the phones and type letters on an IBM Selectric typewriter with its pivoting typeball.

Using only freelance accountants, I bought an off-the-rack software program for the accounting functions and did my own accounting. But because of my tenure working at a shopping center company, I had enough expertise in all the different areas of the business to oversee the accounting, property management, leasing, marketing and preparing financial reporting to investors.

I took some ICSC courses and pursued my ICSC professional designations, studying late into the nights. That first year in business, I raised $490,000 from my 14 partners, each of whom put in $35,000 to invest with me in the purchase of my first retail property.

As I brought more properties into my portfolio, I added different people to my business in different areas, but for my first center, I handled all of these responsibilities myself. And so can you, acting on your own or with a compatible partner. Keep in mind that the entity that manages the property is often a different entity from the one that owns the property. While I own my management company, my properties are owned by separate entities that I also own, but with various partners that are not affiliated with my management company.

The first step to creating an entity to purchase and hold the real estate asset is to determine the type of entity you want to establish. Most of the entities that are appropriate for a small number of investors to hold a single asset will not be advertising to the masses as opposed to securities of public companies, which are widely held by tens of thousands of shareholders. Therefore, entities such as privately held limited liability companies do not need to be registered with the U.S. Securities and Exchange Commission (SEC) or most state regulatory authorities, all of which typically entail enormous expenses to comply with securities disclosures and maintenance requirements.

For example, the Sarbanes-Oxley Act of 2002 does not obligate these nonpublic shopping center companies to undertake costly measures to comply with its specific mandates and requirements for financial reporting. Instead, most of these entities will be issued pursuant to exemption under

U.S. Federal Securities Act of 1933 (as amended) and applicable state securities laws.

When you review the various options for establishing your entity, you will need to consider tax implications, securities laws, state laws, liability and other issues of importance to the investor group.

Nontax Considerations, State Law and Liability Considerations

A number of entity forms are available for investing in real estate properties. These entities can also conduct development and management of the properties. None is the perfect choice. Instead, the choice of entity depends on the nature and size of the enterprise that you intend to establish, the source and type of income, equity and financing you would expect, the number of family members and other investors you plan to involve, and whether your entity will manage and control the assets.

Your primary options available are sole proprietorship, general partnership, limited partnership, limited liability company (LLC), S corporation and C corporation. Each will provide you with different advantages and challenges with respect to liability, management, transferability, continuity, financing and taxes.

Tax Considerations, Single Level of Taxation for Partnerships and Co-ownership

When choosing the business entity, three of your principal tax considerations are:

1. The avoidance of double taxation of income
2. The ability to distribute money and property on a tax-deferred basis
3. The deductibility of losses

An entity generates losses when its deductible expenses exceed its income in a given year. Typical deductible expenses from real estate operations include depreciation or cost recovery, interest expense, property taxes and normal operating expenses, such as utilities, repairs and maintenance, insurance and wages of employees.

Choosing a Legal Entity

The list of legal entities you can select from is long, each of which has advantages and disadvantages. Regardless of which you choose, the owner's objective is paramount in which entity you choose to establish.

Some entities allow you to run the real estate as the sole owner and to report the asset's earnings on your individual income tax return. Others are intended for running the property's business activities as a separate taxpayer while limiting your personal liability to your initial invested amount. Let us review the options.

Sole Proprietorship

The sole proprietorship is the most basic form of business organization, one with no identity separate from you as the owner. By definition, sole proprietorships can have no more than one owner. Operating as a sole proprietorship would provide you the least amount of protection from liability, as all of your nonprotected assets (as opposed to protected assets such as certain retirement accounts and property considered exempt under state laws) would be at risk.

Sole proprietorships, however, require no documentation (and need only the simplest accounting); by definition, there is no entity to organize or dissolve.

Some sole proprietors choose to register a trade name or "doing business as" name (d/b/a), allowing them to conduct business under a different name and open a separate business account with a bank; for example, John C. Doe d/b/a Sunshine Mall.

Among the more challenging aspects of a sole proprietorship are the tasks involved in planning for the dissolution of the business, which, in the case of a business that cannot exist separate from its owner, essentially means death of the owner. The business itself cannot be transferred. Instead, each individual asset must be transferred, thus invoking difficult and complex estate planning and administration issues.

A sole proprietorship is not considered a separate entity for federal income tax purposes, and all income and expenses are reported on your individual tax return using your individual social security number.

Therefore, as a sole proprietor, you would report income or loss of the proprietorship on your own individual federal income tax return. The operating losses of a proprietorship are deemed your personal tax losses. The business itself need not file a separate income tax return. This results in only one level of tax on the business's profits.

Subject to passive activity loss limitations, operating losses may offset your other income as the proprietor. Those operating losses, which qualify as net operating losses from a trade or business, may be carried back or forward to other years under the rules of Code Section 172.

I do not recommend setting up a shopping center entity as a sole proprietor.

General Partnership

A general partnership can be formed by two or more individuals or business entities. Little documentation is required to organize a general partnership. Much like a proprietorship, the general partnership offers no liability protection.

Unless otherwise agreed to by the partners, all partners in a general partnership manage the business and each is responsible for the debts and liabilities of the entity. By default, each partner has equal rights in the entity's management and operation, and decisions are made by majority vote. Partners generally restrict transfers of partnership interests, with the assignee only permitted to become a partner with the consent of the other partners. Creditors of a general partnership can generally rely on any general partner to bind the entity.

If you choose a general partnership for your legal entity, it would be dissolved upon the death, bankruptcy, departure, insanity, incompetence, a wrong and prejudicial act of any partner or upon the express decision of a partner to dissolve the partnership. The entity must then be wound down upon dissolution.

A joint venture is generally a partnership where the purposes and activities are limited to the single purpose that brought two or more individuals or entities together. The power and authority of the venturers of a joint venture are generally limited to binding the joint venture with respect to pursuit of such single, specific enterprise.

A general partnership, like any partnership under Subchapter K of the tax code, is not taxed as a separate entity, and as a result pays no federal income tax. Therefore, there is only one level of tax on the business' profits. While most state tax laws do not impose any tax on partnerships, state tax laws vary. Some jurisdictions (for example, the District of Columbia) impose an entity-level tax.

As the general partner, you would be required to file an informational tax return on behalf of the partnership stating the name of each partner and each partner's share of partnership income or loss, whether or not any money or property is currently distributed to partners. Because a partnership is not a separate tax-paying entity, items of income, loss, deduction and credit pass through to each partner and must be included on their individual income tax returns. These items can be allocated among the partners in any manner agreed upon so long as the allocation has substantial economic effect.

Subject to the passive loss and capital loss limitation rules, a partner may deduct his or her distributive share of partnership losses up to the amount of his or her adjusted basis in his partnership interest. Unlike shareholders of a corporation, a partner's basis in his or her partnership interest includes his or her share of partnership debt.

Thus, for real estate partnerships with highly appreciated property, this may permit your partners to cash out the value of that appreciation (for example, with refinancing proceeds) without immediate tax consequences.

Upon formation, under IRS Code Section 721, there is generally no gain or loss recognized when contributing property to a partnership in exchange for a partnership interest.

Limited Partnership

In a limited partnership, certain limited partners restrict their power to manage the business in exchange for limited liability. For example, liability exposure is capped at the limited partner's investment in the entity. Limited partnerships must comprise at least two partners, one of which must be a general partner and one of which must be a limited partner. Many shopping centers function in this manner.

You as the general partner manage the business with no limitation on liability (that is, a general partner in a limited partnership has the same unlimited liability that a general partner in a general partnership has). However, in states that allow limited partnerships to convert into limited liability-limited partnerships, state laws grant limited liability for liabilities arising after the date of conversion even to general partners.

Organizational documents, such as a limited partnership agreement, are required to form a limited partnership. The limited partnership agreement can specify restrictions on transfers by limited partners of their interests and may condition transfers upon the general partner's approval. Some partnership agreements require the unanimous consent of all partners.

Unlike a general partnership, the death or other incapacity of a limited partner will not affect the existence of the limited partnership; the death or incapacity of the only general partner of a limited partnership will cause a dissolution, unless a successor general partner is admitted to the limited partnership.

A limited partnership is taxed in the same way as a general partnership with one crucial distinction. Because limited partners are not liable for the debts of a limited partnership, general partners receive the entire basis derived from recourse liabilities. However, if a limited partner contractually has economic risk of loss (for example, by indemnifying a general partner against loss from a part or all of such general partner's liability under partnership recourse debt), such limited partner will receive basis in the amount at risk under such indemnified liability.

Only those partners bearing the economic risk of loss for a recourse liability may include that liability in the basis of their partnership interest. Both limited and general partners receive an increase in their basis for their share of nonrecourse liabilities. Generally, this increase is proportional to their share of partnership profits.

More often, only general partners—not limited partners—are subject to unlimited liability for the debts and obligations of the limited partnership, and only general partners may include recourse liabilities in the basis of their partnership interests.

Accordingly, the limited partners would have a lower basis with which they can take flow-through deductions because a portion of the recourse liabilities will not be allocated to them.

Corporation

Business corporations, as distinguished from municipal or not-for-profit corporations, come in two primary federal income tax formats: S corporation and C corporation. Many jurisdictions have a "close corporation" statute. Close corporations can be taxed as either S corporations or C corporations.

Generally, all corporations are marked by legal characteristics of indefinite life, limited liability for investors (limited to the extent of one's investment in the corporation; remedies to creditors limited to the assets of the corporation), free or limited transferability of share interests, centralized management (by directors elected by the shareholders) and raising of funds through borrowing or through the issuance of shares.

If you set up a corporation, you would be required to file with the state of formation the articles of incorporation or their jurisdictional equivalent, as well as establish bylaws to govern internal operations.

Management by directors means that upon their election to a board of directors, the directors are responsible for the selection and supervision of the corporation's officers and executives, certain financial decisions such as officer compensation, dividends, financing, etc., and proposing and voting on corporate charter and bylaw amendments and fundamental corporate changes including consolidation, merger, liquidation and dissolution.

Close Corporation

Close corporations are often referred to as closed or closely held corporations. They have few shareholders, who often also play the role of officers and directors. Close corporations can be an exception to the free transferability characteristic of corporations, often resembling partnerships with buy-sell agreements among shareholders governing the transferability and pricing of share transfers.

Close corporations are typically formed out of tax, as opposed to capital-raising, considerations. Because most states generally dictate a large number of internal governance provisions for corporations, formation as a closely held corporation can cost less than a partnership or limited liability company.

C Corporation

The C corporation (so-called because it is governed by subchapter C of the Internal Revenue Code) is the type of company associated with public trading in stock markets. There is no limit to the number of shareholders in a C corporation.

C corporations are separate taxpaying entities creating two levels of tax (double taxation) on corporate profits. First, the corporation's taxable income is taxed. Then, the after-tax profits of the corporation, to the extent paid to shareholders, are taxed as dividends. Dividends are generally taxable to stockholders as ordinary income.

If the corporation's profits are not paid to shareholders as dividends, the value of those profits is presumably added to the value of the stock, and the shareholder will pay capital gains tax on the value of those profits when he or she sells the shares.

Because of the two levels of tax, I do not recommend you set up your shopping center investment as a C corporation, which is typically not used for real estate ventures.

In contrast to partnerships and S corporations, losses do not flow through to individual shareholders because C corporations are separate taxpaying entities. Instead, losses can only be used by the corporation and are subject to the net operating loss carry-back and carry-forward rules of Section 172.

Under tax code Section 351, contribution of property to a C corporation will generally not result in taxable gain or loss to the shareholder if the contributing shareholders, immediately after such contribution, own at least 80 percent of all voting stock and at least 80 percent of all other stock.

S Corporation

The S corporation (so-called because it is governed by Subchapter S of the Internal Revenue Code) is the form of corporation designed for electing corporations that choose to be S corporations rather than C corporations.

Like limited partners and stockholders in C corporations, stockholders in S corporations are insulated from liability.

The S corporation is a state law corporation that has elected subchapter S tax treatment with the IRS, generally resulting in the pass-through of profits and losses directly to stockholders. Making this election requires the consent of all shareholders.

To be eligible for S corporation status, the corporation must meet six important criteria. An S corporation must:

1. Be a domestic (U.S.–based) corporation
2. Not be an ineligible corporation
3. Not have more than 100 shareholders
4. Generally not have a shareholder that is not an individual or certain eligible trust
5. Not have any nonresident alien shareholders (from outside the United States)
6. Not have more than one class of stock

An ineligible corporation is a financial institution that uses the reserve method of accounting for bad debts; for example, an insurance company, a section 936 corporation, a DISC or former DISC.

The primary benefit of S corporation status is that there is generally a single level of tax on profits. An S corporation, like any entity taxed as a partnership (e.g., a general partnership, a limited partnership, a limited liability company [LLC]), must file an information tax return with the IRS.

Unlike C corporations, S corporations are generally taxed as if they were partnerships in that all corporate income and loss are reported by the shareholders regardless of whether any money or property is actually distributed.

In other words, if you elect S corporation status with the IRS for your shopping center ownership entity, your company receives the benefit for pass-through taxation of the corporation's profits in avoiding taxes at the corporate level. Your corporation's profits would be passed through to the individual tax returns of your investors and your own tax return.

Similar to partners/members in a partnership/LLC, S corporation shareholders may deduct the entity's losses. However, there are two main differences regarding basis creation and proportionate economic sharing.

S corporation debt is treated differently than partnership debt. S corporation shareholders do not get to increase their stock basis by third-party debt (such as a mortgage loan) borrowed by the S corporation unless the shareholder is the lender. As a result, a shareholder in a highly leveraged S corporation, where the loans are not from the shareholder, will have less basis and therefore less ability to either receive tax-deferred distributions or to deduct the entity's losses compared to a partner/member in a highly leveraged partnership/LLC.

In the event that the shareholder lends money to an S corporation, the shareholder would have a separate basis in the debt. If the S corporation has losses, first the shareholder's stock basis would be reduced by losses but not below zero. Second, the shareholder may then deduct additional pass-through losses by reducing his indebtedness basis but not below zero.

After the taxpayer has reduced his debt basis in order to take additional losses, any further losses may be carried over indefinitely until the shareholder has an increase in basis or any gain allocated to the shareholder.

Unlike partnerships or LLCs, which provide flexibility in how distributions are shared and how income and loss are allocated, S corporation shareholders must proportionately share (based on their stock ownership) the S corporation's items of income, deduction, loss and credit; otherwise, the S corporation would violate the one class of stock rule and lose its S corporation status.

Contributions of property to an S corporation follow C corporation rules. Under tax code Section 351, contribution of property to an S corporation will generally not result in taxable gain or loss to the shareholder if the contributing shareholders, immediately after such contribution, own at least 80 percent of all voting stock and at least 80 percent of all other stock.

Limited Liability Company

If you are starting a company to acquire a shopping center, I recommend you consider setting it up as a limited liability company. It is a relatively new form of entity organization. The LLC has become popular among real estate investors because of its inherent flexibility. Internal operations of LLCs under state law are similar to limited partnerships; IRS check-the-box provisions allow LLCs to choose whether to be taxed as partnerships with pass-through taxation or as corporations (C or S).

If an LLC has only one member, it is a disregarded entity and is treated as the same taxpayer as its sole member, making it essentially a sole proprietorship owned by the sole member, albeit with limited liability.

LLC investors, or members, benefit from limited liability whether they choose to manage the entity themselves or elect managers (who are paid for their services, even if they are members) to do so.

Interests in LLCs are freely transferable, though the transfer of membership rights requires the consent of the other members. Another feature of an LLC is that the legal ownership entity can exist indefinitely or for a prescribed term.

To form an LLC, you would need to file the articles of organization or a certificate of formation. An operating agreement among the members would govern the entity. Membership can comprise one or an unlimited number of members. Different classes of membership are permitted. Like any entity taxed as a partnership, LLC members can choose to allocate and distribute profits in whatever manner is agreed to in the operating agreement.

Because LLCs combine a single level of taxation with limited liability and because LLCs have fewer formalities than an S corporation does and more flexibility regarding entity allocations, LLCs have become a popular entity form for doing business.

For tax treatment of a single-member LLC that is disregarded for federal income tax purposes, refer to the information relating to sole proprietorships. For tax treatment of an LLC that is taxed as a partnership, refer to information relating to general partnerships. For tax treatment of an LLC that is taxed as a C corporation, see information regarding C corporations, which I covered previously in this chapter.

Unless I specifically indicated otherwise, all references to an LLC within this chapter will assume that an LLC is taxed as a partnership.

Tenancy-in-Common

A tenant-in-common (TIC) owns an undivided fractional interest in property. Thus, a tenant-in-common may generally freely dispose of his or her interest, making the transferee a cotenant with the other tenants-in-common.

Each tenant-in-common is required to report his or her share of income or loss produced by the property. Since each tenant-in-common is only liable for his or her share of expenses, that amount is all he or she may deduct, even if he or she actually paid more. When the property is sold, the gain or loss realized is divided between the tenants-in-common in proportion to their respective interests.

A benefit of a TIC interest in real estate property is that, unlike partnership interests or interests in REITs, TIC interests may qualify for like-kind exchanges under IRS Section 1031. Section 1031 provides for nonrecognition of gain or loss when property that is held for use in trade or business or for investment is exchanged solely for property of a like-kind.

If business activity conducted by the TIC with respect to the property resembles a partnership, the IRS may claim that in actuality such TIC is a partnership and deny access to Section 1031.

Revenue Procedure 2002–22 is a safe harbor for qualifying joint ownership of real estate as a TIC (and not a partnership) and sets forth 15 factors the IRS considers when differentiating between a TIC and a partnership.

Key factors that determine whether the entity is a TIC or a partnership include:

1. A TIC may not have more than 35 co-owners.
2. Each tenant-in-common must hold title to TIC property as a tenant-in-common under local law.
3. No business activities other than those customarily performed with the maintenance and repair of rental real estate property may be conducted with respect to the property. This prohibition includes real estate development.

Real Estate Investment Trust

A real estate investment trust (REIT) is an entity that typically owns, operates and manages income-producing commercial properties. Contrary to popular belief, REITs are not necessarily publicly traded companies. Instead, REITs are structured especially for tax purposes, in order for the tax burden to fall under the responsibility of the owners rather than the entity that controls the underlying real estate business.

REITs are generally taxed as C corporations, but there are a number of important differences. The most important is that the REIT is allowed a deduction for dividends paid to shareholders, thereby avoiding double taxation of that income.

The deduction for dividends paid causes the REIT to resemble a partnership or an S corporation because there is no entity-level tax on amounts that are distributed to shareholders. Conversely, the important difference between a REIT and a true pass-through entity is that other items, like net operating losses, do not pass through to shareholders.

Qualifying as a REIT requires satisfying strict statutory requirements under IRS Code Sections 856 through 859. The intent of these requirements is to limit REIT status to those entities holding a diversified portfolio of passive real estate investments, as opposed to conducting an active trade or business.

The requirements for you to qualify your entity as a REIT are too numerous and complicated to cover in this chapter. If you desire to structure your business as a REIT, you should confer with legal counsel regarding specifics of the investment property or properties and the owners' objectives.

Generally, to qualify as a REIT, the entity must:

1. Be managed by a board of directors or by trustees
2. Be structured as a domestic corporation
3. Have transferable shares or certificates of interests
4. Be owned by 100 or more people
5. Pay at least 90 percent of its taxable income every year to shareholders
6. Invest at least 75 percent of its total assets in real estate
7. Generate 75 percent or more of its gross income from investments in or mortgages on real property

Business Trust

Business trusts resemble living trusts or *inter vivos,* Latin for "between the living." This type of trust is usually created during a person's lifetime to either save money on taxes or set up long-term management of a person's property.

The business trust (sometimes called a Massachusetts trust) is a variation of the traditional *inter vivos* trust set up for the purposes of conducting a business. The trustee simply holds and manages the trust property to generate a profit for the beneficiaries whose beneficial interests are represented by freely transferable certificates.

The federal tax code makes no special provision for business trusts. Rather, business trusts are taxed as a corporation, partnership or ordinary trust, depending on which it most closely resembles.

Thus, the beneficial owners of the business trust must look to the tax provisions governing the form that the trust is taxed in order to determine its tax treatment.

The major difference between a business trust and a REIT is that the business trust could be taxed as any number of types of entities while the REIT will be taxed under the tax law previously described.

Lender Considerations

Lenders for large loan or property-specific transactions often prefer that borrowing entities be organized as single-purpose or special-purpose entities (SPEs), which are deemed to be bankruptcy remote if sufficient protections are built into their core organizational documents, as well as into specific transaction documents.

However, a 2009 decision by the U.S. Bankruptcy Court for the Southern District of New York has put a cloud on the bankruptcy-remote status of SPEs by allowing solvent, SPE subsidiaries of a bankrupt parent company, General Growth Properties, Inc. (GGP), to maintain its Chapter 11 bankruptcy cases, raising several important issues related to the use of SPEs structured to be bankruptcy-remote.

In this precedent-setting case, the Court denied a motion by lenders and servicers of certain commercial mortgage-backed securities (CMBS) lenders to dismiss the bankruptcy cases of 20 of GGP's SPE debtors, which were cash-flow positive, evidencing that the financial problems of a parent company can indeed result in the bankruptcy filing of a solvent, bankruptcy-remote SPE.

The goals of lender provisions relating to SPEs, which are deemed to be bankruptcy remote, are to minimize the possibility that:

1. The borrowing entity will become insolvent.
2. The possible insolvency of the entity's shareholders, partners or members will affect the borrower's solvency.
3. Economic issues unrelated to the transaction will affect the quality of the real property collateral.
4. The entity will file for or be compelled to file for bankruptcy.

Typical lender requirements include:

1. Restrictions on certain powers and purposes: These are limited to activities necessary for the transaction contemplated.

2. Debt and bankruptcy limitations: Restrictions on incurring debt other than what is necessary to back the project or unsecured trade payables; borrower agrees not to put the borrower into bankruptcy or join any bankruptcy filing.

3. Independence: At least one director, manager or member, as the case may be, independent from the entity's parent or any affiliate, whose vote is necessary for certain actions, including those that would affect bankruptcy.

In the case of a partnership or LLC, a lender may require a general partner or member to be an SPE with its own independent director, manager or member to avoid the problem that bankruptcy or insolvency of non-SPE members could cause the bankruptcy, insolvency or dissolution of the borrowing entity. In a single-member LLC, a noneconomic member can be the required independent manager or member.

4. No merger or reorganization: No merger or consolidation with a non-SPE, and no reorganization, dissolution, liquidation or sale of substantially all of the entity's assets may be permitted without the lender's consent.

5. Separateness: The entity must hold itself out as separate to avoid either the judicial concept of piercing the corporate veil, alter ego or substantial consolidation. The entity must also maintain separate books, records and accounts, etc.

6. No amendments: The lender would create prohibitions on amendments to organizational and/or transaction documents unless the lender consents.

Now that you have considered the appropriate entity to set up to acquire and own a retail property, you will need to get a lawyer to draft up the documents and set up the legal entity. A competent legal and financial specialist can also advise you as to which entity is best for you.

CHAPTER VI

Setting Up the Deal

Putting Together the Deal

ONCE YOU HAVE YOUR INVESTORS LINED UP, you have found the ideal
real estate property to purchase and have financing sources in place, then
what? You are ready to turn your proposal and your ideas into reality by getting a commitment from your investors, the bank loan arranged and the real
estate purchase under way.

When you have an actual property that you hope to purchase, you
should immediately start preparing ARGUS runs or Excel spreadsheets. This
way you will have real numbers to work with, in terms of calculating the purchase price, costs of improvements and the anticipated rewards of income
and appreciation.

Of course, if you do not have ARGUS, you still can prepare all your pro
formas with Excel or some similar program, but it will be more time-consuming and cumbersome. Another alternative is to outsource this project to
an accounting firm that specializes in commercial real estate acquisitions.

Additionally, you will now be able to develop specific plans for how you
are going to increase the value on the property over time. After already developing numerous practice packages, it should not be difficult to prepare
the package on the real deal based on real-life details of this property.

When you have the package completed, you will need to make duplicate
copies to present to the proposed investors that you have lined up in order
to get each of them to agree to the deal. Without a moment to spare, you

need to be talking to your bank about obtaining a loan for the balance of the property's cost to move quickly on the acquisition.

Perhaps the bank can set aside a line of credit for you to draw upon for your redevelopment costs, which would include tenant allowances, tenant buyouts, architectural and construction drawings, and other soft and hard costs relating to construction.

You will have to move fast in the competitive market in which we live. Deals can close quickly. Many shopping centers that I have bought had a short 30-day study period, and maybe only another 30 days to close on the property.

You can tell both the investors and the banks that you do not have the property under contract yet but that you are confident that you will get it. After all, if you are not able to get the property for some reason—for example, if another buyer locks it in before you can pull together the various parts of your deal or if you are outbid—going through this procedure will only arm you with further experience for the next deal.

My students are surprised when I tell them that I would do all this work without even having the property under contract. Yes, it is a tremendous amount of work to do on speculation and there are costs involved. I have file drawers filled with packages of deals that I was unable to bring to fruition.

You do not have to buy many properties to be a successful real estate developer. You might have to repeat this exercise many times, but once you succeed in one deal, you are on your way.

I consider all of the extra work a cost of doing business and professional education. On balance, if I am able to acquire one shopping center a year, no matter how many times I have tried and failed throughout the year, then at the end of 10 years, I have 10 shopping centers. That is not too shabby for a small developer.

Financing the Deal

You will need funds to acquire the property beyond the amount you put up or receive from your investors. Your choices are endless. You can arrange for financing from many available programs including permanent loans, bridge loans, construction loans and other financing structures to take you from acquisition to redevelopment.

These can come from local, regional, national or foreign banks. There are other sources of funds, including government agencies, insurance companies, hedge funds and pension funds.

I prefer to deal with a regional banker I know—and one who knows me—but I still desire the loan to be competitive, nonrecourse, if possible, with either fixed- or variable-rate financing, depending on the terms and market conditions.

Capital Formation

The *Sources and Uses of Funds* example (Table 6.1, p. 100) summarizes the initial amount of capital you need to purchase the property and how you are planning to use the capital. The amount of capital you need and the proportion of debt and equity from which the capital is derived are summarized in the *Sources of Funds* section.

How you will deploy that capital to accomplish your business goals for the investment property for items such as the purchase of the property, the upgrades to the property, inducement allowances you allocate for tenant improvements and leasing commissions to attract desirable retailers is outlined in the *Uses of Funds* section.

This is one of the main reports that any sophisticated investor and, surely, the debt lender are expecting you to feature prominently in your package. Like a balance sheet in a financial statement where assets equal liabilities, your *Sources of Funds* must always equal your *Uses of Funds*.

Once you determine the total amount of capital you require, you must decide how much should come from debt financing and how much should come from raising equity. In defining the proper sources of capital, you must be realistic. Even if you wished to obtain, for example, 95 percent of the capital as debt and 5 percent as equity, you have to recognize that legitimate debt sources will not lend you such a large percentage of the capital required. However, maybe you can get the lender to lend you up to 80 percent of the capital required.

You must ask yourself the right questions when planning your debt and equity financing and none have easy answers. Should you borrow 80 percent? What if a secondary debt source, a mezzanine lender, is willing to lend you an additional 10 percent of the capital required, but due to the risk involved, the mezzanine piece comes at a much higher interest rate or with onerous loan terms? The more capital you borrow, the less equity you will need to raise.

Consider this: The cheapest money is the first-trust debt backed by a first-trust deed, which is the modern-day version of the mortgage. It is a legal document that gives your mortgage lender the right to foreclose and sell your property if you fall behind on your mortgage payments.

The second most expensive is the mezzanine financing, and the most expensive money is the equity. Thus, the more you borrow as debt and the less equity you have to raise, the larger returns of cash flow and appreciation you can accrue to the equity and to yourself.

However, the more debt you place on the property, the more risk you place on the deal for investors and for yourself. It is a balance, and I have always leaned toward reasonable debt and reasonable financing risk. I usually try to obtain 75 percent of the required capital as debt and 25 percent of the required capital as equity.

I have consistently refused to place a mezzanine piece of initial debt on my acquisitions. I believe that placing such high-cost financing on a deal makes it more difficult for me to raise equity because many of my investors perceive the risk to be unwarranted, despite the higher projected returns of cash flow and appreciation I can build into the model.

Lender Requirement

The lender is more likely going to lend you no more than 75 percent of the required capital, and you are most likely going to be required to personally sign on this loan as a guarantor. The lender will hold a first mortgage deed of trust on the property, which will be the lender's primary form of security. If that security diminishes in value to less than the debt, the lender will look to you as the guarantor to make sure it is fully repaid when the loan is due.

If your deal is such that the lender is looking for you to make it whole, then in addition to your investors and you losing all your investment, you will be faced with an additional liability that can be very burdensome.

The risk of personal liability, if it is required, should never be taken lightly and, especially in many of your initial deals, will most likely be a requirement of loan approval. Requirement of personal guarantees is another reason why

75 percent debt, 25 percent equity has been the highest level of debt I am willing to set on my deals.

By contrast, your investors' risk is only the amount each of them invested. While any partnership can have exceptions to what one usually sees, often the investors invest their money for a share in the ownership of the partnership, and if the partnership fails, the investors can lose all their investment but not more than that investment.

The investor is usually not guaranteeing the debt or any other guarantees that you as the managing partner will need to guarantee. For example, besides the debt that you probably will be guaranteeing, you might be required to personally guarantee bonds or other requirements by the county, city, township or pertinent municipality in order to accomplish the upgrades you are planning for the property. That is another reason why the sharing arrangement involving the property's cash flow and appreciation is more favorable to you if the deal is successful. After all, you take risks that the investors do not take, and it is your sole responsibility to improve the asset.

As your required capital is the total of debt borrowed and equity raised, you must ask yourself if you have enough of a track record and/or financial net worth to allow you to borrow the amount of debt you are projecting to borrow, say 75 percent of the total required capital. If you do not, can you borrow part of the required capital? If not, is there another person, possibly one of your investors, who has the track record and/or solid financial statement and is willing to cosign with you in order for the loan to be approved?

I have not needed to share my added cash flow or appreciation with someone as added compensation for the risk to borrow the debt, but I know it is done at times. The amount you would have to share with a cosigner of the debt is whatever you can negotiate.

As to the equity portion, the amount you can raise sets the size of the deal you can eventually complete. For example, if you are able to raise $1 million and you are borrowing debt of 75 percent of the capital required, then you can complete a deal that has a *Sources and Uses* of $4 million.

In every deal I have completed over a quarter of a century, I have raised the equity by holding one-on-one meetings with my potential investors until I raised the funds needed to satisfy the lender. On only one occasion I had someone help me raise the additional equity. It was in 1986, in my third deal. After raising $490,000 on my first deal in 1984 and $2.25 million in my second deal in 1985, I had the opportunity to purchase a property that required me to raise equity of $5.5 million.

At the time, I was unable to raise that much equity. I was introduced to a gentleman whose business was working continually with a large group of well-to-do Washingtonians who were looking to invest in real estate and to help them find good opportunities. They trusted this gentleman because of his previous track record and understood that his business was to review multiple real estate opportunities and present to them only the opportunities he thought were worthwhile. His investors usually invested between $100,000 and $200,000 in a deal. These investors recognized that his acumen was helping them find superior investments and for that, they were willing to grant him a portion of their investment's profits.

Since his investor group was primarily made up of Washingtonians, I had a personal relationship with some of them. Others I had heard of and some of them had learned of my success to date. Because I trusted this gentleman who led the investor group, I structured a sharing arrangement with him.

We prepared a private placement memorandum (PPM) and outlined in the PPM what this man would receive for raising the $5.5 million. The deal called for him to receive an asset management fee of 1 percent of the partnership's monthly gross operating receipts to be paid to him monthly, for as long as the partnership was in existence.

In addition, this man was to get 10 percent of the distribution payable to me of the extra cash flow and appreciation over the preferred return if the deal was successful, for as long as the partnership remained in existence.

As it turned out, we sold 40 operating partnership units at $137,500 each. I bought one unit and this man bought another unit, *pari passu*, along with the other 38 investors he brought into the deal. This enabled us to acquire what was then a diamond in the rough, which we later turned into a gem that has made money for all the partners year after year.

Today, we still own this shopping center and this man still receives a monthly check for his asset management fee, part of the asset's cash flow and appreciation commensurate with his 10 percent back-end interest, plus cash flow and appreciation commensurate with the unit he purchased.

All partners including myself are happy to pay his fees because we are all getting handsome returns that none of us would be getting if it were not for his initial contribution in helping to structure the equity portion of the deal.

Today, I no longer need to make those kinds of deals in new ventures because I am able to take the risks and raise the equity in addition to using my management and development skills to improve the asset.

Throughout the years, I have learned that arranging the initial debt on a property most likely has to be with a commercial bank and with personal guarantees. That loan with your personal financial exposure has to carry the property until you complete the upgrades you are planning. This includes the remerchandising of the center, which involves renegotiating renewals for the existing leases, signing new leases and opening new stores. Once the property's income is stabilized, you can place a permanent loan on the property and only have to sign personally as to the standard nonrecourse carveouts without a personal guarantee.

Your first loan, the acquisition loan or acquisition/construction loan, is the loan you need to purchase the property and begin implementing your plan to increase the value of the property.

As you prepare to close on the property, the bank will require that all your equity is raised and deposited in the partnership account by the settlement date planned for the purchase of the property. Upon settlement, the bank will convey the funds owed to the seller but will most likely not advance you the monies you have allocated in your *Sources and Uses of Funds* for work still to be completed such as upgrades to the shopping center, tenant improvements or leasing commissions.

These monies will be disbursed as you complete each phase of your work or lease or re-lease the center. This is not usually a problem as the commercial bank is accustomed to distributing money in this manner. The bank typically distributes funds for this type of work promptly as the bank and you have agreed.

Generally, you have all the investor money in the partnership account on the day the bank funded the initial loan. Additionally, if the bank is lending you 75 percent of the *Use of the Funds*, they will lend you 75 percent of the line items of the bank loan that pertains to the purchase settlement. The bank will then continue to disburse 75 percent of the line items that pertain to the items that you will be completing after the purchase of the property as the work progresses and you need the money.

A commercial bank loan is usually for three to five years at most and possibly with one or two one-year extensions. Thus, in most cases, in no later than five years, you will have to complete your upgrading and plan to sell the property to repay the initial short-term mortgage or refinance with a permanent loan.

As I do not typically sell my investment properties, my business plan calls for a refinance of the initial commercial bank loan. It is in my best interest to do this as soon as possible, as I always wish to be released from my personal guarantee.

After the property's income is stabilized, this second loan can be obtained from a permanent lender. This permanent lender is usually an institutional lender, such as an insurance company, a pension fund or a lending source, that aggregates your loan as part of a commercial mortgage-backed securities (CMBS), a pool of loans that it will later sell to investors to spread the risk. The amount of this second loan is based on stabilized NOI (the financial statement line before debt service), which when applied to the cap rate will typically equate to a higher value than the scenario you presented to the commercial lender of your program to increase value in the future by borrowing money from the bank.

These loans are usually 75 percent of asset value. If your plans to increase value have been successful, the refinancing should not be a problem. Hopefully, you have increased value over the monies you have borrowed (as that is why you purchased this particular property) and even with changes in the market to interest rates or fluctuating cap rates, you should still be able to refinance for at least the amount of the existing debt.

Traditionally, this permanent loan only requires nonrecourse carve-outs. That means you have no personal recourse guarantees in case the partnership is unable to pay the monthly debt service or unable to pay back the loan in full when it is due.

It is worthwhile noting that the concept of nonrecourse carve-outs in a loan document is often misunderstood. The common misconception regarding nonrecourse loans is that the lender will not hold the borrower and/or guarantor personally liable on the loan in the event of a monetary default. In other words, people take the nonrecourse term to mean that if you default on your loan payments, the lender's only remedy is to foreclose on your property as the sole collateral you put up as security for the loan.

While that is the general intent, the carve-outs give the lender other options for ensuring you repay the loan principal and all the interest. The lender can cite specific carve-outs for bad faith acts, which obligate you as the borrower and any guarantors to take full liability for the loan balance.

Mortgage agreements are lengthy and complicated. Review the list of carve-outs (e.g., enumerated landlord actions or omissions in the loan document) before agreeing to them to make sure they are not broad or unreasonable.

Most nonrecourse loans include these exceptions or carve-outs within the loan documents that result in full-recourse liability to the borrower and the guarantor when certain "bad-boy" behaviors are cited.

What you are guaranteeing with the nonrecourse carve-outs is that there will be no "bad-boy" behaviors such as:

- You have not hidden or lied about anything you know about the property that would cause the lender to not lend on the property.
- You will continue to tell the lender of issues as defined in the loan documents and obtain the prior written consent of the lender where required.
- You do not permit waste occurring to or on the mortgaged property.
- You do not exhibit gross negligence or undertake criminal acts that result in the forfeiture, seizure or loss of any portion of the mortgaged property.
- You have not misapplied or misappropriated rents, insurance proceeds or condemnation awards you may receive after the occurrence and during the continuance of an event of default.
- You will comply with the lender agreement regarding any other disclosures.
- You will not defraud the partnership or the lender.

This is quite a difference from the recourse liabilities you assume on the initial commercial bank loan.

Some of these carve-outs in the promissory note can make the loan balance fully recourse to the borrower in the event that the borrower fails to obtain prior written consent from the lender on an assignment of an anchor tenant, for example.

In citing these carve-out provisions in a defaulting nonrecourse loan, the lender can foreclose on the property and go after you as the borrower and guarantor to mitigate its losses. My experience has led me to have my permanent loans securitized, thus minimizing my risks.

Sources and Uses of Funds

Table 6.1 below is a sample financing structure of a deal, which depicts the sources of capital and how I would use the capital. In this example, I am personally investing $100,000 and bringing in nine other investors, each in-

Table 6.1   Sample Shopping Center, Financial Analysis, Sources and Uses of Funds

SAMPLE SHOPPING CENTER
Financial Analysis
SOURCES AND USES OF FUNDS

SOURCES OF FUNDS

EQUITY				
Investor I - Sponsor	10%		100,000	
Investor Group (9 Other Investors)	90%		900,000	
TOTAL EQUITY				1,000,000
DEBT				
Acquisition Loan	75% of total cost		3,000,000	
TOTAL DEBT				3,000,000
TOTAL SOURCES OF FUNDS				4,000,000

USES OF FUNDS

ACQUISITION COSTS			
Purchase of Property		3,000,000	
Broker's Commission		0	
TOTAL ACQUISITION COSTS			3,000,000
SETTLEMENT COSTS			120,000
POINTS AND FEES			
Acquisition fee (RMC)	1%	30,000	
Debt Origination Fee (Lender)	0.75%	22,500	
TOTAL POINTS AND FEES			52,500
PROPERTY UPGRADES			800,000
WORKING CAPITAL RESERVE			27,500
TOTAL CASH REQUIREMENT AT SETTLEMENT			4,000,000
TOTAL USES OF FUNDS			4,000,000

vesting $100,000, for a total equity investment of $1 million. As equity owners, we are borrowing $3 million to acquire an existing shopping center valued at $3 million. It is just a coincidence that the purchase price is the same as the bank loan. The reason we are borrowing that much money is that we are planning to spend $800,000 in property upgrades, $120,000 in settlement costs, $52,500 in points and fees and $27,500 to fund a working capital reserve.

Note the information depicted under the heading of Sources of Funds. The first subheading under it is Equity. My typical Sources of Funds section separately depicts my equity and the equity of my partners. My equity partners collectively make up the Investor Group and I am the Sponsor. In the first few deals I structured, I set up my investment to match the dollar amount as the individual shares I was trying to sell to my investors. Bear in mind that I do not need to come up with all the cash to acquire my equity share because the actual cash I need for this initial investment is reduced by the commission fees I earn as acquisition fees for putting the deal together.

Actually, I am investing real cash in the sum of $100,000 less the acquisition fee of $30,000, which amounts to $70,000 in this example. I always disclose this fee in advance to my potential investors and explain to them the justification for the $30,000 fee. More on this will follow, but first let me describe conceptually the rationale behind raising equity.

I sell the concept to my investors by telling them that I have an investment valued at $1 million and that this investment is available for purchase in shares. There are 10 shares, each worth $100,000, available for purchase in my investment. I am conveying the opportunity to share in my investment, of which I would purchase one of the shares, aligning our interests and risks equally among us.

I tell my investors, "I would like you to purchase at least one of the shares." The investor correctly surmises that I am purchasing the same interest as he would be purchasing if he buys a share.

It is not uncommon for investors to buy more than one share. In my first deal, one of my investors acquired more than one share. On the other hand, some investors choose to buy less than a full share. For example, if a potential investor tells me that he can only invest $50,000 even though a share is worth $100,000, then you can always sell him a half share or the proportionate partnership interest equivalent to $50,000.

That becomes your choice, but I caution that the ongoing work involved in courting then later reporting to one partner is the same whether he owns half a share, a full share or more than one share.

In the sample statement, the Total Equity is the total investment. In this case, it would be my $100,000 investment plus the aggregate amount the other nine investors put in as the Investor Group's investment of $900,000. Adding the Investor Group's portion to my investment gives us the total of $1 million in equity.

Now, let us review the debt on this deal under Sources of Funds. In the example, we are planning to borrow only first-trust debt, an acquisition/construction loan and no additional mezzanine loan.

Please note that under Acquisition Loan the first-trust loan is 75 percent of the total $4 million in costs needed to purchase and upgrade the property.

As there is only one type of debt in this example, the $3 million in Total Debt is the same as the Acquisition Loan. When you combine the debt and equity in this example, the Total Sources of Funds is $4 million—$1 million in equity (25 percent) and $3 million in debt (75 percent).

The Uses of Funds section defines how we are planning to use the $4 million we are raising through debt and equity.

Please refer to Acquisition Costs. In this example, we have only two line items, the Purchase of Property and the Broker's Commission. The Purchase of Property is your cost to acquire the shopping center, and in this example, that is $3 million.

The Broker's Commission is shown as zero because in this example the seller is paying 100 percent of the Broker's Commission. There are usually other line items depicted under Acquisition Costs that are not shown in this example but are shown in the case studies to follow. These can include such items as a property appraisal, a roof inspection report, several types of environmental reports, a geotechnical report, an ALTA survey and others.

An ALTA survey is prepared to meet the standards of the American Land Title Association for the title company and the lender. This survey defines the land and location data needed for issuing the title and mortgage insurance. ALTA surveys, like many other costs of acquisition, can cost several thousand dollars and take weeks to complete. For that reason, it is important to define all these costs ahead of time, before you begin raising funds to acquire commercial real estate.

Settlement Costs vary by jurisdiction. They may include transfer taxes, recording fees on the deed and deed of trust (relating to your loan).

Many fees and settlement expenses incurred at settlement become part of your cost basis in the property while other fees and costs are treated outside the cost basis. For example, abstract fees, legal fees for title search and preparing the sales contract and deed, recording fees, surveys and title insurance are typically included in the cost basis.

Costs relating to obtaining a loan are a business expense that can be amortized over the period of the loan but are not considered part of the cost basis. These costs include discount points, loan origination fees, mortgage insurance premiums and fees required by the lender for an appraisal. Therefore, it is advisable to define each settlement cost separately in your plans.

You must be as accurate as possible in projecting all the cost items that are listed under the *Uses of Funds.* For example, settlement cost in Maryland varies by county whereas settlement cost in Virginia does not. Virginia charges a grantor tax that the seller pays. In Maryland, the seller is responsible for paying half of the transfer tax and half of the tax on the deed. The buyer pays the other half of these costs. Mistakes in estimating settlement costs properly can set you back thousands of dollars.

Please refer to the Points and Fees section in our example. I believe a fee of 1 percent of the sales price is reasonable initial compensation for putting together this deal and getting it to the point where the transaction takes place. My investors almost always agree.

I had two instances where I was not able to get this fee. In both cases, an investor was willing to invest a large amount of money with me but with the caveat that I not take an initial acquisition fee. In those instances, he insisted I wait to get my acquisition fee until the property appreciated so that all investors in the deal could profit from the increase in asset value concurrently.

Every deal is, of course, a negotiation, and to obtain a large investment from this investor, I did not take this fee in those two instances. However, this is an important fee to me as it in effect lowers the amount of my initial investment by the same amount. Accordingly, the cash that I choose to invest is actually $100,000 less $30,000, or only $70,000, even though I am still purchasing one share. Refer to Equity Investor I-sponsor.

The $30,000 fee is usually taxable to you and shown as a deductible expense to the partnership. It is wise to consult with your lawyer and accountant on how to treat these types of expenses for minimum tax liability to the partnership entity and you.

Some accountants may suggest that you initially convey to all your investors that the $30,000 fee not be treated as a partnership expense but instead as part of your capital investment. In this case, the initial accounting of the setting up of the partnership and the acquisition of the property should properly account for such as a nontaxable event to you. As with all other tax matters, I suggest you seek professional advice.

The commercial lender often charges a debt origination fee. However, this fee varies. I have obtained loans with no fee, sometimes a fee of just half a point (0.5 percent of the loan principal), sometimes three quarters of a point (0.75 percent of the loan principal), sometimes one point (1 percent of the loan principal) and sometimes even as high as two points (2 percent of the loan amount).

It is a matter of negotiation with the commercial bank as to their overall expected yield in lending you the acquisition/construction loan. These banks achieve their yield by charging an initial origination fee and an interest rate on the outstanding balance of the loan on top of the mortgage loan origination fee.

This Debt Origination Fee is usually charged only once for the term of the loan even though the bank usually charges an additional loan origination fee if you have options on the loan and you pick up those options. In this example, the assumption is that the bank will be charging three-quarters of one percent of the loan amount of $3 million, which is $22,500.

I never use a mortgage broker to obtain acquisition or construction financing because of my extensive banking relationships, some of which date back to my early career as a residential homebuilder. But if you hire a mortgage broker to help you obtain acquisition or construction financing, the charge will range from 50 basis points (0.5 percent) to 100 basis points (1 percent) of the loan amount, which varies according to loan amount, complexity and market conditions. This fee would be in addition to the debt origination fee.

Please refer to the line item on Property Upgrades. This line item covers estimated funds you will need to upgrade the property. In this example, we allocated $800,000 to improve the lighting of the center, repair parts of the roofs, paint and renovate part of the facade, repave some areas of the parking lot, add new landscaping, change the signage, etc.

Note the line item denoting Working Capital Reserve. Working capital is an amount of current assets that exceeds current liabilities needed for the operation of the property. Working capital reserve is nothing more than setting aside some cash you will need from time to time to allow you the necessary cash to offset the difference in the timing of payments and the receipt of a bank draw or a rental payment.

In this example, $27,500 is not a material amount. I usually set my working capital reserve in an amount equal to one month's debt service plus one month of operating expenses.

Structuring the Deal

Here comes the difficult part. The deal has to be right for your partners and you, and must be based on the realities of the property you intend to buy. Any mistakes can be costly, not only initially going into the deal but upon refinancing or disposition many years later.

How you set up your investment agreement with your partners all depends on what kind of returns people would expect to receive on their investments, based on some of the other areas in which they can invest their money. For example, you could invest your money in a certificate of deposit (CD) at a bank and have a solid, noncompounded annual percentage rate of return on your investment of 4 percent, depending on prevailing interest rates, which fluctuate with market conditions.

Alternatively, you could get a higher annual return, say 6 percent, investing in a triple-A rated corporate bond from a stable company such as Exxon or General Electric. A riskier stock might yield you 10 percent on a yearly basis or its share price might decrease, in which case you would lose a portion of the principal. The bottom line is you will need to do your homework and make sure that the investment opportunity that you are proposing is attractive, in terms of both return and risk, compared to some of the other opportunities your investors could pursue with their money.

In my dealings with investors over the years, I find that the type of investor I attract is looking for returns of 15 percent per year spread over the life of their investment. If I want to garner and galvanize investor support for my acquisitions, I have to pledge and achieve those ambitious returns.

Over my 20-year career, I have put together deals that offer returns of anywhere from initial cash returns of 8 percent to 15 percent, and overall returns when one includes appreciation of the property from 12 to 25 percent. These returns depend on many factors such as the size of the deal, the cost of the investment, the amount of money I am trying to raise and my own credibility.

At the end of the day, I just want to make sure I can raise the money based on the deal, and that it be fair and worth my time. I try to attain the deal that is the most favorable to me as the developer and achieve what my investors require.

Your financial arrangement should address some key areas. The percentages that I suggest are based on the numbers that have worked best for me in the past 20 years excluding the financial crisis of 2008–2010. You might wish to adjust these percentages to conform to your own circumstances.

The Equity

In a historical sense, it has worked best for the developer to come up with 25 percent of the equity for the purchase of the property and take on debt for the remaining 75 percent. However, in the recent credit crunch of 2008–2010, the percentage of equity required by commercial mortgage lenders up front has sometimes exceeded 40 percent of the purchase price because valuations plummeted during that financial meltdown. Lack of liquidity prompted lenders to take a cautious approach to protect their loans in case property values declined further.

Regardless, as the developer, I usually invest 10 percent of the property's equity with the other equity partners taking on equal shares of the remainder. In the case of an institutional investor, you would still raise the lender's required equity and invest 10 percent of the equity yourself. The institution would invest the remaining 90 percent equity, when the institutional investor committee feels confident about your asset and has the available funds to invest in commercial real estate in accordance with its internal asset allocation strategy.

The Debt

The remaining 75 percent of the purchase price (less, if the market dictates a lower loan-to-value ratio), the debt, would come from a commercial bank or another commercial lender. This loan would usually come with a personal guarantee during the acquisition/construction phase and a change to non-recourse, maybe securitized loan, once the property is stabilized. You as the sponsor would be the only one signing on the loan. Your investor group's greatest risk is the loss of its investment. Your risk is much greater.

In planning your deal, it is important to understand the different methods of financing the deal. Borrowers can choose from acquisition loans, bridge loans, construction loans and permanent financing—whichever case is appropriate for their income-producing properties. In my model, I pursue an acquisition/construction loan at first, and a few years later, when the cash flow is stabilized, I seek permanent financing on the best terms available. (See "Financing the Deal," on pages 92–93, for details.)

The Fees

During the bad times of the real estate business, there are no large fees for putting together new deals, completing major renovations, completing new construction or signing anchor leases. While fees will never make you wealthy, they provide a base that allows you to survive in rough times and in good times to create substantial assets for yourself through your ownership interests in the properties you have purchased and/or developed.

A typical partnership arrangement calls for monthly fees to be paid out from the asset's monthly net operating income or possibly also from the acquisition/construction loan. Naturally, you must first pay the bank your mortgage payment, then the expenses of running the center. You must also first pay your fees for operating and leasing the property, the costs for the upgrades you are proposing, your fee for completing these upgrades, and then—and only then—are you able to make cash distributions to your investor and yourself—if you still have funds left over.

Here are some of the fees that I collect that are associated with the property, either monthly or on an occasional basis.

Acquisition Fee *(1 percent of purchase price of property):*
The partnership will pay 1 percent of the purchase price of the property upon purchase to the development company, which would be your company,

Whether we manage properties for ourselves or for other owners, the management fee compensates us for the effort of collecting rents and keeping the property well maintained, such as our Festival at Old Bridge shopping center in Woodbridge, Virginia.

for acquiring the property. This fee would be structured to be nontaxable, if possible.

Property Management Fee *(4 percent of gross operating income):* A property management fee is paid on a monthly basis to the management company, which oversees cleaning and other items pertaining to maintaining the center, paying vendors and collecting rents, discussions with the tenants, paying the mortgage, preparing budgets and variance reports, and sending financial reports to the investors.

The TRC standard property management agreement provides for the shopping center ownership entity to employ TRC as the property manager to manage, lease, re-lease, market and maintain the property for a term that renews automatically. At my company, we act as property manager for all of the properties that we own. Thus, my company receives 4 percent of the gross operating revenue monthly. I strongly recommend you plan to perform your own property management.

My property management fee of 4 percent of the monthly gross operating receipts collected, includes prepaid and accelerated rent (excluding insurance proceeds, other than insurance proceeds for business interruption and rental interruption insurance, which insurance proceeds shall be included in monthly gross operating receipts).

Gross operating receipts would include, but not be limited to, payments of minimum base rent, percentage rent, real estate tax reimbursements, common area maintenance (CAM) reimbursements, insurance prorations reimbursed, water billings, pay phone receipts (even though we do not have many pay phones on our centers anymore). My fee would not include condemnation proceeds or proceeds from a sale of the property.

Such fee is in addition to my company being reimbursed for expenses relating to on-site building personnel, if there are any assigned to the property, which includes salaries, benefits and other costs of on-site personnel used in the maintenance and operation of the shopping center.

However, the property manager or any personnel that do not spend 100 percent of their time on-site in a maintenance role are costs of the management company (TRC) and not a partnership cost.

Leasing Commission *(4 to 6 percent on new leases, 2 to 3 percent on renewals):*

Marketing the center to new tenants is paramount to its success. The marketing provision of TRC's standard agreement allows my company to direct-mail pieces to prospective tenants, conduct follow-up of inquiries from mailings, print and send brochures, disseminate handouts, make telephone calls, run newspaper ads and place other media advertising. We assume the duties for leasing and marketing the property aggressively to help grow its income for the owners.

Our agreement also allows my company to cooperate with other outside leasing specialists and cooperating brokers by keeping them apprised of space available for lease in the property and even to co-list the available space to enable the best leasing possible.

TRC's standard property management agreement requires the property owner to compensate my company, as the property manager, for our services in securing tenants for the property. This compensation is standard in the shopping center industry. It is known as a leasing commission, payable on all leases my company procures, whether it involves new tenants to the shopping center or existing tenants that agree to renew their lease or exercise an option on a lease for an extension.

Leasing fees often vary by market. In some areas, leasing commissions are paid as a set amount of dollars per square foot leased, while in other areas, the standard is a fee equal to a percentage of the total base rent over a time period as agreed to between the management company and the property's ownership entity. Sometimes, the leasing fees are applicable to rent anticipated for the full term of the lease with a cap of 10 years for longer leases. Regardless of where your property is located, the important thing for you is to get leasing fees at market rates. In the Washington, D.C. area, market rates dictate leasing fees for our properties.

On new leases, we usually get 4 percent of projected fixed minimum rent if there is no leasing agent representing the tenant. We receive 6 percent on a new lease if there is a leasing agent representing the tenant. In the latter, we, as the leasing agent representing the ownership, would receive 3 percent, and the leasing agent representing the tenant receives the other 3 percent.

This leasing commission is calculated solely on the minimum guaranteed rent (MGR) yield over the full term of the new lease or the negotiated term in leases longer than 10 years. The term *MGR*, often referred to as fixed minimum rent, does not include reimbursements for shopping center operating costs, such as real estate taxes, common area insurance, common area maintenance and marketing fund. For example, we have signed a new lease for a ten-year period at $30,000 in MGR due per year for the first three years, $40,000 per year for the next four years and $50,000 per year for the last three years. This scenario would yield $400,000 MGR over the 10-year period.

Assuming there is no other leasing agent representing the tenant, the property would pay a leasing commission fee of 4 percent of $400,000, which amounts to $16,000.

We would be paid half ($8,000) upon lease execution and the balance ($8,000) when the tenant opens for business. The property management agreement allows us to collect the second half of the leasing commission upon either the tenant taking occupancy or when the tenant commences paying rent, whichever is the earliest. We usually take the fee upon opening.

The leasing commission is less for lease renewals (including the exercise of an option). We usually earn a leasing commission of 3 percent paid in full upon option exercise.

In addition to these commissions, the property reimburses my company up to $5,000 per year for certain budgeted expenses, such as the costs of advertising, promoting, marketing, printing brochures, copying charges and other direct charges incurred in connection with leasing the shopping center.

Marketing/Promotional Administration Fee *(15 percent of tenant and landlord contribution combined)*:

Every partnership I oversee contributes to a marketing fund. This fund pools the landlord's and tenants' monies to help bring more customers to the shopping center. I am a strong believer that marketing of our open-air centers has unique advantages. It differentiates our centers from others, brings more customers to our shopping centers, makes us a stronger part of the communities we serve and sometimes helps us when we need community support.

When we apply for a zoning variance or a special exemption approval to expand the shopping center or need a drive-thru feature installed for one of our tenants, the goodwill we have created in our community through local marketing is helpful. These are merely ancillary benefits of a strong marketing program.

The partnership usually matches a percentage of all marketing charges that the tenants contribute to the shopping center. The combination of landlord and tenant contributions comprises 100 percent of the marketing budget. My partnerships have traditionally contributed 25 percent of the tenants' contributions to the marketing fund. However, in the second half of the 2000s and beyond, my partnerships have been contributing as high as 50 percent, 75 percent and in some cases, a full match of the tenants' contributions to the marketing fund.

For many of our properties, the annual marketing budget is around $50,000. For example, if the tenants contribute $25,000, the ownership entity matches the tenant's contribution by also contributing $25,000, which makes up the total marketing budget of $50,000. My company charges a fee of 15 percent of the marketing budget or $7,500 to execute the marketing plan. Thus, after we take our fee to oversee, there is actually $42,500 in the plan to spend.

Construction Supervision Fee *(percentage varies according to scope of service):*

The construction supervision fee can be high if you are doing substantial work as in new development or a major renovation, yet this fee yields income to the management company ongoing during the operation of a shopping center because there is always construction that needs to be overseen.

This is an important fee to The Rappaport Companies, the operating company that oversees all the properties I own, as well as those I do not own but oversee, for which my company receives such fees.

If you are renovating, expanding or developing the property, the partnership will pay your company a fee to oversee the construction process. However, TRC, as do all other full-service retail property management companies, routinely oversees construction work such as the re-demising of one store space into two or combining two store spaces into one. Other routine construction includes demolishing interior fit-out in a space, building out a restroom in a space, reconfiguring a new store to a vanilla-box condition, replacing a storefront and many other items that pertain to getting a space ready for a new tenant.

The partnership compensates TRC for such activity as working with the architect and engineers to draw the plans, overseeing the obtaining of the necessary permits, bidding out the job to several general contractors, selecting the general contractor, overseeing the construction and paying the construction bills.

TRC is paid a percentage of the hard costs of the construction. We are not paid on the soft costs, including but not limited to the architectural, engineering, permit fee or interest costs involved in construction projects.

This fee is payable ratably during the pendency of construction as follows:

- For construction up to $10,000, my management company provides supervision at no cost to the ownership entity.
- For construction over $10,000 but less than $500,000, my management company receives a fee of 7 percent of hard costs.
- For construction over $500,000 but less than $1 million, my company receives 6 percent of hard costs.
- On construction costing more than $1 million, my company receives 5 percent of hard costs.

Partnership Supervisory Fee *(1 percent of gross operating income):*

The ownership entity of each property pays a monthly partnership supervisory fee to me as remuneration for overseeing the partnership responsibilities to make ongoing ownership decisions. In my partnerships, I look after the interests of ownership because it would make no sense to assemble 10 or 20 investors together to approve leases and address other day-to-day issues that property management companies bring to ownership for approval. Small investors do not have the time, skills or inclination to do this type of work. In essence, I function as the managing partner, and this fee is my compensation for taking on the added responsibility.

The fee is equal to 1 percent of the monthly gross operating receipts excluding insurance proceeds, condemnation proceeds or proceeds from a sale of the property. It is calculated on the same receipts as the property management fee is calculated on. This partnership supervisory fee is in addition to the property management fee. The partnership supervisory fee compensates me to:

- Set and approve the long-range plan for the property
- Approve the budget
- Approve all capital expenditures
- Set the future tenant mix
- Evaluate all new leasing opportunities
- Execute all leases
- Monitor partnership tax liability
- Determine the direction and future of the shopping center
- Create value
- Deal with partnership issues
- Prepare and send out reports to investors
- Respond to all investor inquiries
- Meet with investors as necessary

In my experience, my partnership supervisory fee is the same whether the deal is with individual investors or institutional investors. It is a reasonable and market-rate fee. Both individual and institutional partners recognize that it takes considerable skills, experience and time to carry out this responsibility.

Financing Fee *(varies according to the amount financed):*

In consideration for assisting the property owner with respect to the closing of any third-party financing, my company would receive a fee that is negotiated between ownership and the management company, depending on the complexity of the financing. This fee compensates my company for such services as:

- Preparing the financial analysis
- Completing the lender due diligence
- Preparing and collecting estoppel certificates
- Preparing subordination, nondisturbance and attornment (the agreement of a tenant to acknowledge the purchaser of the real estate as its landlord) agreements

I have seen some partnerships structured with this fee being 1 percent of the financing amount. Thus, on a financing or refinancing of $10 million, The Rappaport Companies would receive a fee of $100,000, and on $20 million, a fee of $200,000.

Unlike others, I have never charged such a large fee to my partnerships. The typical fee I charge for my company's time is in the range of $25,000.

Equity Sources Considerations: Fund/Nonfund

There are many considerations you need when structuring your deal. Let us examine some of these critical areas, starting with your equity sources and debt strategy.

Some investment companies create an investment fund to raise equity for the expected purchase of several deals. As such, they have equity available when the opportunity to purchase arises.

If you are working on your first deal, raising a fund is probably not a consideration, but after a few successful deals, it might be. If, on the other hand, you have worked for a shopping center company and gained development, leasing and management expertise but have never put together your own deal, then a fund may be a possibility.

Several of my investors recommended I put together a fund. I know that if I wanted or needed to, I could, but I have not had the necessity to do so.

The benefits of a fund would include access to immediate monies for the deposit, the due diligence costs and, of course, the equity needed for the acquisition. It would possibly allow you to buy larger properties that you would not otherwise be able to buy. So why have I not decided to create such a fund?

Maybe it is because by raising money ahead of time, you do not have much strength in structuring the sharing arrangements with the people or institutions that are eager to invest with you. It is more difficult to find the right property than to secure the equity. I prefer to take on risk in order to get that better sharing arrangement.

Therefore, I have always put up the deposit, spent the early diligence money and spent additional funds on a deal that did not come to fruition. When I am controlling the deal, I am also in a better position to have a bigger sharing of the cash distributions and appreciation than I would with a fund.

You might have heard the cliché, "I seem to be only working for fees." That is because the sharing arrangement is such that aside from the fees you might never really obtain any meaningful ownership interest in the property, surely not as much ownership interest as when you control the deal.

I believe I have meaningful ownership interests in all my properties, and I am content with my model. It might not be for everyone, but it works for me.

Institutional or Noninstitutional?

I have structured two dozen partnerships, three-quarters with individuals and a quarter with institutional investors. If I were able to raise all the equity I needed for my deals from individuals, I would never do a deal with an institution. However, that is not always possible, so I continue to do deals with both.

Why would I rather do deals only with individual investors? The sharing arrangements of cash distributions of cash flow and appreciation upon a refinancing are much better for me with individuals and the partnership documents give me much greater rights as to partnership decisions.

However, the time requirements for raising cash between the two equity sources vary substantially. How much of my time can I spend with multiple individual investors and how much time do I need to spend to find the next great opportunity to purchase? How much time does it take to raise, for example, $100,000 from nine investors each versus raising $900,000 from one institutional investor in one shot?

Is it even possible for me to raise $1 million each from nine investors for a total of $9 million versus $9 million from one institutional investor? Not typically. I would be restricted on the size of deals I could do if I only relied on individual investors.

Presently, when I need less than $5 million in equity, I look to individuals for the money, and for deals larger than $5 million, I look to raise the equity from institutions.

Management Rights

I usually assume absolute decision-making rights for running a partnership made up exclusively of individual partners. The only right the individual partners have is to approve the sale of the property. In cases where half or more of the total ownership interests are being transferred, excluding my interest, the partners must approve the sale in proportion to their interests, meaning a partner with two shares has two votes while a partner with one share has one vote.

If I do not receive majority approval, we have an issue that has to be resolved, yet our partnership agreement does not make provisions for resolving that type of dispute. I have never encountered such an issue in any of my partnerships.

As long as the property is performing in accordance with my projections, there is usually no problem with institutional partners. The institutional partner might require more ongoing operational information than the individual partner might, but if there is no significant negative deviation from the plan, the institutional partner is almost always satisfied.

Institutional investors pool large sums of money to invest. They act as experienced investors on behalf of themselves or other investors and contribute substantial dollar amounts to qualify for preferential treatment in any type of investment they choose.

Because of this expertise and fiduciary responsibility, they require information to transform into a reporting format that is satisfactory to their investors, many of which hold many types of investments. For that reason, institutional investors will have an enormous influence, if necessary, in the management of your property.

They know very specifically the level of risk and return they are willing to accept for themselves and their partners or their clients whose money they are investing. If the deal is not right going in, they are not interested.

If it fits their model and they invest with you, they expect you to give them their returns as you projected. If you are *performing*, they pretty much will let you do what you do best. If not, they are going to do whatever they need to do to protect and enhance their investment.

This is understandable because the institutional investor will have a significant ownership share in your property. As much as 90 percent of the equity invested comes from one source. This one source, the institutional investor, has much greater rights to protect its investment, including taking over the management, leasing and construction management of the property.

The institutional investor typically reserves these extended rights because of its fiduciary duty with its principal investors. This duty is a legal or ethical relationship of trust regarding ensuring the proper management of money the institutional investor is investing with you.

The partnership documents are very onerous to the interests of the institutional investor regarding management rights. That is just one of the issues you need to recognize if you want to enter into a partnership with a more sophisticated partner that can invest all the capital you need to put a deal together.

Institutional investors typically have a time horizon (exit strategy) planned. You must always have a timeline to complete your plan and stabilize the property. This would be the time when your upgrades, renovation, expansion and/or remerchandising are complete.

Once the property and the NOI are stabilized, you will know if the higher returns commensurate with the risks you have taken to upgrade and remerchandise/re-lease the property can be achieved.

If you are unable to do so, it is this time period when you must plan your disposition strategy. The sale of your asset is the defining event where the appreciation in property value is fully realized. This appreciation in asset value is a major component of the overall return on the initial investment that your equity partners put up to acquire the property. This window of time is usually between three and five years.

However, I have never sold a property. So how does that fit in with the time horizon that would show the highest return to the investors?

First, whether I am planning to sell or not, I assume in my initial projections a time period that would provide the highest returns to the investors. If I can stabilize the property in three years, then I show a three-year deal. If it takes four years, it becomes a four-year deal. If it takes five years to stabilize, then it becomes a five-year deal. The faster I can complete my plan, the higher my returns will probably be.

Investor Redemption Rights

All my investors know right from the start that I do not sell. Usually, most of my individual investors also wish to own the property for the long term. My institutional investors, contrarily, tend to be much more transactional and are inclined to sell the property as soon as the plan I proposed is completed.

However, with either type of investor, they invariably want to know there is a way they can exit the partnership when needed. They want to have an exit strategy for the same reason office workers want to know there is an emergency exit stairwell nearby even though they are not planning for a fire.

I have devised a mechanism for my individual investor that has worked very well, and I continue to use it in all my partnerships. Although all my partners know that I am never planning to sell, they can exit the partnership by giving me proper notice.

Each of my property entities gives my partners redemption rights. In the LLC agreement, there is a provision stating that with 12 months' notice prior to the maturity date of the existing financing, the ownership gives all partners notice of their rights to redeem their interest in the partnership. Each partner may exercise its redemption right by sending me written notice during the 30-day period immediately following the date of my redemption notice.

The document also explains how the fair market value of the partner's interest will be determined on the applicable redemption date. The LLC agreement provides for the fair market value of the shopping center's assets to be determined based on the all-cash price, which would be paid by a willing buyer to a willing seller in an arm's-length transaction for the purchase of the shopping center and its assets. The value is determined through an independent appraisal, even multiple appraisals if necessary.

The agreement I have with my partners calls for two qualified commercial real estate brokers to help define the value of the property. These brokers would review details about the property such as the NOI and the reliability of the NOI to establish a market-based capitalization rate.

Most appraisers of income-producing retail properties use the income capitalization approach to determine value. This type of appraisal capitalizes the most recent year's net operating income stream before taxes, depreciation and amortization to derive the value. Income capitalization converts anticipated cash flows into present value by capitalizing the NOI by a market-derived capitalization rate.

For example, for a property that yields $280,000 in NOI, which is comparable with other properties in the market where a buyer will require a 7 percent rate of return (capitalization rate), the broker would estimate that the property would sell in the open market for $4 million ($280,000 / 7% = $4 million).

If the two brokers agree on the value, they would jointly render a single written report of their opinion, which we would typically accept to place a value on the specific share the exiting partner or partners want to redeem.

If the two brokers assigned to appraise the property cannot agree upon the value, we would resort to what we call the three-appraisal method. This method involves appointing a third broker to assign value. If the third broker assigns a higher value than the first two, the higher of the first two appraisals prevails. If the third broker assigns a lower value than the first two, the lower of the first two appraisals prevails.

The value of the selling partner's interest is valued with no discount for a sale of a limited partnership interest. It is valued based both on a sale to a nonrelated third party and after proper splits of the assumed distribution proceeds, or what dollar amount the partner/investor would receive.

Once we know the dollar amount of the interest up for redemption, I have several avenues that I can pursue in order to purchase this selling partner's interest. My options:

1. I can, but I am not required to, notify each of the other partners that a partner wishes to sell their interest and that if anyone wishes to buy that interest what the cost is. Existing partners,

knowing the property well, are good potential purchasers of the interest being sold.

2. I can purchase the interest myself. I have done this quite often over the years, usually buying the interests on behalf of my children, and now my grandchildren, with funds they are receiving from earlier gifts of partnership interests I have given them that are now throwing off cash distributions.

3. As financing is coming due within 12 months, I can ask the partners not wishing to sell if they all would wish to own a larger interest in the property by having the partnership borrow enough money as part of the refinancing to both pay off the existing debt and buy the selling partner's interest.

4. I can find a new investor to buy the selling partner/investor's interest.

The LLC agreement restricts the purchase of any partner's interest only upon a refinancing. If it is not possible to purchase any partner's interest at that time, the partnership is required to sell the shopping center. The reason why the partner wishing to sell must give notice almost a year in advance of a refinancing is so that no other partner would have to incur a diminution in his or her value if the shopping center is required to be sold.

In some cases, the partnership could be penalized by being forced to pay off the existing financing before it is due to obtain money to buy out a partner. The penalty for early redemption also acts as a deterrent for partners that could force a sale of the property if no choices to buy out the partner are possible.

I have never had a partner/investor force a sale of a partnership, even though several partners have from time to time expressed a desire to sell their interests. Some of my partnerships today are more than 25 years old.

Estate planning, cash needs of an investor, divorces and deaths (where many times the children of the deceased now own the inherited interest in the properties and want to cash out their inheritance) are good reasons for partners to sell.

While the partnership documents define when the partner wishing to sell must give notice, I have used reasonable steps to accommodate them whenever they have expressed a desire to sell. No one wants an unhappy investor. Whenever a partner has notified me of his intent to sell his interest in one of my partnerships, I have always been able to find a way to enable the transaction.

With an institutional partner, it is a much more complicated issue. It is even more important for me to handle this situation properly, as the institutional partner and I do not usually concur regarding their disposition strategy.

The institutional partner is transactional in nature and yield driven. As a result, my institutional partner's investment time span is always shorter than my holding period, which is, as I mentioned, *forever*.

I know this going into every deal and plan ahead for the eventual purchase of the institution's interest.

The Concept of Sharing

By now, you may be asking, How do you share the cash flow with your investment partners? How do you share the appreciation upon refinancing or sale with your investing partners? The concept is simple: be generous with yourself.

The idea is that you deserve a larger portion than your pro rata share of the money you invested compared to the money your partners invested because you have taken and are continually going to take greater risks. You are the expert that is helping your less-experienced partners achieve handsome returns that they could not otherwise obtain themselves.

Think of sharing the returns in terms of a front-end interest and a back-end interest. The front-end interest is the interest where the real money is placed. In my earlier example, my $100,000, along with my nine investors who in total invested $900,000 for our combined investment of $1 million, is the front-end interest. The back-end interest is your variable incentive compensation that is sometimes called *carried interest, promote, sponsorship* and *bonus*.

This carried interest is solely yours to earn and not for any of your investors. It gives you an interest in the future cash flow and appreciation of the asset, which can be substantial, especially if you do a good job of increasing the property's cash flow and appreciation.

Carried Interest (Back-End Promote)

Carried interest is an important principle in partnerships in which a general or managing partner takes responsibility for managing and developing the property asset for the benefit of all partners. The general partner typically performs a vast array of services for the partnership for which the partners pay fees along the way.

However, the ultimate success of the venture is realized for the entire investor group when the property is eventually sold at an appreciated value or when the property is refinanced after stabilization of income and accrued equity is distributed upon the refinance.

This general partner can then be highly compensated with carried interest, which is a share in the profits of the investment group upon the sale or refinancing. The concept is sometimes referred to as *carry* but I like to call it *back-end promote*.

Generally, upon disposition of the asset, the partnership must return the capital given to it by the limited partners plus any preferential rate of return before the general partner can share in the profits of the project as mentioned earlier. The *preferred return* is a minimum annual rate of return that the sponsor grants to the partners before the sponsor shares in the profits.

The general partner will then receive a 20 percent carried interest, although some general partners specify in the partnership agreement a compensation of carried interest between 25 percent and 30 percent or more.

Carried interest payments are customary in the fund and venture capital industry. They are used to create a significant economic incentive for venture capital fund managers to achieve capital gains.

Because of this, members of the U.S. Congress have debated carried interest payments at length and on several occasions have proposed regulations such as increased reporting requirements, higher taxation of carried interest and restrictions over the use of placement agents. In other words, Congress has considered taxing carried interest as ordinary income, rather than at the lower rate of a long-term capital gain, which would effectively double the developer's personal income tax bill.

This type of regulation would unwittingly punish smaller private equity and venture capital partnerships that invest in retail real estate. Real estate partnerships are often structured with a carried interest provision to help compensate the general partner in the fairest of ways over many years for maximizing the success of the venture such as the grocery-anchored community shopping centers that I acquire and redevelop.

Through my involvement with ICSC's government relations efforts, I have strived to educate members of Congress about higher taxation of carried interest that runs contrary to the shopping center industry's efforts to improve the performance of community centers.

A successful shopping center helps retailers succeed and expand. It helps provide goods and services to communities throughout America. The

Featured here testifying in Washington, D.C., on June 29, 2000, before the U.S. House of Representatives Subcommittee on Commercial and Administrative Law of the Committee on the Judiciary. I predicted that state and local governments could experience a decrease in sales tax revenues that provide essential public services such as education, police and fire protection, and road repairs as the Internet becomes a more acceptable form of retailing. At the hearing, I told congressional leaders that without this taxation, governments that rely heavily on sales tax revenues to fund key programs could potentially face severe budget shortfalls. In 2010, when a congressional subcommittee proposed tax reforms to raise revenues by treating carried interest as ordinary income rather than as a capital gain, my industry colleagues and I met with legislators to caution them of the negative impact this change could have.

center in turn provides more jobs locally. It also pays property, sales and payroll taxes to reduce the tax burden of the citizens.

The general partner is not the only one that benefits from carried interest. Stakeholders in the community also benefit from the success of the shopping center project. The investor group as a whole benefits because it incentivizes you as the general partner to create success before you can be paid for doing so.

Whether your partnerships involve several individuals or one institutional investor, you should structure all your deals with this type of sharing arrangement. Every institutional and individual investor who is knowledgeable about real estate investing considers this arrangement the norm in our industry.

In this sharing arrangement, this front end (of which you are one of the 10 individuals of this group in my previous example) is going to receive a certain minimum percentage return disbursement on the initial investment, and then additional disbursements are going to be shared with the back end (which is only you).

How to Explain the Sharing Arrangements to Your Partners

So what can you say to make your partners understand the rationale? How do we explain this seemingly lopsided sharing? This is what we would need to convey to an individual investor:

For cash distribution, the partnership is going to distribute an 8 percent cumulative noncompounded return, and then future cash distributions over and above the 8 percent will be distributed 50 percent to the equity and 50 percent to the back-end interest.

In a refinance or a sale, the partnership is going to distribute first any shortfall on the 8 percent cumulative noncompounded return, then the equity, and then any cash leftover will be distributed 50 percent to the equity and 50 percent to the back-end interest.

As part of your initial presentation of the deal, for example, you might tell your investors that you are going to give them an 8 percent return on their investment and that you will share disproportionally the additional distributions beyond the 8 percent, as you will be receiving a greater share.

In this example, you are going to give each shareholder (of which you are part by virtue of your $100,000 investment) half of any distributions over the 8 percent returns, and the other half of any distributions are going to go to you as your promote or back-end interest—as I like to call it—for your added risks and the good job you are doing. I will explain this in more detail later.

Now, what do you say to the investor who cannot understand or accept this type of sharing arrangement?

Let me give you an example of the type of investor who cannot be one of my partners. Let us say that three individuals are looking to invest with me. They each have 25 cents and I have 25 cents.

Together we have one dollar to invest. The three investors say to me that they are happy to pay me all my fees; that is, my acquisition fee, my property management fee, my leasing commissions, my construction management fee, my partnership supervisory fee and my financing fee. That may seem like a boatload of fees to compensate me for the work I am doing. However, how am I compensated for the value I am creating?

The biggest obstacle I face is when I come across an investor who thinks my fees are sufficient compensation, and that I should not be given a greater role in sharing cash flow and appreciation.

This potential partner shrugs when I bring up the sponsor's sharing arrangement. He simply cannot understand why, if we each invested 25 percent of the equity, he should not get 25 percent of the cash flow and 25 percent of the appreciation. This type of investor cannot be my partner.

He does not recognize the money and time I spent on several deals before this one came to be presented to them. Furthermore, he does not realize that I am probably personally guaranteeing the bank loan (recourse or even nonrecourse carve-outs), the completion guarantees with the lender or signing on the loans needed from a bonding company per county or city requirements in order to obtain permits to approve the property. He is not cognizant of the personal risk I am taking beyond the other investors.

But most importantly, I believe I am not fairly compensated by receiving fees only for my *expertise*. Just as the surgeon is not paid by the hour, simply because the surgery took only an hour, but rather paid for his years of schooling and performing hundreds of similar surgeries, so is the case with developers.

As we build our credentials, we are paid more for our expertise and for the record of performance we have established over the years. Receiving a greater share of the cash flow and appreciation is the way we are compensated. The better job we do, the more we share in the property's cash flow and appreciation. That is in the best interest of all partners, as their rewards are correlated with my performance and compensation.

Allocation of Cash Flow

Let me clarify one point. When I talk about distributions, I am not referring to the property's NOI or its taxable income. The distributions exclude funds that you feel should be held in the partnership for reserves; for example, to replace the roof, make tenant improvements or pay leasing commissions. You are going to distribute only the excess cash flow.

When all of the operating expenses and developer expenses are paid out, whatever money remains is available for you, as the managing partner, to determine how to distribute. This is typically an annual percentage.

However, as the managing partner, you can determine how frequently you want to distribute it, whether it is semiannually, quarterly or monthly, depending on the language of the partnership agreement and the type of legal entity you set up. In general, the larger the amount of money, the more often we would distribute it.

Let us say that we have promised an 8 percent cumulative noncompounded return on the partners' equity investment. This 8 percent should be paid out first, if possible. Then, you can distribute any additional money that remains, which is the return on the investment after the preferred return. In my deals, I divide it in half, with 50 percent divided among the investors (myself included, if I am an investor), and 50 percent going to back-end promote (also known as carried interest), meaning to my own development company.

The 50 percent that is returned to the development company can be seen as a bonus for a job well done. After all, it is the developer's hard work that created such a surplus of income, and the partners agreed ahead of time to this carried interest bonus payment. I will explain this later.

If, however, the shopping center does not meet the expected goals as demonstrated in the initial investor package, and there is a shortfall on the return of your partners' investment, this amount will be carried forward to the following year.

Remember: although you obviously hope for success, there is no guarantee that the return that you proposed is going to be achieved. Just keep in mind that the promised return must be realized before any money is shared as a bonus or promote with the back end to your development company. If it is time to sell or refinance the property, and you are still not caught up paying that 8 percent return, you need to make up the difference with your partners before any bonus is given to the developer.

This scenario strictly pertains to a partnership made up of individual investors. The numbers are different if you are working with an institution. Instead of 8 percent, the sharing cash flow might be a 12 to 20 percent cumulative compounded return to the equity, which could be compounded quarterly, semiannually or annually.

When it comes to additional cash beyond the return, instead of splitting the carried interest bonus evenly between the investors and the developer, 75 percent of it would go to the investors (the institution and you), with 25 percent going to the back-end promote.

Another concept your investors should consider is that their equity improves from principal amortization. As the principal is paid monthly on the debt, ownership gains equity on the investment. It really is a type of return to the investor in the sense that it builds up equity that is not dependent on appreciation.

Preferred Return Versus *Pari Passu*

Many investors require cash flow to be distributed to them *pari passu* with the investment of the sponsor at a preferred return ("pref"). Thereafter a disproportionate return is weighted in favor of the sponsor.

Pari passu is a Latin phrase that is literally translated as "with equal step." It simply means "fairly" or "without partiality." According to *Black's Law Dictionary*, *pari passu* means "proportionally; at an equal pace, without preference."

It is customary for the investors and the sponsors to split cash flow or proceeds from a sale or refinancing only after payment of all liabilities of the company have been paid to creditors.

It is important to understand the impact that offering a preferred return has on your returns on investment as the general partner and any additional limited partners. This applies in terms of both sharing cash flow and distribution upon the dissolution of the partnership.

Most of the deals I have assembled provide for the institutional investor's equity and my equity to be *pari passu*, and we share pro rata until we both receive our agreed-upon preferred return. Thereafter, I would receive a larger sharing. However, I once structured a deal where the institutional equity was not *pari passu* with me but was in a preferred position. In this case, the institutional equity received its return first and then I received mine. This obviously was something I did not prefer, but in return I received a much greater sharing of the back-end interest.

I structure my institutional deals so that the partnership consists of only the institution and me. I have tried to bring in individual partners along with the institutional money, but none of my private investors wish to invest with the institution investor once they read the partnership agreement. As I am receiving many different types of fees, along with my *pari passu* preferred return and my back-end interest, the rights the institutional investor require are okay with me but not with anyone else I have tried to bring into an institutional deal.

In Chapter VIII, I will illustrate a case study depicting how distribution to partners upon a sale of the asset is different between institutional deals and individual investor deals.

Distributing Cash

Let us review an example in my model for distributing cash to partners. Later I will walk you through the numbers and charts of how I do this. Again, when I talk about distributions, I am not referring to the property's net operating income but the actual cash distributed.

You may choose to hold some cash for upcoming operating expenses that the property needs, such as a roof that needs replacing, tenant improvements, leasing commissions or something else that would be excluded from the calculation. This calculation is linked exclusively to distributing money.

In the example depicted on Table 6.2, page 130, let us suppose your nine investors and you collectively invested $1 million in the property. You could only distribute $60,000 in the first year, after expenses are subtracted from the revenue, and after any monies you want to keep in the partnership are left to remain. However, $60,000 is not 8 percent of a million, and you promised your investors an 8 percent cumulative noncompounded return.

The first year is $60,000. So, how is that sum distributed? We have 10 partners, each of whom put in $100,000. You, as the sponsor, are one of them. Every investor including you gets $6,000. We are cumulating $20,000.

In the second year, the shopping center performs better. Rents are up. Maybe you leased more space at higher rents, and you could distribute $80,000. The first year you had $60,000 of cash flow, which results in an unpaid preferred return of $20,000.

The deals I structure call for an 8 percent cumulative noncompounded return and a 50/50 sharing thereafter. This means that after the 8 percent, 50 percent is going to go to the front-end investor group, of which you are one of ten, and 50 percent is going to go to the back-end group, which is just you as the developer.

At TRC, part of that back-end group includes some of the people who work in the company. I give them bonuses tied to the back-end promote. Most of my deals have been what I refer to as an 8 percent cumulative noncompounded return and thereafter a 50/50 sharing.

In the second year, I promised $80,000, which is exactly 8 percent. However, we have to take into consideration the $20,000 accumulated. Regardless, cash flow allows us to distribute $80,000, so every partner including you as the sponsor receives a check for $8,000.

In the third year, the shopping center does even better, and you can distribute $100,000. It has nothing to do with income. It has to do with cash that you are distributing. You distribute $100,000. Investors first get $8,000 each for a total distribution of $80,000, which is the 8 percent you promised them. But you actually owe them $20,000 from the first year, or $2,000 to each of the nine investors and yourself as the tenth investor. As a result, you will distribute $10,000 to each investor. By the third year, you would have made all investors whole, including you as one of the 10 investors.

In the fourth year, the shopping center continues its performance streak, which will give you the ability to distribute $120,000. How do you distribute $120,000? First, every investor gets $8,000; the total of the group gets $80,000; and you will have to allocate $40,000 in excess funds.

Remember, the deal that we structured calls for an 8 percent cumulative noncompound return and then a 50/50 sharing between the front and back

Table 6.2 Sample Shopping Center, Distribution of Cash Flow

SAMPLE SHOPPING CENTER
Distribution of Cash Flow

Sharing of Cash Flow Distribution

8% Cumulative Noncompounded Return to the Equity

50% Additional Cash to Equity / 50% Additional Cash to Back-End Promote (Sponsor)

Cash Equity	1,000,000	
Cash Equity Preferred Return	8%	

Investor I - Sponsor	10%
Investor Group (9 Other Investors)	90%

For the years ending		Year 1	Year 2	Year 3	Year 4	Year 5*	Year 6
Net Cash Flow		60,000	80,000	100,000	120,000	80,000	100,000
Distribution Level 1							
Cash Equity		1,000,000	1,000,000	1,000,000	1,000,000	0	0
Preferred Return	8%	80,000	80,000	80,000	80,000	0	0
Cumulative Unpaid Preferred Return		80,000	100,000	100,000	80,000	0	0
Cash Distribution – Level 1		**60,000**	**80,000**	**100,000**	**80,000**	**0**	**0**
Remaining Unpaid Preferred Return		20,000	20,000	0	0	0	0
Excess Funds		0	0	0	40,000	80,000	100,000
Distribution Level 2							
Equity Partners (Front End)	50%	0	0	0	20,000	40,000	50,000
Promote - Sponsor (Back End)	50%	0	0	0	20,000	40,000	50,000
Total – Distribution Level 2		**0**	**0**	**0**	**20,000**	**40,000**	**50,000**
Summary of Distributions							
Equity Partners (Front-End)		60,000	80,000	100,000	100,000	40,000	50,000
Promote - Sponsor (Back-End)		0	0	0	20,000	40,000	50,000
TOTAL		**60,000**	**80,000**	**100,000**	**120,000**	**80,000**	**100,000**

*Refinance at the beginning of 5th year.

ends. As one of the 10 investors, you would be in the front, but as the sponsor of the partnership, you would also receive in the back end.

The front would get $20,000 as 50 percent, and you as the sponsor would get $20,000 as the remaining 50 percent. In effect, the front group gets $10,000 each—you get a check for $10,000 as one of the 10 investors, and you get a check for $20,000 for the back end. That is what an 8 percent cumulative noncompounded return and a 50/50 sharing between the front and the back end means.

Whether you are dealing with individuals or institutions, the concept of the front end and the back end are the same because institutions want the developer incentivized to improve the asset and therefore its returns.

Distributing Net Proceeds From a Sale

The only way to fully realize a return on an investment is to sell the property. When you are calculating the return on investment to demonstrate to potential investors how much money they can make, you are basing it on the assumption of the eventual sale of the property.

You will have agreed upon a length of time of the deal, typically 5 years or 10 years, after which the property will be sold if conditions are right and improvements are completed to the point that income can be stabilized and asset value can be maximized.

When the developer feels it is time to refinance or sell the property—whether it is at the end of the pre-agreed investment term or if the conditions are favorable for a windfall—then the proceeds after all the expenses are shared.

First, you will need to make up any shortfall that there might be on the 8 percent cumulative noncompounded return if that was the amount your agreement initially promised the partners.

Second, you will return the original equity that each partner invested. If there is not enough money from the sale of the property to do so, this is considered a shortfall on equity.

But if the property has appreciated to the point that cash remains after the fees and equity are paid out as initially anticipated, you can again divide any remaining cash in half, with 50 percent being distributed *pari passu* among the equity investors and 50 percent being returned to your development company (back-end promote). See example on Table 6.3.

As stated earlier, in the case of an institutional investor, any additional cash might be divided with the institutional investor receiving a more lucrative sharing arrangement, possibly with the institutional partner receiving 75 percent and I, as the back-end promote, receiving 25 percent.

Let us apply the concept to proceeds distributed based on the sale of the asset, assuming a sale for $6 million four years from now and that the shopping center has done well. After the cost of the sale, you will pay off $3 million on the interest-only acquisition/construction loan, and you have net proceeds of $3 million. How do you divide this $3 million of proceeds?

You would first have to return any shortfall on the 8 percent cumulative noncompounded return. In our example, there is no shortfall upon a sale because you gave back the shortfall in the third year. In fact, we gave more than an 8 percent return when we gave in the example $60,000, $80,000, $100,000 and $120,000. If that were not the case, you would have first given that money back to the investors upon the sale, distributing it evenly as 10 percent to each investor including yourself.

Now you must consider returning the initial investment. After you pay off the loan, all investors would get back their initial investment. You would receive your $100,000, as would each of the other nine investors, for a total distribution of $1 million. That leaves you with $2 million to distribute.

Because there is no shortfall on the 8 percent, and this being a 50/50 deal, of this $2 million, the investors collectively would receive $1 million on the front end and you would receive the balance of $1 million as the back-end promote.

Overall, what did the investors receive? From cash distributions over the four years of the deal, the investors received more than 8 percent annual return in cash. Also, each of the 10 investors received $100,000 at the time of sale, or an average for the four years of the deal of $25,000 a year, or 25 percent of their investment per year.

Notwithstanding the time value of money, the investors overall earned over a 33 percent annual percentage rate return on their initial investment of $100,000.

Table 6.3 Sample Shopping Center, Financial Analysis, Proceed Distribution Based on Sale at End of Fourth Year

SAMPLE SHOPPING CENTER
Financial Analysis
Proceed Distribution Based on Sale at End of Fourth Year

Distribution of Sales Proceeds

8% Cumulative Noncompounded Return to the Equity
Return of Net Capital Investment
50% Additional Cash to Equity / 50% Additional Cash to Back-End Promote (Sponsor)

Initial Equity Investment

Investor I - Sponsor	100,000
Investor Group (9 Other Investors)	900,000
Total Equity Investment	1,000,000

Net Sales Proceeds Before Loan Payoff	**6,000,000**
Loan Balance	(3,000,000)
Net Proceeds from Sale	**3,000,000**
Cumulative Nonpaid Return to Equity Group	0
Return of Equity Group Initial Investment	(1,000,000)
Balance to be distributed	**2,000,000**

Distribution to All Equity Investors		
Equity Partners (Front End)	50%	1,000,000
Promote (Back End)	50%	1,000,000
TOTAL DISTRIBUTION	**100%**	**2,000,000**

Distributing Net Proceeds of Incremental Value Upon Refinancing

However, if instead of selling at the end of four years, you had refinanced the property and continue to own it, how do you handle future distributions? Let us assume that instead of selling it for $6 million, you can obtain a loan of $5 million. See example on Table 6.4 on page 134.

You would first pay off the first mortgage of $3 million, leaving excess cash of $2 million from the new mortgage. As with the previous example, there is no shortfall on the 8 percent cumulative noncompounded return, and thus you can distribute $1 million to the investors; every investor gets back their initial investment of $100,000, including you as you are an investor.

The remaining $1 million is split 50/50. The investors receive $500,000 collectively; you as the developer would receive the balance of $500,000, and you continue to own the property. What is most interesting and most lucrative is what happens with the future cash flow distributions.

Let us assume you have $80,000 to distribute in the fifth year. For comparative purposes, that is exactly 8 percent of the initial investment.

How do we distribute the $80,000? Do the investors get $8,000 each? No. Going forward there is no longer an equity investment. The $80,000 would be distributed at 50/50. This means $40,000 goes to the front end and $40,000 goes to you at the back end. See Table 6.5 on page 136.

You would receive $4,000 as one of the 10 investors, and you would receive an extra $40,000 on the back end. Each year would be computed in

Table 6.4 Sample Shopping Center, Financial Analysis, Proceed Distribution Based on Refinancing at the End of Fourth Year

SAMPLE SHOPPING CENTER
Financial Analysis
Proceed Distribution Based on Refinancing at the End of Fourth Year

Distribution of Refinancing Proceeds
- 8% Cumulative Noncompounded Return to the Equity
- Return of Net Capital Investment
- 50% Additional Cash to Equity / 50% Additional Cash to Back-End Promote (Sponsor)

Initial Equity Investment		
Investor I - Sponsor		100,000
Investor Group (9 Other Investors)		900,000
Total Equity Investment		1,000,000

New Loan Amount		**5,000,000**
Loan Balance		(3,000,000)
Net Refinancing Proceeds		**2,000,000**
Cumulative Nonpaid Return to Equity Group		0
Return of Equity Group Initial Investment		(1,000,000)
Balance to be distributed		**1,000,000**
Distribution to All Equity Investors		
Equity Partners (Front End)	50%	500,000
Promote (Back End)	50%	500,000
TOTAL DISTRIBUTION	**100%**	**1,000,000**

the same manner. For example, if in the sixth year you had $100,000 to distribute at 50/50, $50,000 would go to the front group, $50,000 would go to the back end. See Table 6.5 on page 136.

Let us go back to the example we discussed on page 130 regarding our distribution of cash flow in the first four years. In Year Five (as shown in Table 6.2 as column "Year 5"), our net cash flow drops to $80,000 from a previous high of $120,000 because we are assuming a refinancing at the beginning of the fifth year, and the higher debt service will consume a greater share of the funds from operations.

Contrary to the previous years when we had to distribute a cumulative preferred return of 8 percent, we no longer need to do so as the equity has been fully paid back to the investors.

Instead, we are going to use the $80,000 in distributable funds to distribute $40,000 to the investor group (front end), of which the sponsor will receive $4,000, and $40,000 is distributed to the sponsor (back end).

In Year Six (as shown in Table 6.5 as column "Year 6"), we are going to distribute $100,000. Since there is no preferred return, $50,000 will be distributed to the investor group (front end), of which the sponsor will receive $5,000 as part of the investor group and $50,000 is distributed to the sponsor (back end).

Closing the Deal

When you get your investors and loans in concert and win the bid for the property, agents for the settlement company or title company will oversee the closing and purchase of the property. They act as the intermediary, with the money coming in from the investors and the bank. They will deliver funds to the seller, as well as handle other charges related to the transaction, such as transfer charges, consultant costs and legal fees.

Meanwhile, you will need to develop a legal entity agreement for each individual investor to execute. Depending on the size of the investments that your partners are making, you probably will be exempt from the rigors that are inherent with securities laws.

The legal entity agreement will verify the amount of money that each of your partners is putting into the deal and their promise to contribute this

Table 6.5 Sample Shopping Center, Distribution of Cash Flow

SAMPLE SHOPPING CENTER
Distribution of Cash Flow

Sharing of Cash Flow Distribution
- 8% Cumulative Noncompounded Return to the Equity
- 50% Additional Cash to Equity / 50% Additional Cash to Back-End Promote (Sponsor)

Cash Equity	1,000,000	Investor I - Sponsor	10%
Cash Equity Preferred Return	8%	Investor Group (9 Other Investors)	90%

For the years ending	Year 1	Year 2	Year 3	Year 4	Year 5*	Year 6
Net Cash Flow	60,000	80,000	100,000	120,000	80,000	100,000
Distribution Level 1						
Cash Equity	1,000,000	1,000,000	1,000,000	1,000,000	0	0
Preferred Return 8%	80,000	80,000	80,000	80,000	0	0
Cumulative Unpaid Preferred Return	80,000	100,000	100,000	80,000	0	0
Cash Distribution - Level 1	**60,000**	**80,000**	**100,000**	**80,000**	**0**	**0**
Remaining Unpaid Preferred Return	20,000	20,000	0	0	0	0
Excess Funds	**0**	**0**	**0**	**40,000**	**80,000**	**100,000**
Distribution Level 2						
Equity Partners (Front End) 50%	0	0	0	20,000	40,000	50,000
Promote - Sponsor (Back End) 50%	0	0	0	20,000	40,000	50,000
Total - Distribution Level 2	**0**	**0**	**0**	**40,000**	**80,000**	**100,000**
Summary of Distributions						
Equity Partners (Front End)	60,000	80,000	100,000	100,000	40,000	50,000
Promote - Sponsor (Back End)	0	0	0	20,000	40,000	50,000
TOTAL	**60,000**	**80,000**	**100,000**	**120,000**	**80,000**	**100,000**

*Refinance at the beginning of 5th year

money at the time of settlement. They can arrange to wire their funds to the title company a few days prior to closing.

Most investors will show the agreement to their lawyers for approval. While they are, of course, welcome to comment or request changes, in my experience most investors will sign what I send to them because I strive to present them with a fair and thorough document that protects their interests and outlines all responsibilities.

CHAPTER VII

Case Study Number 1: Ground-Up Development–Land Acquisition and New Development (Noninstitutional Partners)

Land Acquisition and Entitlement

IN THIS LEARNING MODULE, I am going to walk you through the financial aspects of building from the ground up, which entails acquiring the land, getting your entitlements in place, developing the real estate, building it, leasing it and opening the shopping center.

From acquisition of the land through stabilization of a fully leased and fully operating shopping center, I structure two completely separate partnerships, consecutively, not concurrently.

The first partnership covers the period from acquisition of the land until the start of construction—right up to the day we are ready to put a shovel in the ground. During this time period, you as the sponsor would apply for rezoning of the land (if necessary); complete all the construction drawings, including all civil, engineering and architectural drawings; and obtain all the required preconstruction entitlements, including but not limited to site plan approval and building permits.

By this stage of predevelopment, you would have obtained signed leases with the anchor tenant(s) and have enough leases executed for nonanchor tenants to allow you to secure financing to start construction. You would have obtained debt financing for the new construction as well as equity financing as necessary. As the sponsor, you must have everything in place in order to move to Phase 2, the construction of the new shopping center. This is when the second partnership comes in.

The second partnership would be responsible for constructing the shopping center, leasing all otherwise nonleased store spaces, opening the shopping center to the public, operating the center for a period of time in order to show a history of sales for the tenants and selling the shopping center. In my model, this involves refinancing the shopping center with a nonrecourse permanent loan.

Why do I set up two partnerships instead of one during the development phases? It is because there are two very different levels of risk and thus two very different levels of expected returns in the phases of the development. As well, there is a much lesser amount of debt and equity needed for the first phase, the predevelopment phase, versus the construction phase.

The type of investor who is willing to invest in Phase 1 of the project is willing to take a higher level of risk to achieve a higher return. That investor might or might not be the same investor who wishes to invest in the construction and lease-up of the shopping center.

The reverse is also true. The investor who wishes to invest in the construction and lease-up of the shopping center may or may not want to invest in Phase 1, the entitlement phase.

Throughout this chapter I have prepared tables to illustrate the various stages of the process: for example, Phase 1, the land acquisition and preconstruction period, and Phase 2, the construction, lease-up and stabilization of the shopping center.

Let us analyze the entitlement process in Phase 1 by reviewing Table 7.1, *Sources and Uses of Funds* on page 141, which shows that we are buying a parcel of land for $5 million. We are able to borrow 60 percent of the cost of the land and the costs of the entitlement process from a debt source. We are raising the remaining 40 percent of the land cost and the costs of the entitlement process from investors who are looking to take an equity share in the project.

In looking at the lower section of the table titled *Uses of Funds,* we project that our total costs to purchase the land and obtain all the entitlements will run at $7.8 million. We are projecting it will take us two years to obtain these entitlements, and accordingly we are showing interest carry and real estate taxes for the two-year period.

Look at the top section called *Sources of Funds*. Note that we have a

Table 7.1 ABC Shopping Center, Financial Analysis, Sources and Uses of Funds, Entitlement Process

ABC SHOPPING CENTER
Financial Analysis
Sources and Uses of Funds
Entitlement Process

SOURCES OF FUNDS

EQUITY

Investor I - Sponsor	10%	312,000	
Investor Group	90%	2,808,000	
TOTAL EQUITY			3,120,000

DEBT

Acquisition/Entitlement Loan	60% of total cost	4,680,000	
TOTAL DEBT			4,680,000
TOTAL SOURCES OF FUNDS			7,800,000

USES OF FUNDS

ACQUISITION COSTS

Land Acquisition		5,000,000	
Broker's Commission (paid by seller)		0	
TOTAL ACQUISITION COSTS			5,000,000

DUE DILIGENCE COST

Appraisal		10,000	
ALTA Survey		7,500	
Environmental Survey		15,000	
Other Consultants		10,000	
TOTAL DUE DILIGENCE COST			42,500

SETTLEMENT COSTS			85,000

ENTITLEMENT / PRECONSTRUCTION COST

Architectural		500,000	
Civil Engineering		500,000	
Cultural Resource Analysis		60,000	
Environmental		50,000	
Forestation Credits/Fees		150,000	
Geotechnical Studies		100,000	
Legal - Environmental		25,000	
Legal - Corporate		25,000	
Legal - Land Use		100,000	
Legal - Leasing		60,000	
Permit Fees / Bond Fees		100,000	
Real Estate Taxes (2 years)		75,000	
Traffic Studies		50,000	
Utility Design (Dry Utilities)		60,000	
Wetland Studies		50,000	
Contingency	10% **	190,500	
TOTAL ENTITLEMENT/PRECONSTRUCTION			2,095,500

FINANCING COSTS

Loan Origination Fee	1% of loan amount	46,800	
Interest Carry (2 years)	6.25%	500,000	
TOTAL FINANCING COST			546,800

WORKING CAPITAL RESERVE			30,200

TOTAL USES OF FUNDS			7,800,000

Property Acreage	20	Acres
Property Square Footage	871,200	Sq Ft

**10% of entitlement/ preconstruction cost

total of $7.8 million in funds. We believe we can borrow 60 percent of the total costs or $4,680,000.

The bank will hold the sponsor responsible for the debt and will not front all the money at once. While not depicted in this schedule, the assumption is that I, as the sponsor, will have to personally guarantee this loan, and that the bank will disburse over the two-year period 60 percent of the costs as the costs are incurred.

The required equity is 40 percent of the $7.8 million or $3,120,000. The sponsor invests 10 percent ($312,000), and the remaining investors, which we call the Investor Group, invests 90 percent ($2,808,000) of the equity.

Let us review each line item in Table 7.2, on page 143, *Assumptions to Financial Analysis & Calculation of Sales Proceeds, Entitlement Process*.

1. *Financial Assumptions*: We assume the interest rate on the debt is 200 basis points (a basis point is equal to one-hundredth of one percentage point, or 0.01 percent; thus, 200 basis points equal 2 percent) over the 30-day Libor with an overall floor rate of 6.25 percent. At this time, the rate on the loan is 6.25 percent. Often, U.S. commercial real estate adjustable-rate mortgages use a spread over U.S. dollar Libor rates as the benchmark interest rate to determine the floating interest rates the borrower will pay. Libor, which stands for London interbank offered rate, is a daily reference rate based on the interest rates at which many worldwide banks borrow unsecured funds from other banks in the London wholesale money market (or interbank market). This rate better reflects market conditions than the federal funds target rate, which is determined by a meeting of the members of the U.S. Federal Open Market Committee, which uses this rate to regulate inflationary force.

2. *Distribution of Recapitalization*: This event occurs when Phase 1 is complete and the project is ready to start construction. The land ready for construction is then valued. This new value less all costs to date is the added value that has been created through the entitlement process.

   This is the amount the Phase 1 partnership would be compensated for "selling" the land to an unrelated third party if it were

Table 7.2 ABC Shopping Center, Assumptions to Financial Analysis & Calculation of Sales Proceeds, Entitlement Process

ABC SHOPPING CENTERS
Assumptions to Financial Analysis & Calculation of Sales Proceeds
Entitlement Process

FINANCIAL ASSUMPTIONS

Loan Type	Amount	Period	Term	Interest Rate	Points & Fees	Amortization
Acquisition / Entitlement Loan	4,680,000	xx/xx/xx - xx/xx/xx	2 Years	6.25%	1%	N/A

◆ Interest Rate is based on 30-Day Libor + 200 basis points with floor of 6.25%
◆ For the Purposes of this Analysis Assumed an Interest Rate of 6.25% (assumed Libor + spread will not be greater than floor)

DISTRIBUTION OF RECAPITALIZATION

Recapitalization will occur once the property is ready for construction. Property will be fully entitled with a lease in place for an anchor tenant. All architectural and civil engineering plans will be complete.

Distribution of Sales Proceeds
a. Any unpaid preferred 8% annual cumulative, noncompounded return *pari passu*
b. Return of Net Capital Investment
c. 50% to Equity Group/50% to promote

SALES PROCEEDS

Initial Equity Investment

Investor I - Sponsor	10%	312,000
Investor Group	90%	2,808,000
Total Equity Investment	100%	3,120,000

Projected Sales Price — **10,500,000**

Additions to Sales Proceeds (Working Capital Reserve)		30,200
Estimated Cost of Sale	1.50%	(157,500)
Loan Balance		(4,680,000)
Net Proceeds from Sale		5,692,700
Cumulative Nonpaid Return to Equity Group	8% Per Year	(499,200)
Return of Equity Group Initial Investment		(3,120,000)
Balance to be distributed		2,073,500

Distribution to All Equity Investors

Investor I - Sponsor	5%	103,675
Investor Group	45%	933,075
Distribution to Promote	50%	1,036,750
Total Distributed		2,073,500

Calculation for Return on Investment

Total Proceeds to Equity Investors	4,655,950	*(cumulative nonpaid return to equity group + return of equity group initial investment + distribution to all equity investors (Investor I & Investor Group)*
Less: Initial Investment	3,120,000	
Additional Proceeds over Initial Investment (2 years)		1,535,950
Average Annual Proceeds over Initial Investment		767,975 *($1,535,950 / 2)*
Annual Percentage of Return		24.61% *($767,975 / $3,120,000)*

actually selling the entitled land. Similarly, the Phase 2 partnership would be paying the same amount for "buying" the land from an unrelated party if it were actually buying the land.

The distribution is the distribution of proceeds after all partnership expenses are paid as well as the repayment of the construction loan.

The distribution is as shown:

a) Any unpaid preferred 8 percent annual cumulative, non-compounded return is returned *pari passu* to the Sponsor and the Investor Group. As no distributions were projected nor distributed during the entitlement process, there will be a first distribution for the amount "cumulated."

b) Return of the net capital investment to the Sponsor and the Investor Group

c) 50 percent to the Equity Group (Sponsor and Investor Group on the front end) and 50 percent to the promote (back end).

3. *Sales Proceeds*: We have assumed the entitled parcel is worth $10.5 million. We assumed in the earlier example that the unentitled parcel was worth $5 million and our additional costs were $2.8 million. The total *Sources and Uses of Funds* is $7.8 million. In essence, we created value for our hard work of $2.7 million ($10.5 million − $7.8 million = $2.7 million).

This gives our Investor Group, after all splits with the Sponsor, an annual return of approximately 25 percent. I believe this lucrative return is acceptable and necessary for investors to invest with me on an unentitled parcel of land.

Refer to the subsection *Projected Sales Price*. After setting our sales price of $10.5 million, we added $30,200, the working capital reserve that we started with and should still be in the partnership account, then subtracted an estimate of the cost of selling the land to the new partnership of 1.5 percent of the land value, or $157,500. We then subtracted the debt of $4,680,000. Thus, the net proceeds from sale ready to be shared between the Sponsor and the Investor Group is $5,692,700.

From the $5,692,700, the first deduction is the cumulative nonpaid return computed annually at 8 percent to the Equity Group. Since the total equity investment is $3,120,000 and the entitlement period is assumed to be two years, the cumulative noncompounded return is $3,120,000 x 8 percent x two years = $499,200.

From the $5,692,700, the second deduction is the return to the Equity Group of their initial investment of $3,120,000 and the balance remaining to be distributed is $2,073,500.

For the $2,073,500, 50 percent goes to the Equity Group (front end) and 50 percent goes to the promote (back end). As the Sponsor's share of the total equity is 10 percent, the Sponsor has 10 percent of 50 percent, or 5 percent, and the Investor Group has 90 percent of the remaining 50 percent, or 45 percent. Therefore, of the $2,073,500 balance to be distributed, the sponsor receives $103,675, the investor group receives $933,075 and the promote to the Sponsor is $1,036,750.

To determine the return to the equity investors, we add the total funds the equity investors received as the cumulative preferred return ($499,200), their initial equity investment ($3,120,000) and their 50 percent sharing of the final distribution ($1,036,750) for a total of $4,655,950. From this amount, the initial equity investment ($3,120,000) is subtracted and the *Additional Proceeds over Initial Investment* (over two years) is $1,535,950.

As the entitlement process took two years, the *Average Annual Proceeds over Initial Investment* is $1,535,950 divided by two or $767,975 per year.

Accordingly, the *Annual Percentage Return* was $767,975 / $3,120,000 = 24.61 percent.

At this point, Phase 1 is now complete. We bought a piece of land. We entitled the land. We increased the value with our hard work. We sold the land to the new partnership at a market rate price that gave the Investor Group a fair return for a relatively high-risk investment.

Phase 2 is now ready to start. The Phase 2 partnership is buying a parcel of ground fully entitled for $10.5 million. It has a few executed leases. Financing is in place and the project is ready to start construction.

The risk these investors share in the second phase of development is less than the risk of those who invested in Phase 1. As a result, they are going to expect less than the 25 percent return that the Phase 1 investors expected and received. The return to the Phase 2 Investor Group should be higher than if the Investor Group were buying the center after it was built, fully leased and operating with a stable rent roll and a reliable history of tenant retail sales.

In Phase 2, we will treat the ownership as a new entity—the second partnership. This partnership will be buying 20 acres of land to build a shopping center comprising 147,000 square feet of gross leasable area (GLA). The sponsor will oversee the construction, the lease-up and the operation of the center until the income is fully stabilized with a reliable history of tenant sales and until the property is eventually sold. In my case as the sponsor, I would refinance the property value rather than outright selling the asset, but we must assume a sale in order to show projected return.

Refer to Table 7.3, *ABC Shopping Center, Financial Analysis, Sources and Uses of Funds, Development Process* on page 147. Let us first look at the *Uses of Funds* section with explanations of the line items most relevant:

1. *Acquisition Costs*: The land is being purchased for $10.5 million.
2. *Settlement Costs*: While the table shows $200,000, each state, county, city or town has different recordation or transfer costs pertaining to the purchase of land and the placing of a first deed of trust upon a property. The lender who provides the acquisition and construction funds will want the loan to be secured by a first position deed of trust (mortgage) on the property. It is important to check with your land use attorney to confirm these costs as well as other costs that might be included at closing.
3. *Origination Fee*: The loan origination fee is 1 percent of the construction loan amount of $28,350,000, or $283,500. This is a fee that might be charged by the debt lender as part of lending the acquisition/construction financing.
4. *Hard Costs*: In construction terms, hard costs are distinguished from soft costs in that hard costs are the labor, material and other construction-related costs needed to complete all the land

Table 7.3   ABC Shopping Center, Financial Analysis, Sources and Uses of Funds, Development Process

ABC SHOPPING CENTER
Financial Analysis
Sources and Uses of Funds
Development Process

SOURCES OF FUNDS

EQUITY

Investor I - Sponsor	10%	1,215,000	
Investor Group	90%	10,935,000	
TOTAL EQUITY			12,150,000

DEBT

Acquisition/Construction Loan	70% of total cost	28,350,000	
TOTAL DEBT			28,350,000
TOTAL SOURCES OF FUNDS				40,500,000

USES OF FUNDS

ACQUISITION COSTS

Land Acquisition			10,500,000	
Broker's Commission (paid by seller)			0	
TOTAL ACQUISITION COSTS				10,500,000

SETTLEMENT COSTS				200,000
APPRAISAL	$0.10			15,000
ORIGINATION FEE	1%			283,500

HARD COSTS

Site Development	275,000	per Acre	5,500,000	
Off-Site Improvements			1,200,000	
In-Line Tenants (Vertical Construction)	$80.00	65,000	5,200,000	
In-Line Tenants (Tenant Improvements)	$45.00	65,000	2,925,000	
Grocery Anchor (Capped @ $85 psf)	$85.00	35,000	2,975,000	
Mini-Anchor (Capped @ $75 psf)	$75.00	32,000	2,400,000	
Pad Site (1-5 Ground Leases)	$0.00	15,000	0	
Contingency	5% of hard costs above		1,010,000	
TOTAL HARD COSTS				21,210,000

SOFT COSTS

Architectural	$0.68		100,000	
Civil Engineering	$0.68		100,000	
Development Fees	5% of total hard costs		1,060,500	
Environmental/Other Consultants	$0.34		50,000	
Geotechnical/Inspection Testing	$0.68		100,000	
Legal - Land Use	$0.07		10,000	
Legal Corporate	$0.51		75,000	
Marketing	$0.34		50,000	
Permit Fees/Bond Fees	$0.34		50,000	
Real Estate Taxes (2 years)	$0.85		125,000	
Leasing Commissions			1,750,000	
Construction Interest Carry (2 years)	6.25%		2,800,000	
Tenant Allowance	$3.40		500,000	
Utility Connection Charges	$2.89		425,000	
Water and Sewer Tap Fees	$3.74		550,000	
Contingency	5%		387,275	
TOTAL SOFT COSTS				8,132,775
WORKING CAPITAL RESERVE				158,725
TOTAL USES OF FUNDS				40,500,000

Property Acreage	20	Acres
Gross Leasable Area	147,000	Sq Ft

development and the construction of all the buildings in the shopping center. In this example, we would exclude the construction costs for the pad buildings, which are assumed to be leased as ground leases, and thus the tenants on the pad sites will be responsible to build their own buildings.

5. *Soft Costs*: In contrast to hard costs, soft costs are generally not considered to be directly related to physical construction. Rather, they entail nonconstruction costs such as development fees; architectural and civil engineering fees; any government fees, including the plan approval fee; the cost of the building permit, utility fee such as gas and any electricity, sewer and water hook-up fees and real estate taxes. Soft costs also include marketing expenses and the financing costs, such as interest expense and other financing charges during the construction period.

a) *Development Fee*: The development fee is a fee the Sponsor's company collects for overseeing the development of the project. The fee is 5 percent of the hard costs of construction, 5 percent of $21,210,000, or $1,060,500.

b) *Leasing Commissions*: The leasing commissions are split between the Sponsor's company that is overseeing the leasing for the development and, at times, brokers/sales agents that would be representing certain tenants on an exclusive basis. I estimated that 65 percent of the leasing commissions of $1,750,000 are paid to the Sponsor's company and 35 percent to other brokers/sales agents representing some of the tenants.

c) *Construction Interest Carry*: The interest carry is the estimated interest cost on the acquisition/construction loan for the two-year period that the shopping center is under construction.

6. *Working Capital Reserve*: I usually add a working reserve of about two hundred thousand dollars, as at times bills have to be paid before the lender makes the funds available. Quite honestly, it also rounds out the numbers so that the development, which in this case is $40,500,000, does not appear as a $40,341,275 development.

Now let us turn to the section of Table 7.3 called *Sources of Funds* (p. 147). The *Total Sources of Funds* line item is $40.5 million, which must coincide with the line item titled *Total Uses of Funds*. The *Total Sources of Funds* section should always equal the sum of the *Total Uses of Funds*.

The total equity required is $12,150,000. That is a much greater amount of equity than $3,120,000 that was required when the unentitled parcel of land was purchased. This difference in the equity amount is another reason why I split the development process into two phases.

To raise $12,150,000 at the time the unentitled parcel of land was purchased would be very difficult. The total funds are not needed and would materially change the returns on the equity. However, I do give each of the investors in the Investor Group of Phase 1 the option to become investors in the Investor Group of Phase 2.

In this second phase, we are assuming that we can obtain a loan of 70 percent of the total costs needed for the development. Therefore, the loan is 70 percent of $40.5 million or $28,350.000. I will explain this in greater detail when I review the next chart.

In summary, the equity required is 30 percent of $40.5 million or $12,150,000. The sponsor will be contributing 10 percent of the $12,150,000, or $1,215,000.

This amount is slightly less than the monies received by the sponsor at the transfer/sale of the land into the Phase 2 partnership, so the sponsor has no additional monies needed to invest in order to hold 10 percent of the equity piece. The remaining equity is the Investor Group, which holds 90 percent of the equity with an investment of $10,935,000.

The Investor Group can comprise nine investors each investing $1,215,000 or a larger or a lesser number of investors that in total equals the required equity investment of $10,935,000.

Table 7.4 on page 150, *ABC Shopping Center, Yield Analysis/Refinancing Year (NOI/Total Project Cost)—Development Process*, is one of the templates I created to help me decide if the risk of development is worth the return. This is critical not only for the investors but even more importantly for me, as I will be signing on to guarantee a very large acquisition/construction loan to build the shopping center. Investors of income-producing properties such as shopping centers often use cash-on-cash return as a quick napkin test to evaluate the cash flow and determine if the deal works.

Table 7.4 ABC Shopping Center, Yield Analysis for Sale/Refinancing Year (NOI/Total Project Cost)–Development Process

ABC SHOPPING CENTER

Yield Analysis for Sale/Refinancing Year (NOI/Total Project Cost) - Development Process

Base Assumptions	
NOI (Year 5)	3,847,619
Total Project Cost	40,500,000
Stabilized Yield	9.5%
GLA in Square Feet	147,000

Incremental Increase/Decrease	
NOI	100,000
Cap Rate	7.5%
Value	1,333,333
Spread (bps)	200
Required Project Yield	9.5%

NOI/Cost Sensitivity	Impact on Yield (bps)
$1.33M Cost Reduction / Increase	0.32%
$100K NOI Reduction / Increase	0.25%

9.5% Yield	
Required NOI	3,847,500
Required Project Cost	40,501,253

NOI (Year 5)		PROJECT COST						
		36,500,000	37,833,333	39,166,667	40,500,000	41,833,333	43,166,667	44,500,000
400,000	4,247,619	11.64%	11.23%	10.84%	10.49%	10.15%	9.84%	9.55%
300,000	4,147,619	11.36%	10.96%	10.59%	10.24%	9.91%	9.61%	9.32%
200,000	4,047,619	11.09%	10.70%	10.33%	9.99%	9.68%	9.38%	9.10%
100,000	3,947,619	10.82%	10.43%	10.08%	9.75%	9.44%	9.15%	8.87%
NOI	3,847,619	10.54%	10.17%	9.82%	9.5%	9.20%	8.91%	8.65%
(100,000)	3,747,619	10.27%	9.91%	9.57%	9.25%	8.96%	8.68%	8.42%
(200,000)	3,647,619	9.99%	9.64%	9.31%	9.01%	8.72%	8.45%	8.20%
(300,000)	3,547,619	9.72%	9.38%	9.06%	8.76%	8.48%	8.22%	7.97%

I have learned from experience that if the stabilized NOI before debt service divided by the total project cost—the cash-on-cash return—is not at least 200 basis points (2 percent cash-on-cash return), the *spread,* over the capitalization rate (the rate at which one would expect to purchase the center once stabilized), the risk could be too great to proceed with the deal. In that case, maybe you should not be developing the shopping center.

However, there are many factors to consider, such as your assumptions of rent, project costs, architectural design, etc., to see if you can get within those parameters. Yet these are only parameters.

If you have most of the development pre-leased to credit tenants before you start construction, obviously your risk is less than if you have a small amount of the property preleased.

You would also need to look at the fees you will be receiving because when you add leasing fees, development fees, future property management and partnership supervisory fees, your total fees will be substantial. This could help balance your expected return against your risk. In summary, this 200 basis point spread is only a guide, not a set rule.

For example, if the cash-on-cash return is equal to the cap rate, then you might as well let someone else take the risk of building the shopping center and just buy the shopping center (or some other center with the same risk parameters for the same price) when it is stabilized and operating.

Please examine the different sections of the table.

1. *Base Assumptions*
    a) *Stabilized NOI* will occur in the fifth year and based on Table 7.4 on page 150, which I will explain later, the projected NOI in the fifth year is $3,847,619.
    b) *Total Project Cost*, also based on Table 7.4 is $40,500,000.
    c) *Stabilized Yield* is the cash-on-cash return, which is derived by dividing the NOI by the total project cost. In this example, we are assuming a 7.5 percent cap rate on the sale of the shopping center. Thus, the stabilized yield is 9.5 percent.
    d) *GLA* (gross leasable area) is 147,000 square feet.

2. *NOI (Year 5.)/Project Cost*: The left side of Table 7.4 shows NOI in increments of $100,000 while the top shows the project costs in increments of $1,333,333. Within the chart are numbers that pertain to the NOI/ Project Cost, or the cash-on-cash return.

Shaded in blue are the numbers that are 9.5 percent or higher. These blue-shaded areas are NOI and Project Cost numbers that allow the project to be developed on a profitable basis.

The numbers boxed in yellow depict the NOI and project costs that are assumed to be achievable in this development. The cash-on-cash return with this NOI of $3,847,619 and the project costs of $40,500,000 equal 9.5 percent.

Any of the figures highlighted in blue will allow the center to be developed. Note that toward the left columns where the project cost is reduced and toward the top rows where the NOI is increased, the cash-on-cash return increases. For example, the top row, left column, has the lowest project cost of $36,500,000 and the highest NOI on the table, $3,847,619 + $400,000; as a result it generates the highest cash-on-cash return.

3. *Incremental Increase/Decrease, NOI/Cost Sensitivity,* and *9.5 Percent Yield*: These sections summarize the preceding discussion.

This table lets you balance how conservative or aggressive your rental income assumptions can be. It also allows you, as the sponsor, to decide how much you can spend on project costs.

While land development costs might be set, what about the type of retaining or landscaping walls you should build? How much can you afford to spend on block, brick or stone? What type of architectural design can you afford to undertake? What type of insulation and finish materials should you plan to use in the exterior of the building, Dryvit, brick or stone? What type of roofs, what type of lights in the parking lot, what type of sidewalk, underneath canopies, and other building improvements can you afford?

Obviously, these choices can make a material difference in project cost and cash-on-cash return. This table allows me to continually value-engineer the project through the design process and even during the construction phase. As I define the exact costs, I can make adjustments to the table to learn how much money I can spend and where to spend it where it will add the most value.

You might be in the design phase or even under construction. However, if you are renting at higher rents than first projected, you can implement changes and re-figure your cash-on-cash return. You might decide to add some of the features that at first you thought you could not afford. At the very least, this table will let you recognize that you will be obtaining a higher cash-on-cash return than you first projected.

On the other hand, if you are renting at lease rates that are lower than you originally projected, this Excel spreadsheet allows you to reduce the costs during design or during construction to meet your cash-on-cash goals.

Table 7.5, *ABC Shopping Center, Financing Capacity, Development Process* on page 154, helps us determine the maximum acquisition/construction financing we can most likely obtain. There are three calculations lenders perform when reviewing your deal to determine how much they are going to lend you. These ratios are *Loan to Cost, Loan to Value* and *Debt Service Coverage.* The lender will then generally lend on the calculation that shows the lowest loan amount acceptable to lend.

Note in the table:

1. *Loan to Cost*: We are assuming that the total project cost is $40.5 million and that the lender will lend 70 percent of the total project costs, or $28,350,000. At times, I have seen lenders lend as much as 85 to 100 percent of total project costs but in the 2008–2010 credit crunch, they were lending no more than 65 percent of total project costs, if at all. However, for this historical example we are assuming they will lend 70 percent.

2. *Loan to Value*: The top of the table shows the stabilized NOI, which I will say takes place in Year 4. We divide that NOI by three different cap rates in order to arrive at three possible values. With a stabilized NOI in Year 4 of $3,813,360, we show the reasonable values at $52,598,069 using a cap rate of 7.25 percent; $50,844,800 using a cap rate of 7.50 percent and $49,204,645 using a cap rate of 7.75 percent.

   We then look at three different possible percentages that a lender might lend; for example, 65 percent, 70 percent and

Table 7.5 ABC Shopping Center, Financing Capacity, Development Process

ABC SHOPPING CENTER
Financing Capacity
Development Process

	Cap Rate		
	7.25%	**7.50%**	**7.75%**
NOI - Year 4	3,813,360	3,813,360	3,813,360
Capitalized Value	52,598,069	50,844,800	49,204,645

Loan to Cost

Total Development Cost	40,500,000	
75%	30,375,000	
70%	**28,350,000**	
65%	26,325,000	

Loan to Value

75%	39,448,552	38,133,600	36,903,484
70%	**36,818,648**	**35,591,360**	**34,443,252**
65%	34,188,745	33,049,120	31,983,019

Debt Service Coverage Ratio

		Debt Constant [1]		
		7.73%	**7.98%**	8.23%
NOI - Year 4	3,813,360			
1.25	3,050,688	39,465,563	38,229,173	37,067,898
1.20	**3,177,800**	**41,109,961**	**39,822,055**	**38,612,394**
1.15	3,315,965	42,897,351	41,553,449	40,291,193

(1) Debt Constant computed on a 7% Interest Rate, fully amortizing loan, 30-year amortization

75 percent of value. Of these nine possible loan amounts, I project that the lender will lend me 70 percent of the value derived from a cap rate of 7.5 percent or $35,591,360.

3. *Debt Service Coverage Ratio (DSCR)*: This ratio is the amount of cash flow available to meet your annual interest and principal payments on debt. It is based on interest rate and amortization, after discounting for a margin of safety to make sure a borrower can pay the debt service on the loan.

   The lender sets assumptions as to interest rate and amortization even if it is different from the rate it is charging you. For example, the annual percentage interest rate a lender might charge on a loan could be 6 percent or less while in this ratio the lender may be computing your DSCR using a 7 percent annual percentage rate (APR).

   The lender is setting a rate that pertains as much to refinancing probable rates as today's construction rates. Using the same logic, the construction loan will almost definitely be interest only, but as to this ratio the lender would set a 30-year amortization and maybe even a harsher 25-year amortization.

   Then the lender sets an arbitrary coverage factor that it deems appropriate as a DSCR on your projections. For example, a DSCR of less than one would mean a negative cash flow after debt service. A DSCR of .90 means that you have only enough NOI to cover 90 percent of the annual debt payments.

   A coverage factor of 1.0 would indicate that the expected NOI would be exactly enough to pay the debt service. In essence, the lender is looking for a coverage factor that is higher than one. If one or two stores default on the rent or you miss your leasing targets, the margin of safety that the lender sets on your coverage to determine your loan amount accounts for that loss in income when your lender is projecting your DSCR. A coverage factor of 1.10 gives a lender a little safety factor at 1.20, a slightly larger safety factor at 1.30, a greater safety factor, etc.

   Our assumption is that the lender would lend at a minimum interest rate of 7 percent, a minimum amortization of 30 years and a 1.20 coverage factor. Based on a stabilized fourth year NOI of $3,813,360, the lender would lend $39,822,055.

Thus, when we look at the three calculations, the lender on each of the three would lend:

Loan to Cost—$28,350,000
Loan to Value—$35,591,360
Debt Service Coverage Ratio—$39,822,055

This is the rationale for assuming that the lender will lend $28,350,000 in this example the lowest of the three ratios.

Table 7.6 on page 157 shows the revenue and expenses and subsequent cash flow for the proposed third and fourth years of the development. While the table actually shows eight years of information, the assumption is that the development is a four-year project with an expected sale on the first day of the fifth year.

The left column lists all the revenue categories, all the operating expense categories, the NOI, a list of the nonoperating expenses, net cash flow before debt service, debt service and cash flow after debt service. Let us review what we are expecting for each year of the development:

- Column Year 1: We assume the site work is completed.
- Column Year 2: We assume the vertical construction, or the construction of the buildings, is completed.
- Column Year 3: This is the first year the shopping center is open and operating. All the stores are not expected to be leased, open, operating and paying rent for the full year. Therefore, the revenue is substantially less than the revenue in the following years of operation.
- Column Year 4: This is the second year of operation and the first year that the shopping center is assumed that all spaces are fully leased, tenants operating and paying rent. We call this year the *stabilized year*.
- Column Year 5: The NOI line item is boxed and shaded, as this is the dollar amount we use to determine the targeted value by applying a reasonable cap rate. Here we are assuming a sale of the shopping center during the fourth year with a settlement planned for the first day of the fifth year based on the NOI of Year 5 projected at $3,847,619.

Table 7.6 ABC Shopping Center, Financial Analysis, Schedule of Prospective Cash Flow—Development Process

ABC SHOPPING CENTER
Financial Analysis
Schedule of Prospective Cash Flow—Development Process

For the period ending	Rate	Year 1	Year 2	Year 3 Lease-Up	Year 4 Stabilized	Year 5 Sale / Refinancing*	Year 6	Year 7	Year 8
REVENUE									
Base Rental Revenue				4,125,624	4,149,552	4,187,155	4,225,881	4,265,775	4,449,753
Absorption & Turnover Vacancy				(1,243,376)	0	0	0	0	0
Percentage Rent				0	0	0	0	0	0
Common Area Maintenance	3%			185,760	251,451	255,233	262,887	270,774	278,891
Real Estate Taxes				134,445	179,935	182,632	188,112	193,750	199,566
Insurance				28,011	37,490	38,049	39,187	40,360	41,573
Promotion				0	0	0	0	0	0
Miscellaneous				0	0	0	0	0	0
TOTAL POTENTIAL GROSS REVENUE				3,230,464	4,618,428	4,663,069	4,716,067	4,770,659	4,969,783
Collection Loss/Additional Vacancy	3%			(96,914)	(138,553)	(139,892)	(141,482)	(143,120)	(149,093)
EFFECTIVE GROSS REVENUE				3,133,550	4,479,875	4,523,177	4,574,585	4,627,539	4,820,690
OPERATING EXPENSES									
Common Area Maintenance	$1.66			179,255	239,912	243,511	250,816	258,340	266,091
Real Estate Taxes	$1.24			134,441	179,934	182,633	188,112	193,755	199,568
Insurance	$0.26			28,009	37,486	38,049	39,190	40,366	41,577
Management Fees	4%			125,342	179,195	180,927	182,983	185,102	192,828
General and Administration	$0.10			11,203	14,994	15,219	15,676	16,146	16,631
Legal and Accounting				11,203	14,994	15,219	15,676	16,146	16,631
TOTAL OPERATING EXPENSES				489,453	666,515	675,558	692,453	709,855	733,326
NET OPERATING INCOME				2,644,097	3,813,360	**3,847,619**	3,882,132	3,917,684	4,087,364
NONOPERATING EXPENSES									
Partnership Supervisory Fee	1%			31,336	44,799				
Tenant Improvements (1)				0	0				
Leasing Commissions (1)				0	0				
Reserves (Capital/TI/LC) (2)	$0.25			0	0				
TOTAL NONOPERATING EXPENSES				31,336	44,799				
NET CASH FLOW BEFORE DEBT SERVICE				2,612,761	3,768,561				
ADDITIONAL FUNDS									
Proceeds from Refinancing				0	0	0			
Working Capital Adjustments				0	0	0			
TOTAL ADDITIONAL FUNDS				0	0	0			
DEBT SERVICE									
Interest Payments (3)				1,771,875	1,771,875	1,771,875			
Principal Payments				0	0				
Origination Points and Fees				0	0				
TOTAL DEBT SERVICE				1,771,875	1,771,875	1,771,875			
NET CASH FLOW AFTER DEBT SERVICE				840,886	1,996,686				
Cash on Cash Return				6.92%	16.43%				
NOI/Total Project Costs				6.53%	9.42%				

Year 1 – Year 2: SITE WORK, VERTICAL CONSTRUCTION

PROPERTY SOLD OR REFINANCED AT THE BEGINNING OF YEAR 5

(1) Leasing Commissions and Tenant Improvements paid by Construction Loan
(2) Effective upon refinancing
(3) Interest Carry is paid from the construction loan the first 2 years

*Sale/refinancing at the beginning of the year

Table 7.7 on page 159 lists the basic assumptions to the financial analysis and is self-explanatory.

Please turn to Table 7.8, *ABC Shopping Center, Distribution of Cash Flow—Development Process* on page 160, which shows the accrual of cash distributions and previously distributed share of cash flow.

- Column Year 1 is the year where the site work is under construction. There is no cash flow this first year. We initially targeted $972,000 as preferred return, or 8 percent of the Equity Group's investment of $12,150,000. We are accruing this amount as depicted in the chart as *Remaining Unpaid Preferred Return*.

- Column Year 2 is the year the buildings in the shopping center are constructed. We also anticipated no cash flow during this second year. We now owe $972,000 for another year of preferred return on the 8 percent of the Equity Group's investment of $12,150,000. We are again accruing this amount as depicted in the table as *Remaining Unpaid Preferred Return,* which by now has grown, with $972,000 (owed in Year 1) and $972,000 (owed in Year 2), to $1,944,000.

- Column Year 3 depicts the year when the shopping center has opened and is now operating, but it is not fully leased. The cash flow is $840,886. The cash flow is not sufficient to pay the 8 percent preferred return of $972,000. The difference between $972,000 and $840,886, or $131,114, is added to the prior unpaid preferred return. Thus, at the end of the third year the *Remaining Unpaid Preferred Return* has increased to $2,075,114.

- Column Year 4 shows the stabilized year when the shopping center is fully leased and all tenants are paying a full year of rent. The cash flow now is $1,996,686. That cash flow now exceeds the annual preferred return of 8 percent, or $972,000. The difference between the cash flow of $1,996,686 and the preferred return of $972,000 is $1,024,686. We subtract that difference from the prior unpaid preferred return [$1,024,686 − $2,075,114 = ($1,050,428)]. Thus, at the end of the fourth year, the *Remaining Unpaid Preferred Return* is $1,050,428.

Table 7.7 ABC Shopping Center, Assumptions to Financial Analysis, Development Process

ABC SHOPPING CENTER
Assumptions to Financial Analysis
Development Process

FINANCIAL ASSUMPTIONS

Loan Type	Amount	Period	Term	Interest Rate	Points & Fees	Amortization
Construction Financing	28,350,000	xx/xx/xx - xx/xx/xx	4 Years	6.25%	1%	N/A

Interest Rate is based on 30-Day Libor + 200 basis points with floor of 6.25%
For the Purposes of this Analysis Assumed an Interest Rate of 6.25% (assumed LIBOR + spread will not be greater than floor)
For details see funding capacity schedule

CASH FLOW ASSUMPTIONS

Vacancy Factor	3%
Management Fee	4%
Partnership Supervisory Fee	1%
Capital Expenditures Reserves	$0.25
Renewal Rate	75%
Tenant Sales Escalation	1.50% Annually

Tenant Improvements	
New Leases	$10.00
Renewal Leases	$2.00
Leasing Commissions	
New Leases	6%
Renewal Leases	2%
Market Rent Escalations	3% Annually

IRR ASSUMPTIONS

Terminal Capitalization Rates	
Low	7.25%
Medium	7.50%
High	7.75%

DISTRIBUTION ASSUMPTIONS

Cash Flow Distributions
1. 8% Preferred Return Cumulative Noncompounded to Equity
2. 50% Distribution to Equity/50% Distribution to Sponsor

Sale/Refinancing Distributions
1. Unpaid 8% Preferred Return Cumulative Noncompounded to Equity
2. Return of Equity
3. 50% Distribution to Equity/50% Distribution to Sponsor

Table 7.8   ABC Shopping Center, Distribution of Cash Flow—Development Process

ABC SHOPPING CENTER
Distribution of Cash Flow - Development Process

Sharing of Cash Flow Distribution
- 8% Cumulative Noncompounded Return to the Equity
- 50% Additional Cash to Equity/50% Additional Cash to Back-End Promote (Sponsor)

Cash Equity	12,150,000	Investor I - Sponsor	10%
Cash Equity Preferred Return	8%	Investor Group	90%

For the years ending		Year 1	Year 2	Year 3	Year 4
Net Cash Flow		0	0	840,886	1,996,686
Distribution Level 1					
Cash Equity		12,150,000	12,150,000	12,150,000	12,150,000
Preferred Return	8%	972,000	972,000	972,000	972,000
Cumulative Unpaid Preferred Return		972,000	1,944,000	2,916,000	3,047,114
Cash Distribution - Level 1		0	0	840,886	1,996,686
Remaining Unpaid Preferred Return		972,000	1,944,000	2,075,114	1,050,428
Excess Funds		0	0	0	0
Distribution Level 2					
Equity Partners (Front End)	50%	0	0	0	0
Promote - Sponsor (Back End)	50%	0	0	0	0
Total - Distribution Level 2		0	0	0	0
Summary of Distributions					
Equity Partners (Front End)		0	0	840,886	1,996,686
Promote - Sponsor (Back End)		0	0	0	0
TOTAL		0	0	840,886	1,996,686

As ownership has been unable to reward its investors with the 8 percent preferred return per year by the fourth year, all of the cash distributions are distributed to the Equity Group and the Sponsor. No distributions will go to the promote (back end).

Please see Table 7.9 on page 161, *ABC Shopping Center, Financial Analysis, Rate of Return—Development Process, Based on Sale at the Beginning of the Fifth Year.* This schedule assumes the shopping center will be sold at the beginning of the fifth year. It shows the distribution of sale proceeds and the percentage return that the investors, which include the Investor Group and Sponsor, are expected to receive. Note the details:

Table 7.9   ABC Shopping Center, Financial Analysis, Rate of Return—Development Process, Based on Sale at the Beginning of the Fifth Year

ABC SHOPPING CENTER
Financial Analysis
Rate of Return - Development Process
Based on Sale at the Beginning of the Fifth Year

Initial Equity Investment

Investor I - Sponsor	10%	1,215,000
Investor Group	90%	10,935,000
Total Equity Investment	100%	12,150,000

NOI Year 5	3,847,619
Loan Balance end of Year 4	28,350,000

Deductions from Sales Price		**Additions to Sales Proceeds**	
Estimated Cost of Sale	1.5%	Working Capital Reserve	158,725
Exit Fees (Lender)	0.0%	Real Estate Tax Escrow	-
		Insurance Escrow	-
		Year Five	1,996,686
		Total Additions	2,155,411

Capitalization Rate	**7.25%**	**7.50%**	**7.75%**
Projected Sales Price	53,070,607	51,301,587	49,646,697
Additions to Sales Proceeds	2,155,411	2,155,411	2,155,411
Deductions From Sale	(796,059)	(769,524)	(744,700)
Loan Balance	(28,350,000)	(28,350,000)	(28,350,000)
Net Proceeds from Sale	26,079,959	24,337,474	22,707,407
Cash Flow Y4	(1,996,686)	(1,996,686)	(1,996,686)
Cumulative Nonpaid Return to Equity Group	(1,050,428)	(1,050,428)	(1,050,428)
Return of Equity Group Initial Investment	(12,150,000)	(12,150,000)	(12,150,000)
Balance to be Distributed	10,882,845	9,140,360	7,510,293

Distribution to All Equity Investors				
Investor I - Sponsor	5%	544,142	457,018	375,515
Investor Group	45%	4,897,280	4,113,162	3,379,632
Distribution to Promote	50%	5,441,422	4,570,180	3,755,147

Rate of Return for Equity Investors **			
Total Proceeds to Equity Investors	20,638,536	19,767,294	18,952,261
Annual Rate of Return	19.20%	17.40%	15.73%
IRR (compounded annually)	15.48%	14.29%	13.13%
Initial Investment	(12,150,000)	(12,150,000)	(12,150,000)
Year 1	0	0	0
Year 2	0	0	0
Year 3	840,886	840,886	840,886
Year 4 Sale / Refinance	20,638,536	19,767,294	18,952,261

Distribution of Sales Proceeds
1. Any unpaid preferred 8% annual cumulative, noncompounded return *pari passu*
2. Return of Net Capital Investment
3. 50% to Net Capital Investment/50% to promote

**Does not include promote returns

1. *Initial Equity Investment*
   a) Shows the *Sponsor* has invested 10 percent of the equity investment of $12,150,000, or $1,215,000
   b) Shows the *Investor Group* has invested 90 percent of the equity investment of $12,150,000, or $10,935,000
2. *Deductions from Sales Price/Additions to Sales Proceeds*
   a) Shows the *NOI* in Year 5 as sales price is based on the year going forward from the expected sale date of day one of Year 5
   b) *Loan Balance* is the same as the original loan amount as the loan was interest-only during the construction of the shopping center
   c) *Estimated Cost of Sale*, including all transfer charges, sales commission, legal fees, etc., is 1.5 percent of the sales price
   d) *Working Capital Reserve* is the same as in the initial *Sources and Uses of Funds*: $158,725
   e) *Cash Flow Year 4* is the cash flow from Year 4 that is assumed to be distributed upon settlement of disposition of the shopping center
3. *Capitalization Rate*
   a) *Sales Price,* and thus distributions and returns, are based on three assumptions of cap rates. The middle column is the cap rate that I believe to be the market rate (7.5 percent). The lower cap rate (7.25 percent) is more aggressive and the higher cap rate (7.75 percent) is more conservative on the part of the seller.
   b) *Projected Sales Price*: Here we take the NOI in Year 5 and divide it by the cap rate to derive the *Sale Price*. ($3,847,619 / 7.25% = $53,070,607; $3,847,619 / 7.5% = $51,301,587 and $3,847,619 / 7.75% = $49,646,697)
   c) *Net Proceeds from Sale* is the sale price plus the working capital reserve, plus the cash flow in Year 4, less the cost of sale and less the loan balance.
   d) *Balance to be Distributed* is the *Net Proceeds* from sale, less the cash flow from Year 4, less the shortfall on the 8 percent preferred return of $1,050,428, less the return of the Equity Group's initial investment.

This balance is distributed 50 percent to the Equity Group (45 percent to the Investor Group and 5 percent to the Sponsor on the front end) and 50 percent to the promote on the back end, which goes to the Sponsor.

4. *Rate of Return for Equity Investors* is the rate of return the Investor Group and the Sponsor receive, which excludes the promote.

These returns are shown at the bottom of the same Table 7.9 on page 161 as *Annual Rate of Return* and *Internal Rate of Return (IRR)*.

a) *Annual Rate of Return* is the distributions divided by the equity investment with the result divided by the number of years of the development. For the middle column where the cap rate is 7.50 percent, the distributions provide the equity investors with an annual rate of return of 17.40 percent calculated as follows: $840,886 (Year 3) + $19,767,294 (Year 4 sale proceeds and operating cash flow) – $12,150,000 (in returning the equity investors' initial investment) = $8,458,180 (in total returns over the life of the investment) / $12,150,000 (the equity investors' initial investment / 4 (years) = 17.40 percent annual return on initial investment.

b) *Internal Rate of Return (IRR)* The IRR is a discount rate that investors use to make the net present value of all cash flows from the project equal to zero. The IRR ratio figures in the time value of money at the same annual rate as the IRR turns out to be. The rate, in this example, would always be less than the *Annual Rate of Return*, as the majority of the funds distributed to the Equity Group occurs at the end of the project instead of evenly spread throughout the life of the investment. In our example, the IRR compounded annually is 14.29 percent.

Let us summarize this development example illustrated in two phases. While the annual rate of return for the entitlement phase was 25 percent, the annual rate of return for the development phase was less, at 17.40 percent using a 7.50 percent cap rate.

This is considered to be on the lower side of an acceptable return. In my ventures, I strive to give the Investor Group a return closer to 20 percent per year on a development project. If instead of a ground-up development this had been an existing center with reasonable risk, I would more likely be striving to give my Investor Group a 15 percent annual rate of return.

In the next chapter I will illustrate how the financials play out for an existing center and show you how returns are shared differently when your group of investors is one single institution rather than the nine investors we used to illustrate this case study of a new development project.

CHAPTER VIII

Case Study Number 2: Acquisition of an Existing Shopping Center (Noninstitutional vs. Institutional Partners)

Key Points of the Deal

THE FOLLOWING CASE STUDY illustrates the fundamental financial structural differences between acquiring a shopping center with noninstitutional partners as compared to acquiring a shopping center with an institutional partner. It is intended to demonstrate how the financial terms are different between deals you make with noninstitutional partners as compared to two different structures of deals made with institutional partners. Institutional structure "A" compared to Institutional structure "B" is closer to the structure with a noninstitutional partner. Institutional structure "B" is more complicated and is what is known as a "waterfall" structure of sharing.

Case Study Number 2 shows the purchase of an existing operating shopping center with leases that are below market coming up for renewal. In this case, rents can be increased if the owner repairs or replaces many of the deferred maintenance issues and upgrades the shopping center. This could involve adding lighting, improving landscaping and undertaking a minor facade renovation, that involves painting and new signage.

The sharing of cash flow and appreciation with institutional partners are materially different from sharing with noninstitutional partners. The noninstitutional structure is much more beneficial to the sponsor.

In a noninstitutional structure versus an institutional structure:

1. The preferred return is lower with the noninstitutional partner; thus, the sponsor reaches the promote (back end) sharing arrangement faster than with the institutional partner.
2. The preferred return is noncompounded with the noninstitutional partner. The preferred return is compounded with the institutional partner. This difference also allows the sponsor on the noninstitutional structure to achieve the promote (back end) sharing arrangement faster than with the institutional partner. Noncompounded means there is no interest calculated on any shortfall on the preferred return while compounded means there is interest calculated at the preferred interest rate on the shortfall of the preferred return. Such cumulative interest rate can be calculated annually, semi-annually, quarterly or even monthly. The more frequent the compounding, the less the sharing with the promote (back end) and the less the sponsor receives.

I caution you not to confuse compounding with cumulative. Cumulative refers to accrual of the preferred return. Both institutional and noninstitutional deals—regarding every deal I have seen—are done on a cumulative basis. However, the major difference between the institutional and noninstitutional deals is the compounding, which is the accrual of interest on the unpaid accrued preference. Most institutional structures compound interest on an annual basis.

3. In the noninstitutional structure, if there is cash flow after the preferred return to be distributed, the additional cash flow is distributed to the Equity Group and the promote (back end).
   The institutional partner does not typically allow the distribution of cash flow to be shared with the promote (back end). Institutional investors are afraid that if they distribute cash to the promote (back end) in early successful years and if there should be a shortfall of the preferred return in subsequent not so successful years, they might never receive their full preferred return.

4. Once the preferred return is reached, the sharing arrangement is also different, with the sponsor receiving a greater sharing of the cash flow and the appreciation with the noninstitutional partner than the institutional partner.

Sharing of Cash Flow Distributions

a) *Noninstitutional*: Preferred return is usually between 8 and 10 percent, cumulative, noncompounded, and then 50 percent additional cash distributed to the Equity Group and 50 percent to the promote (back-end Sponsor).

b) *Institutional*: Preferred return is usually anywhere between 10 and 20 percent, cumulative, compounded, and then maybe 75 percent additional cash distributed to the Equity Group and 25 percent to the promote (back-end Sponsor). However, the sharing can be anywhere from 50 percent to the Equity Group, 75 percent to the Equity Group or even 90 percent to the Equity Group.

Sharing of Appreciation at Refinancing and/or Sale

a) *Noninstitutional*: Same structure as per our previous examples. First distribution is the shortfall on the preferred return, then the return of the equity and then a 50/50 sharing between the Equity Group and the promote (back-end Sponsor).

b) *Institutional*: Same structure as with noninstitutional. First distribution is the shortfall on the preferred return, then the return of the equity, and then a 75 percent to 25 percent sharing between the Equity Group and the promote (back-end Sponsor).

Note in Table 8.1, *XYZ Shopping Center, Equity & Debt Assumptions* on page 168, the equity, debt and fee assumptions and how some are different and others are the same when the sponsor structures the deal with a noninstitutional partner. Also note two alternative deal structures: one deal

Table 8.1 XYZ Shopping Center, Equity & Debt Assumptions

XYZ SHOPPING CENTER

NONINSTITUTIONAL PARTNERSHIP	INSTITUTIONAL PARTNERSHIP (DEAL A)	INSTITUTIONAL PARTNERHIP (DEAL B)

EQUITY & DEBT ASSUMPTIONS

NONINSTITUTIONAL PARTNERSHIP	INSTITUTIONAL PARTNERSHIP (DEAL A)	INSTITUTIONAL PARTNERHIP (DEAL B)
Equity 10% Sponsor 90% Noninstitutional Partner **Debt** 1. Initially Commercial Bank 30-Day Libor + 200 Basis Points Floating, Floor of 6.25% *(Assumed Libor + spread will not be greater than Floor)* 3-4 Year Loan Sponsor's Personal Guaranty 2. Stabilized – Securitized Loan Fixed Rate 10-Year Treasury + 300 Basis Points, Floor of 7.25% *(Assumed Treasury + Spread will not be greater than Floor)* 10-Year Loan 30-Year Amortization Nonrecourse	**Equity** 10% Sponsor 90% Institutional Partners **Debt** 1. Initially Commercial Bank 30-Day Libor + 200 Basis Points Floating, Floor of 6.25% *(Assumed Libor + spread will not be greater than Floor)* 3-4 Year Loan No Personal Guaranty 2. Stabilized – Securitized Loan Fixed Rate 10-Year Treasury + 300 Basis Points, Floor of 7.25% *(Assumed Treasury + Spread will not be greater than Floor)* 10-Year Loan 30-Year Amortization Nonrecourse	**Equity** 10% Sponsor 90% Institutional Partners **Debt** 1. Initially Commercial Bank 30-Day Libor + 200 Basis Points Floating, Floor of 6.25% *(Assumed Libor + spread will not be greater than Floor)* 3-4 Year Loan No Personal Guaranty 2. Stabilized – Securitized Loan Fixed Rate 10-Year Treasury + 300 Basis Points, Floor of 7.25% *(Assumed Treasury + Spread will not be greater than Floor)* 10-Year Loan 30-Year Amortization Nonrecourse

FEES (Noninstitutional & Institutional)

1% of Sales Prices/Acquisition Fee (Paid at Purchase)
5% Development Fee of Hard Costs (Paid as Construction Progresses)
4% Management Fee of Gross Income (Paid Monthly)
4-6% Leasing Fee (calculated on Base Rent of Initial Lease Term or 10 years if lower); 2% on Renewals
1% Partnership Supervisory Fee of Gross Income (Paid Monthly)

SHARING OF CASH FLOW DISTRIBUTIONS

NONINSTITUTIONAL PARTNERSHIP	INSTITUTIONAL PARTNERSHIP (DEAL A)	INSTITUTIONAL PARTNERHIP (DEAL B)
8% Cumulative Non-Compounded Return to the Equity 50% Additional Cash to Equity / 50% Additional Cash to Back-End Promote (Sponsor)	12% Cumulative Compounded Return to the Equity 75% Additional Cash to Equity/25% Additional Cash to Back-End Promote (Sponsor)	N/A - Sharing is *Pari Passu* N/A - Sharing is *Pari Passu*

with an institutional partner (Deal A) and a slightly different deal with an institutional partner (Deal B).

- *Equity*: In all previous examples with noninstitutional partners, the sponsor is investing 10 percent and the Investor Group is investing the remaining 90 percent of the equity.

An institutional partner usually requires the same ratio of equity from the sponsor; in this case, that would be 10 percent. In most partnerships with an institutional partner, the institutional investor expects the sponsor to invest around 10 percent.

In my first institutional partnership deal, my institutional partner required me to invest 20 percent. On the next two deals with institutional partners, they required me to invest 10 percent of the equity.

My record of accomplishment with these institutions has helped build a trust whereby the institutions are not quite as demanding. In my last institutional partnership deal, the institution required me to invest only 5 percent of the equity and it took on the remaining 95 percent stake. And just prior to the 2008–2010 credit crunch, several institutions offered to put up 100 percent of the equity to entice me to sponsor the deal.

In the period that immediately followed the credit crunch, the institutional partner again began to require me to put up a minimum of 10 percent equity investment. Thus, in this example, there is no difference between a noninstitutional and institutional partner as it pertains to the percentage of equity investment by the sponsor.

- *Initial Debt from a Commercial Bank*: In regard to the purchase and upgrading of the shopping center, the acquisition/renovation loan is usually with a commercial bank, whether the equity comes from noninstitutional or institutional sources. Regardless of whether the equity comes from noninstitutional or institutional sources, the loan duration is the same.

These intermediate-term loans are made for the planned completion of the proposed upgrading of the property and the projected increases in rents, which stabilizes the income so that the sponsor can obtain permanent financing at more favorable terms. The intermediate-term loans are usually between three and four years.

However, the significant difference between intermediate-term loans and permanent financing is the cost, or interest rate, of the loan and the requirement for the sponsor to give a personal guaranty.

I have never balked at personally guaranteeing a loan in a partnership with noninstitutional partners. I certainly recognize that I am taking a much greater risk in personally guaranteeing a loan than if I were not required to do so. Without doubt, I would never want to guarantee a loan when given the choice, but that is one of the reasons why I receive the sharing arrangement that I do for cash flow and appreciation.

I also have an agreement with my noninstitutional partners that gives me many rights that the institutional partnership documents do not. The differences in the partnership documents are so materially different that I have never signed on debt financing when my partner is an institution.

There is another benefit to the investor group when the sponsor personally guarantees the initial loan. The interest rate on the loan is often lower when the sponsor personally guarantees the loan than when the sponsor does not. When, I, as the sponsor, personally guarantee the loan, it is usually 200 basis points (2 percent) over Libor, and in 2010 there was a floor of between 5.5 percent and 6.5 percent.

In this example I have set the floor at 6.25 percent. When I do not personally guarantee the loan, I have still been able to borrow debt financing but at a higher price, usually 400 basis points over Libor, perhaps with a floor of 6.25 percent.

In 2010, following the trough of the financial crisis, it was possible but not necessarily probable to obtain debt financing without personal guarantees. These came with tougher lender requirements, such as a larger percentage of available space preleased and/or a lower loan-to-value ratio.

The partnership documents give the institution strong rights to protect its investment. If the deal is going as you projected, the institutional partner will allow you to operate the partnership as promised. But if the partnership is not doing as well as projected, those documents are going to give the institutional partner the right, at some point, to take over the operations of the partnership in order to protect its investment.

Your equity investment is still *pari passu* with your institutional partner, but the protection of its investment is your partner's priority over your personal guaranty on the debt. A good friend once told me that if you guarantee the debt with an institutional partner as your equity partner, you are in the game with two 800-pound gorillas: the debt lender and the institutional partner. And if things do not go as you projected, you are going to get "squished like a bug" by one or both of the 800-pound gorillas. That is one advice I have never forgotten.

- *Debt—Stabilized Loan*: Once the property is stabilized, following the three- or four-year period of the initial construction loan, depending how you structured the deal, the time is right to sell the property.

As my model is to hold and not to sell, this is the time to put a permanent nonrecourse loan on the property, which gives ownership the advantage to draw upon the "added value" equity. If some or all of my noninstitutional partners want to sell, I will bring in new noninstitutional partners. If my institutional partner wishes to sell, which they probably will, I will bring in new partners, noninstitutional or institutional, and refinance the debt.

However, if the partner, whether it be noninstitutional or institutional, wishes to maintain its ownership interest, in both cases, the permanent loan would have the same terms and conditions. There is no difference in the permanent financing whether my partner is noninstitutional or institutional.

- *Fees (Noninstitutional and Institutional)*: All the fees that the sponsor receives are the same whether the partner is noninstitutional or institutional. As the sponsor's fees are market rate, I have found institutional partners, in almost all cases, quite willing to pay my company's fees, including the acquisition fee and the partnership supervisory fee.
- *Sharing of Cash Flow Distributions*: This example shows you how distribution of excess cash flow differs with noninstitutional partners compared with institutional investors.

  1. *Noninstitutional*
     a) 8 percent cumulative noncompounded return to the equity and then

    b) 50 percent additional cash flow to the equity and 50 percent additional cash flow to the back-end promote (sponsor); the same as the previous examples.

2. *Institutional Deal A*

    a) 12 percent cumulative compounded return to the equity and then

    b) 75 percent additional cash flow to the equity and 25 percent additional cash flow to the back-end promote (sponsor)

3. *Institutional Deal B*

    Sharing is *pari passu.* There is no cash distribution to the back-end promote. The calculation in regards to sharing is only calculated at the time of refinance or sale at the end of the deal.

In comparing noninstitutional with Institutional Deal A, increasing the preferred return from 8 to 12 percent increases the amount of cash flow and appreciation that is shared *pari passu* before the sponsor receives the disproportionate incentive-sharing arrangement.

There are other aspects that influence the sharing of cash flow. Compounding the preferred return is another way to share more of the cash flow and appreciation on a *pari passu* basis before the sponsor shares on the disproportionate sharing arrangement.

The compounding effect on the cash flow also impacts what your partners receive and what ends up available to distribute to the back-end promote. I have seen deals that distribute cash compounded annually, quarterly and even monthly. The shorter the time period of the compounding, the greater the cash flow and appreciation that is ultimately shared *pari passu* and the less shared with the back-end promote.

Let us review Table 8.2 on page 173, *Sharing of Appreciation at Refinancing and/or Sale:*

1. *Noninstitutional Deal*

    a) Shortfall on 8 percent cumulative noncompounded return (if any)

    b) Return of equity

    c) 50 percent additional cash to equity; 50 percent additional cash to back-end promote (sponsor)

Table 8.2 XYZ Shopping Center, Sharing of Appreciation at Refinancing and/or Sale

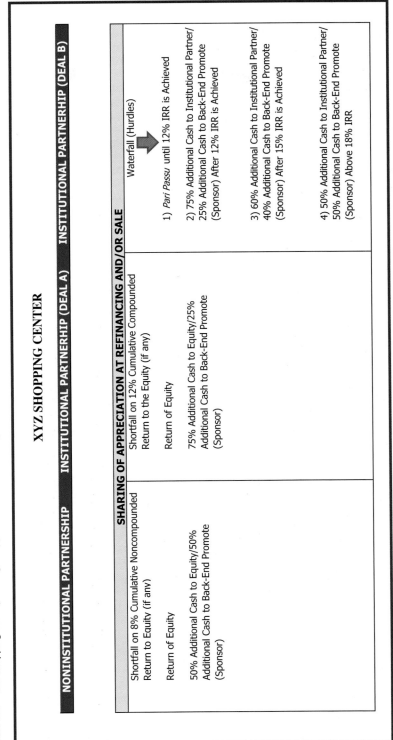

XYZ SHOPPING CENTER

NONINSTITUTIONAL PARTNERSHIP	INSTITUTIONAL PARTNERSHIP (DEAL A)	INSTITUTIONAL PARTNERHIP (DEAL B)
SHARING OF APPRECIATION AT REFINANCING AND/OR SALE		
Shortfall on 8% Cumulative Noncompounded Return to Equity (if any)	Shortfall on 12% Cumulative Compounded Return to the Equity (if any)	Waterfall (Hurdles)
Return of Equity	Return of Equity	1) *Pari Passu* until 12% IRR is Achieved
50% Additional Cash to Equity/50% Additional Cash to Back-End Promote (Sponsor)	75% Additional Cash to Equity/25% Additional Cash to Back-End Promote (Sponsor)	2) 75% Additional Cash to Institutional Partner/ 25% Additional Cash to Back-End Promote (Sponsor) After 12% IRR is Achieved
		3) 60% Additional Cash to Institutional Partner/ 40% Additional Cash to Back-End Promote (Sponsor) After 15% IRR is Achieved
		4) 50% Additional Cash to Institutional Partner/ 50% Additional Cash to Back-End Promote (Sponsor) Above 18% IRR

2. *Institutional Deal A*
   a) Shortfall on 12 percent cumulative compounded return (if any)
   b) Return of equity
   c) 75 percent additional cash to equity; 25 percent additional cash to back-end promote (sponsor)

3. *Institutional Deal B featuring a waterfall return*
   a) *Pari passu* until 12 IRR percent return in achieved
   b) 75 percent additional cash to institutional partner; 25 percent additional cash to back-end promote (sponsor) after 12 IRR percent is achieved
   c) 60 percent additional cash to institutional partner; 40 percent additional cash to back-end promote (sponsor) after 15 percent return is achieved
   d) 50 percent additional cash to institutional partner; 50 percent additional cash to back-end promote (sponsor) above 18 IRR percent return

The main difference between the noninstitutional deal and Institutional Deal A is the interest rate applied to the preferred return and the percentage used in the sharing of the appreciation. The sharing concept involving the excess cash flow is the same.

Let's look at Institutional Deal B to learn about two concepts of structuring the sharing arrangement. In previous examples, we talked about a disproportional sharing of cash flow and appreciation between the equity and the back-end promote (sponsor). For example, if the sponsor represents 10 percent of the equity and receives a 50 percent back-end promote, then after the preferred return has been paid, the sponsor will receive 55 percent of the additional cash flow and appreciation: 10 percent of the 50 percent of the front end (the total equity investment) and 50 percent of the back-end promote, for a total of 55 percent.

Note that in Institutional Deal B, the back-end promote to the sponsor is 25 percent, as is customary in many institutional deals. However, the example illustrates how the sponsor's interest goes from 10 percent *to* 25 percent; *not* 10 percent *and* 25 percent.

If the sharing is as shown in Institutional Deal A, the sponsor would receive 10 percent of 75 percent or 7.5 percent of the front end and 25 percent of the back end, for a total of 32.5 percent of the cash flow distributed after the preferred return has been distributed.

If the sharing is as shown in Institutional Deal B the sponsor would receive 25 percent of the excess cash flow after the preferred return is met. Obviously, this deal would not be as favorable to the sponsor.

This is a very important concept to understand. Make sure your institutional partner and you are correctly defining the split right from the start. I once had a situation where my institutional partner and I had been negotiating for weeks, whereby each of us were unwittingly interpreting the sharing arrangement differently until my letter of intent set forth the terms clearly in writing. That is when the misunderstanding came to light.

We finally worked it out, but it added a level of stress to the deal that could have been avoided had I understood the effect these two concepts have on cash distributions. Henceforth, when an institutional partner starts to talk about preferred returns splits in future deals, I always make sure we are both clear on how I intend to calculate the split.

In the example, please note how we define the sharing after distributing the preferred return in Institutional Deal B. We refer to sharing with the institutional partner *not* to the equity, quite contrary to the way we explain the sharing arrangement in the noninstitutional deal and Institutional Deal A.

The second concept to be mindful about is that there is not only one split after the preferred return but multiple splits directly tied to the prosperity of the project. This concept aligns the interest of the institutional partner with the sponsor and provides for multiple splits that reward for various levels of return. As the institutional partner's return increases, a larger percentage of the sharing goes to the sponsor. We refer to this as a *waterfall return*.

In your splitting arrangement, you can set up waterfall returns to split the excess cash flow into different levels. This deal structure is appropriate because the institutional partner puts in most of the capital for the project and thus takes on the greatest share of the risk on the front end.

Why is a waterfall return arrangement as depicted in Institutional Deal B fair to both, the institutional partner and the sponsor partner? The concept is simple although the mechanics sound complicated. The institutional investor comes in to a deal with a required rate of return (RRR).

This is necessary because the institution often has to provide its investors a rate of return that is high enough to induce them to invest in your project, plus cover its own internal investment and management costs—hence the institution's RRR.

After you give your institutional partner on the front end of the deal its fair return or RRR for the initial risk, you can begin to shift your splits so that you are increasingly giving yourself more on the back end of the cash flow for achieving success—hence the various waterfall levels of distribution.

In this example on Table 8.2 on page 173, after the institutional partner receives an IRR of 12 percent, additional appreciation can be shared 75 percent to the institutional partner and the sponsor goes from 10 percent to 25 percent until we reach the 15 percent IRR hurdle.

If the project has an IRR over 15 percent, any distributions over the 15 percent and up to 18 percent are distributed 60 percent to the institutional partner and 40 percent to the sponsor. If the project has an IRR of over 18 percent, any distribution over the 18 percent is distributed 50 percent to the institutional partner and 50 percent to the sponsor.

The waterfall split sounds complicated, but the concept is simple.

Table 8.3, *XYZ Shopping Center, Yield Analysis (NOI/Total Project Cost)*, on page 177, is another template I created to help me decide if the risk of doing a deal is worth the return. (*See* also Table 7.4, *ABC Shopping Center, Yield Analysis (NOI/Total Project Cost)—Development Process* on page 150.)

Please examine the different sections of the chart and note the similarities and differences between this example and Table 7.4.

1. *Base Assumptions*
   a) *Stabilized NOI* will occur in the fourth year, and based on the more detailed Table 8.6 on page 184, which I will explain later, the projected NOI in the fourth year is $2,019,098.
   b) *Total Project Cost*, also based on Table 8.3, is $21,350,000.
   c) *Stabilized Yield* is the cash-on-cash return. In this example, we are assuming a 7.5 percent cap rate on the sale of the shopping center. Thus, the required stabilized yield rounds up to 9.5 percent.
   d) *GLA*—Gross leasable area is 153,690 square feet.

Table 8.3   XYZ Shopping Center, Yield Analysis (NOI/Total Project Cost)

XYZ SHOPPING CENTER

Yield Analysis (NOI/Total Project Cost)

Base Assumptions

Stabilized NOI (Year 4)	2,019,098
Total Project Cost	21,350,000
Stabilized Yield	9.46%
GLA	153,690

Incremental Increase/Decrease

NOI	**50,000**
Cap Rate	7.5%
Value	666,667
Spread (bps)	**200**
Required Project Yield	9.5%

NOI/Cost Sensitivity

	Impact on Yield
$0.67M Cost Reduction/Increase	**0.27%**
$50K NOI Reduction/Increase	**0.23%**

9.5% Yield

Required NOI	**2,028,250**
Required Project Cost	**21,253,663**

Stabilized NOI (Year 4) vs **PROJECT COST**

		19,350,000	20,016,667	20,683,334	**21,350,000**	22,016,667	22,683,334	23,350,000
200,000	2,219,098	11.47%	11.09%	10.73%	10.39%	10.08%	9.78%	9.50%
150,000	2,169,098	11.21%	10.84%	10.49%	10.16%	9.85%	9.56%	9.29%
100,000	2,119,098	10.95%	10.59%	10.25%	9.93%	9.62%	9.34%	9.08%
50,000	2,069,098	10.69%	10.34%	10.00%	9.69%	9.40%	9.12%	8.86%
NOI	**2,019,098**	10.43%	10.09%	9.76%	**9.46%**	9.17%	8.90%	8.65%
(50,000)	1,969,098	10.18%	9.84%	9.52%	9.22%	8.94%	8.68%	8.43%
(100,000)	1,919,098	9.92%	9.59%	9.28%	8.99%	8.72%	8.46%	8.22%
(150,000)	1,869,098	9.66%	9.34%	9.04%	8.75%	8.49%	8.24%	8%

2. *NOI (Year 4. Project Cost*: The left side of Table 8.3 shows NOI in increments of $50,000 while the top shows the project costs in increments of $666,667. Within the table are numbers that pertain to the NOI/Project Cost, or the cash-on-cash return.

   Shaded in blue are the numbers that are 9.5 percent or larger. These blue-shaded areas are NOI and Project Cost numbers that allow the project to be acquired.

   The numbers boxed in yellow depict the NOI and project costs that are assumed to be obtainable in this acquisition and redevelopment. The cash-on-cash return in the NOI row depicting $2,019,098, and the project costs column depicting $21,350,000 equal 9.46 percent.

   Any of the figures highlighted in blue will allow the center to be acquired and redeveloped. Note that toward the left columns where the project cost is reduced and toward the top rows where the NOI is increased, the cash-on-cash return increases. For example, the top row, left column, has the lowest project cost of $19,350,000 and the highest NOI on the table, $2,019,098 + $200,000 of incremental NOI = $2,219,098. As a result, it generates 11.47 percent, which is the highest cash-on-cash return.

Table 8.3 allows you to balance how conservatively or aggressively your assumptions relate to rental income. It also reveals how much you can spend on project costs. It can also let you value-engineer the project through the design process and even during the construction phase.

Similar to the *ABC Shopping Center, Yield Analysis (NOI/Total Project Cost)—Development Process* example, Table 7.4, on page 150, Table 8.3 allows you to recognize that you will be obtaining a higher cash-on-cash return than you first projected or, if you are renting at lease rates that are lower than you originally projected, this Excel spreadsheet allows you to reduce the costs during design or construction to meet your cash-on-cash goals.

3. *Incremental Increase/Decrease, NOI/Cost Sensitivity, 9.5 Percent Yield*: These sections summarize what we just discussed.

In Table 8.4, *XYZ Shopping Center, Financial Analysis, Sources and Uses of Funds* on page 179, we are purchasing an existing shopping center. We will

Table 8.4   XYZ Shopping Center, Financial Analysis, Sources and Uses of Funds

XYZ SHOPPING CENTER
Financial Analysis
SOURCES AND USES OF FUNDS

SOURCES OF FUNDS

EQUITY

Investor I - Sponsor	10%	872,065		
Investor Group	90%	7,848,582		
TOTAL EQUITY			8,720,647	

DEBT

1st Deed of Trust (see funding capacity)	70% LTV	12,629,353		
TOTAL DEBT			12,629,353	
TOTAL SOURCES OF FUNDS				21,350,000

USES OF FUNDS

ACQUISITION COSTS

Purchase of Property	7.5%	18,041,933		
Broker's Commission (Paid by Seller)		0		
TOTAL ACQUISITION COSTS			18,041,933	
SETTLEMENT COSTS			103,792	

DUE DILIGENCE COSTS

Accounting	$0.10	15,000		
Appraisal	$0.08	12,000		
Architectural	$0.05	8,000		
Civil Engineering (ALTA/ACSM)	$0.07	10,000		
Environmental / Other Consultants	$0.13	20,000		
Legal - Land Use	$0.16	25,000		
Miscellaneous	$0.10	15,000		
TOTAL DUE DILIGENCE COSTS			105,000	

POINTS AND FEES

Acquisition Fee	1%	180,419		
Equity Financing Fee	0%	0		
Debt Financing Fee (Broker)	0%	0		
Debt Origination Fee (Lender)	1%	126,294		
Legal Corporate		200,000		
TOTAL POINTS AND FEES			506,713	
WORKING CAPITAL RESERVE			143,302	
TOTAL CASH REQUIREMENT AT SETTLEMENT				18,900,740
LEASING COMMISSIONS				233,580
TENANT IMPROVEMENTS				215,680
DEFERRED MAINTENANCE/PROPERTY UPGRADES				2,000,000
TOTAL USES OF FUNDS				21,350,000

spend $2 million to upgrade the center. We plan to improve the tenant mix, and in the process, we would bring existing rents up to market. This scenario shows us selling the shopping center at the end of the third year.

Let us first look at the *Uses of Funds* section on Table 8.4, page 179, with explanations of the most relevant line items:

1. *Acquisition Costs*: We are purchasing the shopping center for $18,041,933, using a 7.5 percent cap rate.
2. *Settlement Costs*: While the chart shows $103,792, this amount varies by jurisdiction. Each state, county, city or town has different recordation or transfer costs pertaining to the purchase of a property and the placing of a first deed of trust upon the property. The lender that provides the acquisition and construction funds will want the loan to be secured by a first deed of trust (mortgage) on the property. It is important to check with your land use attorney to confirm these costs as well as other costs that might be included at closing.
3. *Acquisition Fee*: The acquisition fee, which is 1 percent of the purchase price of $18,041,933, or $180,419, is a fee that I, as the sponsor, charge for putting together the deal.
4. *Origination Fee*: The loan origination fee of $126,294, which is 1 percent of the acquisition/renovation loan amount of $12,629,353, is a fee that might be charged by the debt lender as part of lending the acquisition/renovation financing.
5. *Leasing Commissions/Tenant Improvements*: In this example, leasing commissions in the amount of $233,580 and tenant improvements in the amount of $215,680 are estimated amounts needed for the first three years of the deal. Raising these funds as part of the initial equity does require raising more equity than if you solely relied on future cash flow to fund these critical expenses. However, by raising this additional equity up front, the overall return for the partners would be slightly less than if this additional equity were not raised. Conversely, the cash distributions during the first three years would be greater.
6. *Working Capital Reserve*: I usually set aside a working reserve, as at times bills have to be paid before the lender makes the

funds available. The amount set aside for the capital reserve also allows me to round out the numbers so that the development, which in this case is $21,350,000, does not appear as a $21,206,698 development, if no funds were allocated for working capital.

The Total Sources of Funds line item is $21.35 million, which must coincide with the line item titled *Total Uses of Funds*. The Total Sources of Funds section should always equal the sum of the Total Uses of Funds.

In this second phase, we are assuming that we can obtain a loan of 70 percent of the acquisition price. Therefore, the loan is 70 percent of $18.04 million, or $12,629,353. I will explain this in greater detail when I review the next table.

In summary, the equity required is $8,720,647. The sponsor will be contributing 10 percent of the $8,720,647 or $872,065. The Investor Group can comprise nine investors of $872,065 or a larger or a lesser number of investors that in total equals the required equity investment of $7,848,582.

Table 8.5, XYZ *Shopping Center, Financing Capacity* on page 182, helps us determine the maximum acquisition/renovation financing we can most likely obtain as used in Table 7.5 on page 154.

Here, we again consider three calculations lenders make when reviewing your deal to determine how much they are going to lend you. These ratios are Loan to Cost, Loan to Value and Debt Service Coverage Ratio. As we said previously, the lender will generally lend on the calculation that shows the lowest loan amount acceptable to lend.

Refer to the following headings in Table 8.5:

1. *Loan to Cost*: We are here assuming that the total project cost is $21.35 million and that the lender will lend 70 percent of the total project costs, or $14,945,000.

2. *Loan to Value*: The top of the table shows the NOI that the lender will use to underwrite the loan (Year 1 NOI). We look at that NOI with three different cap rates in order to arrive at three possible values. Using Year 1 NOI of $1,353,145, we show the reasonable values at $18,664,069 at a cap rate of 7.25 percent, $18,041,933 at a cap rate of 7.50 percent and $17,459,935 using a cap rate of 7.75 percent.

Table 8.5   XYZ Shopping Center, Financing Capacity

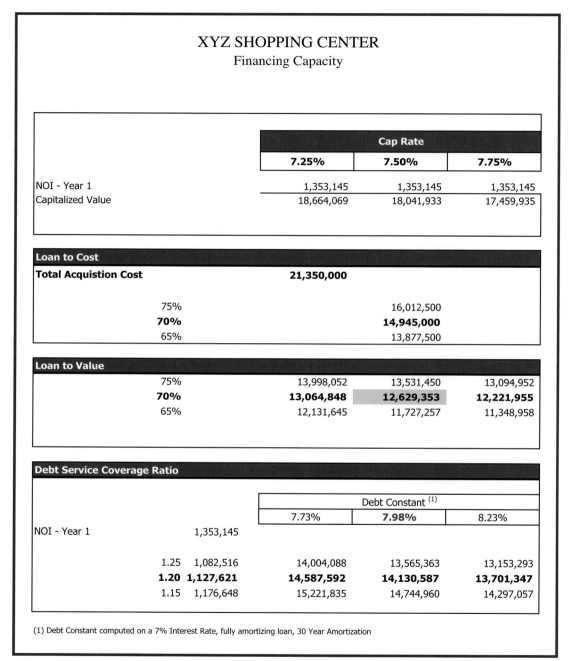

XYZ SHOPPING CENTER
Financing Capacity

	Cap Rate		
	7.25%	**7.50%**	**7.75%**
NOI - Year 1	1,353,145	1,353,145	1,353,145
Capitalized Value	18,664,069	18,041,933	17,459,935

Loan to Cost

Total Acquistion Cost	**21,350,000**	
75%	16,012,500	
70%	**14,945,000**	
65%	13,877,500	

Loan to Value

75%	13,998,052	13,531,450	13,094,952
70%	**13,064,848**	**12,629,353**	**12,221,955**
65%	12,131,645	11,727,257	11,348,958

Debt Service Coverage Ratio

		Debt Constant [1]		
		7.73%	**7.98%**	8.23%
NOI - Year 1	1,353,145			
1.25	1,082,516	14,004,088	13,565,363	13,153,293
1.20	**1,127,621**	**14,587,592**	**14,130,587**	**13,701,347**
1.15	1,176,648	15,221,835	14,744,960	14,297,057

(1) Debt Constant computed on a 7% Interest Rate, fully amortizing loan, 30 Year Amortization

We then look at three different possible percentages that a lender might lend; for example, at 65 percent, 70 percent and 75 percent of value. Of these nine possible loan amounts, I project that the lender will lend me 70 percent of the value derived from a cap rate of 7.5 percent, or $12,629,353.

3. *Debt Service Coverage Ratio (DSCR)*: This ratio is the amount of cash flow available to meet your annual interest and principal payments on debt. It is based on interest rate and amortization, after discounting for a margin of safety to make sure a borrower can pay the debt service on the loan.

   As I indicated for ABC Shopping Center, Financing Capacity, a coverage factor of 1.0 would indicate that the expected NOI would exactly be enough to pay the debt service. The lender is looking for a coverage factor that is higher than one. A coverage factor of 1.10 gives the lender a little safety factor, 1.20 a large safety factor, 1.30 a greater safety factor, etc.

   Our assumption is that the lender would lend at a minimum interest rate of 7 percent, a minimum amortization of 30 years, and a 1.20 coverage factor. Based on Year 1 NOI of $1,353,145, the lender would lend $14,130,587.

Let us take a look at the three calculations that the lender on each of the three would lend:

Loan to Cost—$14,945,000
Loan to Value—$12,629,353
Debt Service Coverage Ratio—$14,130,587

This is the rationale for assuming that the lender will lend $12,629,353, which is the lowest amount under the three parameters that provide the lender the least amount of risk on the debt we are placing on this deal.

Table 8.6, *XYZ Shopping Center, Financial Analysis, Schedule of Prospective Cash Flow*, on page 184, shows the revenue and expenses and subsequent cash flow for the proposed fourth year of the acquisition/renovation. While the chart actually shows five years of information, the assumption is that we

Table 8.6 XYZ Shopping Center, Financial Analysis, Schedule of Prospective Cash Flow

XYZ SHOPPING CENTER
Financial Analysis
Schedule of Prospective Cash Flow

For the period ending		Year 1	Year 2	Year 3	Year 4	Year 5
REVENUE						
Base Rental Revenue		1,557,591	1,775,738	1,973,166	2,210,848	2,301,444
Absorption & Turnover Vacancy		(71,888)	(149,582)	(16,974)	(14,991)	(5,492)
Percentage Rent		50,488	48,825	49,749	0	0
Common Area Maintenance		245,921	263,767	309,298	322,563	336,138
Real Estate Taxes		206,458	209,134	231,779	238,574	246,539
Insurance		31,009	31,820	35,324	36,359	37,575
Miscellaneous		500	500	500	500	500
TOTAL POTENTIAL GROSS REVENUE		2,020,079	2,180,202	2,582,842	2,793,853	2,916,704
Collection Loss/Additional Vacancy	4.00%	(80,803)	(87,208)	(103,314)	(111,754)	(116,668)
EFFECTIVE GROSS REVENUE		1,939,276	2,092,994	2,479,528	2,682,099	2,800,036
OPERATING EXPENSES						
Common Area Maintenance	$1.40	215,405	221,867	228,523	235,380	242,439
Insurance	$0.22	33,396	34,398	35,430	36,493	37,587
Real Estate Taxes	$1.43	219,121	225,695	232,466	239,439	246,622
Management Fees	4.00%	77,571	83,720	99,181	107,284	112,001
General and Administration	$0.10	15,319	15,779	16,252	16,739	17,242
Legal and Accounting	$0.10	15,319	15,779	16,252	16,739	17,242
Advertising and Promotion	$0.07	10,000	10,300	10,609	10,927	11,255
TOTAL OPERATING EXPENSES		586,131	607,538	638,713	663,001	684,388
NET OPERATING INCOME		1,353,145	1,485,456	1,840,815	**2,019,098**	2,115,648
NONOPERATING EXPENSES						
Partnership Supervisory Fee	1%	19,393	20,930	24,795	26,821	28,000
Tenant Improvements		0	0	0	18,292	5,856
Leasing Commissions		0	0	0	14,327	5,249
Capital Improvement Reserves	$0.10	15,319	15,319	15,319	15,319	15,319
TOTAL NONOPERATING EXPENSES		34,712	36,249	40,114	74,759	54,424
NET CASH FLOW BEFORE DEBT SERVICE		1,318,433	1,449,207	1,800,701	1,944,339	2,061,224
REFINANCING PROCEEDS		0	0	0	257,742	0
DEBT SERVICE						
Interest Payments		789,335	789,335	789,335	897,950	888,486
Principal Payments		0	0	0	130,908	140,372
Origination Points and Fees		0	0	0	257,742	0
TOTAL DEBT SERVICE		789,335	789,335	789,335	1,286,600	1,028,858
NET CASH FLOW AFTER DEBT SERVICE		529,098	659,872	1,011,366	915,481	1,032,366
Cash-on-Cash Return		6.07%	7.57%	11.60%	10.50%	11.84%
NOI/Total Project Costs		6.34%	6.96%	8.62%	9.46%	9.91%

are planning the acquisition/renovation as a three-year project with an expected sale on the first day of the fourth year.

The left column lists all the revenue categories, all the operating expense categories, the NOI, then a list of the nonoperating expenses, net cash flow before debt service, debt service and net cash flow after debt service. Let us review what we are expecting for each year of the development:

- Column Year 1: We purchase the shopping center, start working on obtaining the permits and maybe start some of the renovation work, but we have not made major rent increases or tenant re-merchandising as the renovation work is not materially complete.
- Column Year 2: We assume the renovation work is complete and rents are able to start increasing, greater than CPI, based on the work we have completed. However, due to the loss depicted under the revenue line item "Absorption & Turnover Vacancy" in the amount of $149,582, one can see that stabilization of the property with a new lease structure where possible is not complete until the end of Year 2.
- Column Year 3: This is the first year the shopping center's renovation is complete for a full year. Due to the diminishing loss on the revenue line item, "Absorption & Turnover Vacancy" is now only $16,974. One can see that stabilization of the property with a new lease structure is now complete. We call this year the *stabilized year*.
- Column Year 4: The NOI line item is shown in bold in the shaded Year 4 column as this is the dollar amount we use to determine the targeted value by applying a reasonable cap rate. Here we are assuming a sale of the shopping center during the third year with a settlement planned for the first day of the fourth year based on the NOI of Year 4 projected at $2,019,098.

Please refer to Table 8.7, *XYZ Shopping Center, Assumptions to Financial Analysis*, page 186. This table lists the basic assumptions to the financial analysis depicted previously. Among the key assumptions is the acquisition financing of $12,629,353 for three years at a 6.25 percent interest plus 100 basis points for points and fees in an interest-only note and a subsequent ten-year

Table 8.7 XYZ Shopping Center, Assumptions to Financial Analysis

XYZ SHOPPING CENTER
Assumptions to Financial Analysis

FINANCIAL ASSUMPTIONS

Loan No.	Loan Type	Amount	Period	Term	Interest Rate	Points & Fees	Amortization
01	Acquisition Financing	12,629,353	xx/xx/xx - xx/xx/xx	3 Years	6.25%	1%	N/A

☒ Interest Rate is based on 30-Day Libor + 200 basis points with floor of 6.25%
☒ Interest only for the first three years and then amortized over 30 years
☒ For the Purposes of this Analysis Assumed Interest Rate of 6.25% (assumed Libor + spread will not be greater than floor)
☒ For details see funding capacity schedule

Loan No.	Loan Type	Amount	Period	Term	Interest Rate	Points & Fees	Amortization
02	Permanent Financing	12,887,095	xx/xx/xx - xx/xx/xx	10 Years	7.25%	1%	30 Years

☒ Interest Rate is based on 10-Year Treasury + 300 basis points with floor of 7.25%
☒ Interest only for the first three years and then amortized over 30 years
☒ For the Purposes of this Analysis Assumed Interest Rate of 7.25% (assumed Libor + spread will not be greater than floor)

Payoff Existing Loan		12,629,353
Points and Fees		257,742
New Loan Amount		12,887,095

NOI - Year 4	2,019,098	
CAP Rate	7.50%	
Shopping Center Value	26,921,307	
Loan Amount	47.87% LTV	12,887,095

CALCULATION FOR DEBT COVERAGE RATIO

Interest Rate	7.25%
Debt Constant	8.19%
Amortization	30 Years
Annualized Debt Service	1,054,952
NOI - Year 4	2,019,098
Debt Coverage Ratio	**1.91**

CASH FLOW ASSUMPTIONS

Vacancy Factor	4%	Tenant Improvements		
Management Fee	4%	New Leases		$10.00
Partnership Supervisory Fee	1%	Renewal Leases		$2.00
Capital Expenditures Reserves	$0.10	Leasing Commissions		
Renewal Rate	75%	New Leases		6%
Tenant Sales	1.50% Annually	Renewal Leases		2%
Market Rents	3% Annually			

IRR ASSUMPTIONS

Terminal Capitalization Rates	
Low	7.25%
Medium	7.50%
High	7.75%

note for permanent financing of $12,887,095 at 7.25 percent plus points and fees of 100 basis points and calculated with a 30-year amortization schedule.

We arrived at a value of $26,921,307 for the shopping center using a 7.5 percent cap rate to capitalize the $2,019,098 projected NOI for Year 4.

The permanent loan we are taking in the amount of $12,887,095 in this example covers the minimum amount to pay off the balance on the existing loan of $12,629,353 we are taking for the acquisition and to cover $257,742 in financing expenses for points and fees. The new loan has an attractive loan-to-value (LTV) ratio of 47.87 percent.

The calculation for debt coverage ratio of 1.91, cash flow assumptions and IRR assumptions using three separate cap rates in the chart are self-explanatory.

Now turn to Table 8.8, *XYZ Shopping Center, Distribution of Cash Flow (Noninstitutional),* on page 188, which shows the accrual of cash distributions and previously distributed share of cash flow.

- Column Year 1 depicts the first year of operation since the shopping center was purchased. The cash flow is $529,098. The cash flow is insufficient to pay the 8 percent preferred return of $697,652. The difference between the two is $168,553, the unpaid preferred return. This amount will cumulate and carry over to the next year, Year 2.
- Column Year 2's cash flow is $659,872. The cash flow is still not sufficient to pay the 8 percent preferred return of $697,652. The difference between the two is $37,780, the unpaid preferred return. We add this deficiency to the first year's unpaid preferred return [$168,553 + $37,780 = $206,333]. Thus, at the end of the second year, the *Remaining Unpaid Preferred Return* is $206,333.
- Column Year 3 shows the stabilized year when the shopping center's renovation is complete, the center is fully leased and some spaces with new tenants and some spaces with existing tenants are paying higher rent due to leases being renewed after the renovation is complete. The cash flow in Year 3 is $1,011,366. That cash flow now exceeds the annual preferred return of 8 percent, or $697,652. The difference between the two is $313,714. We subtract that difference from the prior unpaid preferred return

Table 8.8   XYZ Shopping Center, Distribution of Cash Flow (Noninstitutional)

XYZ SHOPPING CENTER
Distribution of Cash Flow (Noninstitutional)

Sharing of Cash Flow Distribution
- 8% Cumulative Noncompounded Return to Equity
- 50% Additional Cash to Equity/50% Additional Cash to Back-End Promote (Sponsor)

Cash Equity	8,720,647	Investor I - Sponsor	10%
Cash Equity Preferred Return	8%	Investor Group	90%

For the years ending	Year 1	Year 2	Year 3**	Year 4	Year 5
Net Cash Flow	**529,098**	**659,872**	**1,011,366**	**915,481**	**1,032,366**
Distribution Level 1					
Cash Equity (8%)	8,720,647	8,720,647	8,720,647	8,720,647	8,720,647
Preferred Return	697,652	697,652	697,652	697,652	697,652
Cumulative Unpaid Preferred Return	697,652	866,205	903,984	697,652	697,652
Cash Distribution - Level 1	**529,098**	**659,872**	**903,984**	**697,652**	**697,652**
Remaining Unpaid Preferred Return	168,553	206,333	0	0	0
Excess Funds	**0**	**0**	**107,382**	**217,829**	**334,714**
Distribution Level 2					
Equity Partners (Front End) 50%	0	0	53,691	108,915	167,357
Promote - Sponsor (Back End) 50%	0	0	53,691	108,915	167,357
Total - Distribution Level 2	**0**	**0**	**53,691**	**108,915**	**167,357**
Summary of Distributions					
Equity Partners (Front End)	529,098	659,872	957,675	806,566	865,009
Promote - Sponsor (Back End)	0	0	53,691	108,915	167,357
TOTAL	**529,098**	**659,872**	**1,011,366**	**915,481**	**1,032,366**

**Refinance at the End of the Third Year

[$206,333 – $313,714 = ($107,381)]. Thus, at the end of the third year, there is no *Remaining Unpaid Preferred Return;* instead, there are *Excess Funds* rounded to $107,382. These additional funds are to be distributed 50 percent, or $53,691, to the equity partners (front end), *pari passu* (of which you are Investor I-Sponsor holding a 10 percent share of the Equity Partners) and 50 percent, $53,691, are distributed to you as the Promote-Sponsor *(back end)*.

- Even though the shopping center is sold at the end of the third year, Columns Year 4 and 5 show that if the shopping center was not sold but instead refinanced with no return of equity as part of the refinancing, the cash flow would continue to exceed the 8 percent preferred return of $697,652. In both Years 4 and 5, the Equity Group first receives $697,652, and the remaining cash flow is split 50 percent to the Equity Partners (front end) and 50 percent to the Promote-Sponsor (back end).

Please turn to Table 8.9, *XYZ Shopping Center, Financial Analysis, Rate of Return (Noninstitutional), Based on Sale at the End of the Third Year,* page 190. This schedule assumes the shopping center will be sold at the end of the third year. It shows the distribution of sale proceeds and the percentage return that the Investor Group is expected to receive.

1. *Initial Equity Investment*
   a) Shows the Sponsor has invested 10 percent of the equity investment of $8,720,647, or $872,065
   b) Shows the Investor Group has invested 90 percent of the equity investment of $8,720,647, or $7,848,582
2. *Deductions from Sales Price/Additions to Sales Proceeds*
   a) Shows the *NOI* in Year 4 as sales price; is derived by applying a cap rate to the NOI on the year going forward from the expected sale date of day one of Year 4
   b) *Loan Balance* is the same as the original loan amount because the loan was interest-only during the acquisition/renovation of the shopping center.

Table 8.9 XYZ Shopping Center, Financial Analysis, Rate of Return (Noninstitutional), Based on Sale at the End of the Third Year

XYZ SHOPPING CENTER
Financial Analysis
Rate of Return (Noninstitutional)
Based on Sale at End of Third Year

Initial Equity Investment

Investor I - Sponsor	10%	872,065
Investor Group	90%	7,848,582
Total Equity Investment	100%	8,720,647

NOI Year 4	2,019,098
Loan Balance end of Year 3	12,629,353

Deductions from Sales Price		**Additions to Sales Proceeds**	
Estimated Cost of Sale	1.5%	Working Capital Reserve	143,302
Exit Fees (Lender)	0.0%	Real Estate Tax Escrow	-
		Insurance Escrow	-
		Cash Flow Y3 Q4	252,842
		Total Additions	396,144

Capitalization Rate		**7.25%**	**7.50%**	**7.75%**
Projected Sales Price		**27,849,628**	**26,921,307**	**26,052,877**
Additions to Sales Proceeds		396,144	396,144	396,144
Deductions From Sale		(417,744)	(403,820)	(390,793)
Loan Balance		(12,629,353)	(12,629,353)	(12,629,353)
Net Proceeds from Sale		**15,198,673**	**14,284,277**	**13,428,875**
Cash Flow Y3 Q4		(252,842)	(252,842)	(252,842)
Cumulative Nonpaid Return to Equity Group		0	0	0
Return of Equity Group Initial Investment		(8,720,647)	(8,720,647)	(8,720,647)
Balance to Be Distributed		**6,225,185**	**5,310,789**	**4,455,386**
Distribution to All Equity Investors				
Investor I - Sponsor	5%	311,259	265,539	222,769
Investor Group	45%	2,801,333	2,389,855	2,004,924
Distribution to Promote	50%	3,112,592	2,655,394	2,227,693

Rate of Return for Noninstitutional Partner			
Total Proceeds to Investor Group	**10,877,473**	**10,465,995**	**10,081,063**

Annual Rate of Return	20.15%	18.41%	16.77%
IRR (compounded quarterly)	18.46%	17.09%	15.78%
Initial Investment	(7,848,582)	(7,848,582)	(7,848,582)
Year 1	476,189	476,189	476,189
Year 2	593,885	593,885	593,885
Year 3 Sale / Refinance	11,523,904	11,112,426	10,727,494

Distribution of Sales Proceeds
  1. Any unpaid preferred 8% annual cumulative, noncompounded return *pari passu*
  2. Return of Net Capital Investment
  3. 50% to Net Capital Investment/50% to promote

c) *Estimated Cost of Sale*, including all transfer charges, sales commission, legal fees, etc., are 1.5 percent of the sales price.

d) *Working Capital Reserve* is the same as in the initial *Sources and Uses of Funds*, $143,302.

e) *Cash Flow Year 3, Quarter 4* is the cash flow that is assumed to be distributed upon settlement of disposition of the shopping center, $252,842.

3. *Capitalization Rate*

a) *Sales Price*, and thus distributions and returns, are based on three assumptions of cap rates. The middle column is the cap rate that I believe to be the market rate (7.5 percent). The lower cap rate (7.25 percent) is more aggressive, and the higher cap rate (7.75 percent) is more conservative on the part of the seller.

b) *Projected Sales Price*: Here we take the NOI in Year 4 and divide it by the cap rate to derive the *Sale Price*. ($2,019,098 / 7.25% = $27,849,628; $2,019,098 / 7.5% = $26,921,307 and $2,019,098 / 7.75% = $26,052,877)

c) *Net Proceeds from Sale* is the sale price plus the working capital reserve, plus the cash flow in Year 3, Quarter 4, less the cost of sale and less the loan balance.

d) *Balance to Be Distributed* is the *Net Proceeds* from the sale, less the cash flow from Year 3, Quarter 4, and less the return of the Equity Group's initial investment. There is no shortfall on the 8 percent preferred return.

This balance is distributed 50 percent to the Equity Group (45 percent to the Investor Group and 5 percent to the Sponsor on the front end) and 50 percent to the Promote on the back end, which goes to the Sponsor.

4. *Rate of Return for Noninstitutional Partner* is the rate of return the *Investor Group* receives.

These returns are shown as *Annual Rate of Return* and *Internal Rate of Return (IRR)*.

a) *Annual Rate of Return* is the distributions divided by the equity investment with the result divided by the number of years of the development. For the middle column where the cap rate is 7.50 percent, the distributions provide the noninstitutional partner with an annual rate of return of 18.41 percent calculated as follows: $476,189 (Year 1) + $593,885 (Year 2) + $11,112,426 (year 3 sale proceeds and operating cash flow) – $7,848,582 (in returning the noninstitutional partner's initial investment) = $4,333,918 (in total returns over the life of the investment) / $7,848,582 (the non-institutional partner's initial investment)/3 (years) = 18.41 percent annual return on initial investment.

b) *Internal Rate of Return (IRR):* The IRR compounded quarterly is 17.09 percent. The formula for calculating IRR is not simple and depending how you calculate it, you may end up with different results. Keep in mind that IRR is an *effective* rate of return. The Excel IRR function calculates a *nominal* return. The Excel IRR function works well in calculating the IRR when compounding annually because the nominal and effective returns are the same (compounds only once). When you attempt more frequent compounding, a spread develops between the nominal and effective rate of return. In order to use the Excel IRR function for quarterly compounding, you should translate its result into an effective rate of return. The superior function for compounding more than once a year is Excel's XIRR. In this function, it calculates an effective rate of return by properly inserting the dates when the cash flow is distributed.

Please turn to Table 8.10, *XYZ Shopping Center, Distribution of Cash Flow (Institutional Deal A),* page 193, which shows the planned allocation of cash distributions. Turn your attention to the row depicting the net cash flow of the project and observe the columns illustrating five years of operation.

- Column Year 1 depicts the first year of operation since the shopping center was purchased. The cash flow is $529,098. The cash flow is not sufficient to pay the 12 percent preferred return of $1,046,478. The difference is $517,379, the unpaid preferred return, and will cumulate and compound and be carried over to the next year, Year 2.

Table 8.10 XYZ Shopping Center, Distribution of Cash Flow (Institutional Deal A)

XYZ SHOPPING CENTER
Distribution of Cash Flow (Institutional Deal A)

Sharing of Cash Flow Distribution
- 12% Cumulative Compouned Return to Equity
- 75% Additional Cash to Equity / 25% Additional Cash to Back-End Promote (Sponsor)

Initial Cash Equity	8,720,647	Investor I - Sponsor	10%
Cash Equity Preferred Return	12%	Investor Group	90%

For the years ending	Year 1	Year 2	Year 3**	Year 4	Year 5
Net Cash Flow	529,098	659,872	1,011,366	915,481	1,032,366
Distribution Level 1					
Initial Cash Equity	8,720,647	8,720,647	8,720,647	8,720,647	8,720,647
Unpaid Preferred Return		517,379	966,070	1,117,110	1,382,159
Ending Equity Balance (Capital)	8,720,647	9,238,026	9,686,717	9,837,756	10,102,806
Preferred Return 12%	1,046,478	1,108,563	1,162,406	1,180,531	1,212,337
Cumulative Unpaid Preferred Return	1,046,478	1,625,942	2,128,476	2,297,640	2,594,496
Cash Distribution - Level 1	529,098	659,872	1,011,366	915,481	1,032,366
Remaining Unpaid Preferred Return	517,379	966,070	1,117,110	1,382,159	1,562,130
Excess Funds	0	0	0	0	0
Distribution Level 2					
Equity Partners (Front End) 75%	0	0	0	0	0
Promote - Sponsor (Back End) 25%	0	0	0	0	0
Total - Distribution Level 2	0	0	0	0	0
Summary of Distributions					
Equity Partners (Front End)	529,098	659,872	1,011,366	915,481	1,032,366
Promote - Sponsor (Back End)	0	0	0	0	0
TOTAL	529,098	659,872	1,011,366	915,481	1,032,366

**Refinance at the End of the Third Year

- Column Year 2's cash flow is $659,872. The preferred return is now $1,108,563, not $1,046,478 as in Year 1. Year 2 preferred return is 12 percent on the initial investment of $8,720,647, or $1,046,478 + 12 percent on the Year 1 *Remaining Unpaid Preferred Return* of $517,379, or $62,086, a total of $1,108,563. The cash flow is still insufficient to pay the *Preferred Return* of $1,108,563. The difference between $1,108,563 and $659,872, or $448,691, is the unpaid preferred return. We add this difference to the first year's unpaid preferred return [$517,379 + $448,691 = $966,070]. Thus, at the end of the second year, the *Remaining Unpaid Preferred Return* is $966,070.

- Column Year 3 shows the stabilized year when the shopping center's renovation is complete, the center is fully leased and there are some spaces with new tenants and some spaces with existing tenants paying higher rent due to leases being renewed after the renovation was completed. The cash flow in Year 3 is $1,011,366. That cash flow still does not exceed the annual cumulative compounded preferred return of 12 percent, or $1,162,406. The difference between the cash flow of $1,011,366 and the cumulative compounded preferred return of $1,162,406 is $151,040. We add that difference to the prior unpaid preferred return [$966,070 + $151,040 = $1,117,110]. Thus, at the end of the third year, the *Remaining Unpaid Preferred Return is* $1,117,110.

- Even though the shopping center is sold at the end of the third year, Columns Year 4 and 5 show that if the shopping center were not sold but refinanced with no return of equity as part of the refinancing, the cash flow would continue to be less than the 12 percent cumulative compounded preferred return. In both Years 4 and 5, the Equity Group first receives 100 percent of the cash flow while the *Remaining Unpaid Preferred Return* continues to accumulate.

See Table 8.11, *XYZ Shopping Center, Financial Analysis, Rate of Return (Institutional Deal A), Based on Sale at the End of the Third Year,* on page 195. This schedule assumes the shopping center will be sold at the end of the third year. It shows the distribution of sale proceeds and the percentage return that the Investor Group is expected to receive.

Table 8.11   XYZ Shopping Center, Financial Analysis, Rate of Return (Institutional Deal A), Based on Sale at the End of the Third Year

XYZ SHOPPING CENTER
Financial Analysis
Rate of Return (Institutional Deal A)
Based on Sale at End of Third Year

Initial Equity Investment		
Investor I - Sponsor	10%	872,065
Investor Group	90%	7,848,582
Total Equity Investment	100%	8,720,647

NOI Year 4	2,019,098
Loan Balance end of Year 3	12,629,353

Deductions from Sales Price		Additions to Sales Proceeds	
Estimated Cost of Sale	1.5%	Working Capital Reserve	143,302
Exit Fees (Lender)	0.0%	Real Estate Tax Escrow	-
		Insurance Escrow	-
		Cash Flow Y3 Q4	252,842
		Total Additions	396,144

Capitalization Rate	7.25%	7.50%	7.75%
Projected Sales Price	**27,849,628**	**26,921,307**	**26,052,877**
Additions to Sales Proceeds	396,144	396,144	396,144
Deductions From Sale	(417,744)	(403,820)	(390,793)
Loan Balance	(12,629,353)	(12,629,353)	(12,629,353)
Net Proceeds from Sale	**15,198,673**	**14,284,277**	**13,428,875**
Cash Flow Y3 Q4	(252,842)	(252,842)	(252,842)
Cumulative Nonpaid Return to Equity Group	(1,117,110)	(1,117,110)	(1,117,110)
Return of Equity Group Initial Investment	(8,720,647)	(8,720,647)	(8,720,647)
Balance to Be Distributed	**5,108,075**	**4,193,679**	**3,338,277**

Distribution to All Equity Investors				
Investor I - Sponsor	7.50%	383,106	314,526	250,371
Investor Group	67.50%	3,447,951	2,830,734	2,253,337
Distribution to Promote	25%	1,277,019	1,048,420	834,569

Rate of Return for Institutional Partner			
Total Proceeds to Investor Group	**12,529,489**	**11,912,272**	**11,334,875**
Annual Rate of Return	27.32%	24.70%	22.25%
IRR (compounded quarterly)	23.77%	21.89%	20.07%
Initial Investment	(7,848,582)	(7,848,582)	(7,848,582)
Year 1	476,189	476,189	476,189
Year 2	593,885	593,885	593,885
Year 3 Sale/Refinance	13,212,161	12,594,944	12,017,547

Distribution of Sales Proceeds
1. Any unpaid preferred 12% annual cumulative, compounded return *pari passu*
2. Return of Net Capital Investment
3. 75% to Net Capital Investment/25% to promote

1. *Initial Equity Investment*
   a) Shows the Sponsor has invested 10 percent of the equity investment of $8,720,647, or $872,065
   b) Shows the Investor Group has invested 90 percent of the equity investment of $8,720,647, or $7,848,582

2. *Deductions from Sales Price/Additions to Sales Proceeds*
   a) Shows the *NOI* in Year 4 as sales price, and is derived from applying a cap rate on the NOI for the year going forward from the expected sale date of day one of Year 4
   b) *Loan Balance* is the same as the original loan amount because the loan was interest-only during the acquisition/renovation of the shopping center.
   c) *Estimated Cost of Sale*, including all transfer charges, sales commission, legal fees, etc., is 1.5 percent of the sales price.
   d) *Working Capital Reserve* is the same as in the initial *Sources and Uses of Funds*, $143,302.
   e) *Cash Flow Year 3, Quarter 4* is the cash flow from Year 3, Quarter 4 that is assumed to be distributed upon settlement of disposition of the shopping center, $252,842.

3. *Capitalization Rate*
   a) Similar to our previous example depicting a deal with noninstitutional partners, the sale price, and thus the distributions and returns, are based on three assumptions of cap rates. The middle column is the cap rate that I believe to be the market rate (7.5 percent). The lower cap rate (7.25 percent) is more aggressive, and the higher cap rate (7.75 percent) is more conservative on the part of the seller.
   b) *Projected Sales Price*: Here we take the NOI in Year 4 and divide it by the cap rate to derive the *Sale Price*. ($2,019,098 / 7.25% = $27,849,628; $2,019,098 / 7.5% = $26,921,307 and $2,019,098 / 7.75% = $26,052,877)
   c) *Net Proceeds from Sale* is the sale price plus the working capital reserve, plus the cash flow in Year 3, Quarter 4, less the cost of sale and less the loan balance.
   d) *Balance to Be Distributed* is the *Net Proceeds* from sale, less the cash flow from Year 3, Quarter 4, less the shortfall

on the 12 percent cumulative compounded preferred return of $1,117,110, less the return of the Equity Group's initial investment.

This balance is distributed 75 percent to the equity group (67.5 percent to the Investor Group and 7.5 percent to the Sponsor on the front end) and 25 percent to the Promote on the back end, which goes to the Sponsor.

4. *Rate of Return for Institutional Partner* is the rate of return the *Investor Group* receives.

These returns are shown as *Annual Rate of Return* and *Internal Rate of Return (IRR)*.

a) *Annual Rate of Return* is the distributions divided by the equity investment with the result divided by the number of years of the development. For the middle column where the cap rate is 7.5 percent, the distributions provide the institutional partner with an annual rate of return of 24.70 percent calculated as follows: $476,189 (Year 1) + $593,885 (Year 2) + $12,594,944 Year 3 sales proceeds and operating cash flow − $7,848,582 (in returning the Institutional Partner's initial investment) = $5,816,436 (in total returns over the life of the investment) / $7,848,582 (the institutional partner's initial investment) / 3 (years) = 24.70 percent (annual return on initial investment). As you can see, this annual rate of return of 24.70 percent is superior to the noninstitutional partner annual rate of return of 18.41 percent as depicted in the previous example describing a similar deal with noninstitutional partners.

b) *Internal Rate of Return (IRR):* The rate in this example is consistent with the previous example depicting a noninstitutional deal in that it would always be less than the *Annual Rate of Return* because the majority of the funds received by the Equity Group occurs at the end of the project instead of evenly spread throughout the life of the investment. However, in this example, the IRR compounded quarterly is 21.89 percent for the institutional partner compared to 17.09 percent for the noninstitutional partner as shown in the previous example.

Table 8.12, *XYZ Shopping Center, Distribution of Cash Flow (Institutional Deal B),* page 199, shows the planned allocation of cash distributions. Turn your attention to the row depicting the net cash flow of the project and observe the columns illustrating five years of operation.

- Column Year 1 depicts the first year of operation since we purchased the shopping center. The cash distribution is $529,098. There is a *pari passu* sharing of the cash distribution between the Investor Group (90 percent of the equity investment) and Investor I-The Sponsor (10 percent of the equity investment, which is my investment). There is no preferred return with regard to cash distribution, and thus there is no disproportional sharing of cash distribution after the preferred return. Accordingly, there is also no unpaid preferred return. The $529,098 in cash distribution is prorated with $52,910 (10 percent) going to Investor I-Sponsor and $476,189 (90 percent) going to the Investor Group.
- Column Year 2's cash flow is $659,872. As in Year 1, there is a *pari passu* sharing of the cash distribution between the Investor Group (90 percent of the equity investment) and Investor I-Sponsor (10 percent of the equity investment, my investment). There is no preferred return regarding cash distribution, and thus there is no disproportional sharing of cash distribution after the preferred return. As a result, we have no unpaid preferred return. The $659,872 in cash distribution is prorated $65,987 (10 percent) to Investor I-Sponsor and $593,885 (90 percent) to the Investor Group.
- Column Year 3 shows the stabilized year when the shopping center's renovation is complete, the center is fully leased and there are some spaces with new tenants and some spaces with existing tenants paying higher rent due to leases being renewed after the renovation was completed. The cash distribution in Year 3 is $1,011,366. As in Year 1 and 2, there is a *pari passu* sharing of the cash distribution between the Investor Group (90 percent of the equity investment) and Investor I-Sponsor (10 percent of the equity investment, my investment). There is no preferred return with regard to cash distribution and thus there is no disproportional sharing of cash distribution after the preferred return. This also results

Table 8.12   XYZ Shopping Center, Distribution of Cash Flow (Institutional Deal B)

XYZ SHOPPING CENTER
Distribution of Cash Flow (Institutional Deal B)

Sharing of Cash Flow Distribution
◆ Funds Distributed *Pari Passu*

Initial Cash Equity	8,720,647	Investor I - Sponsor	10%
Cash Equity Preferred Return	N/A	Investor Group	90%

For the years ending		Year 1	Year 2	Year 3**	Year 4	Year 5
Net Cash Flow		**529,098**	**659,872**	**1,011,366**	**915,481**	**1,032,366**
Distribution Level 1						
Initial Cash Equity		8,720,647	8,720,647	8,720,647	8,720,647	8,720,647
Unpaid Preferred Return		N/A	N/A	N/A	N/A	N/A
Ending Equity Balance (Capital)		8,720,647	8,720,647	8,720,647	8,720,647	8,720,647
Preferred Return	N/A	0	0	0	0	0
Cumulative Unpaid Preferred Return		0	0	0	0	0
Cash Distribution – Level 1		**0**	**0**	**0**	**0**	**0**
Remaining Unpaid Preferred Return		0	0	0	0	0
Excess Funds		**529,098**	**659,872**	**1,011,366**	**915,481**	**1,032,366**
Distribution Level 2						
Investor I - Sponsor	10%	52,910	65,987	101,137	91,548	103,237
Investor Group	90%	476,189	593,885	910,230	823,933	929,129
Total – Distribution Level 2		**529,098**	**659,872**	**1,011,366**	**915,481**	**1,032,366**
Summary of Distributions						
Investor I - Sponsor		52,910	65,987	101,137	91,548	103,237
Investor Group		476,189	593,885	910,230	823,933	929,129
TOTAL		**529,098**	**659,872**	**1,011,366**	**915,481**	**1,032,366**

**Refinance at the End of the Third Year

in no unpaid preferred return. The $1,011,366 in cash distribution is prorated and allocates $101,137 (10 percent) to Investor I-Sponsor and $910,230 (90 percent) to the Investor Group.

- Even though the shopping center is sold at the end of the third year, Columns Year 4 and 5 show cash distributions of $915,481 and $1,032,366 respectively, as if the center were not sold. These cash distributions are shared in the same way as I explained relating to Years 1, 2 and 3.

Table 8.13, *XYZ Shopping Center, Financial Analysis, Rate of Return (Institutional Deal B), Based on Sale at End of Third Year,* on page 201, assumes the shopping center will be sold at the end of the third year. It shows the distribution of sale proceeds and the percentage return that the Investor Group is expected to receive. However, unlike Deal A (Table 8.11, page 195), this deal provides for a waterfall return structure.

Let us review how this structure rewards the sponsor after the institutional investor receives its fair preferred return compensation.

1. *Initial Equity Investment*
   a) Shows the *Sponsor* has invested 10 percent of the equity investment of $8,720,647, or $872,065
   b) Shows the *Investor Group* has invested 90 percent of the equity investment of $8,720,647, or $7,848,582
2. *Deductions from Sales Price/Additions to Sales Proceeds*
   a) Shows the *NOI* in Year 4 as sales price and is derived from establishing a cap rate and dividing it by the NOI for the first full year that follows the anticipated sale date. In this case, the transaction is planned for Day 1 of Year 4.
   b) *Loan Balance* is the same as the original loan amount as the loan was interest-only during the acquisition/renovation of the shopping center.
   c) *Estimated Cost of Sale*, including all transfer charges, sales commission, legal fees, etc., is 1.5 percent of the sales price.
   d) *Working Capital Reserve* is the same as in the initial *Sources and Uses of Funds*, $143,302.
   e) *Cash Flow Year 3, Quarter 4* is the cash flow from the fourth quarter of the third year of operation, amounting to $252,842

Table 8.13 XYZ Shopping Center, Financial Analysis, Rate of Return (Institutional Deal B), Based on Sale at End of Third Year

XYZ SHOPPING CENTER
Financial Analysis
Rate of Return (Institutional Deal B)
Based on Sale at End of Third Year

Initial Equity Investment

Investor I - Sponsor	10%	872,065
Investor Group	90%	7,848,582
Total Equity Investment	100%	8,720,647

NOI Year 4	2,019,098
Loan Balance end of Year 3	12,629,353

Deductions from Sales Price		**Additions to Sales Proceeds**	
Estimated Cost of Sale	1.5%	Working Capital Reserve	143,302
Exit Fees (Lender)	0.0%	Real Estate Tax Escrow	-
		Insurance Escrow	-
		Cash Flow Y3 Q4	252,842
		Total Additions	396,144

Capitalization Rate		**7.25%**	**7.50%**	**7.75%**
Projected Sales Price		27,849,628	26,921,307	26,052,877
Additions to Sales Proceeds		396,144	396,144	396,144
Deductions From Sale		(417,744)	(403,820)	(390,793)
Loan Balance		(12,629,353)	(12,629,353)	(12,629,353)
Net Proceeds from Sale		**15,198,673**	**14,284,277**	**13,428,875**

1st Hurdle - Proceeds Split *Pari Passu* Until 12% Return Is Achieved

Investor I - Sponsor	10%	998,505	998,505	998,505
Investor Group	90%	8,986,549	8,986,549	8,986,549
Total Distribution in 2nd Hurdle		9,985,055	9,985,055	9,985,055
Remaining Proceeds to Distribute After 1st Hurdle		5,213,619	4,299,223	3,443,820

2nd Hurdle - Proceeds Split 75% to Investor Group and
25% to Sponsor Until 15% Return Is Achieved

Investor I - Sponsor	25%	277,989	277,989	277,989
Investor Group	75%	833,967	833,967	833,967
Total Distribution in 2nd Hurdle		1,111,956	1,111,956	1,111,956
Remaining Proceeds to Distribute After 2nd Hurdle		4,101,663	3,187,266	2,331,864

3rd Hurdle - Proceeds Split 60% to Institutional and 40% to
Sponsor Until 18% Return Is Achieved

Investor I - Sponsor	40%	587,317	587,317	587,317
Investor Group	60%	880,975	880,975	880,975
Total Distribution in 3rd Hurdle		1,468,292	1,468,292	1,468,292
Remaining Proceeds to Distribute After 3rd Hurdle		2,633,371	1,718,974	863,572
Investor I - Sponsor	50%	1,316,685	859,487	431,786
Investor Group	50%	1,316,685	859,487	431,786
Total Distribution in 3rd Hurdle		2,633,371	1,718,974	863,572

SUMMARY			
Investor I - Sponsor	3,180,497	2,723,299	2,295,597
Investor Group	12,018,177	11,560,979	11,133,277
Total Distribution	**15,198,673**	**14,284,277**	**13,428,875**

Rate of Return for Institutional Partner			
Total Proceeds to Equity Investors	12,018,177	11,560,979	11,133,277
Annual Rate of Return	25.15%	23.21%	21.39%
IRR (compounded quarterly)	22.22%	20.79%	19.42%
Initial Investment	(7,848,582)	(7,848,582)	(7,848,582)
Year 1	476,189	476,189	476,189
Year 2	593,885	593,885	593,885
Year 3 Sale / Refinance	12,700,849	12,243,651	11,815,950

Distribution of Sales Proceeds
See Detail of Hurdles Above

that is assumed to be distributed upon settlement of the disposition of the shopping center.

3. *Capitalization Rate*

   a) *Sale Price:* Similar to our previous example depicting a deal with noninstitutional partners or as in Institutional Deal A, the sale price, and thus the distributions and returns, are based on three assumptions of cap rates. The middle column is the cap rate that I believe to be the market rate (7.5 percent). The lower cap rate (7.25 percent) is more aggressive, and the higher cap rate (7.75 percent) is more conservative on the part of the seller.

   b) *Projected Sales Price:* Here we take the NOI in Year 4 and divide it by the cap rate to derive the *Sale Price*. ($2,019,098 / 7.25% = $27,849,628, $2,019,098 / 7.5% = $26,921,307 and $2,019,098 / 7.75% = $26,052,877)

   c) *Net Proceeds from Sale* is the sale price plus the working capital reserve, plus the cash flow in Year 3, Quarter 4, less the cost of sale and less the loan balance.

Let us now examine the effect of waterfall returns on the investor's IRR to illustrate the concept explained on page 175. The waterfall relates to the order and terms by which distributions are paid to the institutional partner and the sponsor.

As I stated previously, there is no standard waterfall formula for distribution of excess cash relating to your institutional partner's unpaid equity. Discuss a waterfall distribution formula with your institutional partner and describe it in your LLC documents to ensure that both parties are in agreement with the exact method for distributing the unpaid equity from the project's cash flow.

The Institutional Deal B shopping center consists of two investors, the institutional investor and the developer, which would be you or me as the sponsor. In this case, the institutional investor contributed 90 percent of the required project equity and you or I as the developer sponsor contributed the remaining 10 percent.

In this model that I structured as Institutional Deal B, the cash flow is distributed according to a set of parameters specifying cash flow percentage allocations and IRR targets set up as a cash flow waterfall.

In this example, I am describing one waterfall method that I consider fair and works well for my institutional partners and me. The method involves various hurdles. Upon reaching a particular hurdle, the distribution of excess cash flow is distributed according to a waterfall formula. It is structured like this:

- *Hurdle 1*: The institutional investor receives 90 percent of the monthly cash flows and the sponsor 10 percent, proportional to their respective overall equity contributions on a *pari passu* basis, until both investors achieve a 12 percent IRR, which when reached becomes Hurdle 1. IRR is typically calculated from the date the funds are provided to the partnership or LLC entity.
- *Hurdle 2*: Upon reaching the 12 percent IRR, the institutional investor receives 75 percent of the excess monthly cash flows and the sponsor receives 25 percent, which begins to pay the sponsor's promote until the institutional investor achieves a 15 percent IRR.
- *Hurdle 3*: Upon reaching the 15 percent IRR, the institutional investor receives 60 percent of the excess monthly cash flows and the sponsor receives 40 percent, which helps to pay the sponsor's promote until the institutional investor achieves an 18 percent IRR.
- The *Final Split* or *Hurdle 4*: Upon achieving an 18 percent IRR, the allocation of monthly cash flow is 50/50, or half going to each investor.

Refer to the line items in the exhibits to see the effect of waterfall returns for the institutional investor as well as the sponsor.

1. *First Hurdle:* The initial method of sharing distributions is on a *pari passu* sharing, 90 percent to the Investor Group and 10 percent to Investor I-Sponsor until a 12 percent IRR return is achieved. This is called the *first hurdle* or *Hurdle 1*. In all three columns, Investor I-Sponsor receives $998,505 and the Investor Group receives $8,986,549 of the total first hurdle distribution of $9,985,055.

2. *Second Hurdle:* The second method for sharing the unpaid equity upon satisfying Hurdle 1 is 75 percent to the Investor Group and 25 percent to Investor I-Sponsor until a 15 percent IRR return is achieved. This is called the *second hurdle* or *Hurdle 2.* In all three columns, the Investor Group receives $833,967 and Investor I-Sponsor receives $277,989 of the total Hurdle 2 distribution of $1,111,956. This is a different sharing arrangement from the Noninstitutional deal and Institutional Deal A where the sponsor receives 10 percent of the Equity Group and then 25 percent as part of the promote. In this case, the sponsor goes from sharing 10 percent to sharing 25 percent, *not a 10 percent sharing and a 25 percent additional sharing as the promote.*

3. *Third Hurdle:* The third method for sharing distributions is 60 percent to the Investor Group and 40 percent to Investor I-Sponsor until an 18 percent IRR return is achieved. This is called the *third hurdle* or *Hurdle 3.* In all three columns, the Investor Group receives $880,975 and Investor I-Sponsor receives $587,317 of the total third hurdle distribution of $1,468,292.

4. *Remaining Proceeds:* The remaining proceeds upon reaching Hurdle 3 are shared 50 percent to the Investor Group and 50 percent to Investor I-Sponsor. While the dollar amount in the three columns is different depending on the cap rate, the distribution is shared evenly between the Investor Group and Investor I-Sponsor.

5. *Rate of Return for Institutional Partner* is the rate of return the *Investor Group* receives. These returns are shown as *Annual Rate of Return* and *Internal Rate of Return (IRR).*

   a) *Annual Rate of Return* is the distributions divided by the equity investment with the result divided by the number of years of the development. For the middle column where the cap rate is 7.5 percent, the distributions provide the institutional partner with an annual rate of return of 23.21 percent calculated as follows: $476,189 (Year 1) + $593,885

(Year 2) + $12,243,651 (Year 3 sales proceeds and operating cash flow) − $7,848,582 (in returning the institutional partner's initial investment) = $5,465,143 (in total returns over the life of the investment) / $7,848,582 (the institutional partner's initial investment) / 3 (years) = 23.21 percent annual return on initial investment. As you can see, this annual rate of return of 23.21 percent is superior to the noninstitutional partner annual rate of return of 18.41 percent as depicted in the previous example describing a similar deal with noninstitutional partners. Compared to Institutional Deal A, the return is very close to the Institutional Deal A having a yearly return of 24.7 percent.

b) *Internal Rate of Return (IRR):* The rate in this example is consistent with the previous examples depicting the noninstitutional deal and the Institutional Deal A in that the IRR return would always be less than the Annual Rate of Return, as the majority of the funds received by the Equity Group occur at the end of the project instead of evenly spread throughout the life of the investment. In this example, the IRR compounded quarterly is 20.79 percent for the institutional partner compared to 17.09 percent for the noninstitutional partner and 21.89 percent for the institutional partner in Deal A.

See Table 8.14, *XYZ Shopping Center, Financial Analysis, Fees and Returns at the End of the Third Year* on page 206. This chart compares the sharing of fees, cash flow, appreciation and promote between the investor group and myself in the three different deal structures previously discussed: Noninstitutional, Institutional Deal A and Institutional Deal B.

Note that Table 8.14 shows a comparison illustrating how in Institutional Deal A the sponsor only receives $2,434,280, or 29.5 percent of the deal, when adding fees, cash flow sharing, appreciation and promote. By contrast, in Institutional Deal B, the partner receives $2,785,573—$351,293 more cash than in Deal A—or 33.76 percent of the deal.

This table gives you a broad comparison at a glance of how much the

Table 8.14 XYZ Shopping Center, Financial Analysis, Fees and Returns at the End of the Third Year

XYZ SHOPPING CENTER
Financial Analysis
Fees and Returns at the End of the Third Year

	Noninstitutional			Institutional - Deal A			Institutional - Deal B		
	Sponsor	Inv. Group	Total	Sponsor	Inv. Group	Total	Sponsor	Inv. Group	Total
Equity Contribution	10%	90%	100%	10%	90%	100%	10%	90%	100%
Fees	739,589	0	739,589	739,589	0	739,589	739,589	0	739,589
Cash Flow	268,356	1,931,982	2,200,337	220,034	1,980,304	2,200,337	220,034	1,980,304	2,200,337
Appreciation	265,539	2,389,855	2,655,394	426,237	3,836,132	4,262,369	**	3,484,839	3,484,839
Promote	2,655,394	0	2,655,394	1,048,420	0	1,048,420	1,825,950	0	1,825,950
Total	3,928,879	4,321,837	8,250,715	2,434,280	5,816,436	8,250,715	2,785,573	5,465,143	8,250,715
Percentage	47.62%	52.38%	100%	29.50%	70.50%	100%	33.76%	66.24%	100%

**Included in Promote

sponsor receives in the three different partnership structures I outlined, Noninstitutional, Institutional Deal A and Institutional Deal B. For easy comparisons, all three partnership structures contribute equity in the same manner, 10 percent coming from the sponsor and 90 percent coming from the Investor Group.

However, how you structure the exact arrangement in the partnership agreement matters greatly and it is not limited to the waterfall return. Whether the returns you promise are cumulative and compounded makes a difference in the total returns your partners and you will receive.

Just as important is how you propose to compound the returns, such as whether you will have them compounded quarterly or annually. What would happen if the returns are compounded annually (once a year) instead of quarterly (four times a year)? Your investors' money would grow much faster at quarterly compounding than when annually compounded.

In our example, the preferred return is 8 percent and is cumulative, but it is not compounded in the noninstitutional partnership structure.

The institutional deals are different. Institutional Deal A reflects a partnership structure where the preferred return is 12 percent, cumulative and compounded quarterly. Institutional Deal B represents a partnership structure where the preferred return is likewise 12 percent, cumulative, compounded quarterly but with a waterfall structure of returns as I explained earlier. (*Table 8.14 on page 206.*)

Let us compare some of the line items:

1. *Fees*: We show $739,589 in fees. These fees payable to the sponsor's development and management company comprise the sum of the acquisition fee, property management fee, leasing commissions, construction supervision fee, partnership supervisory fee and financing fee for the three years of the partnership structure. The fees are the same for all three partnership structures, whether noninstitutional or institutional. Essentially, these fees are market-based rate fees and are customarily acceptable to all partners, whether individuals or institutions.

2. *Cash Flow*
   a) *Noninstitutional:* The sponsor receives $268,356 of the total $2,200,337 distributed. This is greater than 10 percent, which

is the amount invested as equity by the sponsor, as the sponsor had some of the cash flow distributed as carried interest promote incentive.

b) *Institutional Deal A and Deal B:* From the same cash flow distribution of $2,200,337 as described in the Noninstitutional deal, we owe the institutional partner the cumulative compounded preferred return of 12 percent. However, as we were unable to fully distribute the preferred return in the earlier period, the sharing of the cash flow is exactly as the equity investment, 10 percent to the sponsor and 90 percent to the Investor Group. However, because of the 12 percent preferred return, the sponsor gets a lower amount of the total cash to be distributed ($220,034) in both Institutional A and B deals compared to the Noninstitutional deal where the sponsor gets $268,356.

3. *Appreciation*

a) *Noninstitutional and Institutional Deal A:* The sponsor and Investor Group share *pari passu*, in the same ratio as their investment, 10 percent to the sponsor and 90 percent to the Investor Group. The total appreciation amount of $2,655,394 in Noninstitutional Group is less than the $4,262,369 in Institutional Deal A. This is because in the Noninstitutional partnership structure the "cumulative" preferred return is 8 percent while in the Institutional Deal A partnership structure the "cumulative compounded" return is 12 percent. This compounding and higher preferred return structure as well as the sharing arrangement is 75 percent to the equity and 25 percent to the promote in the institutional deal versus 50 percent to the equity and 50 percent to the promote in the Noninstitutional deal, allocating more of the proceeds upon sale to be shown as appreciation and not promote.

b) Institutional Deal B: Because the waterfall structure appreciation is shown as part of the promote, in these examples, the returns were substantial, so Institutional Deal B showed a greater return to the sponsor than Institutional Deal A. If the deal was not very successful, Institutional Deal A would have been more substantial than Institutional Deal B for the sponsor.

4. *Promote*: The promote goes fully to the sponsor. In the noninstitutional partnership structure, there is more cash to be allocated to the promote than cash allocated in either Institutional Deal A or Deal B.

In summary, the sponsor gets more of the upside when dealing with noninstitutional rather than institutional partners. When you examine the line items "total" and "percentage," the sponsor in the noninstitutional partnership structure receives materially more cash than in either of the institutional partnership structures.

I am often asked who I would rather have as an investment partner, a noninstitutional group of private investors or an institutional partner. My answer, purely from the economics outcome of the structure, would always be to go with a noninstitutional group of private investors. From the rights granted to me as a sponsor in the documents governing the legal entity, I would also always prefer a noninstitutional group of private investors.

So why would one ever want to deal with an institutional partner? Because institutions have the money—and the money in the larger amounts that allow one to do larger deals. Our time is limited and precious. Is our time better spent raising money from many private investors or finding the next opportunity to own and improve retail properties? Is it better to do fewer deals with a better sharing arrangement or more deals with a less advantageous sharing arrangement? Is it better doing a large deal with an institutional partner that would be too difficult for you to raise the money from many individual investors even if you had the time?

I believe doing more deals and spreading your investment over multiple real estate ventures makes owning any individual deal less risky. That is why I advocate that it is better to own 10 percent of 10 deals than 100 percent of one deal, especially from the standpoint of spreading risk as well as the fees I can collect. Unquestionably, fees on 10 properties are greater than fees on only one.

For these reasons, I continue to structure partnerships with noninstitutional partners and institutional partners depending on the size and type of deal. It seems to work well for my company and for me personally.

CHAPTER IX

Case Study Number 3:
Cameron Chase Village Center,
Ashburn, Virginia

A Real-Life Example: Asset Preservation

IN THIS CASE STUDY, I will review the details of my real-life acquisition of Cameron Chase Village Center to give you the opportunity to learn some of the principles we have covered thus far in planning an acquisition and pro-jecting returns. I acquired this shopping center with equity I raised from a group of individual investors (noninstitutional partners).

Cameron Chase Village Center—Ashburn, Virginia

This property was a unique one that needed little fixing, so the example illustrates asset enhancement and asset preservation through proper management. We set aside in our pro forma less than $122,000 for property upgrades and $160,000 for tenant improvement allowances and leasing commissions. This is a relatively small amount of the $14.4 million purchase. (In

Chapter X, we will cover the details of an acquisition that requires much greater upgrades and remerchandising efforts.)

I deleted some data in this case study, such as specific tenant rents, to preserve confidentiality where appropriate. I also altered some of the information to illustrate some of the learning points I depicted in the sample cases throughout this writing.

The Project

Cameron Chase Village Center (CCVC) is a small but highly productive neighborhood shopping center. The 29,380-square-foot project is located in the rapidly growing Ashburn section of Virginia's Loudoun County. Our project is part of a larger nonowned retail development that includes an ice park, a Shell gas station, a Goodyear Tire & Battery store, a future site for the Navy Federal Credit Union, a future restaurant and bank pads.

The project's juxtaposition in the northwest quadrant of Farmwell Road and Smith Switch Road is very attractive to retail and other commercial tenants because of its desirable location, which ranks among the fastest-growing suburban areas in the Washington, D.C., metropolitan area.

Wegmans Grocery Store, at the corner of Route 28 and Waxpool Road (Waxpool Road turns into Farmwell Road), is two miles east of the project. Food Lion Center, located at the entrance to the 5,072 residential unit Ashburn Village at Farmwell Road and Ashburn Village Boulevard, is only one-half mile to the west. The property sits nestled among the corporate campuses of America Online (AOL) and Verizon, the Washington Redskins Park and other highly successful office buildings. Because of its proximity to this commercial hub, the shopping center draws an abundance of office workers in the daytime as well as the more typical nighttime traffic.

When we acquired CCVC, the project had been recently built and opened for business, with the first tenant opening for business on August 29, 2005. Upon acquisition, the center was 95.2 percent leased, with only one store space of 1,400 square feet vacant.

The project and adjacencies are zoned as Planned Development-Industrial Park (PD-IP). The project is approved as a retail development the way it was built and leased. Even though the zoning category is more restrictive regarding retail uses than if the zoning category were designated as a strictly

Cameron Chase Village Center features alternative users such as MBH Settlement Group L.C., a leading settlement company in Virginia that assists home buyers and sellers with title insurance and closing services.

retail zoning category, we were not concerned this would pose material restrictions in expanding our retail mix.

Service Star, Inc., a Colorado-based developer in a partnership with Shell Oil, originally developed all the parcels in this development, with the exception of the Ice House (an ice park that has been operating for many years). Service Star, Inc. had intended to develop the remaining parcels. Other than the Shell Oil Station and the Goodyear Tire & Battery, which are owned by Shell Oil, Service Star's plan was to sell off the remaining parcels when complete.

The parcel for the future Federal Navy Credit Union had been sold when we acquired the project and the CCVC parcel was sold shortly thereafter. The future restaurant and bank pads will eventually be sold.

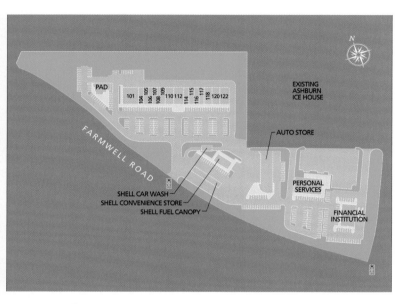

Figure 9.1 Cameron Chase Village Center site plan depicting the strip-shaped center at the top with various pad sites to the left and lower portions of the site.

The CCVC ownership entity selected The Rappaport Companies (TRC) before the start of construction to oversee the leasing and the property management. TRC has a deep knowledge of the tenants, the present income and expenses of the property and the construction of the building.

Let us review more specific information about Cameron Chase Village Center, such as its location and the market it serves.

The Market

Cameron Chase Village Center is uniquely positioned to serve a mostly affluent and rapidly growing market in Loudoun County, Virginia. Households in Loudoun are now considered among the wealthiest in the United States,

Cameron Chase Village Center welcomes customers with a large pylon sign listing all tenants.

having a median income of more than $98,000. Not far behind are nearby Fairfax, Howard and Montgomery counties. The region has the second-highest income of any major metropolitan area in the country, falling behind wealthy San Jose, California, households.

Within a three-mile radius of Cameron Chase Village Center, the population in the last census projections was 66,783 at the time we acquired the property

Beef O'Brady's Family Sports Pub anchors the Cameron Chase Village Center.

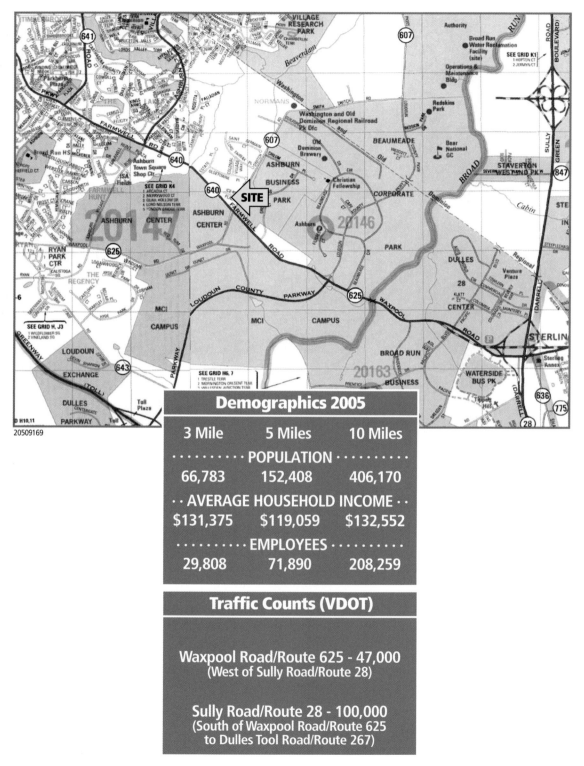

Figure 9.2 The Cameron Chase Village Center investor book highlights demographics and vehicular traffic counts.

Cameron Chase Village Center
Farmwell Rd AT Smith Switch Rd
Ashburn, VA 20147

Site Map

Latitude: 39.0175
Longitude: -77.4682

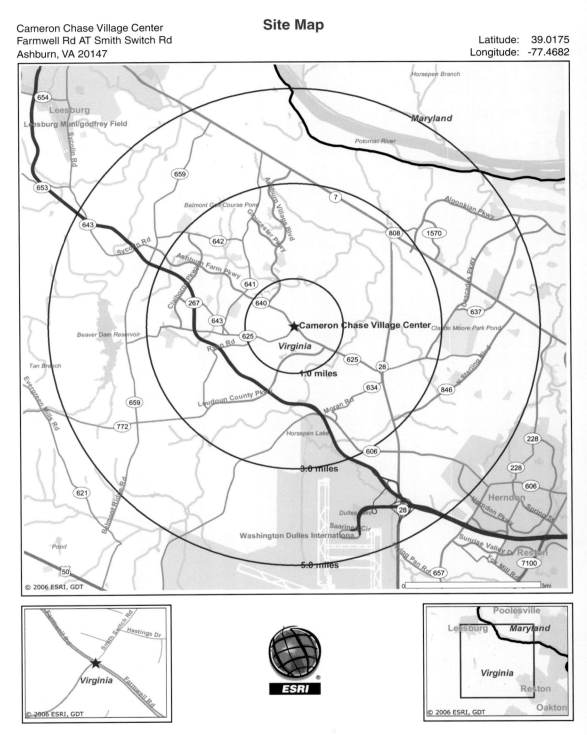

Figure 9.3 The Cameron Chase Village Center site map

Demographic and Income Profile

Cameron Chase Village Center
Farmwell Rd at Smith Switch Rd
Ashburn, VA 20147

Latitude:	39.0175
Longitude:	-77.4682
Radius:	1.0 miles

Site Type: Radius

Summary	2000	2005	2010
Population	2,819	5,046	7,880
Households	893	1,650	2,600
Families	737	1,348	2,092
Average Household Size	3.16	3.06	3.03
Owner Occupied HUs	768	1,450	2,306
Renter Occupied HUs	125	200	294
Median Age	30.9	31.4	31.1

Trends: 2005–2010 Annual Rate	Area	State	National
Population	9.32%	1.55%	1.22%
Households	9.52%	1.74%	1.27%
Families	9.19%	1.6%	1.00%
Owner HHs	9.72%	2.01%	1.46%
Median Household Income	3.54%	4.19 %	3.25%

	2000		2005		2010	
Households by Income	**Number**	**Percent**	**Number**	**Percent**	**Number**	**Percent**
< $15,000	12	1.3%	14	0.8%	15	0.6%
$15,000–$24,999	33	3.7%	37	2.2%	29	1.1%
$25,000–$34,999	47	5.2%	52	3.1%	50	1.9%
$35,000–$49,999	60	6.7%	83	5.0%	112	4.3%
$50,000–$74,999	109	12.2%	146	8.8%	170	6.5%
$75,000–$99,999	139	15.5%	233	14.1%	266	10.2%
$100,000–$149,999	302	33.7%	499	30.2%	657	25.3%
$150,000–$199,000	119	13.3%	300	18.2%	583	22.4%
$200,000+	76	8.5%	287	17.4%	719	27.6%
Median Household Income	$105,303		$126,112		$150,084	
Average Household Income	$118,188		$151,832		$192,983	
Per Capita Income	$38,483		$49,486		$62,991	

	2000		2005		2010	
Population by Age	**Number**	**Percent**	**Number**	**Percent**	**Number**	**Percent**
0–4	385	13.7%	647	12.8%	955	12.1%
5–14	527	18.7%	1,179	23.4%	1,843	23.4%
15–19	120	4.3%	260	5.2%	572	7.3%
20–24	93	3.3%	129	2.6%	225	2.9%
25–34	570	20.2%	631	12.5%	703	8.9%
35–44	687	24.4%	1,268	25.1%	1,691	21.5%
45–54	274	9.7%	615	12.2%	1,310	16.6%
55–64	110	3.9%	229	4.5%	410	5.2%
65–74	37	1.3%	62	1.2%	128	1.6%
75–84	12	0.4%	22	0.4%	35	0.4%
85+	3	0.1%	5	0.1%	7	0.1%

	2000		2005		2010	
Race and Ethnicity	**Number**	**Percent**	**Number**	**Percent**	**Number**	**Percent**
White Alone	2,312	82.0%	4,032	79.9%	6,209	78.8%
Black Alone	214	7.6%	385	7.6%	609	7.7%
American Indian Alone	5	0.2%	9	0.2%	15	0.2%
Asian Alone	178	6.3%	375	7.4%	628	8.0%
Pacific Islander Alone	0	0.0%	0	0.0%	1	0.0%
Some Other Race Alone	48	1.7%	103	2.0%	176	2.2%
Two or More Races	63	2.2%	141	2.8%	242	3.1%
Hispanic Origin (Any Race)	140	5.0%	322	6.4%	562	7.1%

Data Note: Income is expressed in current dollars.

Source: U.S. Bureau of the Census, 2000 Census of Population and Housing. ESRI forecasts for 2005 and 2010.

Figure 9.4 The Cameron Chase Village Center investor book highlights demographic information on the market (above and opposite page).

Demographic and Income Profile

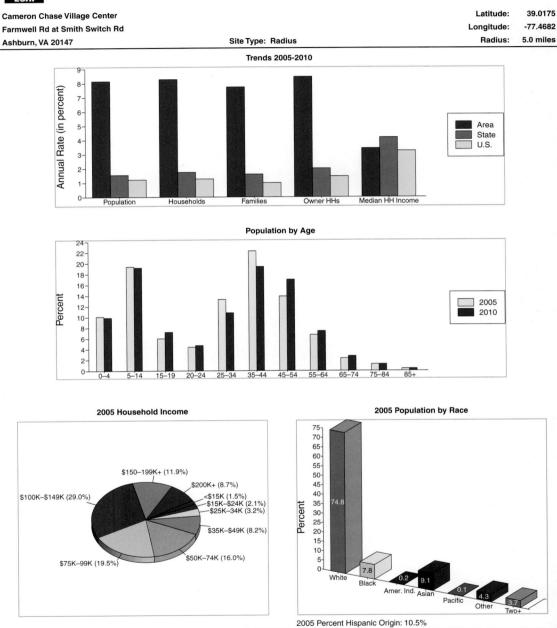

Cameron Chase Village Center
Farmwell Rd at Smith Switch Rd
Ashburn, VA 20147

Site Type: Radius

Latitude:	39.0175
Longitude:	-77.4682
Radius:	5.0 miles

Figure 9.5 The Cameron Chase Village Center demographic data show how the center's immediate trade area was projected to grow in population, number of households, number of families and ownership of homes as compared to the state of Virginia and the national statistics.

CAMERON CHASE VILLAGE CENTER
Ashburn, Virginia

Eastern Loudoun County Map

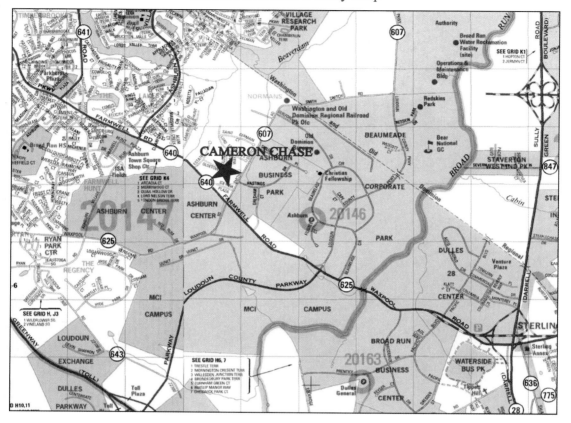

Figure 9.6 The Cameron Chase Village Center investor book has maps to highlight location.

in the mid-2000s, with an average household income of $131,375. Because of the commercial activity nearby, there were also 28,808 employees working in the immediate three-mile radius.

As we look beyond the immediate primary market for a neighborhood center, the market potential is equally attractive for retail. Within a five-mile radius, 152,408 persons live in households that have an average household income of $119,059 and 71,890 employees work in the area. In a ten-mile radius, the population is 406,170, earning $132,552 in annual average household income, and 208,259 persons are employed in the area.

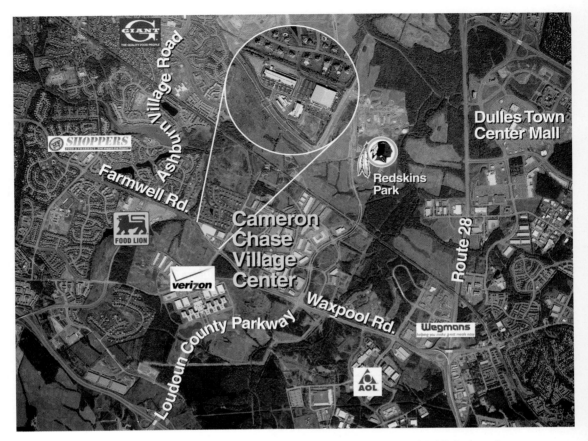

Figure 9.7 The Cameron Chase Village Center investor book has maps to highlight location.

Traffic counts according to the Virginia Department of Transportation (VDOT) bear out the viability of the center. Waxpool Road/Route 625 has 47,000 vehicles driving by each day (west of Sully Road/Route 28). On Sully Road/Route 28, the vehicle count is 100,000 daily (south of Waxpool Road/Route 625 to Dulles Toll Road/Route 267).

Please refer to Table 9.1, Equity Term Sheet, page 225, for a summary of terms agreed to by the equity partners.

In the case of CCVC, my investment partners contributed 75 percent of all cash to fund the acquisition and development costs not funded by the lender. As sponsor, I contributed the remaining 25 percent of the equity cash.

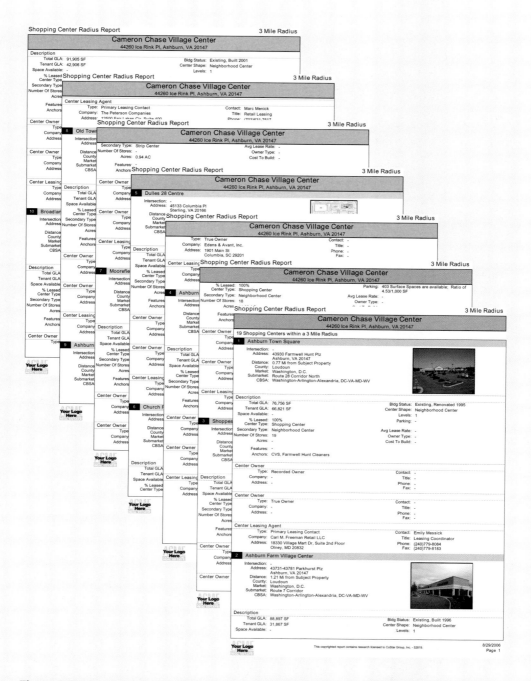

Figure 9.8 Excerpt sample of competitive analysis from Co-Star Group, Inc., depicting information about each competitive shopping center. As part of our due diligence to acquire this property, we gathered key competitive data from Co-Star Group, Inc. The material covers every competitive shopping center within three miles of Cameron Chase Village Center. Co-Star Group is a provider of information, marketing and analytic services to commercial real estate.

Cameron Chase Village Center
44260 Ice Rink Pl, Ashburn, VA 20147

19 Cascades Plaza

Intersection:
Address: 21944-21950 Cascades Pky
          Sterling, VA 20164
Distance
County
Market
Submarket
CBSA

Description
Total GLA
Tenant GLA
Space Available
% Leased
Center Type
Secondary Type
Number Of Stores
Acres
Features
Anchors

Shopping Center Radius Report   3 Mile Radius

Cameron Chase Village Center
44260 Ice Rink Pl, Ashburn, VA 20147

Company: -   Title: -
Address: -   Phone: -
                                     Fax: -

Center Owner
   Type

Center Leasing
   Company
   Address

Shopping Center Radius Report   3 Mile Radius

Cameron Chase Village Center
44260 Ice Rink Pl, Ashburn, VA 20147

Description
Total GLA: 1,411,000 SF   Bldg Status: Existing, Built 1999
Tenant GLA: 435,775 SF   Center Shape: Super Regional Mall
Space Available: 8,394 SF   Levels: 2
% Leased
Center Type
Secondary Type
Number Of Stores
Acres

Center Leasing Agent
   Type: Primary Leasing Contact   Contact: Keith Summers
   Company: Grubb & Ellis   Title: Vice President
   Address: 8020 Towers Crescent Dr, Suite 200   Phone: (703)918-0252

18 Sterling/…

Shopping Center Radius Report   3 Mile Radius

Cameron Chase Village Center
44260 Ice Rink Pl, Ashburn, VA 20147

Secondary Type: Neighborhood Center   Avg Lease Rate: -
Number Of Stores: 17   Owner Type: -
Acres: 7.00 AC   Cost To Build: -
Features:
Anchors

15 Dulles T…

Shopping Center Radius Report   3 Mile Radius

Cameron Chase Village Center
44260 Ice Rink Pl, Ashburn, VA 20147

12 Broadlands Village Center

Intersection: Claiborne Pky
Address: 43150 Broadlands Center
          Ashburn, VA 20148
Distance
County
Market
Submarket
CBSA

17 Ashbroo…

14 Augusta

16 Dulles T…

13 Sterling

Cameron Chase Village Center
44260 Ice Rink Pl, Ashburn, VA 20147

Company: -   Title: -
Address: -   Phone: -
                                     Fax: -

Center Owner
   Type: True Owner   Contact: -
   Company: Saul Centers, Inc.   Title: -
   Address: 7501 Wisconsin Ave, Suite 1500   Phone: -
             Bethesda, MD 20814   Fax: -

Center Leasing Agent
   Type: Primary Leasing Contact   Contact: Diana Shipley
   Company: Saul Centers, Inc.   Title: Agent
   Address: 7501 Wisconsin Ave, Suite 1500   Phone: (301)986-6200
             Bethesda, MD 20814   Fax: (301)986-6023

11 Broadlands Village Center

Intersection: Claiborne Pky
Address: 43150 Broadlands Center
          Ashburn, VA 20148
Distance: 2.36 Mi from Subject Property
County: Loudoun
Market: Washington DC
Submarket: Route 28 Corridor North
CBSA: Washington-Arlington-Alexandria, DC-VA-MD-WV

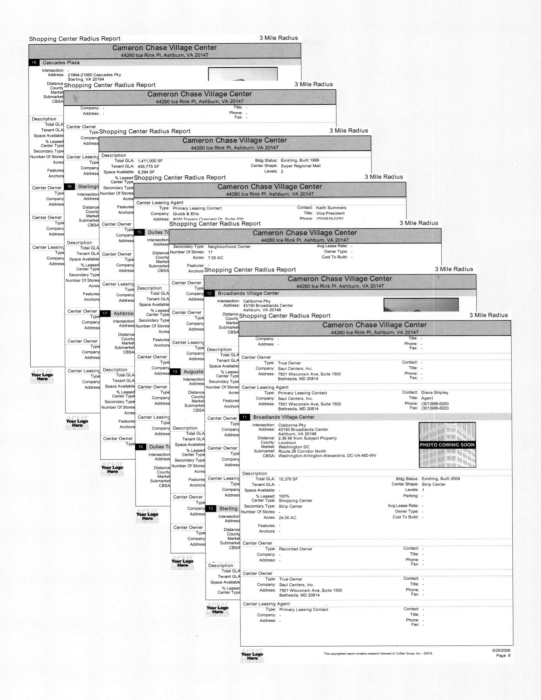

PHOTO COMING SOON

Description
Total GLA: 15,376 SF   Bldg Status: Existing, Built 2004
Tenant GLA: -   Center Shape: Strip Center
Space Available: -   Levels: 1
% Leased: 100%   Parking: -
Center Type: Shopping Center
Secondary Type: Strip Center   Avg Lease Rate: -
Number Of Stores: -   Owner Type: -
Acres: 24.00 AC   Cost To Build: -
Features: -
Anchors: -

Center Owner
   Type: Recorded Owner   Contact: -
   Company: -   Title: -
   Address: -   Phone: -
                                    Fax: -

Center Owner
   Type: True Owner   Contact: -
   Company: Saul Centers, Inc.   Title: -
   Address: 7501 Wisconsin Ave, Suite 1500   Phone: -
             Bethesda, MD 20814   Fax: -

Center Leasing Agent
   Type: Primary Leasing Contact   Contact: -
   Company: -   Title: -
   Address: -   Phone: -
                                    Fax: -

Your Logo Here

Shopping Center Radius Report   3 Mile Radius

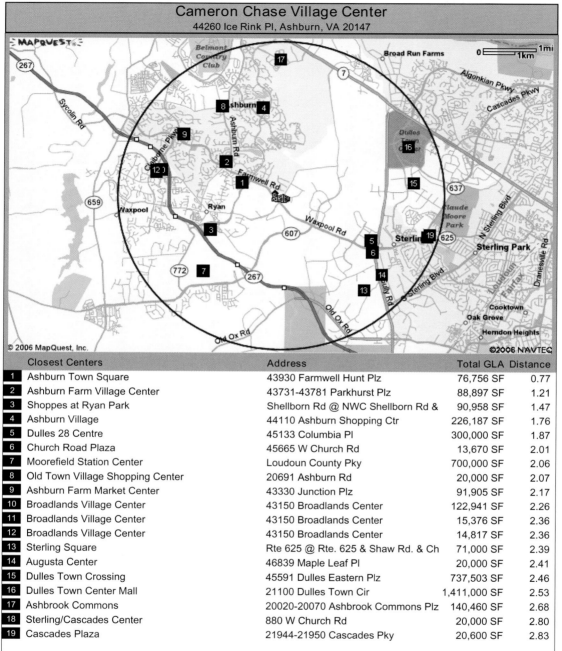

Cameron Chase Village Center
44260 Ice Rink Pl, Ashburn, VA 20147

	Closest Centers	Address	Total GLA	Distance
1	Ashburn Town Square	43930 Farmwell Hunt Plz	76,756 SF	0.77
2	Ashburn Farm Village Center	43731-43781 Parkhurst Plz	88,897 SF	1.21
3	Shoppes at Ryan Park	Shellborn Rd @ NWC Shellborn Rd &	90,958 SF	1.47
4	Ashburn Village	44110 Ashburn Shopping Ctr	226,187 SF	1.76
5	Dulles 28 Centre	45133 Columbia Pl	300,000 SF	1.87
6	Church Road Plaza	45665 W Church Rd	13,670 SF	2.01
7	Moorefield Station Center	Loudoun County Pky	700,000 SF	2.06
8	Old Town Village Shopping Center	20691 Ashburn Rd	20,000 SF	2.07
9	Ashburn Farm Market Center	43330 Junction Plz	91,905 SF	2.17
10	Broadlands Village Center	43150 Broadlands Center	122,941 SF	2.26
11	Broadlands Village Center	43150 Broadlands Center	15,376 SF	2.36
12	Broadlands Village Center	43150 Broadlands Center	14,817 SF	2.36
13	Sterling Square	Rte 625 @ Rte. 625 & Shaw Rd. & Ch	71,000 SF	2.39
14	Augusta Center	46839 Maple Leaf Pl	20,000 SF	2.41
15	Dulles Town Crossing	45591 Dulles Eastern Plz	737,503 SF	2.46
16	Dulles Town Center Mall	21100 Dulles Town Cir	1,411,000 SF	2.53
17	Ashbrook Commons	20020-20070 Ashbrook Commons Plz	140,460 SF	2.68
18	Sterling/Cascades Center	880 W Church Rd	20,000 SF	2.80
19	Cascades Plaza	21944-21950 Cascades Pky	20,600 SF	2.83

Figure 9.9 Excerpt sample of map depicting 19 shopping centers located within a three-mile radius compiled by research company Co-Star Group, Inc.

Table 9.1   Sample of Equity Term Sheet for Cameron Chase Village Center

Equity Term Sheet

Purpose

Formation of limited liability company to acquire shopping center/land to be developed as a shopping center

Capital Contributions

Investors—75% of all cash to fund acquisition and development costs not funded by third-party financing

Sponsor (or his designees)—25% of all cash to fund acquisition and development costs not funded by third-party financing

Distributions

Cash Flow
(i) Preferred 8% Distribution on capital contributions *pari passu* (cumulative and noncompounded);
(ii) 50% to capital *pari passu*
     50% to sponsor (or his designees)

Sale/Refinancing Proceeds
(i) Unpaid Preferred Distribution on capital contributions
(ii) Return of capital *pari passu*;
(iii) 50% to capital *pari passu*
      50% to sponsor (or his designees)

Preferred Distribution calculated at 8% per annum from and after date of contribution

Property Management and Leasing Agreement

Management Fee   5% of gross receipts (payable monthly on actual receipts collected)
Leasing Fee   6% (4% without co-broker) of base rent
                              2% on renewals
Marketing Fee   15% of marketing budget

Partnership Supervisory Fee
Development Fee

1% gross receipts to sponsor (payable monthly on actual receipts collected)
5% of hard costs

You will note in Table 9.1 that we planned the cash flow distributions for this deal as a preferred 8 percent distribution on capital contributions *pari passu* (cumulative and noncompounded); one-half of capital distributing *pari passu* to all partners and the other half going to me and my family as the sponsor's interest.

In planning the distribution from an outright sale or a refinancing, the deal requires the proceeds to be distributed as follows:

- Unpaid preferred distribution on capital contributions (cumulative and noncompounded)
- Return of capital *pari passu*
- 50 percent to capital Investors *pari passu*
- 50 percent to me as Sponsor (or my designees)
- Preferred distribution calculated at 8 percent per year from and after date of contribution

TRC management fees and leasing commissions are:

- Management fee of 5 percent of gross receipts (payable monthly on actual receipts collected)
- Leasing commission of 6 percent of base rent divided equally with co-broker (4 percent if no co-broker is involved); 2 percent on renewals
- Marketing fee of 15 percent of marketing funds collected from tenants and landlord
- Partnership supervisory (asset management) fee of 1 percent of gross receipts to TRC (payable monthly on actual receipts collected)
- Development fee of 5 percent of construction hard costs

In the third quarter of 2006, I formed an LLC and purchased CCVC for $13,625,000 using a cap rate of 6.86 percent on the first year's projected NOI of $934,288 (see Table 9.2 on page 227). The settlement costs were $123,330. Additionally, I had due diligence costs of $63,750, as well as points and fees related to the financing of $236,250.

As part of this acquisition, I set up a reserve of $160,000 for tenant improvement inducements and other leasing costs, a general capital reserve of $70,000 for contingencies and a reserve of $121,670 for capital expenditures relating to property upgrades. This meant that my total cash requirement at settlement would amount to $14.4 million.

The equity investment was eight shares of half a million dollars each for a total of $4 million. My family and I invested a fourth of the equity with our $1 million investment. I structured the equity piece in a manner that all investors combined contributed about one-quarter of all cash to fund the

Table 9.2   Cameron Chase Village, Financial Analysis—Purchase Price ($13.625 Million), Sources and Uses of Funds

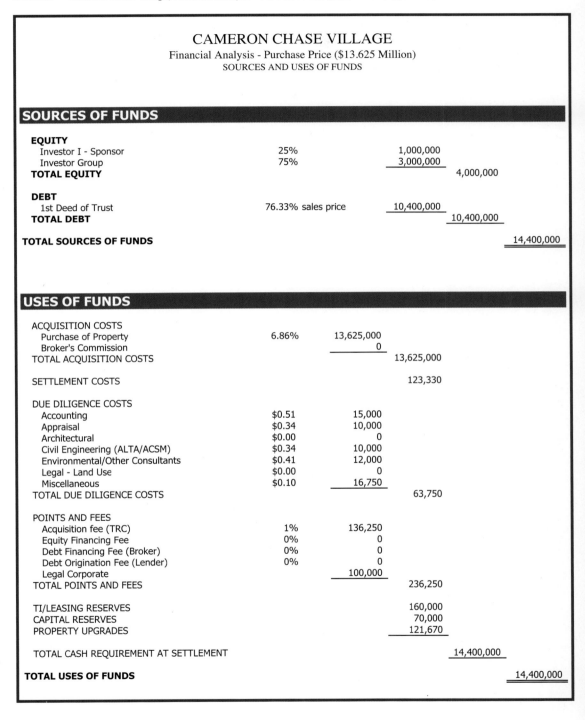

CAMERON CHASE VILLAGE
Financial Analysis - Purchase Price ($13.625 Million)
SOURCES AND USES OF FUNDS

SOURCES OF FUNDS

EQUITY			
Investor I - Sponsor	25%	1,000,000	
Investor Group	75%	3,000,000	
TOTAL EQUITY			4,000,000
DEBT			
1st Deed of Trust	76.33% sales price	10,400,000	
TOTAL DEBT			10,400,000
TOTAL SOURCES OF FUNDS			14,400,000

USES OF FUNDS

ACQUISITION COSTS			
Purchase of Property	6.86%	13,625,000	
Broker's Commission		0	
TOTAL ACQUISITION COSTS			13,625,000
SETTLEMENT COSTS			123,330
DUE DILIGENCE COSTS			
Accounting	$0.51	15,000	
Appraisal	$0.34	10,000	
Architectural	$0.00	0	
Civil Engineering (ALTA/ACSM)	$0.34	10,000	
Environmental/Other Consultants	$0.41	12,000	
Legal - Land Use	$0.00	0	
Miscellaneous	$0.10	16,750	
TOTAL DUE DILIGENCE COSTS			63,750
POINTS AND FEES			
Acquisition fee (TRC)	1%	136,250	
Equity Financing Fee	0%	0	
Debt Financing Fee (Broker)	0%	0	
Debt Origination Fee (Lender)	0%	0	
Legal Corporate		100,000	
TOTAL POINTS AND FEES			236,250
TI/LEASING RESERVES			160,000
CAPITAL RESERVES			70,000
PROPERTY UPGRADES			121,670
TOTAL CASH REQUIREMENT AT SETTLEMENT			14,400,000
TOTAL USES OF FUNDS			14,400,000

acquisition and development costs. I arranged for third-party financing to fund the remaining cash required of $10.4 million.

We placed a nonrecourse first deed of trust loan of $10.4 million on the property at time of purchase. The loan was a 10-year fixed rate loan with interest only for the first three years; thereafter it converted to a 30-year amortization. The annual percentage interest rate of the loan was 5.855 percent.

In our investor package, we created a spreadsheet covering the first 11 years following the acquisition. (See Table 9.3 on page 229.) In that period, we planned to grow our NOI from $934,288 to $1,209,598. We projected our net cash flow before debt service to grow at a healthy clip per year from $905,486 in Year 1 to $1,141,623 in Year 11. This allowed us to begin paying down the principal on our debt starting in Year 4 while still maintaining a satisfactory net cash flow after debt service, starting with $298,126 in Year 1 and ending with $406,173 in Year 11.

Our model allowed me to distribute cash-on-cash return of 6 percent ($240,000) of each equity partner's investment in Year 1, progressively increasing the annual cash-on-cash return for each of the partners in the succeeding years and ending with 10 percent ($400,000) cash-on-cash return in Year 11.

One important factor that my investors want to know is how their investment would perform in a disposition of the asset and upon a refinancing. To clarify this in my initial investor package, I provide details on a hypothetical sale at the end of the fifth year. (See Table 9.4 on page 231.)

Distributions of cash flow are only one measure of returns. You must combine the annual distributions from operations with the distribution resulting from the disposition of the asset (or the distribution from equity realized upon a refinancing) to get the real picture in evaluating the return on your investors' investment.

The first step will involve appraising the asset at the appropriate point in time. In our investor package for Cameron Chase Village, we will project a hypothetical appraisal after five years of ownership. To determine the shopping center's projected sale price at the end of Year 5 (for the sake of deriving a distribution of equity in the event of a sale or refinancing), we look at two key figures: the NOI projected in Year 6, which is $1,073,361 and the loan balance at the end of Year 5, which is $10,128,958.

Based upon current transactions of similar types of properties in the market and considering the changes we plan to make to improve the prop-

Table 9.3   Cameron Chase Village Financial Analysis—Purchase Price ($13.625 Million), Schedule of Prospective Cash Flow

CAMERON CHASE VILLAGE
Financial Analysis - Purchase Price ($13.625 Million)
Ashburn, Virginia
Schedule of Prospective Cash Flow

For the period ending		Dec-2007 Year 1	Dec-2008 Year 2	Dec-2009 Year 3	Dec-2010 Year 4	Dec-2011 Year 5	Dec-2012 Year 6	Dec-2013 Year 7	Dec-2014 Year 8	Dec-2015 Year 9	Dec-2016 Year 10	Dec-2017 Year 11
REVENUE												
Base Rental Revenue		983,573	1,011,664	1,044,370	1,073,026	1,102,362	1,132,187	1,166,017	1,201,001	1,229,986	1,244,679	1,280,012
Absorption & Turnover Vacancy		0	0	0	0	(11,161)	(4,463)	0	0	(46,627)	(7,992)	(7,056)
Percentage Rent		0	0	0	0	0	0	0	0	0	0	0
Common Area Maintenance		165,913	170,786	176,006	181,178	183,941	189,905	196,360	202,266	199,470	208,839	214,725
Real Estate Taxes		72,231	74,396	76,624	78,930	80,489	83,403	86,249	88,834	88,048	93,684	96,495
Insurance		10,803	11,124	11,457	11,802	12,033	12,473	12,900	13,283	13,168	14,004	14,430
Promotion		0	0	0	0	0	0	0	0	0	0	0
Miscellaneous - Water		0	0	0	0	0	0	0	0	0	0	0
TOTAL POTENTIAL GROSS REVENUE		1,232,520	1,267,970	1,308,457	1,344,936	1,367,664	1,413,505	1,461,526	1,505,384	1,484,045	1,553,214	1,598,606
Collection Loss/Additional Vacancy	4%	(49,301)	(50,719)	(52,338)	(53,797)	(43,546)	(52,077)	(58,461)	(60,215)	(12,735)	(54,137)	(56,888)
EFFECTIVE GROSS REVENUE		1,183,219	1,217,251	1,256,119	1,291,139	1,324,118	1,361,428	1,403,065	1,445,169	1,471,310	1,499,077	1,541,718
OPERATING EXPENSES												
Common Area Maintenance	$3.63	106,740	109,942	113,243	116,639	120,136	123,742	127,454	131,277	135,214	139,271	143,449
Insurance	$0.37	10,800	11,124	11,458	11,801	12,155	12,520	12,896	13,283	13,681	14,092	14,514
Real Estate Taxes	$2.46	72,230	74,397	76,629	78,928	81,296	83,734	86,246	88,834	91,499	94,244	97,071
Management Fees	5%	59,161	60,863	62,806	64,557	66,206	68,071	70,153	72,258	73,566	74,954	77,086
TOTAL OPERATING EXPENSES		248,931	256,326	264,136	271,925	279,793	288,067	296,749	305,652	313,960	322,561	332,120
NET OPERATING INCOME		934,288	960,925	991,983	1,019,214	1,044,325	1,073,361	1,106,316	1,139,517	1,157,350	1,176,516	1,209,598
NON OPERATING EXPENSES												
Advertising and Promotion (LL Contribution)	$0.14	4,200	4,200	4,200	4,200	4,200	4,200	4,200	4,200	4,200	4,200	4,200
General and Administration	$0.16	4,770	4,913	5,060	5,212	5,369	5,530	5,696	5,866	6,042	6,224	6,410
Legal and Accounting	$0.27	8,000	8,240	8,487	8,742	9,004	9,274	9,552	9,839	10,134	10,438	10,751
Asset Management Fee	1%	11,832	12,173	12,561	12,911	13,241	13,614	14,031	14,452	14,713	14,991	15,417
Tenant Improvements		0	0	0	0	11,030	4,544	0	0	33,520	21,737	7,902
Leasing Commissions		0	0	0	0	36,850	14,736	0	0	107,347	74,382	23,295
TOTAL NONOPERATING EXPENSES		28,802	29,526	30,308	31,065	79,694	51,898	33,479	34,357	175,956	131,972	67,975
NET CASH FLOW BEFORE DEBT SERVICE		905,486	931,399	961,675	988,149	964,631	1,021,463	1,072,837	1,105,160	981,394	1,044,544	1,141,623
ADDITIONAL PROCEEDS												
Proceeds from Refinancing		0	0	0	0	0	0	0	0	0	0	0
TI/Leasing Commission Reserve		0	0	0	0	0	0	0	0	0	0	0
TOTAL ADDITIONAL PROCEEDS		0	0	0	0	0	0	0	0	0	0	0
DEBT SERVICE												
Interest Payments		607,360	607,360	607,360	603,875	595,982	587,616	578,747	569,347	559,383	548,821	537,625
Principal Payments		0	0	0	131,575	139,468	147,834	156,702	166,103	176,067	186,629	197,825
Origination Points and Fees		0	0	0	0	0	0	0	0	0	0	0
TOTAL DEBT SERVICE		607,360	607,360	607,360	735,450	735,450	735,450	735,450	735,450	735,450	735,450	735,450
NET CASH FLOW AFTER DEBT SERVICE		298,126	324,039	354,315	252,699	229,181	286,013	337,387	369,710	245,944	309,094	406,173
Proposed Cash Distribution		240,000	240,000	260,000	280,000	280,000	300,000	320,000	320,000	360,000	380,000	400,000
Cash on Cash Return on Proposed Distribution		6%	6%	6.50%	7%	7%	7.50%	8%	8%	9%	9.50%	10%

erty, we projected that a cap rate of 6.25 percent is reasonably achievable to apply to the NOI to derive the projected value.

Since I do not plan to sell, we will use that hypothetical value to establish how much to borrow using a reasonable loan-to-value ratio. However, one cannot predict a precise cap rate so we will look at three cap rate scenarios; ones using 6, 6.25 and 6.5 percent respectively.

The result of dividing each of the three cap rates by the projected NOI gives us three projected sale prices: $17,889,350 using the 6 percent cap rate; $17,173,776 using the 6.25 percent cap rate and $16,513,246 using the 6.5 percent cap rate.

As in all transactions, we have deductions from the sale price and additions to sale proceeds. For deductions, we will estimate the cost of the sale at 1.5 percent. For additions, we anticipate taking the benefit of drawing from our working capital reserve of $160,000, paying the lender no penalty for early retirement of the loan, receiving back our escrow funds for real estate taxes of $12,038, paying insurance of $1,800 and liquidating the cash flow for the fourth quarter of Year 5. This gives us total additions of $243,838.

Note how these additions and deductions affect the net proceeds from the sale in the chart. Using the 6 percent cap rate, we projected net proceeds of $7,735,890. Using the 6.25 percent cap rate, we projected net proceeds of $7,031,050 and $6,380,428 when using the 6.5 percent cap rate.

Once we arrive at net proceeds from a sale, we deduct the cash flow from the fourth quarter of Year 5 ($70,000), the cumulative unpaid returns to the Equity Group ($300,000) and the return of Equity Group initial investment ($4,000,000) to determine the balance to be distributed under each valuation scenario; for example, $3,365,890 at the 6 percent cap rate, $2,661,050 at the 6.25 percent cap rate and $2,010,428 at the 6.5 percent cap rate.

Table 9.4 illustrates how the proceeds are distributed at 50 percent to the Investor Group on the front end and 50 percent to TRC and affiliates as the sponsor on the back end. On the front end, I receive 12.5 percent for my 25 percent ownership and the Investor Group receives 37.5 percent for their three-quarter ownership stake. The example depicts each of our shares based on the three cap rate scenarios.

The box in the table reveals the projected annual returns from cash flow and the returns from the proceeds based on a sale. This combination of annual distributions, with final distributions of cash, results in the Equity Group receiving an annual rate of return of 16.41 percent (6 percent cap rate), 14.65 percent (6.25 percent cap rate) and 13.03 percent (6.5 percent cap rate).

The IRR (compounded quarterly) would be 14.22 percent, 13.02 percent and 11.87 percent respectively.

Table 9.5, page 232, projects similar scenarios based on selling the asset at the end of the tenth year of ownership.

In Table 9.5, we are projecting a hypothetical appraisal after 10 years of ownership instead of 5 years, as distinguished from Table 9.4.

To determine the shopping center's projected sale price at the end of Year 10 (for the sake of deriving a distribution of equity in the event of a sale

Table 9.4 Cameron Chase Village Financial Analysis—Purchase Price ($13.625 Million), Rate of Return/
Refinancing Proceeds, Based on Sale at End of Fifth Year (Dec. 2011)

CAMERON CHASE VILLAGE
Financial Analysis - Purchase Price ($13.625 Million)
Rate of Return/Refinancing Proceeds
Based on Sale at End of Fifth Year (Dec. 2011)

Initial Equity Investment

Investor I - Sponsor	1,000,000
Investor Group	3,000,000
Total Equity Investment	4,000,000

NOI Year 6	1,073,361
Loan Balance end of Year 5	10,128,958

Deductions from Sales Price		**Additions to Sales Proceeds**	
Estimated Cost of Sale	1.5%	Working Capital Reserve	160,000
Exit Fees (Lender)	0.0%	Real Estate Tax Escrow	12,038
		Insurance Escrow	1,800
		Cash Flow Y5 Q4	70,000
		Total Additions	243,838

Capitalization Rate		**6.00%**	**6.25%**	**6.50%**
Projected Sales Price		17,889,350	17,173,776	16,513,246
Additions to Sales Proceeds		243,838	243,838	243,838
Deductions From Sale		(268,340)	(257,607)	(247,699)
Loan Balance		(10,128,958)	(10,128,958)	(10,128,958)
Net Proceeds from Sale		7,735,890	7,031,050	6,380,428
Cash Flow Y5 Q4		(70,000)	(70,000)	(70,000)
Cumulative Nonpaid Return to Equity Group		(300,000)	(300,000)	(300,000)
Return of Equity Group Initial Investment		(4,000,000)	(4,000,000)	(4,000,000)
Balance to Be Distributed		3,365,890	2,661,050	2,010,428
Distribution to All Equity Investors				
Investor I - Sponsor	12.50%	420,736	332,631	251,303
Investor Group	37.50%	1,262,209	997,894	753,910

Rate of Return for Equity Investors **				
Total Proceeds to Equity Investors		6,052,945	5,700,525	5,375,214
Annual Rate of Return		**16.41%**	**14.65%**	**13.03%**
IRR (compounded quarterly)		**14.22%**	**13.02%**	**11.87%**
Initial Investment		(4,000,000)	(4,000,000)	(4,000,000)
Year 1 - Dec-2007		240,000	240,000	240,000
Year 2 - Dec-2008		240,000	240,000	240,000
Year 3 - Dec-2009		260,000	260,000	260,000
Year 4 - Dec-2010		280,000	280,000	280,000
Year 5 - Dec-2011 (Sale / Refinancing)		6,262,945	5,910,525	5,585,214

*Distribution of Sales Proceeds
  1. Any unpaid preferred 8% annual cumulative, noncompounded return *pari passu*
  2. Return of Net Capital Investment
  3. 50% to Net Capital Investment/50% to Sponsor

**Does not include promote returns

Table 9.5 Cameron Chase Village, Financial Analysis—Purchase Price ($13.625 Million), Rate of Return/Refinancing Proceeds, Based on Sale at End of Tenth Year (Dec. 2016)

CAMERON CHASE VILLAGE
Financial Analysis - Purchase Price ($13.625 Million)
Rate of Return/Refinancing Proceeds
Based on Sale at End of Tenth Year (Dec. 2016)

Initial Equity Investment	
Investor I - Sponsor	1,000,000
Investor Group	3,000,000
Total Equity Investment	4,000,000

NOI Year 11	1,209,598
Loan Balance end of Year 10	9,295,622

Deductions from Sales Price		Additions to Sales Proceeds	
Estimated Cost of Sale	1.5%	Working Capital Reserve	160,000
Exit Fees (Lender)	0.0%	Real Estate Tax Escrow	12,038
		Insurance Escrow	1,800
		Cash Flow Y10 Q4	95,000
		Total Additions	268,838

Capitalization Rate	6.00%	6.25%	6.50%
Projected Sales Price	20,159,967	19,353,568	18,609,200
Additions to Sales Proceeds	268,838	268,838	268,838
Deductions From Sale	(302,400)	(290,304)	(279,138)
Loan Balance	(9,295,622)	(9,295,622)	(9,295,622)
Net Proceeds from Sale	10,830,784	10,036,481	9,303,278
Cash Flow Y10 Q4	(95,000)	(95,000)	(95,000)
Cumulative Nonpaid Return to Equity Group	(220,000)	(220,000)	(220,000)
Return of Equity Group Initial Investment	(4,000,000)	(4,000,000)	(4,000,000)
Balance to Be Distributed	6,515,784	5,721,481	4,988,278

Distribution to All Equity Investors				
Investor I - Sponsor	12.50%	814,473	715,185	623,535
Investor Group	37.50%	2,443,419	2,145,555	1,870,604

Rate of Return for Equity Investors **

Total Proceeds to Equity Investors	7,572,892	7,175,740	6,809,139
Annual Rate of Return	16.14%	15.15%	14.24%
IRR (compounded quarterly)	12.30%	11.84%	11.39%
Initial Investment	(4,000,000)	(4,000,000)	(4,000,000)
Year 1 - Dec-2007	240,000	240,000	240,000
Year 2 - Dec-2008	240,000	240,000	240,000
Year 3 - Dec-2009	260,000	260,000	260,000
Year 4 - Dec-2010	280,000	280,000	280,000
Year 5 - Dec-2011	280,000	280,000	280,000
Year 6 - Dec-2012	300,000	300,000	300,000
Year 7 - Dec-2013	320,000	320,000	320,000
Year 8 - Dec-2014	320,000	320,000	320,000
Year 9 - Dec-2015	360,000	360,000	360,000
Year 10 - Dec-2016 (Sale/Refinancing)	7,857,892	7,460,740	7,094,139

*Distribution of Sales Proceeds
1. Any unpaid preferred 8% annual cumulative, noncompounded return *pari passu*
2. Return of Net Capital Investment
3. 50% to Net Capital Investment/50% to Sponsor

**Does not include promote returns

or refinancing), we again focus on the two most important measures of value: the NOI projected in Year 11, which is $1,209,598, and the loan balance at the end of Year 10, which is $9,295,622.

In this example, we also projected a cap rate of 6.25 percent to capitalize the NOI in order to determine the projected value at the end of the tenth year. As cap rates vary with market conditions, we show three cap rates scenarios: ones using 6, 6.25 and 6.5 percent respectively.

The result of dividing each of the three cap rates by the projected NOI gives us three projected sale prices: $20,159,967 using the 6 percent cap rate; $19,353,568 using the 6.25 percent cap rate and $18,609,200 using the 6.5 percent cap rate.

In this transaction, we will estimate most of the deductions from the sale price (as well as additions to the sale proceeds) to be the same as our example for a sale at the end of the fifth year. The difference is the cash flow for the fourth quarter of the last year. In this example, Year 10 is $95,000. This gives us total additions of $268,838.

Note how these additions and deductions affect the net proceeds from the sale in the table. Using the 6 percent cap rate, we projected net proceeds of $10,830,784. Using the 6.25 percent cap rate, we projected net proceeds of $10,036,481, and $9,303,278 when using the 6.5 percent cap rate. By holding the investment for 10 years as compared to 5 years, we benefit from a higher sale price at the end of the term as well as receiving our returns on the investment each year through the sharing of excess cash flow.

How do we distribute the proceeds in this example? We deduct the cash flow from the fourth quarter of Year 10 ($95,000) from the net proceeds from the sale plus the cumulative unpaid returns to the Equity Group ($220,000) and the return of Equity Group initial investment ($4 million) to determine the balance to be distributed under each valuation scenario. Note in the table that the balance we would distribute if we sold at a 6 percent cap rate is $6,515,784; $5,721,481 at a 6.25 percent cap rate and $4,988,278 at the 6.5 percent cap rate.

The proceeds are being distributed at 50 percent to the Investor Group on the front end and 50 percent to TRC and affiliates as the Sponsor on the back end.

On the front end, I receive 12.5 percent for my 25 percent ownership and the Investor Group receives 37.5 percent for their three-quarter ownership stake, which is consistent with the previous example. Both examples depict each of our shares based on the three cap rate scenarios.

The box in the table shows the combination of the projected annual returns from cash flow and the returns from the proceeds based on the sale at the end of the tenth year. This combination of annual distributions, with final distributions of cash, results in the Equity Group receiving an annual rate of return of 16.14 percent (6 percent cap rate), 15.15 percent (6.25 percent cap rate) and 14.24 percent (6.5 percent cap rate). The corresponding IRR (compounded quarterly) would be 12.30 percent, 11.84 percent and 11.39 percent respectively.

The chart also lays out all distributions of cash flow throughout the life of the investment plus the large distribution for Year 10 resulting from a sale of the project at market value.

The latter includes any unpaid preferred return of 8 percent on an annual cumulative basis, returned noncompounded *pari passu*; the return of the net capital investment back to the Equity Group; the 50 percent distribution to the net capital investment; and 50 percent to the promote. All of the promote goes to TRC and affiliates.

The LLC agreement spells out exactly how proceeds are to be distributed so there is never a question in the investors' minds.

Please refer to Table 9.3, *Schedule of Prospective Cash Flow* on page 229. In determining the *Effective Gross Revenue*, you would need to analyze the rents achieved prior to the acquisition, not only for every leasable space but also the future rents you could achieve once the present leases and any options have expired.

When we purchased the shopping center, it had 16 tenant spaces. Table 9.6 on page 236 lists each tenant's name, the gross leasable area of each of the tenant spaces in square feet, the lease commencement date (LCD), the lease termination date (LTD), the base rent (in dollars per square foot based on triple net recoveries) and the annual rent (triple net) (leased area x base rent = annual rent).

Triple net, also known as NNN and net-net-net, is a term that refers to a lease obligation whereby the lessee (the tenant) becomes solely responsible for its pro rata share of all of the costs relating to the operation of the shopping center in addition to the rent applied under the lease, the minimum guaranteed rent (MGR).

The three basic components of operating costs that the lease allows the landlord to recover from the tenant are its share of net real estate taxes, net building insurance and net common area maintenance. The tenant is obligated to pay the net amount of these three types of costs.

All tenants at CCVC are paying triple net charges as opposed to paying fixed charges for operating costs, which can cause the landlord to not fully recover his costs to operate the center.

The base rents and annual rents as shown in the table are the minimum guaranteed rents NNN. In summary, there are 29,380 square feet of gross leasable area in which expected total minimum base rent per the terms of the 16 tenant leases is $964,451.

The column *Market Rent/Option Rent* shows what I believe the base rent would be today if I had to re-lease any of the spaces. I have set the market rents for each of the spaces as the rent the present tenant is paying. I have assumed that each of the tenants is paying market rent for the sake of this analysis. One tenant might be paying slightly more than market rent and one paying slightly less due to the size of an individual space or because of the tenant's use.

Cameron Chase Village Center

Table 9.6 Cameron Chase Village Center, Leasing Assumptions (Note: rents deleted to preserve confidentiality)

CAMERON CHASE VILLAGE
Ashburn, Virginia
Leasing Assumptions

TENANT	SPACE	AREA	LCD	LTD	BASE RENT	Annual Rent	MARKET RENT/ OPTION RENT	FUTURE TERMS/ASSUMPTIONS
Beef O'Brady's	101	3,830	05/26/05	09/30/15			$29.00	Tenant will exercise one 10-year option at fixed rent 10/05 : $————/month 10/08 : $————/month 10/10 : $————/month 10/11: 3% increase annually
Snappy Auctions	104	1,400	10/17/05	12/31/10			$37.00	Tenant will renew at market rent
Medicap Pharmacy	105	1,400	07/28/06	08/31/11			$37.00	Tenant will exercise three 5-year options at fixed rent LY6 $————; then 3% increase annually
Asia Palace	106	1,400	05/26/05	10/31/10			$31.00	Tenant will exercise one 5-year option at fixed rent 11/05: $————/month 11/06: 3% increase annually
Cameron Chase Village Cleaners	107	1,400	05/26/05	06/30/10			$34.00	Tenant will exercise one 5-year option at fixed rent
Smoothie King	108	1,050	08/10/05	11/30/10			$34.00	Tenant will exercise one 5-year option at fixed rent
Quizno's Subs	109	1,750	05/26/05	08/31/10			$33.00	Tenant will exercise first 5-year option at fixed rent and second 5-year option at market rent
Vacant/New Tenant (Butterfly Life Fitness)	110	2,100	11/01/06	10/31/11			$32.00	New Tenant effective 11/01/06 with 5-year option at market rent
MBH Settlement Group	112	2,800	08/24/05	11/30/10			$35.00	Tenant will exercise one 5-year option at fixed rent
Dejure Salon	114	1,400	05/26/05	08/31/10			$32.00	Tenant will exercise one 5-year option at fixed rent
Tiffany's Nail Spa	115	1,400	05/26/05	08/31/10			$34.00	Tenant will exercise one 5-year option at fixed rent
Vacant/New Tenant (Old Package Factory)	116	1,400	01/01/07	12/31/11			$33.00	Open & Operating on 01/01/07
Bean Scene Café	117	1,400	09/21/05	09/30/10			$33.00	Tenant will exercise one 5-year option at fixed rent
Pho Bistro	118	2,100	03/01/06	02/28/11			$35.00	Tenant will exercise one 5-year option at fixed rent
Mirchi's	120	2,100	05/26/05	09/30/12			$30.00	Tenant will exercise one 5-year option at fixed rent
Let's Dish!	122	2,450	05/26/05	08/31/10			$32.00	Tenant will exercise one 5-year option at fixed rent
Total Gross Leasable Area		29,380				$964,451		

♦ Assumed all tenant will be occupied and paying rent effective the analysis date.
♦ Assumed all leasing commissions, tenant improvements and any rent loss for vacant premises will be paid by the seller.
♦ Assumed that tenant will be billed back-management fees, but will not be billed for any administrative fees.
♦ For the purpose of this analysis option rent is dicounted at the rate of 3%.

Overall, I felt it was reasonable to analyze the asset from the standpoint whereby the tenants are considered as if they are paying market rent. This schedule reflects that assumption for the sake of valuating the asset in present-day terms.

This market rate rent for each space is then increased over time to account for inflation, which I will explain in the next exhibit.

However, I only use market rent to calculate rent if:

1. The tenant goes out of business and we need to calculate what a new tenant would pay in MGR, and/or
2. The tenant has an option, and the option does not specify a rent but only states the option rent will be at the market rate, and/or
3. The original lease term or the lease term and the option term(s) expire and we need to provide for this income in our cash flow projection (in this example shown as 11 years)

Future Terms/Assumptions sets the terms of the existing leasing and what I believe will occur in future years.

Table 9.7 on page 239 details the assumptions to the financial analysis. The first section is the assumption on the permanent loan.

When I purchase a shopping center, I frequently borrow the acquisition/redevelopment debt from a commercial bank using my personal guarantee.

With the Cameron Chase acquisition, the property was only a couple of years old. It had no deferred maintenance and was fully leased. This is not the type of center I usually purchase. It was a stable asset, more like an institutional purchase than a purchase where I can renovate, fix deferred items on the center, remerchandise the center by changing the tenant mix or show a relatively higher return to the investors because of the higher risk of that type of investment.

However, five factors convinced me to stray from my model to acquire Cameron Chase Village Center:

1. I had previously overseen the construction and leasing of the center for an out-of-town developer and knew the center and its market potential well.

2. It was a deal size that allowed me to answer the requests of several individual investors who had previously invested with me and wanted to invest with me again.

3. Several individuals who had not previously invested with me had expressed interest in investing with me.

4. Some of these individuals were not interested in short-term investments with higher risk and hopefully higher returns than the more stable investment. These investors were looking to invest their money in long-term investments for the benefit of their retirement or for their children. My pool of investors had increased over time to where I had a more diverse group, such as investors who wanted more stable properties, as well as investors who were more transactional and looking for higher returns.

5. Since the center was leased and stable (to the extent a two-year-old center is stable), I was able to place a very beneficial Commercial Mortgage Backed Securities (CMBS) 10-year permanent loan on the property with a desirable loan amount, interest rate and terms. The loan was nonrecourse, except for standard non-recourse carve-outs (fraud, theft, hiding knowledge of material consequences, etc.). Such a structure, where I do not have to personally guarantee a loan, always interests me because that is where I always want to be eventually anyway. The loan terms are summarized on Table 9.7.

A CMBS loan is a real estate loan that banks bundle together with other real estate loans. It ultimately places the mortgages into a trust with other real estate loans and then sells the trust as bonds to investors. These CMBS products were extremely popular in the early and mid-2000s but immediately after slowed to a crawl when the financial morass of 2008–2010 took a heavy toll on commercial real estate lending.

Borrowers preferred a CMBS loan because it gave them the ability to get a higher mortgage loan at a lower interest cost, often as nonrecourse. It also spurred lending to real estate. With the mortgage liability not held by banks, bankers were able to lend more money to potential borrowers because they collected the money from bondholders, keeping a portion as profit and reinvesting the money into the loan market.

Table 9.7   Cameron Chase Village Center, Assumptions to Financial Analysis

CAMERON CHASE VILLAGE
Ashburn, Virginia
Assumptions to Financial Analysis

FINANCIAL ASSUMPTIONS

Loan No.	Loan Type	Amount	Period	Term	Interest Rate	Points & Fees	Amortization
01	Permanent Financing - Fixed Rate	10,400,000	11/01/06 - 10/31/16	10 Years	5.84%	0%	30 Years

♦ Interest rate is based on ten-year treasury + 105 basis points (Locked effective 08/25/06 ten year treasury = 4.84%)
♦ Loan is interest only for the first three years and then amortized over 30 years.

NOI - Year 1	934,288
CAP Rate	6.86%
Shopping Center Value	13,625,000
Loan Amount	10,400,000
LTV	76.33%

CASH FLOW ASSUMPITONS

Vacancy Factor (Less Absorption & Turnover Vacancy)	4%	Tenant Improvements	
Management Fee	5%	New Leases	$10.00
Partnership Supervisory Fee	1%	Renewal Leases	$2.00
Capital Expenditures Reserves	$0.00	Leasing Commissions	
		New Leases	6%
Renewal Rate	90%	Renewal Leases	2%

IRR ASSUMPTIONS

Terminal Capitalization Rates	
Low	6%
Medium	6.25%
High	6.50%

The second section of the exhibit, *Cash Flow Assumptions*, reflects general assumptions that are the basis of the 11-year cash flow projection.

The third section of the exhibit, *IRR Assumptions*, shows the three exit cap rates we used to determine a sales price upon the assumed sale, which we must show in order to determine return on investment.

In Table 9.2, *Sources and Uses of Funds*, page 227, there is a line item called *Settlement Costs*, which depicts settlement-related costs of $123,330.

Table 9.8 on page 240 shows the details behind the estimated settlement cost. This is a very important template because different jurisdictions sometimes have materially different fees in purchasing or placing debt on a piece of real estate.

In the Washington, D.C., metropolitan area, there is a material difference between a purchase in Virginia and a purchase in Maryland. For example, this $123,330 cost in Virginia, depending on the county, city or town, could rise as high as $400,000 in Maryland.

Table 9.8 Cameron Chase Village Center, Financial Analysis—Purchase Price ($13.625 Million), Settlement Costs

CAMERON CHASE VILLAGE
Financial Analysis - Purchase Price ($13.625 Million)
Settlement Costs

Input Information	
Purchase Price	13,625,000
Total Debt	10,400,000

DESCRIPTION			PURCHASER	SELLER
CLOSING FEES				
Title Examination			1,000	0
Settlement Fee			500	0
Recording Fee			500	0
Misc Fees and Charges			1,000	0
TOTAL CLOSING FEES			3,000	0
PREPAID EXPENSES				
Real Estate Tax Escrow (2 months)			12,038	0
Insurance Escrow (2 months)			1,800	0
TOTAL PREPAID EXPENSES			13,838	0
RECORDATION/GRANTOR'S TAX - DEED				
State Recordation Tax	$2.50	per $1,000	34,063	0
County Recordation Tax	1/3 of the State tax amount		11,354	0
Grantor's Tax	$1.00	per $1,000	0	13,625
TOTAL RECORDATION - DEED			45,417	13,625
RECORDATION TAX - DEED OF TRUST				
State Recordation Tax				
0 10,000,000	$2.50	25,000		
10,000,001 20,000,000	$2.20	880		
20,000,001 30,000,000	$1.90	0		
30,000,001 40,000,000	$1.60	0		
40,000,001 999,999,999	$1.30	0		
Total State Recordation Tax			25,880	0
County Recordation Tax (1/3 of State)			8,627	0
TOTAL RECORDATION - DEED OF TRUST			34,507	0
TITLE INSURANCE - DEED OF TRUST				
Up to 3,000,000	$3.10		0	0
Up to 5,000,000	$2.60		0	0
Up to 10,000,000	$2.10		0	0
Up to 20,000,000	$1.95		26,569	0
Up to 50,000,000	$1.80		0	0
Up to 999,999,999	$1.75		0	0
TOTAL TITLE INSURANCE			26,569	0
TOTAL SETTLEMENT COSTS			123,330	13,625

Table 9.9, *Rent Roll,* page 242, is a summary of some of the relevant financial information from the leases we have with our tenants. Shown are the unit number, the tenant name, lease term, size of store space and minimum guaranteed rent.

The rent roll provides the detail that flows into all financial statements. For example, Space #110 is shown as vacant, whereas Table 9.6, *Leasing Assumptions,* page 236, shows the space rented to a new tenant, Butterfly Life Fitness. This is because the tenant had not yet opened and thus was not yet shown on the rent roll.

As the developer, you should always be thinking of how to increase value, not only by increasing the rent in an individual space but through implementing long-term strategies.

Ask yourself these questions: Does the present tenant mix give the center the highest value in 5 years or even 10 years? Should you plan to subdivide some of the larger spaces into smaller spaces in order to strengthen the tenant mix and increase the rents? Should you plan to combine two or more stores in order to create a space large enough to attract a powerful anchor tenant?

What should you do to make the tenant mix as viable as possible? This is not only to increase cash flow but also to have a center that can be assigned a lower cap rate for refinancing or sale.

Figure 9.10, *Lease Plan with Vacancies* on page 244, highlights the vacant spaces in yellow. Space #116 is the only space presently shown as vacant.

Figure 9.11, *Lease Plan with Current Expirations (Excluding Options),* page 245, along with Figure 9.12, *Lease Plan with Expirations (Including Options),* page 246, allow us to plan and understand, on a macro level, a shopping center's potential for changing tenants in order to increase retail productivity and achieve higher rents.

These two reports allow us to examine on a space-by-space basis adjoining spaces whose leases terminate at about the same time. This awareness permits us to subdivide or combine spaces to upgrade the tenant mix, increase rents and assemble adequate space for an anchor tenant.

An important tool we use to qualify rents is the tenant sales report. It helps us understand if our tenants are successful. From this report, we create other reports that correlate tenant sales to rents.

This allows us to review our tenants' sales, their gross rents and their

Table 9.9   Cameron Chase Village Center, Rent Roll

Rent Roll
CAMERON CHASE VILLAGE
As of August 28, 2006

August 28, 2006
6:10 pm

Vacant units: Market

Unit	Tenant Name	Lease Dates/Term/Type	Unit Square Feet and Percent of Total		Current Rent	Rent Per Square Foot
106	Asia Palace Deposit per Lease: $4,200.00	5/26/2005 to 10/31/2010 Term: 5 Years Retail	1,400	4.7651%	Monthly: Annual:	
117	Bean Scene Cafe Deposit per Lease: $4,433.33	9/21/2005 to 9/30/2010 Term: 5 Years Retail	1,400	4.7651%	Monthly: Annual:	
101	Beef O'Brady's Deposit per Lease: $10,851.66	5/26/2005 to 9/30/2015 Term: 10 Years Retail	3,830	13.0361%	Monthly: Annual:	
107	Cameron Chase Village Cleaners Deposit per Lease: $4,433.33	5/26/2005 to 6/30/2010 Term: 5 Years Retail	1,400	4.7651%	Monthly: Annual:	
114	Dejure Salon Deposit per Lease: $4,258.33	5/26/2005 to 8/31/2010 Term: 5 Years Retail	1,400	4.7651%	Monthly: Annual:	
122	Let's Dish! Deposit per Lease: $7,350.00	5/26/2005 to 8/31/2010 Term: 5 Years Retail	2,450	8.3390%	Monthly: Annual:	
112	MBH Settlement Group Deposit per Lease: $9,333.34	8/24/2005 to 11/30/2010 Term: 5 Years Retail	2,800	9.5303%	Monthly: Annual:	
105	Medicap Pharmacy Deposit per Lease: $5,236.00	Commenced 7/28/2006 Term: Month-To-Month Retail	1,400	4.7651%	Monthly: Annual:	
120	Mirchi's Deposit per Lease: $6,125.00	5/26/2005 to 9/30/2012 Term: 7 Years Retail	2,100	7.1477%	Monthly: Annual:	
118	Pho Bistro Deposit per Lease: $7,000.00	11/9/2005 to 2/28/2011 Term: 5 Years Retail	2,100	7.1477%	Monthly: Annual:	
109	Quizno's Subs Deposit per Lease: $5,541.67	5/26/2005 to 8/31/2010 Term: 5 Years Retail	1,750	5.9564%	Monthly: Annual:	
108	Smoothie King Deposit per Lease: $3,412.50	8/10/2005 to 11/30/2010 Term: 5 Years Retail	1,050	3.5739%	Monthly: Annual:	
104	Snappy Auctions Deposit per Lease: $4,900.00	10/17/2005 to 12/31/2010 Term: 5 Years Retail	1,400	4.7651%	Monthly: Annual:	
116	The Package Factory	5/26/2005 to 7/31/2010 Term: 5 Years Retail	1,400	4.7651%	Monthly: Annual:	
115	Tiffany's Nail Spa Deposit per Lease: $4,433.33	5/26/2005 to 8/31/2010 Term: 5 Years Retail	1,400	4.7651%	Monthly: Annual:	
110	Vacant		2,100	7.1477%	Mkt mth: Mkt ann:	
	Property Totals Total Deposits: $81,508.49		29,380		Monthly: Annual:	

DELETED FOR CONFIDENTIALITY   DELETED FOR CONFIDENTIALITY

Vacant:	2100	Square Feet
Vacancy Percentage:	7%	
Occupied:	27280	Square Feet
Occupied Percentage:	93%	

Dimension Name:	GLA	
Unit Total:	29,380	Square Feet
PropertyTotal:	29,380	Square Feet
Difference:	0	Square Feet
Percent of Total:	100%	

gross rents as a percentage of sales. We call the latter an occupancy cost ratio analysis because it help us compare across various categories what our tenants pay the landlord in rent and extra charges in relation to the revenue they generate.

Why is this important to landlords of retail properties? The occupancy cost ratio helps us determine if our tenants are paying rents that are above, at or below sustainable levels.

The drawings on pages 247 and 248 depict the Cameron Chase lease plan, each colored to reflect gross rent per square foot (Figure 9.13) and gross rent as a percentage of sales (Figure 9.14). These drawings give us an early indication of struggling tenants even while current on their rent.

Rent affordability varies from retailer to retailer. Different uses can afford to pay different percentages of their sales volume in gross rent. For example, a grocery store sells a high volume of merchandise at low profit margins. Carrying a large inventory and turning its mostly perishable inventory stock multiple times a year allows a supermarket to be profitable only if its gross rent is kept between 2 and 3 percent of its annual sales.

Inventory turnover is computed at retail by dividing the annual sales by the average monthly inventory. An item whose inventory is sold (turns over) four to six times a year, such as for many apparel specialty stores, has a higher holding cost than one that turns over in the teens, such as a supermarket.

Generally, retail inventory on hard goods such as appliances, electronics, furniture and sporting goods has low annual stock turns. Soft goods such as clothing, apparel and footwear have medium stock turns, and food and other grocery items move their stock much faster.

A typical supermarket chain's gross profit averages below 30 percent. Gross profit represents the portion of sales revenue remaining after deducting the cost of goods sold including purchase and distribution costs, such as inbound freight charges, purchasing and receiving costs, warehousing costs and other costs associated with distributing the merchandise to the stores. Advertising and promotional expenses as well as vendor allowances may also be accounted for as a component of cost of goods sold by some retail chains.

By contrast, a fashion apparel tenant can pay anywhere between 8 and 12 percent of annual sales in rent depending on the type of fashion tenant and the annual sales volume. Other uses vary even greater. For example, a

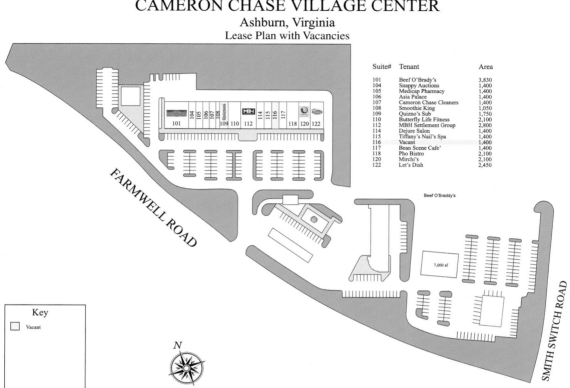

Figure 9.10 Cameron Chase Village Center, Lease Plan with Vacancies

restaurant often pays gross rent that equals between 8 and 10 percent of its annual sales.

Typically, tenants in open-air neighborhood centers pay occupancy cost ratios on the lower end of the scale while tenants in enclosed regional malls pay on the higher end. However, a sizable portion of the mall tenant's occupancy costs are applied to the landlord's recoveries of operating costs. The reason for the discrepancy is that mall specialty shops subsidize the anchors that pay very little of a mall's vast expenses. These include high property taxes and insurance costs as well as the cost to upkeep the center's luxurious amenities, roofs, sprawling parking lots, climate-controlled common areas with mechanical systems for vertical transportation and lavish

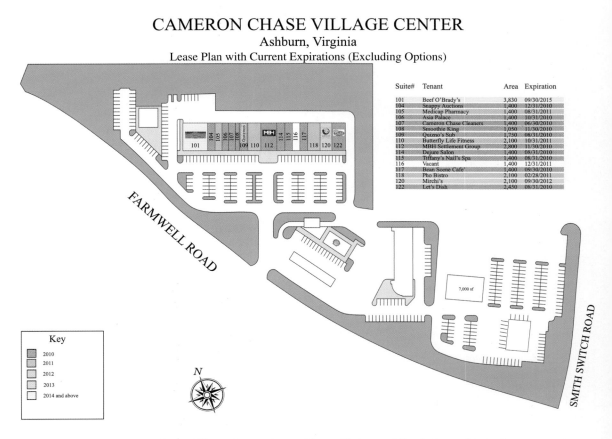

CAMERON CHASE VILLAGE CENTER
Ashburn, Virginia
Lease Plan with Current Expirations (Excluding Options)

Suite#	Tenant	Area	Expiration
101	Beef O'Brady's	3,830	09/30/2015
104	Snappy Auctions	1,400	12/31/2010
105	Medicap Pharmacy	1,400	08/31/2011
106	Asia Palace	1,400	10/31/2010
107	Cameron Chase Cleaners	1,400	06/30/2010
108	Smoothie King	1,050	11/30/2010
109	Quizno's Sub	1,750	08/31/2010
110	Butterfly Life Fitness	2,100	10/31/2011
112	MBH Settlement Group	2,800	11/30/2010
114	Dejure Salon	1,400	08/31/2010
115	Tiffany's Nail's Spa	1,400	08/31/2010
116	Vacant	1,400	12/31/2011
117	Bean Scene Cafe'	1,400	09/30/2010
118	Pho Bistro	2,100	02/28/2011
120	Mirchi's	2,100	09/30/2012
122	Let's Dish	2,450	08/31/2010

Key
- 2010
- 2011
- 2012
- 2013
- 2014 and above

7,000 sf

Figure 9.11 Cameron Chase Village Center, Lease Plan with Current Expirations (Excluding Options)

landscaping throughout—all patrolled by a security force the size of a small town's police department.

There are many factors that affect occupancy cost affordability for tenants of all types of retail properties, but among the most significant are store size, inventory turnover, annual sales volume and the store's gross profit margin.

A full-price retailer that purchases a piece of merchandise at wholesale and sells it at double the cost—keystone markup—can afford to pay you a higher percentage of its sales in gross rent than a discounter that buys the merchandise for $40 and sells it for $65.

Nonetheless, you must consider how total volume relates to rent affordability. A full-price retail tenant achieving $300 per square foot in annual

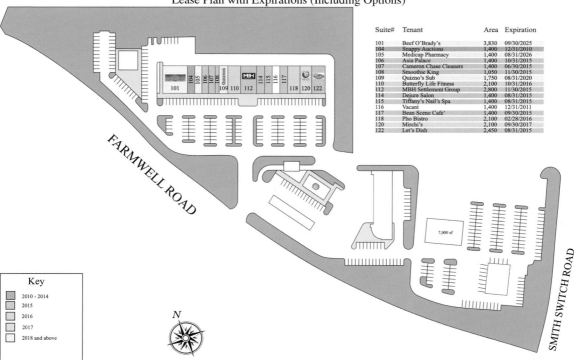

CAMERON CHASE VILLAGE CENTER
Ashburn, Virginia
Lease Plan with Expirations (Including Options)

Suite#	Tenant	Area	Expiration
101	Beef O'Brady's	3,830	09/30/2025
104	Snappy Auctions	1,400	12/31/2010
105	Medicap Pharmacy	1,400	08/31/2026
106	Asia Palace	1,400	10/31/2015
107	Cameron Chase Cleaners	1,400	06/30/2015
108	Smoothie King	1,050	11/30/2015
109	Quizno's Sub	1,750	08/31/2020
110	Butterfly Life Fitness	2,100	10/31/2016
112	MBH Settlement Group	2,800	11/30/2015
114	Dejure Salon	1,400	08/31/2015
115	Tiffany's Nail's Spa	1,400	08/31/2015
116	Vacant	1,400	12/31/2011
117	Bean Scene Cafe'	1,400	09/30/2015
118	Pho Bistro	2,100	02/28/2016
120	Mirchi's	2,100	09/30/2017
122	Let's Dish	2,450	08/31/2015

Key

- 2010 - 2014
- 2015
- 2016
- 2017
- 2018 and above

Figure 9.12 Cameron Chase Village Center, Lease Plan with Expirations (Including Options)

sales paying 8 percent of its sales in gross rent is paying you $24 per square foot in gross rent. A discounter whose volume equals $400 per square foot paying you the same 8 percent is paying you $32 per square foot. Both of these retailers may be achieving a similar total gross profit in their operation, while each is operating within a very different profit margin structure. As a landlord, which would you rather have?

Then you have service-oriented tenants, such as a dentist or a doctor—many of which pay higher rent than conventional retail tenants. Many of these shopping center tenants that mostly offer services instead of goods are destination-type tenants that prefer a retail environment, but since they carry very little inventory, they might be able to pay more than 20 percent of their

CAMERON CHASE VILLAGE CENTER
Ashburn, Virginia
Lease Plan with Gross Rents per Square Foot

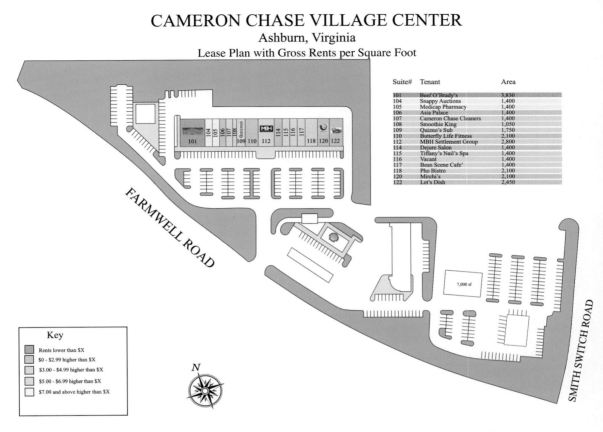

Suite#	Tenant	Area
101	Beef O'Brady's	3,830
104	Snappy Auctions	1,400
105	Medicap Pharmacy	1,400
106	Asia Palace	1,400
107	Cameron Chase Cleaners	1,400
108	Smoothie King	1,050
109	Quizno's Sub	1,750
110	Butterfly Life Fitness	2,100
112	MBH Settlement Group	2,800
114	Dejure Salon	1,400
115	Tiffany's Nail's Spa	1,400
116	Vacant	1,400
117	Bean Scene Cafe'	1,400
118	Pho Bistro	2,100
120	Mirchi's	2,100
122	Let's Dish	2,450

Key

- Rents lower than $X
- $0 - $2.99 higher than $X
- $3.00 - $4.99 higher than $X
- $5.00 - $6.99 higher than $X
- $7.00 and above higher than $X

Figure 9.13 Cameron Chase Village Center, Lease Plan with Gross Rents per Square Foot

sales in gross rent. However, you should not count on professional service tenants agreeing to report sales to you as conventional retailers typically do.

In reviewing the information in these three charts, especially the gross rent as a percentage of sales chart, we can predict which tenants will probably want to leave when their lease expires. Some of these tenants may not even survive to the end of their lease term.

As we continually work to optimize our tenant mix, no matter how small the center, we also always try to choose and work with tenants that have a business model geared to generate the highest sales, which leads to more traffic for all our tenants, which in turn leads to higher rents our tenants can afford. The amount of rent a retailer is willing to pay is ultimately related to

CAMERON CHASE VILLAGE CENTER
Ashburn, Virginia
Lease Plan with Gross Rents as Percentage of Sales

Suite#	Tenant	Area	%
101	Beef O'Brady's	3,830	10.77%
104	Snappy Auctions	1,400	11.71%
105	Medicap Pharmacy	1,400	15.22%
106	Asia Palace	1,400	13.62%
107	Cameron Chase Cleaners	1,400	18.27%
108	Smoothie King	1,050	10.37%
109	Quizno's Sub	1,750	11.04%
110	Butterfly Life Fitness	2,100	N/A
112	MBH Settlement Group	2,800	N/A
114	Dejure Salon	1,400	14.83%
115	Tiffany's Nail's Spa	1,400	17.21%
116	Vacant	1,400	N/A
117	Bean Scene Cafe'	1,400	15.60%
118	Pho Bistro	2,100	15.67%
120	Mirchi's	2,100	13.81%
122	Let's Dish	2,450	3.81%

Key

▪	< 5.00%
▪	6.00% - 8.99%
▪	9.00% - 11.99%
▪	12.00% - 14.99%
▪	15.00% and above
▪	No Sales Data

7,000 sf

FARMWELL ROAD

SMITH SWITCH ROAD

N

Figure 9.14 Lease Plan with Gross Rents as Percentage of Sales

its ability to generate sales and maintain healthy profit margins at a particular location.

In analyzing tenant sales, we also look at our tenants' normal increase in sales as well as the shopping center's escalating operating costs, which we pass on to our tenants. A prolonged decline in tenant sales or an increase in the property's operating costs—or both—can drive the center's average occupancy cost ratio to an unsustainable level. This spells trouble for any shopping center.

In the Cameron Chase Village Center case study in Chapter IX, we learned how to make money in a relatively short time horizon using the principles of good financial management for asset preservation and enhancement. However, few properties you acquire will be new, already-polished gems like Cameron Chase Village sitting in an affluent market and churning out cash flow for you to distribute to your partners and yourself.

Let us head east from Cameron Chase Village Center on a 180-degree road trip on the Interstate 495 loop around Washington, D.C., to learn about redevelopment strategies.

The case study in Chapter X features a shopping center in Bowie, Maryland, which I will use to illustrate how you can uncover hidden value in an acquisition by conducting a full repositioning of the property.

Pointer Ridge Plaza—Bowie, Maryland

Case Study Number 4: Pointer Ridge Plaza, Bowie, Maryland

A Real-Life Example—Asset Appreciation

IN THIS CASE STUDY, I will review the details of another real-life acquisition. In this particular case, the project illustrates an example of asset appreciation through the acquisition of undervalued real estate where we maximize its full potential through a redevelopment and remerchandising of the shopping center.

I acquired Pointer Ridge Plaza (PRP) using my own capital and capital allocated as equity for my family. However, I am including charts depicting theoretical returns from noninstitutional equity partners. This will give you a sense of the returns for the equity group, to differentiate my returns as equity owner and my role as the sponsor receiving the additional fees for management services and a promote bonus for improving the investment.

If you are starting your own business as a shopping center developer, you are unlikely to acquire a piece of real estate of this magnitude without equity partners. However, with perseverance and armed with knowledge, you might find a gem in the raw (just as we did in PRP) that can help you make a lot of money. This is the reason I am taking the extra step in this case study to show you how a project like this would perform for your equity partners as well as for you.

Besides modifying the equity piece for learning purposes, I deleted some data, such as specific tenant rents, to preserve confidentiality where appropriate. I also altered some of the information as well, to illustrate other learning points I depicted in earlier samples throughout this book.

I chose this project to demonstrate what you can do to add value in retail real estate development and ownership. However, this is not easy if you are inexperienced in development principles. You have to decide what you can do given the right opportunity.

My company's experience as a shopping center developer and owner gives us the perspective to understand what the retailer wants and what the landlord needs. This expertise is particularly helpful in the early stages of development when we have to plan leasing strategies and merchandising plans to maximize asset value, fill unmet needs and create synergy among retailers.

More important, it allows us to define potential value regardless of present NOI and assigned cap rates because of our vision for creating value, which is the foundation behind the acquisition of Pointer Ridge Plaza.

The Project

Pointer Ridge Plaza (PRP) is a 71,808-square-foot shopping center located on highly traveled Route 301/Crain Highway in Bowie, Maryland. When I first purchased the shopping center, the center was anchored by a 30,000-square-foot Giant Food grocery store, a CVS/pharmacy, a Pizza Hut and an array of service-oriented tenants and restaurants. From the outset of the acquisition I planned a full renovation, re-tenanting and repositioning of this center.

Giant Food, the anchor tenant at PRP, is an anchor in several of the shopping centers I own. I understand this store's business model and I have a good relationship with its real estate people. From previous conversations with representatives of Giant Food, I was aware of the upside of the anchor situation at PRP, which could be leveraged to greatly improve the property.

Upon reading the Giant lease during the due diligence phase, I determined that Giant Food was currently in one of its five-year option periods and the lease had several five-year options remaining. However, this lease did not give Giant Food broad assignment rights, and more importantly, which is very rare even in leases as old as this one was, Giant Food had to continually operate the store. This continuous operating covenant required Giant Food not only to pay the rent but also to operate a grocery store even if it were losing money in operating the store.

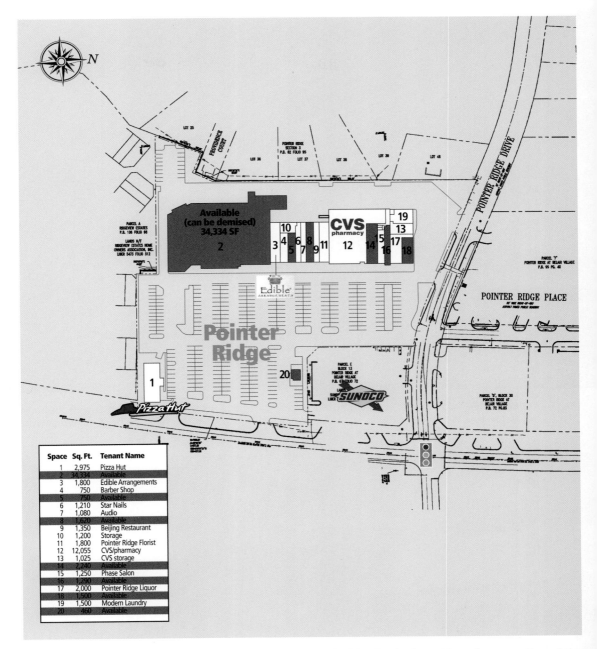

Space	Sq. Ft.	Tenant Name
1	2,975	Pizza Hut
2	34,334	Available
3	1,800	Edible Arrangements
4	750	Barber Shop
5	750	Available
6	1,210	Star Nails
7	1,080	Audio
8	1,620	Available
9	1,350	Beijing Restaurant
10	1,200	Storage
11	1,800	Pointer Ridge Florist
12	12,055	CVS/pharmacy
13	1,025	CVS storage
14	2,240	Available
15	1,250	Phase Salon
16	1,290	Available
17	2,000	Pointer Ridge Liquor
18	1,500	Available
19	1,500	Modern Laundry
20	460	Available

Figure 10.1 The site plan for Pointer Ridge Plaza in Bowie, Maryland, gives a broad perspective of the strip-shaped center, showing the available 34,334-square-foot big-box space from a vacated Giant Food grocery store (Space #2). Most of the store spaces have good visibility from the bustling north-south corridor of Crain Highway and the intersecting Pointer Ridge Drive.

BEFORE—Prior to the acquisition, Pointer Ridge Plaza—with its antiquated storefronts and deferred maintenance items—needed a major renovation and repositioning. The Rappaport Company's strengths could be put to use in undertaking this task.

THE PLAN—We hired Rounds Vanduzer Architects to create renderings of a major facelift of Pointer Ridge Plaza. This helped us to price out the renovation and envision a fresh appearance for the new anchor that we had planned to replace the existing, undersized Giant Food grocery store.

AFTER—The first step of the renovation of Pointer Ridge Plaza involved creating a new facade to give the center a modern look with plenty of curb appeal. In this photo, you can see the first of the new store signs, CVS/pharmacy, placed on the new Dryvett fascia.

Giant Food was operating a store at PRP in an inadequate space that fell short by 25,000 square feet of its then-current prototype of 55,000-plus square feet. With little ability to expand or sublet the store at this center, it was a tremendous opportunity to have Giant Food pay the landlord a substantial amount to cancel the lease instead of having the landlord pay the tenant to terminate the lease.

This meant the tenant could be convinced to close this store as soon as possible but certainly no later than at the conclusion of its present option lease term, which was to expire in about two years. The upside entailed replacing this anchor with a more productive anchor, sized correctly in the current footprint.

The center had been owned by the same individual since it was built over 35 years ago. It was in an excellent location with good visibility and accessibility, but I felt that the owner had become complacent with the center.

The owner was in his late seventies. He was not active in the business of retail real estate anymore. He was living outside of the Washington, D.C., metropolitan area. By then he held no mortgage on the property and was quite content with drawing upon the present cash flow. It was obvious to me that he had no interest in making a major investment in the property in order to bring in stronger tenants and higher rents.

This was a classic example of understanding the owner's objective and the potential inherent in every piece of retail property. Finding an opportunity like this is why I believe real estate is a local business. There will always be a place for the true entrepreneur who does his or her due diligence and gets to really understand the underlying fundamentals of the business.

By driving the local roads, by understanding every submarket in this metropolitan area where I live, by trying to learn about every retail property that maybe fits my model for acquisition, renovation and remodeling, I can find opportunities like Pointer Ridge Plaza that maybe a larger national company would not be able to discover.

One could easily see that the owner had not renovated the center in many years, if ever. On my initial site visit, I saw deferred maintenance items in the parking areas and thought they existed most probably in the roof areas as well. The storefronts and underneath canopies also needed replacing. This property needed a major renovation and repositioning and my company's strengths could be put to use in undertaking the task at hand.

It was obvious the tenant mix was very weak. Upon review of the rent roll, we confirmed the rents were also substantially below the rents of competitive centers. The lease reviews also confirmed that many of the leases were soon expiring, some coming due within five years, including Pizza Hut and CVS. Even with options, the Pizza Hut and the CVS leases would expire within 10 years.

Even though I knew that pharmacies were looking for pad locations with a drive-through service, I learned in a conversation with CVS representatives that the pharmacy had not yet found a new location. Additionally, there were none coming up in the market in the near future that they or I knew about. If, on the other hand, an alternative location became available to CVS after I acquired PRP, by that time I would have completed my renovation and the CVS space could be re-tenanted, most likely at the rent that CVS was paying and maybe even slightly higher.

As of this writing, CVS continues to operate very successfully at PRP and has not yet found a pad location to relocate its PRP store. Now that we have renovated PRP, I expect CVS will continue operating at the center for several more years. If it finds a suitable pad to relocate to, there will be a cancellation fee payable to PRP and we can replace CVS with a higher-paying tenant.

Prescription customers tend to be habitual in nature, and the PRP customer is no different. They will get a haircut at the Pointer Ridge Barber Shop or Phase Salon, buy a bottle of wine from Pointer Ridge Liquor, drop off their laundry at Modern Laundry, get their nails done at Star Nails, pick up their prescription at CVS/pharmacy and stop for lunch at Pizza Hut.

By analyzing the center's potential prior to the acquisition, I believed that if I could obtain the 30,000-square-foot Giant space, complete a major renovation, remerchandise the tenant mix and increase rents as leases expired, I could create substantial additional cash flow and value in the property. With good planning and setting aside the proper capital to make the necessary improvements, this is what we eventually achieved.

The Market

Pointer Ridge Plaza serves a diversified, affluent and growing market in Prince George's County, Maryland. Bowie is a historical example of urbanization, having grown from a small agricultural and railroad town to the largest municipality in the county. It is the fifth most populous city and third largest city by area in the state.

Within a three-mile radius of PRP, the population in 2007 was 27,782 with an average household income of $104,839. Because of the extensive commercial activity in the area and the urban aspect of the market, the daytime population in the immediate three-mile radius was estimated at 19,696.

Within a five-mile radius of this neighborhood center, 69,651 persons lived in households that had an average household income of $110,393, and 34,739 was the daytime population in the area. In a ten-mile radius, the population was 379,591 earning $92,282 in annual average household income and a daytime population of 200,197.

In the immediate three-mile radius of PRP, 1,753 businesses employed 13,319 workers. Within a five-mile radius, 3,060 businesses employed 25,445 workers, and 13,049 businesses employ 171,631 persons in a ten-mile radius.

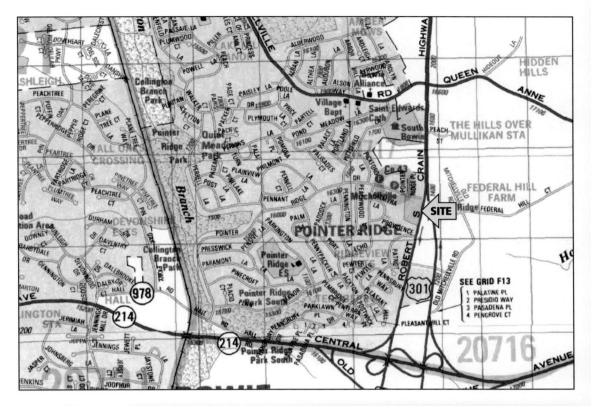

DEMOGRAPHICS 2007	3 MILES	5 MILES	10 MILES
POPULATION	27,782	69,651	379,591
AVERAGE HOUSEHOLD INCOME	$104,839	$110,393	$92,282
EMPLOYEES	13,319	25,445	171,631

TRAFFIC COUNTS
ROUTE 301/CRAIN HIGHWAY (NORTH OF CENTRAL AVENUE) - 60,000
POINTER RIDGE DRIVE - 6,000

Figure 10.2 The Pointer Ridge Plaza investor book highlights demographics and vehicular traffic counts.

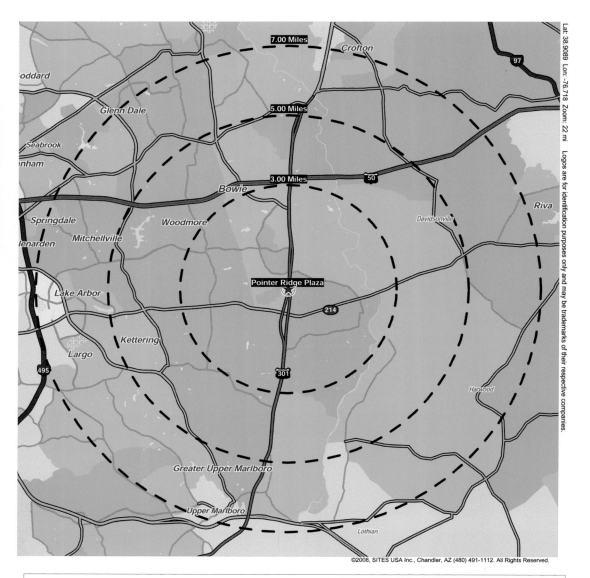

Median HH Income
By Block Groups

- $100,000 or more
- $75,000 to $100,000
- $50,000 to $75,000
- $30,000 to $50,000
- Less than $30,000

Pointer Ridge Plaza
Bowie, Maryland

Current Year Estimated
Median Household Income

September 2008

This map was produced using data from private and government sources deemed to be reliable. The information herein is provided without representation or warranty.

Figure 10.3 The Pointer Ridge Plaza is depicted in a map with median household income in circles of three-, five-, and seven-mile increments.

Figure 10.4 The Pointer Ridge Plaza investor book includes extensive data about the market. Sites USA assembled this data for TRC from census information and other secondary research sources.

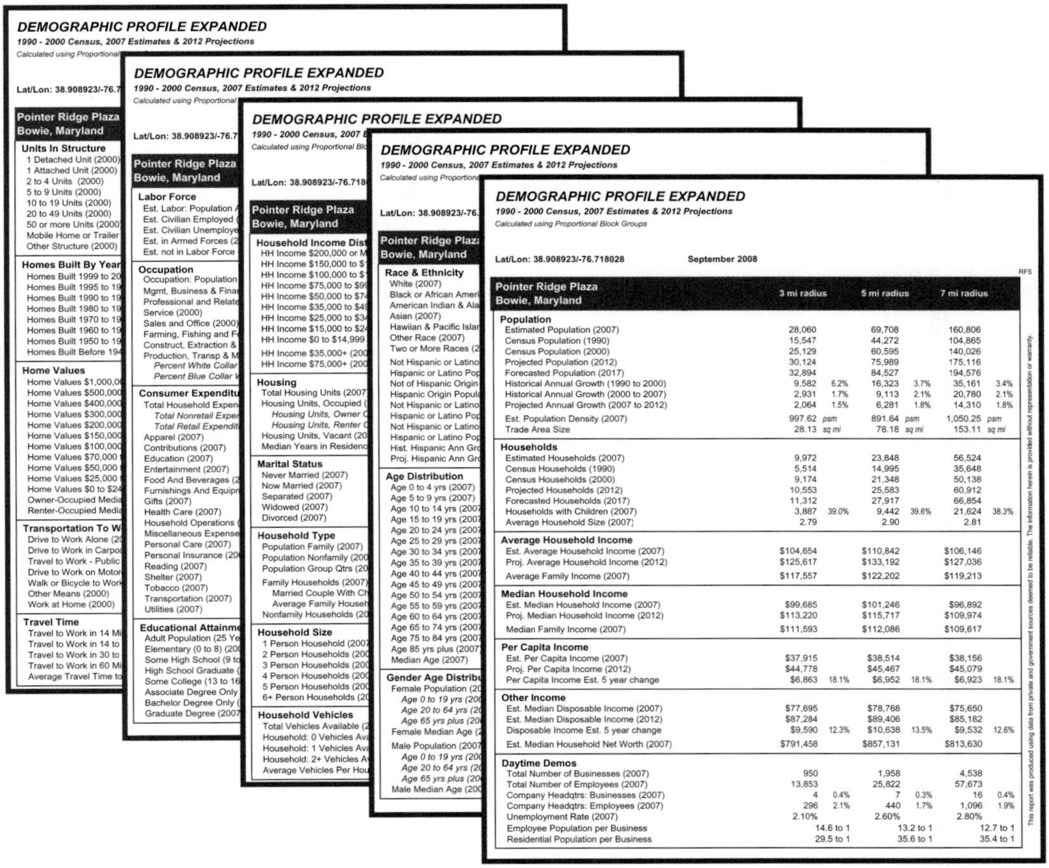

DEMOGRAPHIC PROFILE EXPANDED
1990 - 2000 Census, 2007 Estimates & 2012 Projections
Calculated using Proportional Block Groups

Lat/Lon: 38.908923/-76.718028 September 2008

RF5

Pointer Ridge Plaza Bowie, Maryland	3 mi radius		5 mi radius		7 mi radius	
Population						
Estimated Population (2007)	28,060		69,708		160,806	
Census Population (1990)	15,547		44,272		104,865	
Census Population (2000)	25,129		60,595		140,026	
Projected Population (2012)	30,124		75,989		175,116	
Forecasted Population (2017)	32,894		84,527		194,576	
Historical Annual Growth (1990 to 2000)	9,582	6.2%	16,323	3.7%	35,161	3.4%
Historical Annual Growth (2000 to 2007)	2,931	1.7%	9,113	2.1%	20,780	2.1%
Projected Annual Growth (2007 to 2012)	2,064	1.5%	6,281	1.8%	14,310	1.8%
Est. Population Density (2007)	997.62	psm	891.64	psm	1,050.25	psm
Trade Area Size	28.13	sq mi	78.18	sq mi	153.11	sq mi
Households						
Estimated Households (2007)	9,972		23,848		56,524	
Census Households (1990)	5,514		14,995		35,648	
Census Households (2000)	9,174		21,348		50,138	
Projected Households (2012)	10,553		25,583		60,912	
Forecasted Households (2017)	11,312		27,917		66,854	
Households with Children (2007)	3,887	39.0%	9,442	39.6%	21,624	38.3%
Average Household Size (2007)	2.79		2.90		2.81	
Average Household Income						
Est. Average Household Income (2007)	$104,654		$110,842		$106,146	
Proj. Average Household Income (2012)	$125,617		$133,192		$127,036	
Average Family Income (2007)	$117,557		$122,202		$119,213	
Median Household Income						
Est. Median Household Income (2007)	$99,685		$101,246		$96,892	
Proj. Median Household Income (2012)	$113,220		$115,717		$109,974	
Median Family Income (2007)	$111,593		$112,086		$109,617	
Per Capita Income						
Est. Per Capita Income (2007)	$37,915		$38,514		$38,156	
Proj. Per Capita Income (2012)	$44,778		$45,467		$45,079	
Per Capita Income Est. 5 year change	$6,863	18.1%	$6,952	18.1%	$6,923	18.1%
Other Income						
Est. Median Disposable Income (2007)	$77,695		$78,768		$75,650	
Est. Median Disposable Income (2012)	$87,284		$89,406		$85,182	
Disposable Income Est. 5 year change	$9,590	12.3%	$10,638	13.5%	$9,532	12.6%
Est. Median Household Net Worth (2007)	$791,458		$857,131		$813,630	
Daytime Demos						
Total Number of Businesses (2007)	950		1,958		4,538	
Total Number of Employees (2007)	13,853		25,822		57,673	
Company Headqtrs: Businesses (2007)	4	0.4%	7	0.3%	16	0.4%
Company Headqtrs: Employees (2007)	296	2.1%	440	1.7%	1,096	1.9%
Unemployment Rate (2007)	2.10%		2.60%		2.80%	
Employee Population per Business	14.6 to 1		13.2 to 1		12.7 to 1	
Residential Population per Business	29.5 to 1		35.6 to 1		35.4 to 1	

This report was produced using data from private and government sources deemed to be reliable. The information herein is provided without representation or warranty.

The market is highly diversified. About half of the population residing in the immediate three-mile radius is white (47 percent), with the balance representing various ethnic groups: 40 percent African American, 3.7 percent Asian and Pacific Islander, 2.8 percent other races and 9 percent Hispanic or of Hispanic origin. The population in this three-mile radius is highly educated with almost two-thirds (65.2 percent) having attended college or having attained a college undergraduate or graduate degree.

Traffic counts on Route 301/Crain Highway (north of Central Avenue) show 60,000 vehicles driving by each day adjacent to the property's frontal road of Pointer Ridge Drive, which averages 6,000 in daily vehicle count.

Figure 10.5 through Figure 10.13 The Pointer Ridge Plaza investor book depicts various charts, maps and figures that inform a prospective investor about existing and projected demographics that illustrate the shopping center's market potential.

Population Density

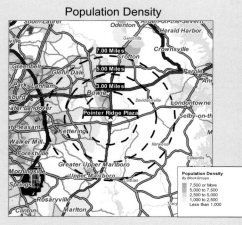

Figure 10.5

Median Income

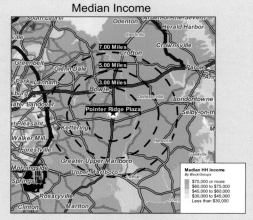

Figure 10.6

Retail Expenditure

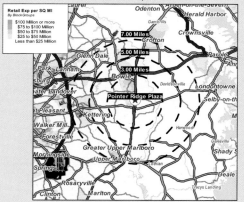

Figure 10.7

Employment Density

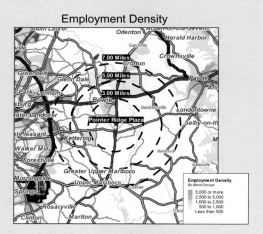

Figure 10.8

College Educated

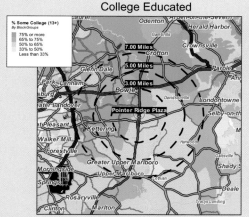

Figure 10.9

5-Year Projected Population

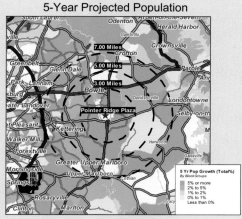

Figure 10.10

Population Growth

2005 Estimated Population	602,572
2010 Projected Population	638,322
2000 Census Population	552,111

Figure 10.11

Median Household Income

- $35,000 to 49,999
- $50,000 to 74,999
- $75,000 to 124,999
- $125,000 or more

2005 Est. Median HH Income	$78,734
2005 Est. Average Household Income	$87,629
2005 Est. Per Capita Income	$31,991

Figure 10.12

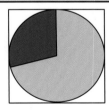

Employment Density

☐ White Collar ■ Blue Collar

2005 Estimated Population	602,572
Total Number of Businesses	20,464
Total Number of Employees	294,528

Figure 10.13

Figure 10.14 A map of Bowie, Maryland, depicts the location of Pointer Ridge Plaza.

Figure 10.15 In this schematic design by Rounds Vanduzer Architects, prospective tenants can see the shopping center in juxtaposition to the Amber Ridge shopping center, separated by Pointer Ridge Drive. In the near future, TRC will be developing the Amber Ridge shopping center to maximize the retail potential of both sites.

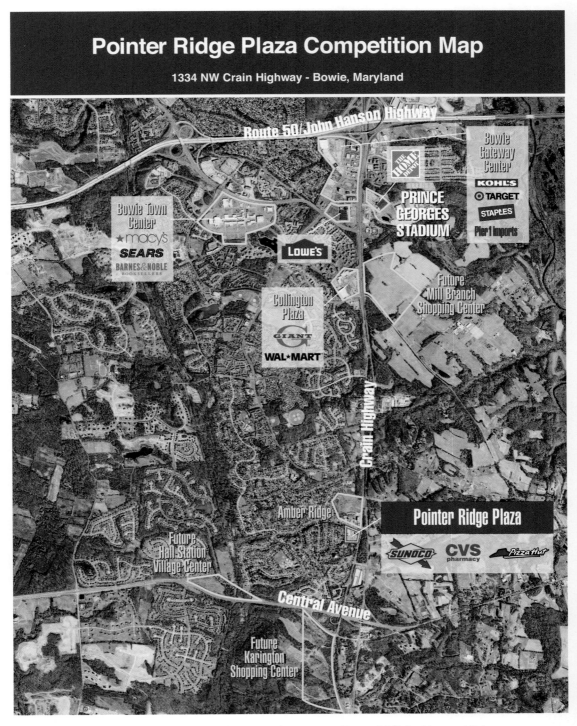

Figure 10.16 Positioned east and west of Crain Highway up to Route 50/John Hanson Highway, the area where Pointer Ridge Plaza is located acts as a retail hub with the regional mall, Bowie Town Center to the north. The area is home to many prominent retailers such as Macy's, Sears, Barnes & Noble, Lowe's, The Home Depot, Safeway, Giant Food, Walmart, Target, Staples and Kohl's.

Figure 10.17 As part of our due diligence to acquire this property, we gather key competitive data. The material covers every competitive shopping center surrounding Pointer Ridge Plaza.

8. Mill Branch Shopping Center (Under Development)

Anchor Tenants: N/A

Retail Square Footage: 200,000 (Estimated)

Developer: Gibraltar Management

Owner: Gibraltar Management

Broker: Gibraltar Management

Notes: Northeast corner of Crain Highway/301 at Mill Branch Road.

9. Wal-Mart Pad (Existing)

Anchor Tenants: Wal-Mart

POINTER RIDGE
Market Analysis
In Alphabetical Order
September 16, 2008

1. Bowie Gateway Center (Existing)

Anchor Tenants: Target / Staples

Retail Square Footage: 250,000 (Estimated)

Developer: Multiple Developers On Property

Owner: Multiple Owners On Property

Leasing Agent: Varies Depending On Ownership

Notes: South of Route 50 at Mitchellville Road.

2. Bowie Town Center (Existing)

Anchor Tenants: Safeway, Sears, Macy's

Retail Square Footage: 684,000

Developer: Simon Properties

Owner: Simon Properties

Leasing Agent: Simon Properties

Notes: Southeast corner of Northview Drive and Collington Road/197.

3. Collington Plaza (Existing)

Anchor Tenants: Giant

Retail Square Footage: 121,765

Developer: Next Realty

Owner: Next Realty

Leasing Agent: Next Realty

Notes: Northwest corner of Crain Highway/301 and Excalibur Road.

4. Hall Station (Under Development)

Anchor Tenants: Rite Aid

Retail Square Footage: 40,500

Developer: Rappaport Companies / Michael Companies

Owner: Rappaport Companies / Michael Companies

Leasing Agent: The Rappaport Companies

Notes: Intersection of Hall Road and Central Avenue.

5. Home Depot Pad (Existing)

Anchor Tenants: Home Depot

6. Karington (Under Development)

Anchor Tenants: N/A

Retail Square Footage:

Developer: The Michael Companies

Owner: The Michael Companies

Broker: The Michael Companies

Notes: Southwest side of Crain Highway/301 and Central Avenue.

7. Lowe's Pad (Existing)

Anchor Tenants: Lowe's

Courtesy of Sam J. Rank

Please refer to Table 10.1, *Equity Term Sheet* (below), for a summary of terms agreed to by the equity partners. As my family and I are the predominant equity owners in Pointer Ridge Plaza, I modified this term sheet to reflect a series on noninstitutional partners and how this deal would be structured in that event.

Table 10.1   Pointer Ridge Plaza, Equity Term Sheet

Equity Term Sheet

Purpose

Formation of limited liability company to acquire and redevelop shopping center

Capital Contributions

Investors—75% of all cash to fund acquisition and development costs not funded by third party financing (Investor Group)

Sponsor (or his designees)—25% of all cash to fund acquisition and development costs not funded by third party financing (Investor 1)

Distributions

Cash Flow
(i) Preferred 8% Distribution on capital contributions *pari passu* (cumulative and noncompounded)
(ii) 50% to capital investor group
      50% to sponsor (or his designees)

Sale/Refinancing Proceeds
(i) Unpaid Preferred Distribution on capital contributions
(ii) Return of capital *pari passu*
(iii) 50% to capital investor group
      50% to sponsor (or his designees)

Preferred Distribution calculated at 8% per annum from and after date of contribution

Property Management and Leasing Agreement

Management Fee   5% of gross receipts (payable monthly on actual receipts collected)
Leasing Fee   6% (4% without co-broker) of base rent
      2% on renewals
Marketing Fee   15% of marketing budget

Partnership Supervisory Fee

1% gross receipts to sponsor (payable monthly on actual receipts collected)
5% of hard costs

Development Fee

1% gross receipts to sponsor (payable monthly on actual receipts collected)
5% of hard costs

For example, this deal calls for investors to contribute 75 percent of all cash to fund the acquisition and development costs of PRP not funded by the lender. The remaining 25 percent of the cash is the responsibility of the sponsor, which is I or my designees, such as my family members.

We planned the cash flow distributions in this deal as an annual preferred 8 percent distribution on capital contributions *pari passu* (cumulative and noncompounded); thereafter, cash flow would be distributed 50 percent *pari passu* to all investment partners (capital Investor Group) and the other 50 percent going to me and my family as the Sponsor's interest. This is different from the example for Cameron Chase Village Center. In the Pointer Ridge Plaza example, my front-end equity investment of 25 percent, as well as my sponsorship interest (back-end interest), increased to 50 percent. If this project were the same as Cameron Chase Village Center, between my front-end interest of 25 percent and my back-end interest of 50 percent, in total I would receive 25 percent of 50 percent (front-end interest). I would also receive 50 percent back-end interest or a total of 12.5 percent plus 50 percent, which would equal 62.5 percent of all cash flow after the 8 percent cumulative noncompounded return and 62.5 percent of all the appreciation after the return of the equity. This project shows another example of how the cash flow and appreciation can be shared.

The distribution at the time of sale or refinancing would be distributed as follows:

- Unpaid preferred distribution on capital contributions (cumulative and noncompounded)
- Return of capital *pari passu*
- 50 percent to capital Investor Group
- 50 percent to me as Sponsor (or my designees)

TRC fees and leasing commissions are:

- Management fee of 5 percent of gross receipts (payable monthly on actual receipts collected)
- Leasing commission of 6 percent of base rent divided equally with co-broker (4 percent if no co-broker is involved); 2 percent on renewals

- Marketing fee of 15 percent of marketing funds collected from tenants and landlord
- Partnership supervisory (asset management) fee of 1 percent of gross receipts to TRC (payable monthly on actual receipts collected)
- Development fee of 5 percent of construction hard costs

Refer to Table 10.2, *Pointer Ridge Plaza, Financial Analysis, Sources and Uses of Funds* (page 270). Let us first look at the *Uses of Funds* section, with explanations of some of the key line items:

1. *Acquisition Costs*: We are purchasing the shopping center for $10,302,000 including the broker's commission. In this case, I hired a broker, whom I knew well and respected for his tact and perseverance, to work as a middleman between the seller and me. I felt that if I dealt directly with the seller, I might have only one opportunity to discuss the purchase, but with this broker I would have many opportunities to keep an open dialogue, if needed. The commission I agreed to pay the broker was 1 percent of the selling price, or $102,000. Accordingly, our total acquisition cost was $10,200,000 to the seller and $102,000 to the broker, for a total acquisition cost of $10,302,000.

2. *Settlement Costs:* Settlement costs in the state of Maryland and especially Prince George's County—where this property is located—are among the most expensive in the region for purchasing commercial real estate and placing debt on a property. This is why it is important to anticipate these costs when structuring your deal.

3. *Points and Fees*
   a) *Acquisition Fee:* The acquisition fee, which is 1 percent of the purchase price of $10,200,000, or $102,000, is a fee that, I, as the Sponsor, charge for putting the deal together.
   b) *Debt Financing Fee:* The debt financing fee of $66,750, which is half of 1 percent of the acquisition/renovation loan amount of $13,350,00, is a financing charge and is part of the lender's profits on the loan.

Table 10.2   Pointer Ridge Plaza, Financial Analysis, Sources and Uses of Funds

POINTER RIDGE PLAZA
Bowie, Maryland
Financial Analysis
Sources and Uses of Funds

SOURCES OF FUNDS

EQUITY			
Investor I - Sponsor	25%	1,112,500	
Investor Group	75%	3,337,500	
TOTAL EQUITY			4,450,000
DEBT			
Acquisition & Construction Loan	75% LTC	13,350,000	
TOTAL DEBT			13,350,000
TOTAL SOURCES OF FUNDS			17,800,000

USES OF FUNDS

ACQUISTION COSTS			
Purchase of Property		10,200,000	
Broker's Commission		102,000	
TOTAL ACQUISTION COSTS			10,302,000
SETTLEMENT COSTS			276,598
POINTS AND FEES			
Acquisition Fee	1%	102,000	
Debt Financing Fee	0.50%	66,750	
Legal Corporate		150,000	
TOTAL POINTS AND FEES			318,750
HARD COSTS			
Façade Renovation		2,562,182	
Landscaping		150,000	
Paving		250,000	
Roofing		433,134	
Signage		120,000	
Site Amenities		50,000	
Space 20 - Pad Site		250,000	
Contingency	5%	190,766	
TOTAL HARD COSTS			4,006,082
SOFT COSTS			
Appraisal		9,425	
Architectural		120,000	
Civil Engineering		60,000	
Construction Management Fee	5%	200,304	
Environmental Cost		500,000	
Legal Land Use		150,000	
Legal Leasing		75,000	
Permits and Inspections		85,000	
Traffic Consultant		30,000	
Miscellaneous		100,000	
TOTAL SOFT COSTS			1,329,729
LC/TI [(1)]			
Leasing Commissions (6 Years)		810,761	
Tenant Improvements (6 Years)		462,420	
TOTAL LC/TI			1,273,181
WORKING CAPITAL RESERVE			293,661
TOTAL PROJECT COSTS			17,800,000

(1) Minimal leasing activity in the 1st two years

c) *Legal Corporate:* This line is an estimate of $150,000 for the legal partnership costs to set up the partnership, consummate the land acquisition, place debt on the property and raise the equity. The previous three items total $318,750.

4. *Hard Costs*: The hard cost of $4,006,082 is a substantial additional investment for a small center of only 71,808 square feet, but this center was in dire need of a major renovation, which entailed $2,562,182 to renovate the facade and to take care of several deferred maintenance items including a complete reroofing of the center and extensive parking lot resurfacing. Also, hard costs were allocated for signage on the new facade, added amenities, the build-out of a pad site and 5 percent contingency factor.

5. *Soft Costs*: The soft costs totaling $1,329,729 are also disproportional for a center of this size notwithstanding costly environmental remediation. Our initial due diligence revealed we needed to set aside half a million dollars to resolve an environmental issue caused by a former dry cleaning tenant. As a condition of the sale, the seller refused to accept an open-ended liability regarding this issue, but reduced the purchase by an amount that was much greater than the expected cost of the remediation. After meeting with representatives from the Maryland Environmental Agency and in revisiting my previous experiences with a similar issue, I decided to take the risk. I also received approval from my lender, who expressed confidence that the environmental issue could be easily resolved.

6. *Leasing Commissions/Tenant Improvements*: In this example, leasing commissions in the amount of $810,761 and tenant improvements in the amount of $462,420 are estimated amounts needed for the first four years of the deal for such expenses. Raising these funds as part of the initial equity does indeed require more equity than solely relying on future cash flow to fund these critical expenses. However, by raising this additional equity up front, the overall return for the partners will be slightly less than if these funds were borrowed or taken from cash flow. Conversely, the cash distributions during the first four years will be greater, and I have found that my partners prefer it this way.

7. *Working Capital Reserve*: I usually set aside a working capital reserve because at times bills have to be paid before the lender
makes the funds available. The amount set aside for the capital
reserve also allows me to round out the numbers so that the
overall plan, which in this case is a $17.8 million acquisition and
redevelopment project, appears as a logical round number with
the ability to fund contingent costs.

Now let us turn to the *Sources of Funds* section of Table 10.2. The *Total
Sources of Funds* line item is $17.8 million, which must coincide with the
line item titled *Total Uses of Funds*. The *Total Sources of Funds* section
should always equal the sum of the *Total Uses of Funds*.

We are assuming that we can obtain a loan of 75 percent of the total
costs needed for the acquisition and redevelopment. Therefore, the loan is
75 percent of $17.8 million, or $13,350,000. I will explain this in greater
detail in my review of the next chart.

In summary, the equity required is 25 percent of $17.8 million, or
$4,450,000. The Sponsor will be contributing 25 percent of the $4,450,000,
or $1,112,500.

The Investor Group can comprise any number of investors that in total
equals the required remaining equity investment of $3,337,500. This could
be 10 shares of $333,750, 12 shares of $278,125, or 15 shares of $222,500.

Table 10.3, *Pointer Ridge Plaza, Financing Capacity* on page 273, helps
us determine the maximum acquisition/renovation financing we can most
likely obtain.

As previously covered in the examples of ABC and XYZ Shopping Center, Financing Capacity (Table 7.5, p. 154, and Table 8.5, p. 182, respectively),
there are three calculations lenders make when reviewing your deal to determine how much they are going to lend you. These ratios are *Loan to
Cost, Loan to Value* and *Debt Service Coverage*. The lender will generally
lend on the calculation that shows the lowest loan amount that bring the
lowest levels of risk to the lender. Let us examine how these parameters
are used to estimate how much of the deal we can expect to finance,
which in turn reveals how much of the required capital will need to be
raised from the Equity Group.

Table 10.3   Pointer Ridge Plaza, Financing Capacity

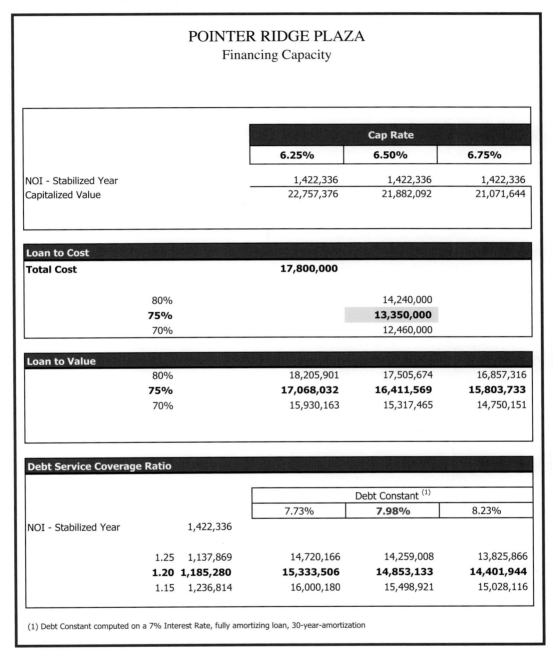

POINTER RIDGE PLAZA
Financing Capacity

	Cap Rate		
	6.25%	**6.50%**	**6.75%**
NOI - Stabilized Year	1,422,336	1,422,336	1,422,336
Capitalized Value	22,757,376	21,882,092	21,071,644

Loan to Cost

Total Cost	17,800,000
80%	14,240,000
75%	**13,350,000**
70%	12,460,000

Loan to Value

	6.25%	6.50%	6.75%
80%	18,205,901	17,505,674	16,857,316
75%	**17,068,032**	**16,411,569**	**15,803,733**
70%	15,930,163	15,317,465	14,750,151

Debt Service Coverage Ratio

		Debt Constant [1]		
		7.73%	**7.98%**	8.23%
NOI - Stabilized Year	1,422,336			
1.25	1,137,869	14,720,166	14,259,008	13,825,866
1.20	**1,185,280**	**15,333,506**	**14,853,133**	**14,401,944**
1.15	1,236,814	16,000,180	15,498,921	15,028,116

(1) Debt Constant computed on a 7% Interest Rate, fully amortizing loan, 30-year-amortization

1. *Loan to Cost*: We are assuming that the total project cost is $17.8 million and that the lender will lend 75 percent of the total project costs, or $13,350,000. In the past, some lenders have lent as much as 85 percent of total project costs, but in the 2008–2010 credit crunch, lenders took a much more conservative approach by lending no more than 65 percent of total project costs, if at all. However, for this center I estimated I could borrow 75 percent of the total capital required.

2. *Loan to Value*: The top of the chart shows the stabilized NOI, which I predicted would take place in Year 6. We then look at that NOI with three different cap rates in order to arrive at three possible values. With a stabilized NOI in Year 6 of $1,422,336, we show the probable values at $22,757,376 based on a cap rate of 6.25 percent, $21,882,092 at a cap rate of 6.5 percent and $21,071,644 using a cap rate of 6.75 percent.

    We then look at three different possible percentages that a lender might lend; for example, at 70 percent, 75 percent and 80 percent of value. This exercise shows nine possible loan amounts. Taking a realistic, albeit conservative approach, I projected that the lender would lend me 75 percent of the value derived from a cap rate of 6.5 percent, or $16,411,569.

3. *Debt Service Coverage Ratio (DSCR)*: This ratio is the amount of cash flow available to meet your annual interest and principal payments on debt. It is based on interest rate and amortization, after discounting for a margin of safety to make sure a borrower can pay the debt service on the loan.

As in the previous examples for ABC and XYZ Shopping Center, Financing Capacity (Table 7.5, p. 154, and Table 8.5, p. 182, respectively), the lender sets assumptions for interest rate and amortization, even if they are different from the rate it is charging you. Our assumption for the Pointer Ridge Plaza acquisition is that the lender would lend at a minimum interest rate of 7 percent, a minimum amortization of 30 years and a 1.20 coverage factor. Based on a stabilized sixth year NOI of $1,422,336, the lender would lend $14,853,133.

Thus, when we look at the three calculations, the lender on each of the three would lend:

Loan to Cost—$13,350,000
Loan to Value—$16,411,569
Debt Service Coverage Ratio—$14,853,133

This is the rationale for expecting that the lender will probably lend $13,350,000 after reviewing the three parameters. The loan-to-cost ratio results in the lowest amount the lender will consider lending in order to mitigate its risk on the debt.

Table 10.5, *Pointer Ridge Plaza, Financial Analysis, Expense Reimbursement Analysis* on page 277 shows tenant reimbursable expenses and revenue. Table 10.4, *Pointer Ridge Plaza, Financial Analysis, Schedule of Prospective Cash Flow* on page 276, shows the revenue and expenses and subsequent cash flow for an 11-year period. Why 11 years? I like to illustrate how the returns materialize on a redevelopment over the period of time it takes to complete the renovation and stabilize the property. This is usually five years, but I also like to show a 10-year time period as well.

For the Pointer Ridge Plaza redevelopment it will take six years to complete the renovation and the re-leasing mainly because of the expirations of existing leases, including lease options. In order to show a return for a 10-year period, I need to project the eleventh year because the sale price is based on the cap rate applied to the NOI budgeted for the 11th year—the year after the sale occurs to conform to industry standards.

The left column lists all the revenue categories, all the operating expense categories and the resulting NOI. It also depicts a list of the nonoperating expenses, net cash flow before debt service, debt service and cash flow after debt service. Let us review the financial results we are expecting each year starting with the acquisition:

- *Column Year 1*: While we can show the first column as a partial year as we did in previous examples and each succeeding year as a calendar year, in this schedule we are going to show each of the columns as full years on a fiscal year basis. There is no difference in the returns, just two different ways to show the numbers. In this example, we purchased the center on March 1, 2007 and thus column 1 is showing information for the fiscal year March 1, 2007–February 29, 2008.

Table 10.4 Pointer Ridge Plaza, Financial Analysis, Schedule of Prospective Cash Flow

POINTER RIDGE PLAZA
Bowie, Maryland
Financial Analysis
Schedule of Prospective Cash Flow

For the period ending	Rate	Feb-2008 Year 1	Feb-2009 Year 2	Feb-2010 Year 3	Feb-2011 Year 4	Feb-2012 Year 5	Feb-2013 Year 6 Stabilized	Feb-2014 Year 7	Feb-2015 Year 8	Feb-2016 Year 9	Feb-2017 Year 10	Feb-2018 Year 11
REVENUE												
Base Rental Revenue		635,760	505,699	656,076	1,012,254	1,293,447	1,430,536	1,449,485	1,474,249	1,559,149	1,597,736	1,635,824
Absorption & Turnover Vacancy		0	0	0	0	0	0	(9,738)	0	(18,294)	(8,266)	0
Percentage Rent		28,469	171,470	178,446	182,208	186,026	189,901	193,835	197,827	201,879	205,993	210,167
Common Area Maintenance		83,270	66,191	91,201	162,242	208,599	218,622	224,129	231,936	242,519	251,963	260,409
Real Estate Taxes		58,198	48,118	62,522	119,113	155,674	163,361	167,700	173,661	177,755	183,985	190,296
Insurance		7,402	6,752	6,866	10,770	12,753	13,148	13,485	13,950	14,761	15,359	15,870
Miscellaneous		0	0	0	0	0	0	0	0	0	0	0
TOTAL POTENTIAL GROSS REVENUE		813,099	798,230	995,111	1,486,587	1,856,499	2,015,568	2,038,896	2,091,623	2,177,769	2,246,770	2,312,566
Collection Loss/Additional Vacancy	4%	(32,524)	(31,929)	(39,804)	(59,463)	(74,260)	(80,623)	(81,556)	(83,665)	(87,111)	(89,871)	(92,503)
EFFECTIVE GROSS REVENUE		780,575	766,301	955,307	1,427,124	1,782,239	1,934,945	1,957,340	2,007,958	2,090,658	2,156,899	2,220,063
OPERATING EXPENSES												
Common Area Maintenance	$2.01	145,000	159,650	196,266	202,154	208,219	214,466	220,900	227,527	234,352	241,383	248,625
Insurance	$0.16	11,300	11,639	11,988	12,348	12,718	13,100	13,493	13,898	14,315	14,744	15,186
Real Estate Taxes	$1.62	117,000	140,000	157,000	161,710	166,561	171,558	176,705	182,006	187,466	193,090	198,883
Management Fees	5%	39,029	38,315	47,765	71,356	89,112	96,747	97,867	100,398	104,533	107,845	111,003
General and Administration	$0.10	7,219	7,435	7,659	7,888	8,125	8,369	8,620	8,878	9,145	9,419	9,702
Legal and Accounting	$0.10	7,219	7,435	7,659	7,888	8,125	8,369	8,620	8,878	9,145	9,419	9,702
Advertising and Promotion		0	0	0	0	0	0	0	0	0	0	0
TOTAL OPERATING EXPENSES		326,767	364,474	428,337	463,344	492,860	512,609	526,205	541,585	558,956	575,900	593,101
NET OPERATING INCOME		453,808	401,827	526,970	963,780	1,289,379	1,422,336	1,431,135	1,466,373	1,531,702	1,580,999	1,626,962
NON OPERATING EXPENSES												
Partnership Supervisory Fee	1%	7,806	7,663	9,553	14,271	17,822	19,349	19,573	20,080	20,907	21,569	22,201
Tenant Improvements		0	0	0	0	0	0	4,500	0	7,438	3,375	0
Leasing Commissions		0	0	0	0	0	0	39,730	0	56,626	25,584	0
Capital Improvement Reserves	$0.50	0	0	0	0	0	36,095	36,095	36,095	36,095	36,095	36,095
TOTAL NONOPERATING EXPENSES		7,806	7,663	9,553	14,271	17,822	55,444	99,898	56,175	121,066	86,623	58,296
NET CASH FLOW BEFORE DEBT SERVICE		446,002	394,164	517,417	949,509	1,271,557	1,366,892	1,331,237	1,410,198	1,410,636	1,494,376	1,568,666
ADDITIONAL FUNDS												
Proceeds from Refinancing		0	0	0	0	0	0	0	0	0	0	0
Lease Termination Fee (Giant)		0	281,000	0	0	0	0	133,500	0	0	0	0
Proceeds from Working Capital		0	0	0	0	0	0	0	0	0	0	0
TOTAL ADDITIONAL FUNDS		0	281,000	0	0	0	0	133,500	0	0	0	0
DEBT SERVICE												
Interest Payments		347,100	373,800	400,500	469,920	496,620	534,000	939,506	929,605	918,988	907,603	895,395
Principal Payments		0	0	0	0	0	38,250	136,967	146,868	157,485	168,870	181,077
Origination Points and Fees		0	0	0	0	38,250	0	133,500	0	0	0	0
TOTAL DEBT SERVICE		347,100	373,800	400,500	469,920	534,870	572,250	1,209,973	1,076,473	1,076,473	1,076,473	1,076,473
NET CASH FLOW AFTER DEBT SERVICE		98,902	301,364	116,917	479,589	736,687	794,642	254,764	333,725	334,163	417,903	492,193
NOI/Total Project Cost		2.55%	2.26%	2.96%	5.41%	7.24%	7.99%	8.04%	8.24%	8.61%	8.88%	9.14%
Cash-on-Cash Return		2.22%	6.77%	2.63%	10.78%	16.55%	17.86%	5.73%	7.50%	7.51%	9.39%	11.06%

Table 10.5 Pointer Ridge Plaza, Financial Analysis, Expense Reimbursement Analysis

POINTER RIDGE PLAZA
Bowie, Maryland
Financial Analysis
Expense Reimbursement Analysis

	Feb-2008 Year 1	Feb-2009 Year 2	Feb-2010 Year 3	Feb-2011 Year 4	Feb-2012 Year 5	Feb-2013 Year 6	Feb-2014 Year 7	Feb-2015 Year 8	Feb-2016 Year 9	Feb-2017 Year 10	Feb-2018 Year 11
OPERATING EXPENSES											
CAM	145,000	159,650	196,266	202,154	208,219	214,466	220,900	227,527	234,352	241,383	248,625
TAXES	117,000	140,000	157,000	161,710	166,561	171,558	176,705	182,006	187,466	193,090	198,883
INSURANCE	11,300	11,639	11,988	12,348	12,718	13,100	13,493	13,898	14,315	14,744	15,186
TOTAL	273,300	311,289	365,254	376,212	387,498	399,124	411,098	423,431	436,133	449,217	462,694
REIMBURSEMENT REVENUE											
CAM	83,270	66,191	91,201	162,242	208,599	218,622	224,129	231,936	242,519	251,963	260,409
TAXES	58,198	48,118	62,522	119,113	155,674	163,361	167,700	173,661	177,755	183,985	190,296
INSURANCE	7,402	6,752	6,866	10,770	12,753	13,148	13,485	13,950	14,761	15,359	15,870
TOTAL	148,870	121,061	160,589	292,125	377,026	395,131	405,314	419,547	435,035	451,307	466,575
PERCENTAGE OF EXPENSES REIMBURSED											
CAM	57.43%	41.46%	46.47%	80.26%	100.18%	101.94%	101.46%	101.94%	103.48%	104.38%	104.74%
TAXES	49.74%	34.37%	39.82%	73.66%	93.46%	95.22%	94.90%	95.41%	94.82%	95.28%	95.68%
INSURANCE	65.50%	58.01%	57.27%	87.22%	100.28%	100.37%	99.94%	100.37%	103.12%	104.17%	104.50%
TOTAL	54.47%	38.89%	43.97%	77.65%	97.30%	99.00%	98.59%	99.08%	99.75%	100.47%	100.84%

During this first year, we work on our renovation drawings and further defining the work we will be doing as part of our renovation. We have allocated a certain amount of dollars for our renovation, and we need to make sure as we start further defining costs with all our consultants and contractors that we are getting the "biggest bang for the buck." We also begin working with the Maryland Environmental Protection Agency on how to remediate the center's environmental issues. We start discussions with our anchor tenant, Giant Food, to determine its plans for leaving the center and if it chooses to do so, we try to ascertain how much we can get from the tenant in lease cancellation fees attributed to its early closing. We would want this amount to at least compensate the landlord for the following: the loss in anchor rent during the downtime, any negative impact on rents for adjacent specialty tenant leases and the cost to re-lease the space. As expected, the anchor confirmed its intent to leave the center when the lease term expires. At this early stage of the first year, we do not yet have any rent increases in place or any tenant remerchandising shown.

- *Column Year 2*: In comparing the first year results with this second year, the base rental revenue is substantially reduced from the first year because we anticipated making a deal to allow Giant Food to terminate its lease. In return the tenant paid us a termination fee of $281,000, which is shown toward the bottom of the second column under *Additional Funds—Lease Termination Fee (Giant)*. However, the *Effective Gross Revenue* remained about the same as Year 1 because we projected CVS to pay $150,000 in percentage rent and about $21,470 in percentage rent from other specialty tenants. As CVS pays percentage rent in arrears and all accounting is on a cash basis and not an accrual basis, Column Year 1 did not show percentage rent as the seller received the percentage rent that was paid in the first year as it covered the time period when the seller owned the property. The projected cash-on-cash return available to distribute after debt service is 6.77 percent because of the Giant Food termination fee. However, without the termination fee, the return would have been about 2 percent, which is consistent with Year 1.

- *Column Year 3:* This is the first year we project that the shopping center will be operating for a full year after the renovation is completed. However, while we have planned to renegotiate the leases for some of the smaller spaces in the center, and plan to re-lease the Giant Food anchor space, the replacement anchor tenant will not be paying rent for any part of Year 3, the fiscal year ending February 2010.

- *Column Year 4*: This year the new anchor tenant is projected to pay rent, but not for the full year. However, we continue to lease or renew small shop leases at higher rents, either to existing tenants or new tenants. This pro forma provides for several tenant spaces that have not yet come up for renewal at higher rents, but enough rollover has occurred and rent on the anchor space is being paid, showing a substantial increases in revenue. The return on equity increases from 2.63 percent in Year 3 to 10.78 percent in Year 4, when the income has begun to stabilize.

- *Column Year 5*: This is the first year that the anchor tenant is projected to pay a full year's rent, the renovation is complete and the rents continue to increase as tenant leases with below-market rents expire and are replaced at market. The net cash flow after debt service continues to increase, with the return on the equity investment increasing to 16.55 percent, even with an assumed higher interest rate and an amortization that is required to extend the commercial bank loan.

- *Column Year 6*: While rents are expected to continue to increase in future years as well, Year 6 is the last year when most of the submarket leases have expired and have been re-leased at higher market rents. The net cash flow after debt continues to increase, with the return on the equity investment increasing to an extraordinary 17.86 percent despite an assumed higher interest rate and an amortization that is required to extend the commercial bank loan for a second extension period.

- *Columns Year 7 through Year 11*: In Year 7, we expect to place a permanent loan on the property and pay off the commercial loan that I personally guaranteed. While I am willing to guarantee the nonrecourse carve-outs on the replacement permanent loan, I will not personally guarantee the debt repayments. Another feature of moving to permanent financing is that the fixed interest rate is assumed to be substantially higher on the permanent loan than the floating rate pegged over Libor for Years 1 through Year 7. Also, we will experience amortization on the loan to help pay down the principal, which was not the case during the time period of the commercial bank loan in Year 1 through Year 4 but was in Years 5 and 6, although not at the same amount as in the permanent loan. As a result, the cash available for distribution in Year 7 through Year 11 will be lower than the return planned in the peak year, Year 6, when the income was stabilized. Accordingly, the returns achieved when taking into consideration the annual cash distributions and amortization increases in Year 7 through Year 11 are perfectly good returns for this level of risk.

Now look at Table 10.6, *Pointer Ridge Plaza, Distribution of Cash Flow,* page 281, which shows the accrual of cash distributions and previously distributed share of cash flow.

- *Column Year 1*: The results for this year depicts the first year of operation of March 1, 2007, through February 29, 2008. The net cash flow for this first year is $98,902. The 8 percent preferred return on the equity investment of $4,450,000 is $356,000. The difference of $257,098, the *Remaining Unpaid Preferred Return,* will cumulate and carry over to the next year, Year 2.
- *Column Year 2*: The second year's cash flow is $301,364. The cash flow is still insufficient to pay the 8 percent preferred return of $356,000. The difference between $356,000 and $301,364, which equals $54,636, is the unpaid preferred return. We add this deficiency to the first year's unpaid preferred return [$257,098 + $54,636 = $311,734]. Thus, at the end of the second year, the *Remaining Unpaid Preferred Return* is $311,734.
- *Column Year 3*: The cash flow in Year 3 is $116,917. Note that this cash flow has fallen compared to Year 2 despite an increase in rental income because we do not yet show income from the Giant Food lease termination as we did in Year 2. Refer back to Table 10.4

Table 10.6 Pointer Ridge Plaza, Distribution of Cash Flow

POINTER RIDGE PLAZA
Distribution of Cash Flow

Sharing of Cash Flow Distribution
◆ 8% Cumulative Noncompounded Return to Equity
◆

Cash Equity	4,450,000	Investor 1 - Sponsor	25%
Cash Equity Preferred Return	8%	Investor Group	75%

For the years ending	Feb-2008 Year 1	Feb-2009 Year 2	Feb-2010 Year 3	Feb-2011 Year 4	Feb-2012 Year 5	Feb-2013 Year 6	Feb-2014 Year 7	Feb-2015 Year 8	Feb-2016 Year 9	Feb-2017 Year 10	Feb-2018 Year 11
Net Cash Flow	**98,902**	**301,364**	**116,917**	**479,589**	**736,687**	**794,642**	**254,764**	**333,725**	**334,163**	**417,903**	**492,193**
Distribution Level 1											
Cash Equity (8%)	4,450,000	4,450,000	4,450,000	4,450,000	4,450,000	4,450,000	4,450,000	4,450,000	4,450,000	4,450,000	4,450,000
Preferred Return	356,000	356,000	356,000	356,000	356,000	356,000	356,000	356,000	356,000	356,000	356,000
Cumulative Unpaid Preferred Return	356,000	613,098	667,734	906,817	783,228	402,541	356,000	457,236	479,511	501,347	439,444
Cash Distribution - Level 1	**98,902**	**301,364**	**116,917**	**479,589**	**736,687**	**402,541**	**254,764**	**333,725**	**334,163**	**417,903**	**439,444**
Remaining Unpaid Preferred Return	257,098	311,734	550,817	427,228	46,541	0	101,236	123,511	145,347	83,444	0
Excess Funds	**0**	**0**	**0**	**0**	**0**	**392,101**	**0**	**0**	**0**	**0**	**52,749**
Distribution Level 2											
Investor 1 - Sponsor (50%)	0	0	0	0	0	196,050	0	0	0	0	26,375
Investor Group (50%)	0	0	0	0	0	196,050	0	0	0	0	26,375
Total - Distribution Level 2	**0**	**0**	**0**	**0**	**0**	**196,050**	**0**	**0**	**0**	**0**	**26,375**
Summary of Distributions											
Investor 1 - Sponsor	24,725	75,341	29,229	119,897	184,172	296,686	63,691	83,431	83,541	104,476	136,236
Investor Group	74,176	226,023	87,688	359,692	552,515	497,956	191,073	250,294	250,622	313,427	355,958
TOTAL	**98,902**	**301,364**	**116,917**	**479,589**	**736,687**	**794,642**	**254,764**	**333,725**	**334,163**	**417,903**	**492,193**

on page 276. The cash flow continues to fall short of meeting the annual preferred return of 8 percent, or $356,000. The difference between the cash flow of $116,917 and the preferred return of $356,000 is $239,083. We add that difference to the prior unpaid preferred return [$311,734 + $239,083 = $550,817]. Thus, at the end of the third year, the *Remaining Unpaid Preferred Return* is $550,817.

- *Column Year 4*: The cash flow in Year 4 is $479,589. That cash flow now exceeds the annual preferred return of 8 percent or $356,000. The difference between the cash flow of $479,589 and the preferred return of $356,000 is $123,589. We subtract that difference from the prior unpaid preferred return [$550,817 – $123,589 = ($427,228)]. Thus, at the end of the fourth year, the *Remaining Unpaid Preferred Return* is $427,228.

- *Column Year 5*: The cash flow in Year 5 now rises to $736,687. This cash flow now exceeds the annual preferred return of 8 percent or $356,000. The difference between the cash flow of $736,687 and the preferred return of $356,000 is $380,687. We subtract that difference from the prior unpaid preferred return [$427,228 – $380,687 = $46,541]. Thus, at the end of the fifth year, the *Remaining Unpaid Preferred Return* is $46,541.

- *Column Year 6*: The cash flow in Year 6 is $794,642. Cash flow continues to exceed the annual preferred return of 8 percent, or $356,000. The difference between the cash flow of $794,642 and the preferred return of $356,000 is $438,642. We subtract that difference from the prior unpaid preferred return [$46,541 – $438,642 = ($392,101)]. Thus, at the end of the sixth year, there is no *Remaining Unpaid Preferred Return;* instead, there are *Excess Funds* of $392,101. These additional funds are distributed 50 percent, or $196,050, to the Investor Group and 50 percent, or $196,050, to you as Investor I-the Sponsor.

- *Column Year 7*: Please note that starting in Year 7 the cash distribution is $254,764, less than 8 percent, or $356,000, which is the preferred return. This is because in Year 7 we are projecting to place a permanent loan that assumes a higher interest rate and a larger amortization than in previous years. As a result, we have less cash available for distribution in this pro forma. This will cause a shortfall to start accruing again. There is no requirement for the Sponsor to return any part of the extra distribution received in Year 6. It is not until Year 11 that the 8 percent preferred return will again catch up in order to have sufficient extra cash flow to be distributed to the Sponsor.

Please see Table 10.7, *Pointer Ridge Plaza, Internal Rate of Return for Refinancing/Sale Proceeds, Year 6 (Feb-2013)*, page 284. This schedule assumes the shopping center will be sold at the end of the sixth year. It shows the distribution of sale proceeds and the percentage return that the Investor Group is expected to receive.

1. *Initial Equity Investment*
    a) Shows the Sponsor has invested 25 percent of the equity investment of $4,450,000, or $1,112,500
    b) Shows the Investor Group has invested 75 percent of the equity investment of $4,450,000, or $3,337,500
2. *Deductions from Sales Price/Additions to Sales Proceeds*
    a) Shows the *NOI* in Year 7 as $1,431,135, which will determine the sale price by applying a cap rate to the NOI on the year going forward from the expected sale date of Day 1 of Year 7
    b) *Loan Balance* is the same as the original loan amount, as the loan was interest-only during the acquisition/renovation of the shopping center. An interest-only commercial bank loan usually covers a set term, such as three to five years, possibly with one or two one-year extensions. The borrower pays only the interest on the principal balance, with the principal balance unchanged. At the end of the interest-only term, a borrower must refinance either as an interest-only mortgage, pay the principal or convert the debt to a principal-and-interest (amortized) loan whereby monthly mortgage payments help to reduce the principal over time.

Table 10.7   Pointer Ridge Plaza, Financial Analysis, Internal Rate of Return for Refinancing/Sale Proceeds, Year 6 (Feb. 2013)

POINTER RIDGE PLAZA

Bowie, Maryland

Financial Analysis

Internal Rate of Return for Refinancing/Sale Proceeds

Year 6 - Feb. 2013

Initial Equity Investment		
Investor I - Sponsor	25%	1,112,500
Investor Group	75%	3,337,500
Total Equity Investment		4,450,000

NOI Year 7	1,431,135	
Loan Balance end of Year 6	13,350,000	

Deductions from Sales Price		Additions to Sales Proceeds	
Estimated Cost of Sale	1.5%	Cash Flow Y6	794,642
Exit Fees (Lender)	0%	Working Capital Reserve	293,661
		Real Estate Tax Escrow	0
		Insurance Escrow	0
		Total Additions	1,088,303

Capitalization Rate		6.25%	6.50%	6.75%
Projected Sales Price		**22,898,160**	**22,017,462**	**21,202,000**
Additions to Sales Proceeds		1,088,303	1,088,303	1,088,303
Deductions From Sale		(343,472)	(330,262)	(318,030)
Loan Balance		(13,350,000)	(13,350,000)	(13,350,000)
Net Proceeds from Sale		**10,292,990**	**9,425,502**	**8,622,273**
Cash Flow Y6		(794,642)	(794,642)	(794,642)
Cumulative Nonpaid Return to Equity Group		0	0	0
Return of Equity Group Initial Investment		(4,450,000)	(4,450,000)	(4,450,000)
Balance to Be Distributed		**5,048,348**	**4,180,860**	**3,377,631**
Distribution to All Equity Investors				
Investor I - Sponsor	50%	2,524,174	2,090,430	1,688,815
Investor Group	50%	2,524,174	2,090,430	1,688,815

Rate of Return for Investor Group			
Total Proceeds to Investor Group	**6,359,630**	**5,925,886**	**5,524,272**
Annual Rate of Return	21.58%	19.42%	17.41%
IRR (compounded annually)	16.14%	14.99%	13.86%
Initial Investment	(3,337,500)	(3,337,500)	(3,337,500)
Year 1 - Feb-2008	74,176	74,176	74,176
Year 2 - Feb-2009	226,023	226,023	226,023
Year 3 - Feb-2010	87,688	87,688	87,688
Year 4 - Feb-2011	359,692	359,692	359,692
Year 5 - Feb-2012	552,515	552,515	552,515
Year 6 - Feb-2013	6,359,630	5,925,886	5,524,272

*Distribution of Sales Proceeds
1. Any unpaid preferred 8% annual cumulative, noncompounded return *pari passu*
2. Return of Net Capital Investment
3. 50% to Investor Group/50% to Promote (Sponsor)

c) *Estimated Cost of Sale*, including all transfer charges, sales commission, legal fees, etc., are planned here to aggregate to 1.5 percent of the sale price.

d) *Working Capital Reserve* is the same as in the initial *Sources and Uses of Funds*, $293,661.

e) *Cash Flow Year 6* is the cash flow that is assumed to be distributed upon settlement of disposition of the shopping center, $794,642.

3. *Capitalization Rate*

a) *Sale Price,* and thus distributions and returns, are based on three assumptions of cap rates. The middle column is the cap rate that I project will be the market rate (6.5 percent). The lower cap rate (6.25 percent) is more aggressive and the higher cap rate (6.75 percent) is more conservative on the part of the seller.

b) *Projected Sales Price*: Here we take the NOI in Year 7 and divide it by the cap rate to derive the *Sale Price*. ($1,413,135 / 6.25% = $22,898,160, $1,431,135 / 6.5% = $22,017,462 and $1,413,135 / 6.75% = $21,202,000)

c) *Net Proceeds from Sale* is the sale price plus the working capital reserve, plus the cash flow in Year 6, less the cost of sale and less the loan balance.

d) *Balance to be distributed* is the *Net Proceeds* from the sale, less the cash flow from Year 6, and less the return of the Equity Group's initial investment. Here we show no shortfall on the 8 percent preferred return.

The balance is distributed 50 percent to the Investor Group and 50 percent to Investor I-the Sponsor.

e) *Rate of Return for Equity Investors* is the rate of return the Investor Group receives. These returns are shown as *Annual Rate of Return* and *Internal Rate of Return (IRR)*.

f) *Annual Rate of Return* equals the distributions divided by the equity investment with the result divided by the number of years of the development. For the middle column where the cap rate is 6.5 percent, the distributions over six years are:

$74,176	*Year 1 distributions*
+ $226,023	*Year 2 distributions*
+ $87,688	*Year 3 distributions*
+ $359,692	*Year 4 distributions*
+ $552,515	*Year 5 distributions*
+ $5,925,886[1]	*Year 6 distributions*
= $7,225,980	*Total distributions*
−$3,337,500	*Subtract the Investor Group's investment*
= $3,888,480	*Subtotal*
÷ $3,337,500	*The Investor Group's investment*
= 1.16508764	*Subtotal*
÷ 6	*Years of holding period*
= 19.42%	*Annual rate of return*

Note[1]: distribution of $5,925,886 in Year 6 =

$497,956	*Cash flow distribution to Investor Group in Year 6 (See previous table, Distribution of Cash Flow, Table 10.6, page 281)*
+ $3,337,500	*The full return of the Investor Group's investment*
+ $2,090,430	*50% distribution to the Investor Group as shown on chart*
= $5,925,886	*Subtotal*

g) *Internal Rate of Return (IRR):* The IRR compounded annually is 14.99 percent.

Please turn to Table 10.8, *Internal Rate of Return for Refinancing/Sale Proceeds, Year 10 (Feb. 2017)*, page 287. In this example for Pointer Ridge Plaza, we are projecting a hypothetical sale after 10 years of ownership instead of six years as illustrated in the previous Table 10.7 on page 284.

In order to determine the shopping center's projected sale price at the end of Year 10 for the sake of deriving at a distribution of equity in the event of a sale or refinancing, we again focus on the two most important measures

Table 10.8 Pointer Ridge Plaza, Financial Analysis, Internal Rate of Return for Refinancing/Sale Proceeds, Year 10 (Feb-2017)

POINTER RIDGE PLAZA

Bowie, Maryland

Financial Analysis

Internal Rate of Return for Refinancing/Sale Proceeds

Year 10 - Feb-2017

Initial Equity Investment		
Investor I - Sponsor	25%	1,112,500
Investor Group	75%	3,337,500
Total Equity Investment		4,450,000

NOI Year 11	1,626,962	
Loan Balance End of Year 10	12,873,311	

Deductions from Sales Price		**Additions to Sales Proceeds**	
Estimated Cost of Sale	1.5%	Cash Flow Y10	473,652
Exit Fees (Lender)	0%	Working Capital Reserve	293,661
		Real Estate Tax Escrow	0
		Insurance Escrow	0
		Total Additions	767,313

Capitalization Rate	**6.25%**	**6.50%**	**6.75%**
Projected Sales Price	26,031,392	25,030,185	24,103,141
Additions to Sales Proceeds	767,313	767,313	767,313
Deductions From Sale	(390,471)	(375,453)	(361,547)
Loan Balance	(12,873,311)	(12,873,311)	(12,873,311)
Net Proceeds from Sale	13,534,924	12,548,734	11,635,596
Cash Flow Y10	(473,652)	(473,652)	(473,652)
Cumulative Nonpaid Return to Equity Group	(83,444)	(83,444)	(83,444)
Return of Equity Group Initial Investment	(4,450,000)	(4,450,000)	(4,450,000)
Balance to Be Distributed	8,527,827	7,541,638	6,628,500
Distribution to All Equity Investors			
Investor I - Sponsor 50%	4,263,914	3,770,819	3,314,250
Investor Group 50%	4,263,914	3,770,819	3,314,250

Rate of Return for Investor Group			
Total Proceeds to Investor Group	7,977,424	7,484,330	7,027,760
Annual Rate of Return	21.36%	19.89%	18.52%
IRR (compounded annually)	14.34%	13.78%	13.23%
Initial Investment	(3,337,500)	(3,337,500)	(3,337,500)
Year 1 - Feb-2008	74,176	74,176	74,176
Year 2 - Feb-2009	226,023	226,023	226,023
Year 3 - Feb-2010	87,688	87,688	87,688
Year 4 - Feb-2011	359,692	359,692	359,692
Year 5 - Feb-2012	552,515	552,515	552,515
Year 6 - Feb-2013	497,956	497,956	497,956
Year 7 - Feb-2014	191,073	191,073	191,073
Year 8 - Feb-2015	250,294	250,294	250,294
Year 9 - Feb-2016	250,622	250,622	250,622
Year 10 - Feb-2017	7,977,424	7,484,330	7,027,760

*Distribution of Sales Proceeds
 1. Any unpaid preferred 8% annual cumulative, noncompounded return *pari passu*
 2. Return of Net Capital Investment
 3. 50% to Investor Group/50% to Promote (Sponsor)

of value: the NOI projected in Year 11, which is $1,626,962, and the loan balance at the end of Year 10, which is $12,873,311.

In this example, we also projected a cap rate of 6.5 percent to capitalize the NOI in order to determine the projected value at the end of the 10th year. As cap rates vary with market conditions, we show three cap rates scenarios: 6.25, 6.5 and 6.75 percent.

The result of dividing each of the three cap rates by the projected NOI gives us three projected sale prices respectively, $26,031,392 using the 6.25 percent cap rate, $25,030,185 using the 6.5 percent cap rate and $24,103,141 using the 6.75 percent cap rate.

In this transaction, we will estimate most of the deductions from the sale price as well as additions to the sale proceeds to be the same as our example for a sale at the end of the sixth year with exception of the cash flow for the last year; in this case, Year 10 is $473,652. This gives us total additions of $767,313, which includes the working capital reserve of $293,661.

Note how these additions and deductions affect the net proceeds from the sale. Using the 6.25 percent cap rate, we projected net proceeds of $13,534,924. Using the 6.5 percent cap rate, we projected net proceeds of $12,548,734 and $11,635,596 when using the 6.75 percent cap rate. By holding the investment for 10 years as compared to 6, we benefit from a higher sale price at the end of the term as well as receiving our returns on the investment each year through the sharing of excess cash flow.

How do we distribute the proceeds in this example? Exactly in half, 50 percent to the Investor Group and 50 percent to the Sponsor.

1. *Annual Rate of Return* equals the distributions divided by the equity investment with the result divided by the number of years of the development. For the middle column, where the cap rate is 6.5 percent, the distributions over six years are:

$74,176	*Year 1 distributions*
+ $226,023	*Year 2 distributions*
+ $87,688	*Year 3 distributions*
+ $359,692	*Year 4 distributions*
+ $552,515	*Year 5 distributions*
+ $497,956	*Year 6 distributions*

+ $191,073	Year 7 distributions
+ $250,294	Year 8 distributions
+ $250,622	Year 9 distributions
+ $7,484,330 [1]	Year 10 distributions
= $9,974,639	Total distributions
− $3,337,500	Subtract the Investor Group's investment
= $6,637,139	Subtotal
÷ $3,337,500	The Investor Group's investment
= 1.9886558	Subtotal
÷ 10	Years of holding period
= 19.89%	Annual rate of return

Note[1] distribution of $7,484,330 in Year 10 =

$313,427	Cash flow distribution to Investor Group in Year 10 (See previous table, Internal Rate of Return for Refinancing/ Sale Proceeds, Table 10.7, page 284)
+ $62,584	75% of cumulative unpaid return
+ $3,337,500	The full return of the Investor Group's investment
+ $3,770,819	50% distribution to the Investor Group as shown on chart
= $7,484,330	Subtotal

2) *Internal Rate of Return (IRR):* The IRR compounded annually is 13.78 percent.

Please refer to Table 10.4, *Schedule of Prospective Cash Flow*, page 276. In determining the Effective Gross Revenue, you would need to analyze the rents achieved prior to the acquisition not only for every leasable space in the shopping center but also the future rents you could likely achieve once the present leases and any options have expired.

Now, turn to Table 10.9, *Financial Analysis, Tenant Assumptions*, page 291. In this table, we list every space at the shopping center. For each space,

Pointer Ridge Plaza, CVS/pharmacy

we look at the retail classification of the tenant presently leasing the space, the square footage, the current rent, the lease term with options and without options, what we think the market rate would be for that space if the space were vacant, what we would need to spend to convert the space into a leasable condition to re-lease it and how much of an inducement in tenant allowance we would need to give a prospective tenant to lease the space.

In this case study, we are dealing with a center that has deep spaces with narrow storefronts. We are planning to reconfigure some of the spaces to create larger spaces so we can have more desirable leasable space. This will result in a fewer number of tenants with a total of the same square footage when the plan is fully implemented.

The assumptions in this table are chief among the assumptions you will make in crafting your pre-acquisition pro forma because they will shape your long-standing rental performance.

Table 10.9   Pointer Ridge Plaza, Tenant Assumptions

POINTER RIDGE PLAZA
Bowie, Maryland
Financial Analysis
Tenant Assumptions

Unit	Tenant	Sq Ft	Modified Sq Ft [3]	Current Rent PSF	Annual Rent	Expiration Date	Future Assumptions	RCD [1]	Delivery	Term	Market Rent PSF	Market Rent	TI	TA	TI (Total)	TA (Total)
01	Pizza Hut	2,975				04/30/10	Tenant will exercise one 5-year option at fixed rent	05/01/10	As-Is	5 Years	30.00	89,250	0.00	0.00	0	0
02	Giant	34,334				Early Termination	Tenant will terminate Lease 04/08. New Tenant effective RCD.	07/01/10	As-Is	20 Years	13.25	454,926	0.00	0.00	0	0
03 [2]	Edible Arrangements	1,800				09/30/13	Tenant will renew at market rent	10/01/13	N/A	5 Years	28.00	50,400	0.00	5.56	0	10,000
04	Barber Shop	750				12/31/10	Tenant will vacate 12/31/10 - Space will be reconfigured	N/A								
06	Star Nails	1,210				12/31/08	Tenant will extend Lease through 12/31/10 at same terms and conditions	01/01/09	As-Is	2 Years	22.76	27,540	0.00	0.00	0	0
05	Vacant	750				N/A	Space will remain vacant through 12/31/10	N/A								
10	Vacant (Storage)	1,200				N/A	Space will remain vacant through 12/31/10	N/A								
RECONFIGURATION OF SPACES 04, 05, 06, 10 AS OF 01/01/11 (See Below)																
04/05/06/10	Vacant as of 12/31/10		1,955			N/A	Reconfiguration of Spaces 04/05/06/10 - New Barber Shop	05/01/11	White Box	10 Years	30.00	58,650	40.00	0.00	78,200	0
04/05/06/10	Vacant as of 12/31/10		1,955			N/A	Reconfiguration of Spaces 04/05/06/10 - New Nail Salon	05/01/11	As-Is [4]	10 Years	30.00	58,650	0.00	20.00	0	39,100
07	Audio	1,080				03/31/09	Tenant will vacate 03/31/09 - New Retail Tenant	07/01/09	As-Is	10 Years	31.00	33,480	0.00	20.00	0	21,600
08	Vacant	1,620				N/A	New Tenant (Concept Deli)	04/01/09	As-Is	10 Years	33.00	53,460	0.00	20.00	0	32,400
09	Beijing Restaurant	1,350				10/31/11	Tenant will renew at market rent	11/01/11	N/A	5 Years	29.00	39,150	0.00	0.00	0	0
11	Pointer Ridge Florist	1,800				MTM	Tenant will vacate 03/31/09 - New Retail Tenant	06/01/09	As-Is	10 Years	26.00	46,800	0.00	20.00	0	36,000
12	CVS	12,055				12/31/09 [6]	Tenant will renew at same terms and conditions	01/01/10	As-Is	10 Years	12.22	147,312	0.00	0.00	0	0
13	CVS (Storage)	1,025				12/31/09 [5]	Tenant will renew at market rent	01/01/10	As-Is	10 Years	14.79	15,160	0.00	0.00	0	0
14	Vacant	2,240				N/A	New Tenant (Concept Mattress Store)	03/01/09	As-Is	10 Years	24.00	53,760	0.00	35.00	0	78,400
15	Phase Salon	1,250				04/30/09	Tenant will vacate 04/30/09 - New Tenant (Concept Salon)	08/01/09	As-Is	10 Years	29.00	36,250	0.00	35.00	0	43,750
16	Vacant	1,290				N/A	New Tenant (Packaging Store)	05/01/09	CDS	10 Years	27.00	34,830	8.00	35.00	10,320	45,150
17	Pointer Ridge Liquor	2,000				12/31/10	Tenant will renew at market rent	01/01/11	N/A	10 Years	26.00	52,000	0.00	0.00	0	0
18	PNC Bank	1,500				10/31/09	Tenant will vacate 10/31/09 - New Tenant (Concept Bank)	06/01/10	As-Is	10 Years	33.00	49,500	0.00	45.00	0	67,500
19	Modern Laundry	1,500				10/31/13	Tenant will exercise one 5-year option at fixed rent	11/01/13	N/A	5 Years	31.00	46,500	0.00	0.00	0	0
20	Available Pad (Up to 1,500 s.f)	460				N/A	New Restaurant	01/01/12	Pad Site	10 Years		100,000	0.00	0.00	0	0
TOTAL		**72,189**										**1,447,617**			**88,520**	**373,900**

[1] RCD = Rent Commencement Date - Includes any downtime necessary for delivery and fixturing period. For Options and Extensions date is the next day after the termination date.
[2] Initial Rent is $___ psf, upon completion of renovation rent will increase to $___ psf.
[3] Total square footages for the reconfiguration spaces 04, 05, 06 and 10 remain the same (3,910 sq ft).
[4] Delivery will be as-is with demising wall. Cost for the demising wall is included in the adjacent barber shop space.
[5] Expiration date for the Storage space 03/31/09 for the purposes of this analysis assumed that the lease will be coterminus wi th the CVS Store
[6] Base Rent at $___ PSF and Percentage Rent 4% over $150 PSF of Sales

(RENT INFORMATION OMITTED FOR CONFIDENTIALITY)

Please refer to Table 10.10, *Pointer Ridge Plaza, Assumptions to Financial Analysis*, page 293. This table lists the basic assumptions to the financial analysis depicted previously. Among the key assumptions is an acquisition/re-development loan of $13,350,000 for four years at a rate of 30-day Libor + 215 basis points, a floor of 4.0 percent interest (assuming Libor + spread will not exceed floor), interest only and a fee of 50 basis points of the loan amount. The loan has two one-year options with terms and conditions as explained in the table. This loan was obtained from a commercial bank, which I personally guaranteed.

Subsequent to the acquisition/redevelopment loan—assuming I have not sold the property at the beginning of the seventh year—I plan to place a ten-year permanent nonrecourse loan of $13,483,500 at 7.00 percent plus points and fees of 250 basis points and calculated with a 30-year amortization schedule.

We arrived at a value of $13,483,500 for the shopping center using a 6.5 percent cap rate to capitalize the $1,431,135 projected NOI for Year 7, a loan-to-value ratio (LTV) of 61.24 percent.

The permanent loan we will be borrowing in the amount of $13,483,500 covers the minimum amount to pay off the balance on the existing loan of $13,350,000 we are planning to take for the acquisition and to cover $133,500 in financing expenses for points and fees.

The calculations for debt coverage ratios, cash flow assumptions and IRR assumptions using three separate cap rates in the chart are self-explanatory.

In Table 10.11, *Pointer Ridge Plaza, Financial Analysis, Settlement* Costs, page 294, there is a line item called *Total Settlement Costs* depicting settlement-related costs of $276,598 for the purchaser and $190,740 for the seller.

Table 10.11 shows the details that back up the estimated cost. As different jurisdictions sometimes have materially different fees involving purchasing or placing debt on a piece of real estate, my settlement costs were substantially higher for Pointer Ridge Plaza in Prince George's County, Maryland, than they were in Cameron Chase Village Center located in Loudoun County, Virginia, featured in Chapter IX.

Figure 10.18 on page 295 shows the site plan of the center with each tenant's location and square footage.

Figure 10.19 on page 296 highlights the vacant spaces in red, depicting opportunities for changing tenants and maximizing rents. However, in

Table 10.10 Pointer Ridge Plaza, Assumptions to Financial Analysis

POINTER RIDGE PLAZA
Bowie, Maryland
Financial Analysis
Assumptions to Financial Analysis

FINANCIAL ASSUMPTIONS

Loan No.	Loan Type	Amount	Period	Term	Interest Rate	Points & Fees	Amortization
01	Acquisition & Construction Loan	13,350,000	03/18/07 - 02/28/11	4 Years	4%	30-Day Libor + 215	0.50% N/A

◆ For the Purposes of this Analysis Assumed 4% Interest Rate
◆ Two 12 month options to extend (See Loan Documents for full details)
  ◆ Extension fee (nonrefundable)　$ 38,250.00
  ◆ Loan shall be in Balance (See Section 3.3 of the loan documents)
  ◆ Option 1 - Debt Service Coverage Ratio on the then-existing maturity date is not less than 1.00:1.00)　Maturity - 02/28/12
  ◆ Option 2 - Debt Service Coverage Ratio on the then-existing maturity date is not less than 1.15:1.00)　Maturity - 02/28/13

OPTION 1 (Effective 03/01/11)		OPTION 2 (Effective 03/01/12)	
Interest Rate	7%	Interest Rate	7%
Debt Constant	7.98%	Debt Constant	7.98%
Amortization	30 Years	Amortization	30 Years
Annualized Debt Service	1,065,815	Annualized Debt Service	1,065,815
NOI (Feb-2012)	1,289,379	NOI (Feb-2013)	1,422,336
Debt Coverage Ratio	**1.21**	**Debt Coverage Ratio**	**1.33**
DCR Required	**1.00**	**DCR Required**	**1.15**

03	Permanent Financing	13,483,500	03/01/13 - 02/28/23	10 Years	7%	1%	30 Years

◆ Interest Rate is based on 10-Year Treasury + 250 basis points
◆ For the Purposes of this Analysis Assumed 7% Interest Rate

NOI - Year 5 (Dec-2013)	1,431,135	Payoff Existing Loan	13,350,000
CAP Rate	6.50%	Points and Fees	133,500
Shopping Center Value	22,017,462	New Loan Amount	13,483,500
Loan Amount	13,483,500		
61.24% LTV			

CASH FLOW ASSUMPTIONS

Vacancy Factor	4%	Tenant Improvements (see tenant assumptions)	
Management Fee	5%	New Leases	
Asset Management Fee	1%	Renewal Leases	
Capital Expenditures Reserves	$0.76	Leasing Commissions	
		New Leases	6%
Renewal Rate	75%	Renewal Leases	4%

IRR ASSUMPTIONS

Terminal Capitalization Rates	
Low	6.25%
Medium	6.50%
High	6.75%

Table 10.11   Pointer Ridge Plaza, Financial Analysis, Settlement Costs

POINTER RIDGE PLAZA
Financial Analysis
Settlement Costs - Prince George's County, MD

Input Information	
Purchase Price	10,200,000
Total Debt	13,350,000

Description			Purchaser	Seller
CLOSING FEES				
Title Examination			500	0
Settlement Fee			300	0
Real Estate Tax Escrow			0	0
Insurance Escrow			0	0
TOTAL			800	0
RECORDATION / GRANTOR'S TAX - DEED				
Recordation Tax	$4.40	per $1,000	22,440	22,440
Transfer Tax - County	1.40%		142,800	142,800
Transfer Tax - State	0.50%		25,500	25,500
TOTAL			190,740	190,740
RECORDATION / GRANTOR'S TAX - DEED OF TRUST (Debt Recordation) (1)				
Recordation Tax	$4.40	per $1,000	13,860	0
Transfer Tax - County	1.40%		44,100	0
Transfer Tax - State	0.50%		15,750	0
TOTAL			73,710	0
TITLE INSURANCE - DEED OF TRUST				
Up to	$3,000,00	$2.00	0	0
Up to	$5,000,00	$1.50	0	0
Up to	$10,000,000	$1.00	0	0
Up to	$20,000,000	$0.85	11,348	0
Up to	$50,000,000	$0.80	0	0
TOTAL			11,348	0

Total Settlement Costs	276,598	190,740

(1) only calculated on the amount greater than purchase price

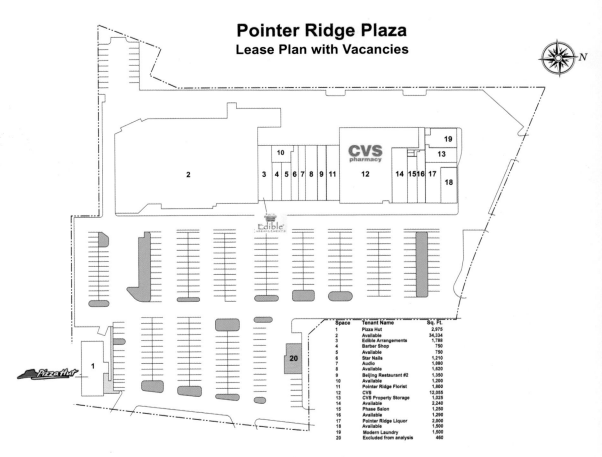

Figure 10.18 Pointer Ridge Plaza, Lease Plan with Vacancies

planning an upgrade, you would need to look at this drawing in conjunction with a drawing that shows expirations with and without options.

Figure 10.20, *Lease Plan with Current Expirations* on page 298, and Figure 10.21, *Lease Plan with All Expirations (Including Options)* on page 299, allow us to plan and understand, on a macro level, a shopping center's potential for changing tenants to increase retail productivity and achieve higher rents.

These two reports allow us to examine on a space-by-space basis the adjoining spaces that have leases terminating around the same time so that we

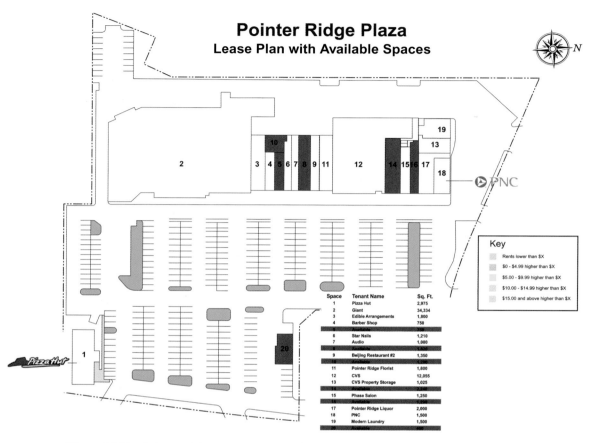

Figure 10.19   Pointer Ridge Plaza, Lease Plan with Available Spaces

can, as appropriate, subdivide or combine spaces to upgrade the tenant mix, increase rents and assemble adequate space for an anchor tenant.

One of the observations we made prior to acquiring this property proved to be right on the money. We recognized we had an opportunity to substantially increase the rent if we could combine spaces 4, 5, 6 and 10 into two large spaces. The way the spaces were presently configured with narrow storefronts and strange L-shaped configurations was not conducive for successful retail stores.

We also saw an opportunity to add value by reconfiguring spaces 13, 17 and 18 and adding new storefronts on the side of the center facing Pointer

Ridge Drive. By recognizing that these three leases came due about the same time, it allowed us to identify this opportunity early on to put plan into motion.

Gross rent as percentage of sales (see Figure 10.23, page 301) is essential information to determine how successful or unsuccessful a tenant's business is at the shopping center. Percentage rent clauses in retail leases are usually based on base rent, not gross rent, but, I believe, base rent does not show how a tenant business is performing as much as gross rent. Two centers could have materially different costs for real estate tax and common area maintenance, and those different costs can be the difference of a successful or unsuccessful store for a tenant. Accordingly, I monitor the *Gross Rent as Percentage of Sales* chart quite closely.

Gross rent per square foot (see figure 10.22, page 300) and *Sales Per Square Foot* (not shown here to protect proprietary sales information) are two charts that one can prepare and review, but it is *Gross Rents as Percentage of Sales* that best shows how a tenant business is performing.

Long before a tenant stops paying rent, or the tenant asks for a rent reduction, a rent abatement or eventually goes out of business, *Gross Rents as Percentage of Sales* can show you the early signs of a tenant that is not be doing well.

As I previously explained, each business that can allow the tenant to survive has a maximum percentage of gross rent as a percentage of sales. By understanding what different tenants can pay as gross rent based on their sales and continually reviewing these percentages, you can continually remerchandise your shopping center and maintain strong tenants that can continue to pay higher rents as their sales increase. When you come across an existing tenant that is not doing well, depending on the strength of the center and the number of potential new tenants waiting to lease spaces, you can either ask a weaker tenant to leave (which they might want to do if they are not doing well), not renew the lease, or just be ready to re-lease the space immediately upon the tenant failing or asking for a rent reduction or abatement. I consider this the most important of all the charts we use because it sets in motion the long-term planning for all our centers.

Pointer Ridge Plaza is proof that you do not have to complete many renovation/remerchandising projects of retail real estate properties in order

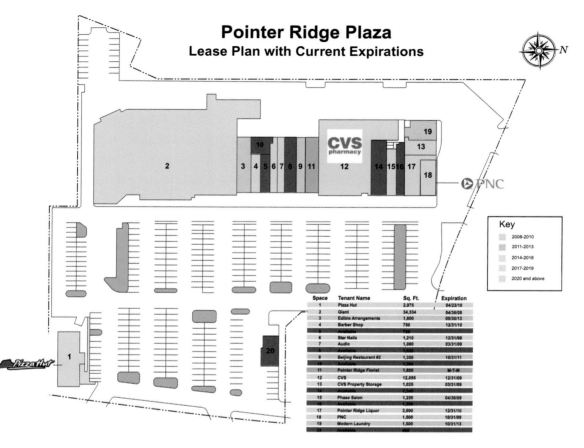

Figure 10.20 Pointer Ridge Plaza, Lease Plan with Current Expirations

to create substantial increases in cash flow and value. This case study also demonstrates the value of having years of experience and why it is critical that you conduct proper due diligence in order to put together a plan that you can accomplish after you complete the acquisition.

When I think of the base information I started with—that is, knowing every competitive center, the future growth plans of projects in the marketplace, all the future major planned roads and all the future planned probable competitive retail properties—I had a good base to start looking for opportunities.

Only then did I add this center to my list of possibilities and try to meet with the owner. It took several years from the first time I corresponded with the owner until he finally sold me the center. During those years, I did more

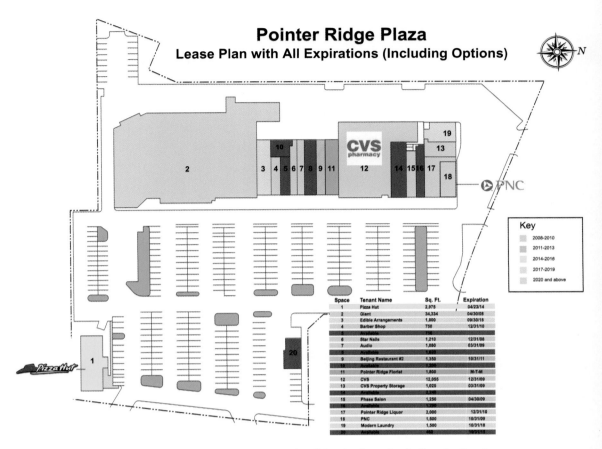

Figure 10.21 Pointer Ridge Plaza, Lease Plan With All Expirations (Including Options)

due diligence on the property than buyers typically do during a feasibility study. By the time I bought the center I felt pretty secure as to all my assumptions.

Overall, Pointer Ridge Plaza demonstrated that the more detail-oriented you are and the more due diligence you are able to complete, the better chance you will have to be successful.

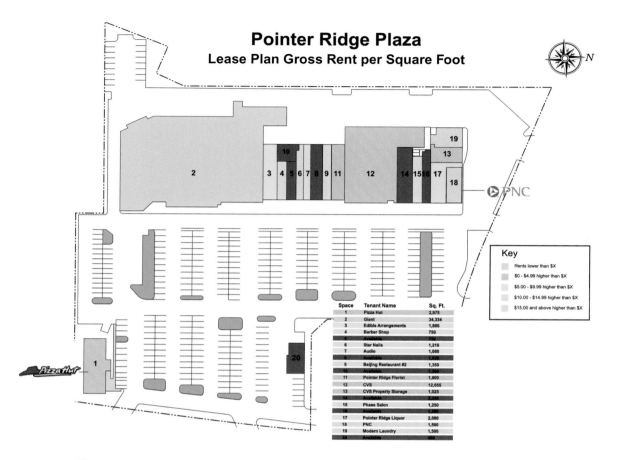

Figure 10.22 Pointer Ridge Plaza, Lease Plan Gross Rent per Square Foot

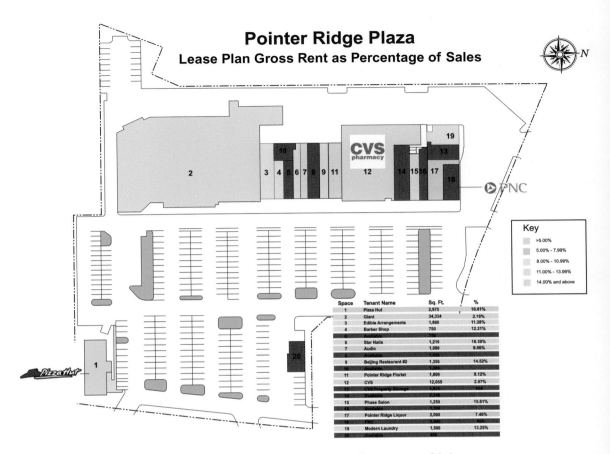

Figure 10.23 Pointer Ridge Plaza, Lease Plan Gross Rent as Percentage of Sales

CHAPTER XI

Maintaining Partner Relations

Communicating With Partners

ALTHOUGH YOU HAVE finalized assembling your partners, closed on the property and started working on your plans to grow their investment, your work with your investors is far from over.

Finding investors was the easy part. Keeping them happy is the key to being successful in this business. You will need to communicate with them frequently and professionally, and most important, you will have to ensure the property performs as you projected.

It should come as no surprise why most publicly traded companies have dedicated investor relations officers to oversee most aspects of communications with investors. In my company, the function ranks among the most important ones we perform, and I personally take on the role of investor relations officer.

However, I do not stop there. Many of my key executives play that role as well because being responsive to partners is paramount for a growing and successful shopping center development company. It is essential to keep your investors informed of what is going on with the property—and this means keeping them abreast of both good news and bad.

I hope that when you purchase your first shopping center, it will make money as you had projected and that you will be distributing cash to the investors every year with the value of the property appreciating for many years. However, when things go wrong and you have bad news to report, do so in a timely fashion and be honest. An investor will generally understand that things will not necessarily turn out exactly as you had originally projected, particularly if you keep them apprised of what is occurring. You also need to share with them ideas on how you plan to rectify the difficulties you encounter along the way.

You could have a perfectly functioning center and be affected by outside forces. Few could have predicted in the early to middle 2000s that Linens N' Things and Circuit City would shutter their stores after decades of profitability. Well, that could have affected your investment.

If they had been anchors in your shopping center, your investment would have suffered financially, and the retail tenants nearby would have also undergone great duress from lack of traffic near the dark big-box location. Tenants could have gone to you asking for rent relief, which if you had granted, would have deteriorated your property's net operating income, a significant measure of asset valuation, cash flow and return to investors.

It is adversities like this that you need to communicate to your investors. However, do not wait until the quarterly reporting when it hits your books financially. Inform them as soon as you become concerned that an important tenant is a credit risk. It is a good idea to write a detailed letter to each investor every three months with an update of the financial situation of the center. If there is a relatively small group of investors, such as five or fewer, you can take more time and effort and send them a monthly package with financial information and an executive summary on the state of the project.

In recent years, the ease with which all of us send and receive large reports of information, I have started sending all my investors in my newest partnerships full reports monthly, including a detailed executive summary. However, whether your information is sent monthly or quarterly, by e-mail or by regular mail, it is imperative that your investors are always well informed about what is occurring.

Personalize your letter, address it directly to the investor and sign it yourself. Use the opportunity to update them on finance, leasing, marketing, renovation and other issues or news pertaining to the property.

You could also include different reports, such as a financial statement and leasing status report, to give them extensive details pertaining to the property. I also like to include a site plan and a lease plan of the center, which show every space and every tenant, and indicate anything that might be going on with each space, such as lease expirations coming up or new tenants moving in. Other pieces to include in the packet might be marketing materials, such as copies of newspaper articles on the center, advertisements or promotional mailers.

Your letter should also address how the center is performing compared to budget, as well as how it is doing compared to your original pro forma. Are you earning and distributing what you promised? Why or why not? Your investors will want to know.

If you are not candid and detailed in your reporting, then you run the risk that if things suddenly do not go well, investors can start questioning your actions and doubting what you are doing for them and why they were not informed in advance of impending problems.

In terms of distributing cash, there is no hard rule as to its frequency, unless you specify a distribution schedule in your original partnership agreement. I never set a specific distribution schedule in my partnership agreements. If this is your first deal, you would likely have quite a few investors and their investment portions might be relatively low, in which case you might want to build up the investor returns in the partnership account and distribute them every six months.

In that case, I advise that you send them a personal report and letter every three months. If the center unexpectedly earns a larger amount than you predicted, there is no rule that says you cannot send a financial report with distribution payments on a monthly basis. The only drawback is that there is more bookkeeping and effort involved with disbursements that are more frequent.

Partner meetings are a matter of personal preferences. In my partnerships where I have more than five or six investors, I do not set partnership meetings. Instead, I send out detailed information on how the center is operating quarterly. Of course, I am always available to speak or meet with any partner who requests to do so. Usually with at least five or six partners no one partner has more than a 25 percent interest in the investment.

However, in the partnerships where I have less than five or six partners, I meet with all the partners once a year. This meeting usually takes place in the late fall, after we have completed the budget for the coming year. The meetings usually last around three hours. We hold the meetings in our office so that we can have our key people who work on the center attend. Many of them make presentations pertaining to their areas of responsibilities such as leasing and accounting, which helps to reinforce to the partners how many of us work on *their* property.

We use a detailed agenda that includes reviewing the year-to-date operations compared to budget, the leasing activity during the year and projected for the coming year, marketing for the year to date and for the coming year, capital expenditures completed for the year to date and for the coming year, distributions for the year to date and proposed for the coming year, present cash reserve, and comparisons of distributions against projections.

All in all, we want the partners to feel like we have a strong control of the property. We use the opportunities of these partners' meetings to get their thoughts, constructive criticism and/or votes of confidence. Overall, these are very productive meetings even though they are very time-consuming to prepare and present.

The effort also benefits all of the employees of our management company as they know they are working for real people who care what they think and how they perform.

At times, I will visit a property with a partner but not frequently. Preparing a formal site visit for your partners is a time-intensive endeavor. However, senior management must inspect a property together if you want your properties to be the best they can be.

I recently spent four hours walking through one of our larger properties with a group of at least ten people. It included the property manager, the divisional property manager, the vice president of property management, the senior vice president of construction, the leasing representative, the executive vice president of real estate (who oversees all leasing), the chief financial officer and the chief operating officer.

Usually, we do not have that many people inspecting a property, nor do I spend that much time on one property, but the visit was very worthwhile. It reinforced to the top management of our company my philosophy of how we should be taking care of our properties.

We walked into every store, whether with an operating tenant or a vacancy. We spoke to every tenant and noted lots of items for further follow-up. I surely cannot do this type of visit every year for every one of the 50 centers we presently oversee, but I always strive to get out enough to inspect and teach.

However, I do require different members of management to formally inspect all the properties a specific number of times per year, depending on the size of the centers and the level of leasing or development activity occurring there. I also select a number of properties to visit throughout the year depending on what needs my personal oversight the most. As all our properties are within a two-hour drive of our office, it is surely easier to make frequent site inspections than if our properties were more spread out. We can never be too busy to visit our properties, and that goes for our management team as well as investors that live nearby.

Parting Ways With an Investor

No matter how hard you try, occasions arise in which an investor needs or wants to leave the project and cash out. In most cases, if the investor wants to sell his share within the terms of the partnership agreement, he or she could transfer his interest to an immediate family member.

However, under my model partnership agreement he or she would not have the right to sell his share outside of an immediate family member without the managing partner's approval. After all, you would not want a new partner whom you do not already know, and you would want to have comfort that his or her interests are aligned with the rest of the investment group.

My noninstitutional partnership requires me to give notice to all of my partners 12 months before any loan in place becomes due. Any partner has an option to notify me if he or she wishes to sell his or her interest. If that partner does so, I must buy or have someone buy that interest or the partner can force a sale of the partnership. This notice is only prior to a time of refinancing, so no partner is penalized by having a loan paid off early due to a forced sale. I have never had a forced sale even though there have been several instances where partners have given me notice that they wished to sell. I have also never let this notice provision prevent an investor from selling his or her interest whenever he or she wished to do so.

If an investor comes to me and tells me he or she wants to sell his or her interest, I try to place a fair value on his or her partnership interest. I then notify the rest of the partners of the opportunity to buy his or her share, particularly the ones who are most involved with or most knowledgeable about the project.

If none of them expresses interest, my choice is to purchase his or her share myself or to bring in one or more partners to buy. I have never had a partner or investor who has wanted to sell his or her share with whom I have not been able to agree upon a fair price, nor have I ever been unable to find a willing investor to buy the share at the same agreed-upon price.

In this situation, you as the managing partner wield considerable power. The partner has no legal right to sell the share on his or her own because you have the right to approve the buyer.

The best way to have happy partners when one of them is leaving is to value the shares in a fair and equitable manner and to try to find someone who is willing and able to buy that share. This is in the best interest of all partners and is an assurance to the remaining partners to be able to exit if needed.

Adding New Investors

What if your deal is established with a group of partners and a new potential partner approaches you and wants in?

In some cases, you can add a new partner after the deal is completed. One such occasion is the previous example. The other is if your asset is having financial troubles.

When you need additional cash and the existing partners are not able or willing to contribute more money to invest, and a second mortgage is not advisable, you might have to search for additional investors. In such case, the majority approval from your existing partners is needed to issue additional equity shares in the partnership.

However, if one of these two situations does not occur, you can simply tell an interested investor that you will inform him or her when your next deal comes along.

CHAPTER XII

Contracts, Agreements, Legal Correspondence and Exhibits

Understanding the Legal Documents

AS YOU EMBARK on your new role as the sponsor of an investment group to acquire, reposition and develop retail properties, you will want to become familiar with several forms, legal documents and agreements that are pertinent to retail development and partnerships. With your input, lawyers and accountants will draft these forms for your use, but I am including a few examples for studying purposes.

Letter of Intent for Purchasing

The letter of intent (LOI) for purchasing property serves the same purpose as the LOI to lease space. It shows you are a serious buyer and outlines the terms that the buyer and seller have agreed on in order to assist the attorneys in drafting a legally binding purchase/sale agreement.

The LOI must identify your buyer entity, the property you are intending to buy, the proposed purchase price with down payment and terms, any conditions you would impose, the time you need to complete your due diligence and when you plan to close. Consider the LOI as your preliminary offer to the seller. See Figure 12.1 on page 310.

Once your LOI is approved by the seller, you need to move quickly on the due diligence, finalize deals with your investors and apply for your

Figure 12.1 Pointer Ridge Plaza Letter of Intent to Purchase

January 13, 2007

By Messenger

Pointer Ridge Plaza
c/o Mr. John A. Smith, Senior Vice President
XYZ Corporation
111 Main Street, Suite 200
City, State 11111-1111

Re: Pointer Ridge Plaza (the "Property")
     Bowie, Maryland
     LETTER OF INTENT

Dear Gentlemen:

This letter of intent (the "Letter") sets forth certain terms and conditions pursuant to which Gary D. Rappaport on behalf of a limited partnership or limited liability company ("Purchaser") and the owner of the Property ("Seller") agree to enter into a contract (the "Contract") for the purchase and sale of the Property (including, without limitation, all improvements thereon and leases thereto).

The Contract shall reflect the following terms and conditions to which Seller and Purchaser have agreed:

1. Purchase Price. The Purchase Price of the Property shall be Ten Million Two Hundred Thousand Dollars ($10,200,000).

2. Deposit. The term "Deposit" in this Letter shall refer to the amount actually delivered to Purchaser to the "Escrow Agent" (as hereinafter defined), in the form of one or more good checks.

mortgage. A contract between the seller and buyer would follow soon after the seller approves the LOI. The lawyers will use the LOI as a guideline.

The LOI often acts as a starting point for negotiation of terms and purchase price without cumbersome legal details, although a lawyer should draft your LOI for such things as to ensure it is nonbinding. All data would be subject to verification later.

Mr. John A. Smith
January 13, 2007
Page 2

3.   At such time as both Purchaser and Seller execute a Contract and Seller delivers (or causes to be delivered) to Purchaser all Due Diligence Materials (as defined herein), Purchaser shall deliver a check in the amount of Three Hundred Thousand Dollars ($300,000) to Commonwealth Land Title Insurance Company (the "Escrow Agent"), to be held by the Escrow Agent in accordance with the terms of the Contract (as defined herein). Upon expiration of the Feasibility Period, an additional Three Hundred Thousand Dollars ($300,000) shall be delivered to the Escrow Agent. All such funds shall become the "Deposit" under the Contract.

(a)   Any checks delivered to Escrow Agent shall be placed or invested in interest bearing accounts or certificates of deposit with such banks, savings and loans, or money markets funds as may be designated by Purchaser from time to time. Any interest earned on the Deposit shall be deemed to be part of the Deposit.

(b)   The entire Deposit shall be returned by the Escrow Agent to Purchaser upon the request of Purchaser (i) if the Purchaser elects to terminate this Letter or the Contract pursuant to paragraph 3 below, (ii) if Purchaser elects to terminate the Contract pursuant to any right granted therein or as a result of Seller's default, or (iii) if Purchaser fulfills its obligations at the Closing. Purchaser shall have the right to apply the Deposit towards the purchase price or to the return of the Deposit upon the payment of the full purchase price.

(c)   The entire Deposit shall be delivered by the Escrow Agent to Seller if the Contract is terminated by Seller pursuant to a right granted therein as a result of the default of Purchaser. Such return of the Deposit shall be the sole remedy of Seller, and shall constitute the agreed and liquidated damages of the Seller in the event of the Purchaser's default under the Contract.

4.   Feasibility Study Period. Upon the execution of this Letter and the receipt of Due Diligence Materials (as defined herein), Purchaser shall have a period of thirty (30) days in which to inspect and investigate the Property (the "Feasibility Period"). Seller shall provide Purchaser with the following (the "Due Diligence Materials") simultaneously with the execution of this Letter: copies of all title reports, surveys, engineering reports, leases, letters of intent and agreements affecting the Property, and any other information Purchaser may reasonably request. Purchaser shall have the right prior to the end of the Feasibility Period to terminate this Letter or the Contract (if executed) for any reason, if in Purchaser's sole and absolute discretion, Purchaser believes the transaction is not feasible or desirable. Purchaser shall notify Seller of such termination in writing on or before the expiration of the Feasibility Period. If Purchaser so notifies Seller of the termination, the entire Deposit (together with interest earned thereon) shall be returned to Purchaser by Escrow Agent and the parties shall be fully released from all obligations and liabilities under this Letter and/or the Contract shall be terminated and of no further force and effect.

(continued)

Mr. John A. Smith
January 13, 2007
Page 3

    5.   <u>Closing</u>.

    (a)   Upon satisfaction of all conditions precedent, Closing shall occur within fifteen (15) days of the end of the Feasibility Period.

    (b)   At Closing, Seller shall convey fee simple title to the Property to Purchaser by a special warranty deed and clear of all financing liens. Title shall be good and marketable, fully insurable by a reputable title insurance company under a full coverage owner's title insurance policy at standard rates, subject only to restrictions of record, which are acceptable to Purchaser.

    (c)   All recording and transfer taxes for the deed shall be paid fifty percent (50%) by the Seller and fifty percent (50%) by the Purchaser.

    (d)   At Closing, all taxes, rents (including percentage rents) and other charges shall be apportioned between Purchaser and Seller.

    (e)   Closing shall be contingent on fulfillment of all conditions precedent to the obligations of Purchaser set forth in the Contract, including, without limitation there being (i) no material condemnation action proposed or pending, (ii) no material casualty, (iii) no change in zoning or other laws affecting the use or occupancy of the Property, (iv) no change in the environmental condition of the Property subsequent to the execution of the Contract, and (v) no changes in the title subsequent to the execution of the Contract.

    6.   <u>Broker</u>. Seller and Purchaser represent and warrant that XYZ Corporation (the "Broker") is the sole broker in connection with the sale and purchase of the Property and Purchaser shall be solely responsible for the Broker.

    7.   <u>Preparation of Contract</u>. Seller agrees to prepare and deliver to Purchaser a proposed Contract containing the terms and conditions set front herein within three (3) days of the Seller's acceptance of this Letter. Both Purchaser and Seller agree to negotiate in good faith to finalize and execute the Contract within ten (10) days of this Letter. The terms and conditions of the Contract shall be subject to the approval of Purchaser and Seller; provided, that neither Purchaser nor Seller shall have any right to object to the inclusion in the Contract of any terms contained in this Letter; and provided further, that neither Purchaser nor Seller shall have any right to insist that any term be included in the Contract that contradicts any term contained in this letter. Seller agrees that it will not negotiate with any other party for the sale of the Property for a period of ten (10) days from the date of this Letter, or as long as Purchaser and Seller are engaged in good faith negotiations concerning the proposed Contract.

Mr. John A. Smith
January 13, 2007
Page 4

This letter shall be binding upon the parties, and their successors and assign. Please indicate the Seller's consent to the terms and conditions of this Letter in the space provided below.

Sincerely,

Gary D. Rappaport, SCSM/SCMD/CLS
PRESIDENT

On behalf of Purchaser

ACCEPTED AND AGREED
this _____ day of _____, 2007

By:_____

Purchase/Sale Agreement

The purchase/sale agreement is much more detailed than the LOI, and your lawyer, sometimes with the help of the broker's lawyer, will draft it. The agreement acts as a specific contract by which both buyer and seller agree to the terms of the transaction. Some professionals refer to the purchase/sale agreement as the purchase contract, sales contract or sales agreement.

Provisions include such features as the legal description of the property, the seller's representation and warranties, defaults and remedies, risk of loss, escrow handling, etc. See Figure 12.2 on page 314.

Figure 12.2 Real Estate Purchase Agreement

REAL ESTATE PURCHASE AGREEMENT

THIS REAL ESTATE PURCHASE AGREEMENT is made and entered as of the ___ day of _____, by and between _____, a _____ [limited liability company] ("Seller"), and_____, a _____ [limited liability company] ("Purchaser").

W I T N E S S E T H:

WHEREAS, Seller is the owner of that certain real property containing the shopping center known as _____, which is located in _____, _____, as more particularly described on Exhibit A hereto, together with all improvements situated thereon, all appurtenances, rights, easements, rights-of-way, tenements and hereditaments incident thereto (collectively, the "Real Property"), together with all tangible personal property located on and used in connection with the Land (the "Personal Property"), and, to the extent assignable, the name "_____", all "Leases" (as hereinafter defined), "Contracts" (as hereinafter defined), governmental permits, licenses and approvals, warranties and guarantees that Seller has received in connection with any work or service performed with respect to, or equipment installed in, the improvements on the Real Property, tenant lists, advertising material and telephone exchange numbers, directly related to the Real Property (collectively, the "Intangible Property", and collectively with the Real Property and the Personal Property, the "Property"); and

WHEREAS, Purchaser desires to purchase from Seller, and Seller desires to sell to Purchaser, the Property, on and subject to the terms and provisions set forth herein.

NOW, THEREFORE, for and in consideration of the premises and the mutual covenants and agreements herein contained and for other good and valuable consideration, the receipt and sufficiency of which are hereby acknowledged, the parties agree as follows:

1.   Purchase and Sale. Purchaser agrees to purchase, and Seller agrees to sell, the Property, for and in consideration of the purchase price and upon the terms and conditions set forth herein.

2.   Purchase Price. The purchase price for the Property (the "Purchase Price") shall be _____ and 00/100 Dollars ($_____) payable at Closing (as hereinafter defined), after closing adjustments, in cash or wire transfer of immediately available funds.

3.   Deposit.

(a)   Within one (1) business day after the date of delivery to Purchaser of an original of this Agreement executed by Seller (the date of such delivery to Purchaser being the "Acceptance Date"), Purchaser shall deliver to_____. (the "Escrow Agent"), as escrow agent, a check or letter of credit in the amount of _____ and 00/100 Dollars ($_____) (the "Deposit"). If Purchaser fails to deliver the Deposit when required to do so, this Agreement shall become null and void, and the parties hereto shall be relieved of all further liability and obligation to each other.

DOC3#260562-v1

(b)   The Escrow shall immediately provide Seller with written evidence of receipt of the Deposit. Any letter of credit delivered as a part of the Deposit shall be in form acceptable to both Purchaser and Seller. The Escrow Agent shall place any check delivered as a part of the Deposit in an interest-bearing account within one (1) business day after the date of receipt thereof and interest on the Deposit shall accrue to the benefit of the party entitled to the Deposit and shall constitute a part of the Deposit for all purposes hereof. The Deposit shall be held by the Escrow Agent pursuant to the terms and conditions of this Agreement.

(c)   At any time prior to Closing, if Seller or Purchaser provides the Escrow Agent with a certification (a copy of which shall be delivered contemporaneously to the other party) that the Seller or Purchaser, as the case may be, is entitled to the Deposit pursuant to the terms of this Agreement, the Escrow Agent shall deliver the Deposit to such party within seven (7) business days after receipt of said notice, unless the other party disputes such certification by written notice to the Escrow Agent (a copy of which shall be delivered contemporaneously to the other party) delivered within five (5) business days of the Escrow Agent's receipt of the initial certification. In such event, the Escrow Agent shall hold the Deposit pending resolution of such dispute.

(d)   The parties acknowledge that (i) Escrow Agent is acting solely as escrow agent at their request and for their convenience, (ii) Escrow Agent shall not be deemed to be the agent of either of the parties, and (iii) Escrow Agent shall not be liable to either of the parties for any act or omission on its part unless taken or suffered in bad faith, in willful disregard to this Agreement, or involving gross negligence. Seller and Purchaser shall jointly and severally indemnify and hold Escrow Agent harmless from and against all costs, claims, expenses, including reasonable attorneys' fees incurred in connection with the performance of Escrow Agent's duties hereunder, except with respect to actions or omissions taken or suffered by Escrow Agent in bad faith, in willful disregard of this Agreement, or involving gross negligence on the part of Escrow Agent; provided, however, that if any litigation shall arise between Seller and Purchaser in connection therewith, the non-prevailing party shall pay all such costs, claims and expenses of the Escrow Agent. In the event any dispute shall arise between the parties hereto as to the disposition of the Deposit, the Escrow Agent's sole responsibility may be met at the Escrow Agent's option by paying the Deposit into the court in which relevant litigation is pending between the parties or by initiating an interpleader action, and upon payment of the Deposit into court, neither Seller nor Purchaser shall have any further right, claim, demand, or action against the Escrow Agent.

4.   <u>Title</u>.

(a)   At Closing, Seller shall convey to Purchaser absolute fee simple title to the Property free of all liens, encumbrances, judgments, covenants, conditions, restrictions, easements and rights-of-way, recorded or unrecorded; subject, however, to the Leases (defined in Section 6(e)) and those matters (if any) affecting title to the Property which are set forth in the Title Commitment referred to below and accepted by Purchaser (collectively, the "Permitted Exceptions"). Title is to be merchantable, good of record and in fact, and insurable without exceptions (other than Permitted Exceptions) at standard rates by a recognized title insurance company selected by Purchaser (the "Title Company").

2

(continued)

(b)   After execution of this Agreement, Purchaser shall, at its own expense, order a standard 2006 ALTA Form commitment for owner's title insurance for the Property (the "Title Commitment"). If Purchaser, in its sole discretion, finds any of the exceptions to title set forth in the Title Commitment to be objectionable ("Objectionable Exceptions"), Purchaser shall, within the Feasibility Period, give written notice to Seller setting forth the Objectionable Exceptions. If Purchaser fails to give notice of Objectionable Exceptions within the Feasibility Period, Purchaser shall be deemed to have accepted all title exceptions which are reported in the Title Commitment; if Purchaser does give such notice, Purchaser shall be deemed to have accepted all title exceptions reported in the Title Commitment other than the Objectionable Exceptions expressly set forth in the notice.

(c)   Except as provided below, Seller shall have the option to cure or not to cure any Objectionable Exceptions. Within five (5) days after receipt of notice of Objectionable Exceptions, Seller shall give Purchaser written notice whether it will or will not cure the Objectionable Exceptions. The Feasibility Period shall be deemed extended such that such five (5)-day period shall expire at least two (2) business days prior to the expiration of the Feasibility Period. If Seller does not give Purchaser such notice within the five (5)-day period, Seller shall be deemed to have elected to cure all of the Objectionable Exceptions. Despite the foregoing, if the Objectionable Exceptions are reasonably susceptible of being cured prior to Closing at an aggregate cost not to exceed _____ and 00/100 Dollars ($_____) (the "Maximum Cure Cost"), Seller shall be obligated to cure such Objectionable Exceptions (each, a "Mandatory Cure Item"). Notwithstanding the foregoing, Purchaser shall have the right to terminate this Agreement in the event that (i) Seller shall fail promptly to commence and diligently to prosecute thereafter the cure of each Mandatory Cure Item, (ii) Seller notifies Purchaser that Seller reasonably anticipates that the Closing will be postponed in accordance with Section 4(d) below to afford Seller sufficient time to effectuate the cure of any Mandatory Cure Item or (iii) any Mandatory Cure Item is not cured at or prior to Closing. In the event that Purchaser terminates this Agreement pursuant to the foregoing sentence, the Deposit shall be promptly returned to Purchaser and thereafter the parties shall be relieved of further liability to one another, at law or in equity

(d)   If Seller elects or is obligated to cure the Objectionable Exceptions, Closing shall be postponed, if necessary, until fifteen (15) days after such cure is complete. If, however, Seller shall not have succeeded within the Maximum Cure Period in curing the Objectionable Exceptions which it has elected or is obligated to cure, or if Seller, as permitted above, elects in the first instance not to cure any Objectionable Exceptions, Purchaser shall have the right either (i) to waive the Objectionable Exceptions not cured by Seller, with a reduction in the Purchase Price equal to the portion of the Maximum Cure Cost not expended by Seller, or (ii) to terminate this Agreement. In the event of termination pursuant to this Section 4(d), the Deposit shall be promptly returned to Purchaser and thereafter the parties shall be relieved of further liability to one another, at law or in equity. Notwithstanding the provisions of Section 4(c) and this Section 4(d), any deeds of trust, mortgages, judgment liens, and other monetary liens against the Property shall not be deemed to be Permitted Exceptions, whether Purchaser gives written notice of objection or not, and shall be removed by Seller at or before the time of Closing, without regard to the Maximum Cure Cost.

(e)   Purchaser may also, at its own expense, obtain an ALTA/ACSM survey of the Property (the "Survey"). In the event that the Survey reveals any matters that would adversely affect the value of the Property or that are otherwise objectionable to Purchaser, Purchaser shall have the right to notify Seller of such matters during the Feasibility Period. Upon any such notice by Purchaser, such matters shall be treated as if they were Objectionable Exceptions and the procedures of Section 4(c) and 4(d) shall apply.

(f)   After the date of this Agreement, Seller shall not alter or permit the alteration of title to the Property.

(g)   Seller shall (i) execute such affidavits and other instruments as are customary and reasonable in the market in which the Property is located and required by the Title Company for the elimination of any standard or preprinted exceptions in Purchaser's final policy of title insurance, or for compliance with tax reporting requirements, and (ii) furnish such evidence of due formation and good standing of Seller and the power and authority of Seller to consummate this transaction in accordance with this Agreement as are customary and reasonable in the market in which the Property is located and required by the Title Company.

5.   Closing. The closing (the "Closing") of the purchase and sale contemplated herein shall be take place on the date (the "Closing Date") specified by Purchaser on not less than five (5) days notice to Seller, provided that the Closing Date shall not be later than thirty (30) days after the end of the Feasibility Period (as defined and described in Section 14(d) hereof); provided, that if no such day is specified, the Closing Date shall be on the date that is thirty (30) days after the end of the Feasibility Period, provided further, that if such day is not a business day, the Closing Date shall be on the next business day. The Closing shall take place at a location mutually agreed upon by Seller and Purchaser.

6.   Representations and Warranties of Seller. In order to induce Purchaser to enter into this Agreement and to purchase the Property, Seller hereby makes the following representations and warranties, which shall survive Closing for a period of twelve (12) months.

(a)   Authority of Seller. Seller is a limited liability company, duly organized and in good standing under the laws of the State of Delaware. Seller has all necessary power and authority and has taken all necessary corporate action to execute, deliver and perform this Agreement. No consents of any other persons are required for such execution or to enable Seller to consummate the transactions contemplated hereby. This Agreement is the valid and binding obligation of Seller, enforceable against it in accordance with its terms, except that such enforcement may be subject to bankruptcy, receivership, reorganization, insolvency, moratorium, or similar laws or procedures relating to, or affecting creditors' rights generally and to general principles of equity.

(b)   No Conflicting Agreements. The execution and delivery by Seller of, and the performance and compliance by Seller with the terms and provisions of, this Agreement do not violate any of the terms, conditions or provisions of (i) Seller's organizational documents, or (ii) to Seller's knowledge, any judgment, order, injunction, decree, regulation or ruling of any court or other Governmental Authority to which Seller is subject.

4

(continued)

(c)   <u>Title; Property Description</u>. Seller is the sole owner of fee simple title to its Property, free and clear of all liens and encumbrances (except liens and other matters of title to be removed at or prior to Closing), subject only to all covenants, conditions, restrictions, easements and other matters duly of record as of the date hereof.

(d)   <u>Compliance with Existing Laws</u>. Seller has not received any written notice which remains outstanding of any violation of applicable building, zoning, environmental or other ordinances, statutes or regulations of any governmental agency in respect to the ownership, use, maintenance, condition and operation of the Property.

(e)   <u>Leases</u>. True, correct and complete copies of all of the leases of the Property and any amendments thereto (collectively, the "Leases") have been delivered to Purchaser. Attached hereto as <u>Exhibit B</u> is a description of the Leases and a current rent schedule covering the Leases. There are no leases or tenancies of any space in the Property, other than those set forth in <u>Exhibit B</u>.

(f)   <u>Contracts</u>. True, correct and complete copies of all contracts and agreements to which Seller is a party (or which otherwise relate to the Property), including, without limitation, those providing for the management, operation, supply, maintenance, repair, advertising or promotion of the Property, including service agreements, maintenance contracts, cleaning contracts, contracts for the purchase or delivery of labor, services, materials or supplies and equipment rental agreements or leases, and landscaping and lawn maintenance agreements (collectively, "Contracts"), a complete listing of which is attached hereto as <u>Exhibit C</u>.

(g)   <u>Condition of Property</u>. Possession of the Property shall be delivered to Purchaser at Closing in its "as is, where is" condition as of the date of Purchaser's execution of this Agreement. Notwithstanding anything to the contrary contained in this Agreement with respect to the legal, physical and environmental condition of the Property, the Property is being sold and conveyed hereunder (and Purchaser agrees to accept the Property) "as is", "where is" and "with all faults", without any representation or warranty except as expressly set forth herein. Purchaser hereby expressly acknowledges and agrees that (i) Purchaser is solely responsible for determining the status and condition of the Property, including, without limitation, existing zoning classifications, building regulations and development requirements applicable to the Property, and Purchaser will thoroughly inspect and examine the Property to the extent deemed necessary by Purchaser in order to enable Purchaser to evaluate the condition of the Property, and (ii) Purchaser is relying solely upon such inspections, examination and evaluation of the Property by Purchaser in purchasing the Property.

(h)   <u>Condemnation Proceedings</u>. No condemnation or eminent domain proceedings are pending or, to the best of Seller's knowledge, currently threatened in writing against the Property.

(i)   <u>Litigation</u>. No litigation is pending or, to the best of Seller's knowledge, currently threatened, affecting the operation or ownership of the Property.

(j)   <u>No Defaults</u>. Neither the execution of this Agreement nor the consummation of the transactions contemplated hereby will: (i) conflict with or result in a breach of the terms, conditions or provisions of, or constitute a default under any agreement or instrument to which Seller is a party or by which the Seller or the Property is bound, (ii) violate any restriction, requirement, covenant or condition to which the Seller is subject or by which Seller or the Property is bound, or (iii) constitute a violation of any applicable code, resolution, law, statute, regulation, ordinance, rule, judgment, decree or order.

(k)   Hazardous Waste. Except for all matters disclosed by the reports delivered by Seller to Purchaser prior to the expiration of the Feasibility Period, Seller has no knowledge of any discharge, spillage, uncontrolled loss, seepage or filtration (a "Spill") of any flammable, explosive, radioactive or reactive materials, any asbestos (whether friable or non-friable), any pollutants, contaminants or other hazardous, dangerous or toxic chemicals, materials or substances, any petroleum products or substances or compounds containing petroleum products, including gasoline, diesel fuel and oil, any polychlorinated biphenyls or substances or compounds containing polychlorinated biphenyls, and any other material or substance defined as a "hazardous substance," "hazardous material," "hazardous waste," "toxic materials," "contamination," and/or "pollution" within the meaning of any Environmental (as hereinafter defined) (collectively, "Hazardous Materials") on the Property, except as disclosed in writing to Purchaser prior to the expiration of the Feasibility Period (as hereinafter defined). As used herein, the term "Environmental Law" shall refer to any law which regulates the use, generation, handling, storage, treatment, transportation, decontamination, clean-up, removal, encapsulation, enclosure, abatement or disposal of any Hazardous Material, including the Comprehensive Environmental Response, Compensation and Liability Act, 42 U.S.C. Section 9601, et seq., the Resource Conservation and Recovery Act, 42 U.S.C. Sections 6901, et seq., the Toxic Substance Control Act, 15 U.S.C. Sections 2601, et seq., the Clean Water Act, 33 U.S.C. Sections 1251 et seq., the Hazardous Materials Transportation Act, 49 U.S.C., Section 1802, their state analogues, and any other federal, state or local statute, law, ordinance, resolution, code, rule, regulation, order or decree regulating, relating to, or imposing liability or standards of conduct concerning any Hazardous Material (as such laws may be amended from time to time, "Environmental Laws"). Seller has not caused a Spill at, upon, under or within the Property. To the best of Seller's knowledge, there is no proceeding or action pending or threatened in writing by any person or governmental agency regarding the environmental condition of the Property.

(l)   Leasing Commissions and Tenant Improvement Allowances. At Closing there shall be no outstanding or contingent leasing commissions, tenant improvement allowances or fees payable with respect to the Property, except for any leasing commission to be paid by Purchaser under Section 7(b) below.

(m)   Approvals. No authorization, consent, order, approval or license from, filing with, or other act by any Governmental Authority or other Person is or will be necessary to permit the valid execution and delivery by Seller of this Agreement or the performance by Seller of the obligations to be performed by it under this Agreement.

(n)   United States Person. Seller is a "United States person" within the meaning of Sections 1445(f)(3) and 7701(a)(30) of the Internal Revenue Code of 1986, as amended.

(o)   Absence of Bankruptcy. Seller has not commenced (within the meaning of any Bankruptcy Law) a voluntary case, consented to the entry of an order for relief against it in an involuntary case, or consented to the appointment of a custodian of it or for all or any substantial part of its property, nor has a court of competent jurisdiction entered an order or decree under Title 11, U.S. Code, or any similar state law for the relief of debtors that is for relief

6

(continued)

against Seller in an involuntary case or appoints a custodian of Seller or for all or any substantial part of its property.

(p) <u>Operating Statements</u>. The annual and year-to-date Operating Statements (as defined in Section 14(b)(v) below), which were prepared on the cash method of accounting, are in accordance with the books and records of Seller and fairly reflect the income and expenses of the Property for the respective periods covered thereby.

(q) <u>Personal Property</u>. There is no personal property relating to the Property or Seller's use or ownership thereof.

(r) <u>Mechanics' Liens</u>. All bills and claims for labor performed and materials furnished to or for the benefit of the Property for all periods prior to the Closing Date have been (or prior to the Closing Date will be) paid in full, and on the Closing Date there shall be no mechanics' liens or materialmen's liens (whether or not perfected) on or affecting the Property.

(s) <u>Utilities</u>. A list of all utilities servicing the Property and the account numbers of such utilities is set forth on <u>Schedule 3</u> attached hereto.

(t) <u>Licenses, Permits, Certificates</u>. Seller has delivered to Purchaser all licenses, permits and certificates in the possession or control of Seller or its asset manager for the Property in connection with the use and occupancy of the Property, and to the best of its knowledge all such licenses, permits and certificates are in full force and effect.

7. <u>Obligations of Seller Pending Closing</u>. From and after the date of this Agreement until the Closing Date, Seller covenants and agrees as follows:

(a) <u>Maintenance and Operation of the Property</u>. Seller will cause the Property to be maintained in its present order and condition, normal wear and tear and damage by fire or other casualty excepted.

(b) <u>Obligations as to Leases</u>. From and after the date of this Agreement, Seller shall not, without Purchaser's prior written consent (which consent, prior to the expiration of the Feasibility Period shall not be unreasonably withheld or delayed, and thereafter may be withheld in Purchaser's sole and absolute discretion), amend, modify, renew, extend or terminate any Lease, unless required by law or the terms of any Lease, or enter into new leases. In the event Purchaser fails to respond in writing to Seller's notice containing a request for any such consent within five (5) business days after receipt by Purchaser of a notice containing a request for such consent, Purchaser shall be deemed to have granted its consent. If Purchaser consents to a new lease after the Acceptance Date and Closing occurs hereunder, Purchaser shall be responsible for all tenant improvement, costs or allowances, and leasing commissions payable by the landlord under such new lease to the extent that such costs are (i) described in the Seller's solicitation for such consent and (ii) allocable to the portion of the unexpired portion of the term of such lease which remains as of the Closing Date.

(c) <u>Insurance</u>. Seller shall maintain insurance on the Property throughout the Closing Date with an insurance company and in amounts reasonably satisfactory to Purchaser, and shall provide evidence thereof to Purchaser upon Purchaser's request.

(d)   Contracts. Seller shall not enter into any additional Contracts or other similar agreements in connection with the Property and which will continue after Closing hereunder without the prior consent of Purchaser (which consent, prior to the expiration of the Feasibility Period shall not be unreasonably withheld or delayed, and thereafter may be withheld in Purchaser's sole and absolute discretion).

8.   Representations, Warranties and Covenants of Purchaser. In order to induce Seller to enter into this Agreement and to sell the Property to Purchaser, Purchaser hereby makes the following representations, warranties and covenants:

(a)   Authority of Purchaser. This Agreement is the valid and binding obligation of Purchaser, enforceable against it in accordance with its terms, except that such enforcement may be subject to bankruptcy, receivership, reorganization, insolvency, moratorium or similar laws, or procedures relating to or affecting creditors' rights generally, and to general principles of equity.

(b)   No Defaults. Neither the execution of this Agreement nor the consummation of the transactions contemplated hereby will: (i) conflict with, or result in a breach of, the terms, conditions or provisions of, or constitute a default under, any agreement or instrument to which Purchaser is a party, (ii) violate any restriction, requirement, covenant or condition to which the Purchaser is subject, and (iii) constitute a violation of any applicable code, resolution, law, statute, regulation, ordinance, rule, judgment, decree or order.

9.   Conditions to Purchaser's Obligations.

(a)   Purchaser's obligation to settle hereunder is conditioned upon the (i) truth of the representations and warranties of Seller in Section 6 above, (ii) Seller's performance of its obligations pursuant to Section 7 above and Seller's deliver at Closing of the documents and items identified in Section 10 below.

(b)   Purchaser's obligation to settle hereunder also is conditioned upon the receipt by Purchaser at Closing of a tenant estoppel letter in the form attached hereto as Exhibit D or such other commercially reasonable form as is required by Purchaser's lender, dated not more than thirty (30) days prior to the Closing Date (a "Tenant Estoppel Letter"), from one hundred percent (100%) of the tenants under the Leases. If Purchaser does not receive the required tenant estoppel letters at Closing, then Purchaser may terminate this Agreement by giving written notice to Seller, in which event the Deposit shall be returned to Purchaser and neither party shall have any further obligations or liabilities to the other.

(c)   Purchaser's obligation to settle hereunder also is conditioned upon the receipt by Purchaser at Closing of a Subordination, Non-Disturbance and Attornment Agreement executed by the tenant under each of the Leases in the form attached hereto as Exhibit E, (each, an "SNDA").

(d)   Purchaser's obligation to settle hereunder also is conditioned upon there being, subsequent to the date hereof, (i) no change in zoning or other laws affecting the use or occupancy of the Property, (ii) no change in the environmental condition of the Property, and (iii) no change in title to the Property.

8

(continued)

10.   <u>Seller's Deliveries</u>. Seller shall execute and acknowledge, as applicable, and deliver to Purchaser at the Closing the following documents and items:

(a)   a special warranty deed, conveying good and marketable fee simple title to the Property, free and clear of all liens and encumbrances, and subject only to the Permitted Exceptions;

(b)   an assignment of the Leases and Contracts whereby (i) Seller assigns to Purchaser all of Seller's right, title and interest in and to the Leases and the Contracts and indemnifies Purchaser for any cost, damage or expense arising out of any failure of Seller to perform any of its obligations under the Leases and the Contracts prior to the Closing Date, and (ii) Purchaser assumes Seller's obligation under the Leases and the Contracts from and after the Closing Date and indemnifies Seller for any cost, damage or expense arising out of any failure of Purchaser to perform any of its obligations under the Leases and the Contracts from and after the Closing Date;

(c)   a letter executed by Seller advising the tenants of the Property of the sale of the Property to Purchaser and directing that rents and other payments thereafter be sent to Purchaser or as Purchaser may direct;

(d)   the certification of non-foreign status as provided in Treas. Reg. 1.1445-2(b)(2)(iii)(B) or in any other form as may be required by the Internal Revenue Code or the regulations issued thereunder;

(e)   the affidavits and instruments required pursuant to Section 4(g) above;

(f)   a statement certifying that all of the representations and warranties of Seller contained in Section 6 of this Agreement shall be true and correct as of Closing with the same force and effect as if such representations and warranties had been made on and as of such date;

(g)   the Tenant Estoppel Letters required pursuant to Section 9 above;

(h)   an SNDA from the tenant under each Lease, as required pursuant to Section 9 above

(i)   a notice to tenants under all Leases in form and substance acceptable to Purchaser (informing the tenants of the sale of the Property and the change of address to which rents or other notices should be sent), executed by Seller;

(j)   all keys with respect to the Property and other documentation in Seller's custody or control relating to the physical condition and operation of the Property; and

(k)   any other documents required by this Agreement to be delivered by Seller or otherwise reasonably necessary to consummate the Closing.

11.   Purchaser's Performance. At Closing, simultaneously with the deliveries of Seller pursuant to the provisions of Section 10 above, Purchaser shall pay to Seller the Purchase Price in the manner specified in Section 2, whereupon the Deposit, and any interest accrued thereon, shall be returned to Purchaser by Escrow Agent or, at the option of Purchaser, shall be applied against the payment of the Purchase Price.

12.   Settlement Charges; Prorations and Adjustments.

(a)   Purchaser shall pay all costs and expenses related to its purchase of the Property including, without limitation, recording fees and taxes, title charges, surveys, its legal fees, notary fees and other such charges incident to Closing, except that Seller shall pay (i) the [Grantor Tax/ transfer tax] imposed as a prerequisite to recording the deed, (ii) the legal fees of Seller's counsel, and (iii) all costs and expenses incurred by Seller in performing its obligations hereunder.

(b)   The following adjustments and prorations shall be made at Closing with Purchaser having the benefits and burdens of ownership for the day of Closing:

(i)   Taxes. Real estate and personal property taxes shall be adjusted as of the Closing Date.

(ii)   Rent and Security Deposits. Rent for the month of, and any month after, Closing collected by Seller prior to Closing shall be adjusted as of the Closing Date. If any tenant is in arrears in the payment of rent on the Closing Date, rents received from such tenant after the Closing shall be applied in the following order of priority: (a) first, to the payment of current rent then due to Purchaser, (b) second, to delinquent rent for any period after the Closing Date; and (c) third, to delinquent rent for any period prior to the Closing Date. Purchaser shall use reasonable efforts to collect arrearages in rents due from tenants as of the Closing Date. Seller may pursue such arrearages but cannot evict any tenant. If rents or any portion thereof received by Seller or Purchaser after the Closing Date are payable to the other party by reason of this allocation, the appropriate sum, less a proportionate share of any reasonable attorneys' fees, costs and expenses of collection thereof, shall be promptly paid to the other party, which obligation shall survive the Closing.

If any tenant of the Property is obligated to pay percentage rent based upon the calendar year or lease year in which the Closing Date occurs (the "Percentage Rent Year"), Purchaser shall, within thirty (30) days after receipt of such payment with respect to the Percentage Rent Year, remit to Seller that portion which is equal to the number of days which elapse between the commencement date of the Percentage Rent Year for each such tenant and the Closing Date, and the total number of days in such Percentage Rent Year. If Seller has received payments of percentage rent based on any Percentage Rent Year in which the Closing Date occurs in excess of Seller's share as calculated as set forth above in this Section 12(b)(ii), Seller shall promptly pay such excess to Purchaser. Notwithstanding any other provision hereof, the obligations of the parties under this Section 12(b)(ii) shall survive until the date which is three (3)

10

(continued)

months after the last date on which any such percentage rent is paid with respect to such Percentage Rent Year.

(iii)   Miscellaneous. All other charges and fees customarily prorated and adjusted in similar transactions, including utilities and other liabilities incurred in the ordinary course of business to be assumed by Purchaser, shall be adjusted and prorated as of the Closing Date. In the event that accurate prorations and other adjustments cannot be made at Closing because current bills are not obtainable or the amount to be adjusted is not yet ascertainable (as, for example, in the case of utility bills), the parties shall prorate, on the best available information, subject to further adjustment promptly upon receipt of the final bill or upon completion of final computations. Seller shall cause all utility meters read on the Closing Date so as to accurately determine its share of current utility bills.

13.   Risk of Loss. The risk of loss or damage to the Property by fire or other casualty prior to Closing shall be borne by Seller. If, prior to Closing, (i) condemnation proceedings are commenced against all or any material portion of the Property, or (ii) the Property is damaged by fire or other casualty to the extent that (A) the cost of repairing such damage shall be an amount which equals ten percent (10%) of the Purchase Price or more or (B) such damage shall entitle **[IDENTIFY MAJOR TENANTS OR %, OF OTHER TENANTS ENTITLED TO TERMINATE]** to terminate such lease(s), then Purchaser shall have the right upon written notice to Seller, given within thirty (30) days after notice of such condemnation or fire or other casualty, to terminate this Agreement, whereupon the parties shall be released and discharged from any further obligations to each other, and the Deposit shall be refunded to Purchaser. If Purchaser does not elect to terminate this Agreement, or in the event of fire or other casualty or condemnation not giving rise to a right to terminate this Agreement, Purchaser shall be entitled to an assignment of Seller's share of the fire or other casualty insurance proceeds (in which event Seller shall pay to Purchaser any amount for which Purchaser would not be fully compensated by such casualty insurance proceeds, including, without limitation, as the result of the amount of any deductible, co-insurance or self-insurance) or the condemnation award, as the case may be, and Seller shall have no obligation to repair or restore the Property. Notwithstanding the foregoing, Purchaser hereby acknowledges and agrees that Seller shall be entitled to retain any condemnation award in connection with that certain.

14.   Inspection of Property and Feasibility Period

(a)   Delivery of Property Documents. Seller shall deliver to Purchaser within two (2) business days of the Acceptance Date copies of all Property Documents, to the extent such Property Documents are in the possession or control of Seller's or Seller's asset manager for the Property (except that Seller shall not be obligated to deliver the Property Documents described in Section 14(b)(i) below, but shall make such documents available to Purchaser for inspection and photocopying at the Property, at the offices of Seller, or at the offices of Seller's asset manager for the Property) .

(b)   Description of Property Documents. The Property Documents consist of the following items:

(i)   All leases for the Property, including all amendments thereto, listings of reimbursements due from tenants, tenant sales reports, listings of security deposits, a rent roll (containing a list of all current charges for each tenant, including minimum base rent, CAM, real estate taxes, any merchants association fees and insurance), tenant ledgers and any letters of intent;

(ii)   The latest survey of the Property showing all improvements, rights of way, easements, dedications and similar matters;

(iii)   A site plan for the Property;

(iv)   Certificates of insurance for all casualty, liability and other insurance policies currently in effect with respect to the Property;

(v)   Statements of income and expense of the Property, together with detailed statements of payables and receivables (for each tenant), for calendar years [2008 and 2009], and monthly statements of income (including a general ledger) and expense for the Property for the months of January [2010] through [_____ 2010] (the Operating Statements");

(vi)   Bills for real estate affecting the Property for the preceding two (2) full tax years;

(vii)   Copies of all Contracts;

(viii) The most recent owner's title insurance policy issued in connection with the Property and all amendments, endorsements and exhibits thereto, including copies of all easements, rights of way or cross-easements relating to the Property;

(ix)   Engineering, architectural, physical inspection, maintenance, geological and environmental reports related to the Property, including those relating to the presence (or absence) of Hazardous Materials;

(x)   Warranties and guarantees related to the Property which are currently in effect;

(xi)   Copies of the actual utility bills for all utilities serving the Property for the twelve (12) months prior to the date hereof; and

(xii)   Any other documents or information reasonably requested by Purchaser.

(c)   Purchaser's Right of Inspection. Purchaser shall have the right, at its own risk, cost and expense, at any time or times prior to Closing or earlier termination of this Agreement, to enter, or cause its agents or representatives to enter, upon the Property for the purpose of

(continued)

making surveys, investigations and/or studies relating to the Property, during reasonable hours and upon reasonable prior notice to Seller. Purchaser's entry shall be subject to the rights of all tenants of the Property, and Purchaser shall not interfere with the business being conducted by the tenants. Purchaser also shall have reasonable access to all documentation, agreements and other information in the possession of Seller or its asset manager related to the ownership, use and operation construction, occupancy, maintenance or leasing of the Property to the extent that Seller is not required to deliver items pursuant to Sections 14(a) and (b) above and Purchaser shall have the right, at Purchaser's cost, to inspect, review and make copies of such documentation. Purchaser shall carry liability insurance covering personal injury which may result from Purchaser's entry onto the Property. Purchaser shall restore any damage to the Property caused by Purchaser's entry onto the Property to substantially the same condition that existed prior to such entry. Purchaser shall be liable for all damage to real or personal property or injuries to persons caused by Purchaser's actions in inspecting the Property and shall indemnify and hold Seller harmless from any claims related thereto. Purchaser shall not perform any subsurface or other "intrusive" testing on the Property without Seller's prior written consent.

(d)   Feasibility Period. In the event that Purchaser, in its sole discretion, determines that Purchaser's plans for the Property would not be feasible for any reason, then Purchaser shall have the right, at its sole election on or before the expiration of thirty (30) days after the Acceptance Date (the "Feasibility Period"), to terminate this Agreement by giving written notice thereof to Seller prior to the expiration of the Feasibility Period, in which event the Deposit shall be returned to Purchaser and neither party shall have any further liabilities or obligations to the other, except for Purchaser's indemnity and other obligations pursuant to Section 14(c).

15.   Brokerage Commission. Seller and Purchaser represent and warrant to each other that no brokerage fee or real estate commission is or shall be due or owing in connection with this transaction to any broker or other party other than _____ ("Broker"), which Broker Seller has retained pursuant to a separate agreement. Seller and Purchaser hereby indemnify and hold the other harmless from any and all claims of any broker or agent other than Broker so claiming based on action or alleged action of the other. The provisions of this Section 15 shall survive Closing or any termination of this Agreement.

16.   Default Provisions; Remedies.

(a)   Purchaser's Default. If Purchaser fails to consummate the purchase and sale contemplated herein when required to do so pursuant to the provisions hereof, then the Escrow Agent shall deliver the Deposit and all interest thereon to Seller as full and complete liquidated damages, and as the exclusive and sole right and remedy of Seller at law or in equity whereupon this Agreement shall terminate and neither party shall have any further obligations or liabilities to any other party.

(b)   Seller's Default. Except for any breaches waived in writing by Purchaser, if Seller breaches any of its covenants or obligations under this Agreement, which breach shall continue for five (5) business days after receipt by Seller of written notice from Purchaser of such breach, or has failed or refused to consummate the purchase and sale contemplated herein by the Closing Date, then Purchaser shall be entitled to (i) waive such breach or default and proceed to Closing, (ii) pursue specific performance of this Agreement, or (iii) terminate this

13

Agreement, obtain the return of the Deposit, and receive from the Seller reimbursement for the Purchaser's out-of-pocket expenses in connection with its due diligence of the Property, including, without limitation, obtaining the Title Commitment and the Survey; provided, however, that in no event shall such damages exceed _____ and 00/100 Dollars ($_____).

(c)   Attorneys' Fees. In the event that any litigation shall arise between the parties hereto as to the subject matter hereof, the prevailing party in such litigation shall be entitled to recover from the non-prevailing party all of its court costs and reasonable attorneys' fees.

17.   Indemnification.

(a)   By Seller. If Closing occurs, Seller agrees to indemnify, hold harmless and defend Purchaser from and against:

(i)   all debts, liabilities and obligations arising from business done, transactions entered into or other events occurring on or before the Closing Date with respect to the ownership, management, operation, maintenance and repair of the Property, other than the debts, liabilities and obligations which are being adjusted between Seller and Purchaser pursuant to this Agreement;

(ii)   any loss, liability or damage suffered or incurred by Purchaser arising out of or resulting from injury or death to individuals or damage to property sustained on the Property on or before the Closing and caused by the willful or negligent act or omission (where applicable law imposes a duty to act) of Seller;

(iii)   any loss, liability or damage suffered or incurred by Purchaser because any representation or warranty made by Seller in this Agreement, or in any document furnished to Purchaser in connection with the Closing, is false or misleading in any material respect;

(iv)   any loss, liability or damage suffered or incurred by Purchaser because of the non-fulfillment of any covenant or agreement on the part of Seller under this Agreement; and

(v)   all reasonable costs and expenses (including reasonable attorneys' fees) incurred by Purchaser in connection with any action, suit, proceeding, demand, assessment or judgment incident to any of the matters indemnified against in this Section.

(b)   By Purchaser. If Closing occurs, Purchaser agrees to indemnify, hold harmless and defend Seller from and against:

(i)   all debts, liabilities and obligations arising from business done, transactions entered into or other events occurring after the Closing with respect to the ownership, management, operation, maintenance and repair of the Property, other than the debts, liabilities and obligations which are being adjusted between Seller and Purchaser pursuant to this Agreement;

(ii)   any loss, liability or damage suffered or incurred by Seller arising out of or resulting from injury or death to individuals or damage to property sustained on the Property

14

(continued)

after the Closing and caused by the willful or negligent act or omission (where applicable law imposes a duty to act) of Purchaser;

(iii)   any loss, liability or damage suffered or incurred by Seller because any representation or warranty made by Purchaser in this Agreement, or in any document furnished to Seller in connection with the Closing, shall be false or misleading in any material respect;

(iv)   any loss, liability or damage suffered or incurred by Seller because of the non-fulfillment of any covenant or agreement on the part of Purchaser under this Agreement; and

(v)   all reasonable costs and expenses (including reasonable attorneys' fees) incurred by Seller in connection with any action, suit, proceeding, demand, assessment or judgment incident to any of the matters indemnified against in this Section.

(c)   The indemnification obligations of the parties pursuant this Section 17 shall survive Closing for a period of twelve (12) months.

18.   Miscellaneous Provisions.

(a)   Completeness and Modification. This Agreement represents the complete understanding between the parties hereto with respect to the transactions contemplated herein and supersedes all prior discussions, understandings or agreements between the parties. This Agreement shall not be modified or amended except by an instrument in writing signed by both of the parties hereto.

(b)   Binding Effect. This Agreement shall be binding upon and inure to the benefit of the parties hereto and their respective heirs, executors, administrators, personal and legal representatives, successors and assigns.

(c)   Assignment. This Agreement shall not be assignable by Purchaser without the prior written consent of Seller other than to an entity owned and controlled by Purchaser.

(d)   Waiver; Modification. Failure by either party to insist upon or enforce any of its rights hereto shall not constitute a waiver or modification thereof.

(e)   Governing Law. This Agreement shall be governed by and construed under the laws of the [Commonwealth of Virginia].

(f)   Headings. The headings are herein used for convenience or reference only and shall not be deemed to vary the content of this Agreement or the covenants, agreements, representations and warranties herein set forth or the scope of any provision hereof.

(g)   Counterparts. This Agreement may be executed in counterparts and all counterparts shall collectively constitute a single agreement.

(h)   Notices. All notices, requests, consents and other communications hereunder shall be in writing and shall be delivered by hand or mailed by first-class, registered or certified mail, return receipt requested, postage prepaid or delivered by commercial courier or facsimile or overnight courier (e.g., Federal Express) against receipt to the addresses indicated below:

(i)   if to Purchaser:

_____
_____
_____
_____

Telephone: _____
Telecopy: _____

With a copy to:

_____
_____
_____
_____

Telephone: _____
Telecopy: _____

(ii)   if to Seller:

_____
_____
_____

Telephone: _____
Telecopy: _____

(i)   <u>Business Days</u>. A "business day" shall be Mondays through Fridays, less and excepting all legal holidays observed by the United States Government or the Government of the [Commonwealth of Virginia]. Any date specified in this Agreement which does not fall on a business day shall be automatically extended until the first business day after such date.

(j)   <u>Confidentiality</u>. Purchaser agrees and acknowledges that the information provided to it by Seller regarding the Property is confidential and that it will not disclose such information to any third parties, except (A) to its employees, agents, attorneys, accountants, lenders and other consultants or other parties that need to know such information in order for Purchaser to evaluate the transaction contemplated herein, in which case Purchaser shall require that such third parties keep such information confidential, (B) pursuant to compulsion by due process of law, (C) in connection with the resolution of any dispute between Purchaser and Seller, or (D) if such information was obtained or is otherwise available in the public domain or from other sources.

(k)   <u>Time of Essence</u>. Time is of the essence as to all dates contained in this Agreement and as to the performance of all covenants, agreements and obligations hereunder.

[INSERT JURISDICTION-SPECIFIC PROVISIONS AS NECESSARY]

16

(continued)

      IN WITNESS WHEREOF, the parties hereto have executed this Agreement as of the day and year first written above.

PURCHASER:

_____, a _____ limited liability company

By: _____

     _____

Date of execution: _____, [2010]

SELLER:

_____, a _____limited liability company

By: _____(SEAL)
Name: _____
Title: _____

Date of execution: _____, [2010]

ACKNOWLEDGEMENT BY ESCROW AGENT

The undersigned Escrow Agent executes this Real Estate Purchase Agreement solely to acknowledge receipt of the Deposit pursuant to Section 3 hereof and to evidence its agreement to serve as escrow agent pursuant to the terms of the foregoing Agreement.

_____

By:_____
Name:
Title:

Date:_____, [2010]

18

(continued)

LIST OF EXHIBITS

EXHIBIT A   Legal Description of Property

EXHIBIT B   Leases and Rent Schedule

EXHIBIT C   Listing of Contracts

EXHIBIT D   Form of Tenant Estoppel

EXHIBIT E   Form of SNDA

EXHIBIT A

<u>Legal Description of Property</u>

(continued)

EXHIBIT B

Leases and Rent Schedule

EXHIBIT C

Listing of Contracts

DOC3#260562-v1

(continued)

<u>EXHIBIT D</u>

<u>Form of Tenant Estoppel</u>

_____ ("Tenant") certifies to _____, its lender, and each of their successors and assigns, as follows:

1.	The undersigned is the Tenant under the Lease dated_____ (the "Lease"), executed by _____ ("Landlord") as Landlord and the undersigned as Tenant, covering a portion of the property known as _____, located in _____, [Virginia] (the "Property").

2.	Pursuant to the Lease, Tenant has leased approximately _____ square feet of space at the Property, designated as _____ (the "Premises"). The term of the Lease commenced on _____ and the expiration date of the Lease is _____.

3.	The current fixed annual rent payable under the Lease is $_____, and percentage rent at _____ percent (____%) of _____. The rentals due and payable under the Lease commenced to accrue on _____. Tenant has paid rent under the Lease through _____. The next monthly fixed rental payment in the amount of $_____ is due on _____. The next [monthly] percentage rent payment is due on __ _____. Tenant's last percentage rent payment was in the amount of _____ _____. Tenant is also required to pay _____ percent (___%) of all annual operating expenses, taxes, and insurance for the Property. No rent or other charges under the Lease have been paid more than thirty (30) days in advance of their due date. All rentals due under the Lease are currently paid to Landlord.

4.	Tenant has paid to Landlord a security deposit of $_____ in the form of [circle one: cash or an irrevocable letter of credit] which continues to be held by Landlord.

5.	Tenant is not entitled to the use of any reserved or exclusive parking spaces at the Property.

6.	The Lease provides for ____ option(s) to extend the term of the Lease for _____ years each. The number of such options which have not been exercised by Tenant and which remain available for exercise under the Lease is _____. The rental rate for each such remaining extension term is as follows: _____. Except as expressly provided in paragraph __ of the Lease, Tenant does not have any claim to or interest in the premises demised pursuant to the Lease, legal or equitable, including, without limitation, any right or option to renew or extend the term of the Lease, to lease other space at the Property, or to purchase all or any part of the Premises or the Property, whether by option or right of first refusal.

7.	True, correct and complete copies of the Lease, including all amendments, modifications and supplements, are attached to this Certificate. The Lease, as so amended, modified and supplemented, is in full force and effect and represents the entire agreement between Tenant and Landlord with respect to the Premises and the Property and there are no other amendments, modifications or supplements to the Lease, whether oral or written. The

DOC3#260562-v1

amendments, modifications or supplements to the Lease attached to this Certificate are as follows (include the date of such amendment, modification or supplement:

_____

_____

_____.

8.   All space and improvements leased by Tenant have been completed and furnished in accordance with the provisions of the Lease and Landlord has complied with all obligations on its part with respect to constructing, fixturing and equipping same. Tenant has accepted and taken possession of the Premises and currently occupies the Premises. Tenant has not assigned, transferred or encumbered the Lease or any interest therein or subleased all or any portion of the Premises.

9.   The Lease is in full force and effect and Tenant neither has nor asserts any claim of offset, defense or counterclaim to the payment of rent and other charges payable under the Lease and asserts no claim against Landlord in regard to any obligations of Landlord relating to the Premises or the Property. Neither Landlord nor Tenant is in default in the performance of any of the terms and provisions of the Lease nor has there occurred any event which, with notice, lapse of time, or both, would constitute such a default.

10.   There are no credits against rentals payable under the Lease and no free rent periods or rental concessions remain outstanding for Tenant.

11.   Tenant has no knowledge of the presence of, or the processing, use, storage, disposal, release or treatment of, any hazardous or toxic materials or substances upon, within, or beneath the Premises or the Property, other than the storage and use of small amounts of cleaning solvents and like substances customarily used in the operation and maintenance of properties similar to the Property.

12.   Tenant has no knowledge of a prior assignment, hypothecation or pledge or rents or the Lease.

13.   There are no actions, either voluntary or involuntary, pending against the undersigned under the bankruptcy laws of the United Sates, or under the bankruptcy laws of any state.

This Certificate is given to _____ (" "), its lender, and each of their successors and assigns, with the understanding that _____ or its designee will rely on it in connection with the purchase of the Property and that _____'s lender will rely upon this certificate in making a loan to_____. Following conveyance of the Property to_____, Tenant agrees that the Lease shall remain in full force and effect and shall bind and inure to the benefit of_____, its lender, and each of their successors and assigns as if all of them were named as Landlord in the Lease.

DATED: _____, [2010].
TENANT: _____

                          By:_____
                          Name:_____
                          Title:_____

[ATTACH LEASE AND ALL LEASE AMENDMENTS TO THIS CERTIFICATE]

(continued)

EXHIBIT E

Form of SNDA

ATTORNMENT, SUBORDINATION AND NON-DISTURBANCE AGREEMENT

　　　　THIS AGREEMENT made this _____ day of _____, [2010], by and among:

LENDER: _____
　　　　　　 _____
　　　　　　 _____

LESSEE: _____
　　　　　　 _____
　　　　　　 _____

and

OWNER: _____
　　　　　　 _____
　　　　　　 _____

　　　　WHEREAS:

　　　　(1)　　_____ (the "Owner") is the owner of the property described in Exhibit A attached hereto and incorporated herein by reference (the "Property");

　　　　(2)　　_____ (the "Lender") has made a loan (the "Loan") to Owner, and such Loan is secured by a Mortgage and Security Agreement on the Property (as amended from time to time, the "Mortgage");

　　　　(3)　　By Lease dated _____ (the "Lease"), the Owner, as Lessor, is leasing to _____ (the "Lessee") a portion of the Property or the improvements located thereon (the "Leased Premises") for a term of _____ (____) years [with _____ (___) option(s) to extend said lease term for additional periods of _____ (___) year(s) each so that the total or aggregate number of possible lease years under said Lease is a total of _____ (___) years], at the rental and upon the terms and conditions set forth in said Lease;

　　　　(4)　　Lender desires to assure the Lessee possession of the Leased Premises upon the terms and conditions set forth in the Lease for the entire original term and any optional renewal term therein provided without regard to any default under the terms of the Mortgage;

　　　　(5)　　Lessee desires to assure Lender that the Lessee will attorn to the Lender under the circumstances set forth in this Agreement and under the Lease;

(6)   Lender desires to assure Lessee that its possession of the Leased Premises and rights under the Lease will not be disturbed so long as Lessee is not in default under the Lease or the terms of this Agreement;

(7)   Lessee has agreed to subordinate the Lease and its interest therein to the Mortgage.

NOW, THEREFORE, in consideration of _____ and No/100 Dollars ($_____) in hand paid by each of the parties herein to the other, of other good and valuable consideration, and of the mutual promises contained herein, the receipt and sufficiency of which is hereby acknowledged by each of the parties, the Lender, Lessee and Owner covenant and agree as follows:

1.   <u>**SUBORDINATION**</u>. Anything to the contrary in the Lease notwithstanding, the Lease, and all rights of Lessee thereunder, are and shall be subject and subordinate in all respects to the Mortgage, to each and every advance made or hereafter to be made under the Mortgage, and to all renewals, modifications, consolidations, replacements and extensions of the Mortgage. Notwithstanding any provisions of the Lease to the contrary, and for so long as the Mortgage and any modification or extensions thereof shall remain unsatisfied, the Mortgage, the Lease and the rights of the Lessee under the Lease shall be superior to any subsequent financing or other encumbrances with a party other than Lender, its successors or assigns, with respect to the Leased Premises, and Lessee and Owner agree that each will not at any time prior to satisfaction of the Mortgage voluntarily subordinate the Lease to any mortgage or encumbrance to a party other than Lender, its successors or assigns, respecting the Leased Premises which is junior in priority to the Mortgage.

2.   <u>**RIGHT OF LENDER TO CURE DEFAULTS**</u>. If any default shall occur under the Lease on the part of the Owner, which would give Lessee the right (or under which Lessee might claim the right) to cancel or terminate the Lease, Lessee shall promptly give notice thereof to Lender, and Lender shall have thirty (30) days from the date of such notice to cure any such default, or if such default is not reasonably capable of being cured in such period of time, Lender shall have the right within such time to commence remedying such default and shall proceed diligently to complete the same. In the event any such default is so cured, the Lease shall not be deemed to be in default, and Lessee's duties thereunder shall continue unabated. Nothing herein shall be deemed to be a duty on the part of Lender to cure any such default, but only a right on its behalf.

3.   <u>**LESSEE TO ATTORN TO LENDER**</u>.

(a)   In the event that the Lender shall succeed to the interest of Owner under such Lease, the Lease shall continue with the same force and effect as if the Lender, as Lessor, and the Lessee had entered into a Lease for a term equal to the then unexpired term of the Lease, containing the same terms, conditions and covenants as those contained in the Lease, including, but not limited to, any rights of renewal therein, and the Lessee shall be bound to the Lender under all of the provisions of the Lease for the remaining term thereof with the same force and effect as if the Lender were the Lessor under the Lease, and the Lessee hereby attorns and agrees to attorn to the Lender as its landlord, such attornment to be effective and self-operative without the execution

(continued)

of any further instruments on the part of either of the parties hereto immediately upon the succession of Lender to the interest of Owner under the Lease. The Lessee shall be under no obligation to pay rent to the Lender until the Lessee receives written notice from the Lender that an event of default under any of the loan documents relating to the Loan has occurred, or that it has succeeded to the interest of the Owner under the Lease. The Owner and Lessee agree that, upon receiving such notice from Lender, Lessee shall pay all rents directly to Lender without any duty to inquire as to the validity of such notice and without any liability therefor to Owner. Nothing contained herein shall in any manner limit or restrict the right of Lender to have a receiver appointed or to seek any other appropriate relief or remedy under any one or more of the loan documents relating to the Loan. The respective rights and obligations of the Lessee and the Lender upon such attornment and their relationship shall be as tenant and landlord respectively, for the remaining term of the Lease, including any renewal periods set forth in said Lease;

(b)   Lessee agrees that it shall not, without the express consent of Lender, prepay any minimum rental under the Lease to Owner in excess of one (1) month's advance minimum rental; and

(c)   In the event that the Lender shall succeed to the interest of the Owner under the Lease, the Lender agrees to be bound to the Lessee under all of the terms, covenants and conditions of the Lease; provided, however, that Lender shall not be:

  (i)   liable for any act or omission of any prior landlord (including the Owner); or

  (ii)   subject to any offsets which the Lessee might have or thereafter have against any prior landlord (including the Owner); or

  (iii)   bound by any prepayment of more than one (1) month's minimum rental under the Lease to any prior landlord (including the Owner); or

  (iv)   bound by an amendment, modification or surrender of the Lease made without its consent.

4.   LENDER'S RIGHT TO PROCEED AGAINST LESSEE. In the event the Lender shall succeed to the interest of the Owner under the Lease, the Lender will have the same remedies by entry, action or otherwise for the nonperformance of any agreement contained in the Lease, for the recovery of rent, for the doing of any waste or for any other default, as Owner had or would have had if the succession not taken place, and this right shall exist whether or not the Lease is formally terminated; in any such action, Lessee waives the necessity of Owner being made a party to such proceeding.

5.   NON-DISTURBANCE PROVISIONS. In the event the Mortgage shall be foreclosed, or in the event Lender otherwise succeeds to the interest of the Owner under the Lease, and provided that Lessee is not then in default under the Lease, the Lease shall not terminate on account of such foreclosure or other such succession, by operation of law or otherwise, so long as the Lessee continues to pay the rents reserved in the Lease and otherwise does not become in default under the Lease.

6. **LENDER'S APPROVAL OR CONSENT**. Wherever Lender's consent or approval under the Lease is required, Lender agrees to not unreasonably withhold such consent, and it is understood and agreed that Lender shall not be deemed to have unreasonably withheld such consent or approval, wherein Lender's reasonable discretion to give such approval or consent would reduce the value, decrease the size or impair the structural integrity of the Leased Premises and/or the Property or otherwise impair the security granted under the Mortgage.

7. **OWNER'S AND LESSEE'S CERTIFICATION**. Owner and Lessee hereby confirm and certify to Lender the following:

(a) That the Lease is in full force and effect and has not been modified, altered or amended and constitutes a complete statement of the agreement between Owner and Lessee with respect to the leasing of the Leased Premises.

(b) That, as of the date hereof, Lessee has no charge, lien or claim of offset or credit against rentals or other charges coming due under the Lease, nor have rentals been prepaid except as expressly provided by the terms of the Lease.

(c) That Lessee has been notified that the Lease has been or will be assigned to Lender as security for the Loan, and Lessee has no notice of a prior assignment, hypothecation or pledge of rents or the Lease.

(d) That there are no actions, either voluntary or involuntary, pending against the Lessee under the bankruptcy laws of the United States, or under the bankruptcy laws of any state.

(e) That to the knowledge of Owner and Lessee, no party to the Lease is in default thereunder.

(f) That all rentals due or coming due under the Lease are currently paid or due to be paid to the Owner.

(g) That this certification is made with the knowledge that Lender is relying on this certification in making the Loan to the Owner.

8. **SURVIVAL**. This instrument shall survive any foreclosure of the Leased Premises, or any other succession by Lender to the interest of the Owner with respect to the Leased Premises, and shall remain in full force and effect until the end of the Lease term and all exercised optional extension periods, or until satisfaction of the Mortgage and all renewals, modifications, consolidations, replacements, and extensions of the Mortgage, whichever shall first occur.

(continued)

9.   **LIMITATION OF LENDER'S LIABILITY**. Lessee shall look solely to the Property for recovery of any judgment or damages from Lender, its successors and assigns, and neither Lender nor its successors or assigns shall have any personal liability, directly or indirectly, under or in connection with the Lease or this Agreement or any amendment or amendments to either thereof made at any time or times, heretofore or hereafter, and Lessee hereby forever and irrevocably waives and releases any and all such personal liability. The limitation of liability provided in this paragraph is in addition to, and not in limitation of, any limitation on liability applicable to Lender, its successors and assigns, provided by law or by any other contract, agreement or instrument.

10.   **APPROVALS**. The Owner has joined in this Agreement for the purpose of expressing its consent and agreement to be bound by the provisions hereof.

11.   **NOTICES**. All notices or demands hereunder shall be sufficient if sent by United States registered or certified mail, postage prepaid, addressed as follows:

If to Lender: _____
                      _____
                      _____

If to Lessee: _____
                      _____
                      _____

If to Owner: _____
                      _____
                      _____

or such other address as any party may hereafter designate in writing to the other.

12.   **BINDING EFFECT**. This Agreement and all of the covenants, terms, conditions and obligations herein contained are covenants running with the land (the Property and the Leased Premises) and binding thereon and shall be binding upon and shall inure to the benefit of the parties hereto and their respective successors and assigns and successors in title to the Leased Premises and successors in title to the Property.

IN WITNESS WHEREOF, the parties hereto have caused this Attornment, Subordination and Non-Disturbance Agreement to be executed effective on the day and year first above written.

LENDER:

WITNESS:

_____

_____

By:_____
Its:_____

LESSEE:

WITNESS:

_____

_____

By:_____
Its:_____

OWNER:

WITNESS:

_____

_____

By:_____
Its:_____

STATE OF _____)
COUNTY OF _____)

    I, the undersigned, a Notary Public in and for said County in said State, hereby certify that _____, whose name as _____ of _____ , an _____, is signed to the foregoing instrument, and who is known to me, acknowledged before me on this day that, being informed of the contents of said instrument, he, as such officer and with full authority, executed the same voluntarily for and as the act of said _____.

    Given under my hand and official seal, this the _____ day of _____, 20___.

    (SEAL)

_____
Notary Public
My Commission Expires:_____

STATE OF _____)
COUNTY OF _____)

(continued)

I, the undersigned, a Notary Public in and for said County in said State, hereby certify that _____, whose name as _____ of _____, a _____, is signed to the foregoing instrument, and who is known to me, acknowledged before me on this day that, being informed of the contents of said instrument, he, as such _____ and with full authority, executed the same voluntarily for and as the act of said _____.

Given under my hand and official seal, this the _____ day of _____, 20___.

(SEAL)

_____
Notary Public
My Commission Expires:_____

STATE OF _____)
COUNTY OF _____)

I, the undersigned, a Notary Public in and for said County in said State, hereby certify that _____, whose name as _____ of _____, a _____ _____, is signed to the foregoing instrument, and who is known to me, acknowledged before me on this day that, being informed of the contents of said instrument, he, as such _____ and with full authority, executed the same voluntarily for and as the act of said _____.

Given under my hand and official seal, this the _____ day of _____, 20___.

(SEAL)

_____
Notary Public
My Commission Expires:_____

Due Diligence

After you have made a determination of the property you want to invest in and have an agreement on the purchase price, you have the duty to perform an adequate due diligence investigation prior to legally binding the partnership to acquire the property.

A proper due diligence investigation will make you aware of all material facts that can affect the value of the property before and after the acquisition is completed. It will also alert you to the limitations of the asset that you are recommending to your investment partners.

As the general partner and developer, your focus should be to add value by changing the tenant mix of the property to produce a larger income stream and eventually dispose of the property at a much greater selling price than you were able to acquire and redevelop it.

If you can expand your leasable area, so much the better. This will add income-producing tenants in gross building area where none existed. Moreover, rental income translates to higher asset value. The due diligence process can help you determine whether the planned changes through the redevelopment can be accomplished in a cost-effective manner.

The process generally includes creating a checklist to help you answer key questions that will verify the current characteristics represented in the selling prospectus, such as the reliability of the income as well as the potential to grow the income.

Key questions about the property that due diligence can uncover will define exactly what you are buying in terms of land, building, improvements, whether parking is sufficient, the soundness of the structure, environmental problems, entitlement rights, development rights, air rights (in the event you later want to add an office or apartment building), zoning changes or restrictions and other important characteristics.

Due diligence will also identify additional costs you may incur, such as real estate tax assessment contesting, drainage and land corrections, encroachment issues with adjacent property owners, liens and uncured violations of zoning laws or code violations.

Having the property properly inspected by a qualified consultant who performs a property condition assessment (PCA) in accordance with ASTM E 2018 guidelines can help save you money in the long run, and perhaps give you leverage to lower the selling price of the property. ASTM International, formerly known as the American Society for Testing and Materials (ASTM), is a century-old not-for-profit organization that sets U.S. best practices guidelines for conducting a baseline PCA of the improvements located on a parcel of commercial real estate.

The first step involves a walk-through survey whereby an inspector identifies physical deficiencies. The inspector seeks to uncover conspicuous defects or material-deferred maintenance of the shopping center's material systems and components equipment, excluding deficiencies that may be remedied with routine maintenance or by making minor repairs.

The ASTM E 2018 guidelines also call for document reviews, performing research and conducting interviews to augment the walk-through inspection. These actions assist in preparing a comprehensive property condition report (PCR) that includes opinions of probable costs for suggested remedies of the physical deficiencies.

As part of your retail real estate due diligence, checking the leases carefully against the rent roll is crucial. This should cover security deposits, CAM and property tax escrows, tenant options to extend their term at below market rents, maintenance and utilities obligations, and uncollectable delinquent rent accrued as owed, to name a few.

As tedious as the process might be, leases need to be analyzed carefully for such landlord encumbrances as tenant exclusives that prevent you from seeking more productive retailers; lease language that gives existing tenants subordination to a future mortgage, which might not be acceptable to your lender; and lots more.

As the buyer, it will be necessary for you to review the estoppel certificates or estoppel letters that the seller will send to tenants to limit the risk that the property is subject to tenant lease default. These letters request that the tenant you will inherit with the closing of the purchase verifies the terms of their relationship with the current property owner and/or manager.

Your attorney will help draft the estoppel letter that requires the tenant to confirm such things as the term of the lease, the condition of the leased premises, any breach of the lease and any options to renew or extend the lease. Refer back to Exhibit D on page 336.

The terms of rent payment and any adjustment to the rent that the landlord might have agreed to aside from what is stated in the lease, the amount the seller is holding as security deposit and any assignment rights or subletting are also typical provisions of the estoppels.

Most important, the estoppels ascertain from the tenant if the landlord has fulfilled all its obligations. If not, as the new landlord you could face unforeseen liability after you have completed the sale.

Following is the typical checklist I have developed to use as guidance for my due diligence.

Figure 12.3   Due Diligence Checklist

DUE DILIGENCE CHECK LIST

1 Third Party Reports

1.1 Building Condition Survey - LandAmerica {IXIS}

1.2 Phase I Environmental - LandAmerica {IXIS}

1.3 Phase II Enviornmental

1.4 Appraisal

1.4.1 Document List

    Recent Tax Bills

    BOMA Chart

    Lease Abstracts & Actual Leases

    Current Rent Roll

    Leasing Broker Contract

    Pending Lease Data (Signed Leases/LOI)

    Income/Expense Data 2003 to 2006 (YTD & Budget)

    Easement Information

    Argus Model

    Sales & Expense Comps

    TI Expenses (recent leases) & TI Projections

    Environmental Report

    Engineering Report

2 Title work

2.1 Title Report

2.2 ALTA Survey

2.2.1 Title Report - Title company

(continued)

2.2.2 Lender's Survey Requirements

3 Lender

3.1 Document List

3.1.1 Title Insurance

3.1.2 ALTA/ACSM Survey

3.1.3 UCC/litigation/tax/judgment/lien searches

3.1.4 Insurance (fire, hazard, rent loss, business interruption, liability, flood/earthquake)

3.1.5 Opinions of Borrower's counsel

3.1.6 Engineering Report with estimate of any deferred maintenance items

3.1.7 Environmental Report showing no toxic or hazardous waste on the Property

3.1.8 Appraisal showing sufficient value to satisfy LTV requirement

3.1.9 Acceptable property manager, management agreement and manager consent

3.1.10 Site inspection

3.1.11 Tenant estoppels and SNDA from all tenants required by Lender

3.1.12 Ground Lessor recognition agreement & any Lease Amendment

3.1.13 Certificate of Occupancy

3.1.14 Certified Rent Roll for the Property

3.1.15 Evidence of separate tax parcel for the Property

3.1.16 Evidence of utility service and adequate parking (if applicable) for the Property

3.1.17 All permits, licenses and contracts with respect to the Property

3.1.18 All leases and other material agreements with respect to the Property

3.1.19 Credit Report, lien and public records searches on Borrower and all key principals

4 Leasing

4.1 Information on pending deals

4.2 Latest Demographic Information

5 Property Management

5.1 Insurance Review (Early Cassidy)

5.2 CAM Analysis

5.3 Mock Yearly Expense Budget

5.4 Tenant Utility Analysis (i.e. are tenants submetered)

5.5 Trash Analysis

5.6 Real Estate Tax Analysis (PES) {SFA}

6 Construction

6.1 Roof Analysis

6.2 Paving Analysis

6.3 Lighting Analysis

7 Lease Administration

7.1 Abstract Leases

7.1.1 Exclusives

7.1.2 Restrictions

7.1.3 Kick-outs

7.1.4 Co-tenancy

7.1.5 No Build Outs

7.1.6 Security Deposits

7.2 Review Estopples

7.3 Review Receivables

7.4 Tenant Correspondence Files Review

7.4.1 Anything peculiar

7.4.2 Past due notices, default letters, etc

7.4.3 Letters, memos abating rent

(continued)

7.4.4 Ensure we have all amendments, letter agreements, etc.

7.5 Review Tenant Reimbursables

7.5.1 CAM Pools

7.5.2 Look for irregularities

7.5.3 Major tenants

8 Financial Analysis

8.1 Argus

8.1.1 Review Seller's Argus

8.1.2 CAM Reconciliation

8.1.3 Prepare New Reconciliation

8.2 Investor Packages

9 Accounting

9.1 Register Legal Entity

9.2 Set up Bank Account

9.3 Obtain Quote for Cost Segregation

9.4 Create CenterSoft Entity

10 Seller's Deliverables

10.1 Tenant Leases

10.1.1 Tenant Profiles / Abstracts

10.1.2 Correspondence Files

10.2 Architectural Plans

10.3 Civil Plans

10.4 Environmental Reports

10.5 Accounting

10.5.1 Reconciliation

10.5.2 Operating Statements (past 3 years and year to date)

10.5.3 Accounts Receivable

    Current

    Prior 12 Months

    Pending Litigation

10.5.4 Tenant Ledgers

    Summary of Billing YTD and Prior Year

    Cash Receipts YTD and Prior Year

10.5.5 Rent Roll

    Minimum Rent

    CAM

    R/E Taxes

    Merchant Association

    Insurance

    Other

10.5.6 Reimbursements (All files on)

    CAM

    R/E Taxes

    Insurance

    Note when billings are done and when last Recon was completed

10.5.7 Utility Books / Records

10.5.8 Real Estate Tax Assessment and Invoices

10.5.9 Insurance Coverage and Invoices

10.5.10 List of Security Deposits

10.5.11 Sales Reports for the last five years

(continued)

Investor Letters/Correspondence

On page 355 is a typical investor letter I use to keep my partners informed about the progress of the asset over the previous year and what I budgeted for the coming year. In this example, I am reporting the operations on a cash basis rather than accrual to reflect the property's unique financial situation while undergoing a repositioning and adding a major tenant. This helps to reflect the true cash flow and explains the distribution that accompanies my letter.

Depending on the property's situation, I may keep accounting records on a cash, accrual or modified (cash/accrual) basis to reflect the true picture of the investment. I find that my partners are most interested in the leasing efforts that will create the most impact on the investment.

Partnership Operating Agreement for an LLC

The LLC document governs your obligations as the sponsor and the obligations of your investors, the LLC members, who make up the investor group. As with other legal entities, forming an LLC is a relatively easy procedure that your lawyer can help you accomplish by filing articles of organization or a certificate of formation. The operating agreement among the members governs the entity and as such must be worded clearly to avoid disputes that may arise from ambiguity. A sample table of contents of an LLC agreement appears on page 358, in Figure 12.5. Its purpose is to describe the key provisions in the LLC documents that I use for my retail properties.

Property Management, Development and Leasing Agreement

The TRC standard property management agreement provides for the shopping center ownership entity to employ TRC as the property manager to manage, lease, re-lease, market and maintain the property for a term that renews automatically.

My management company acts as property manager for all of the properties that we own; thus, my company receives the 4 percent of the gross operating revenue monthly plus various other fees for services we render. Figure 12.6 on page 359 shows a table of contents that describes our management agreements.

Figure 12.4 Investor Sample Letter

January XX, XXXX

Ms. Jane A. Smith

111 Main Street

City, Street 10000-1000

Re: XYZ SHOPPING CENTER RETAIL, LLC

XYZ Shopping Center

City, State

BUDGET YEAR ENDING 12/31/10
SUMMARY OF PARTNERSHIP OPERATIONS

FOR THE TWELVE MONTHS ENDING DECEMBER XX, XXXX

Dear Jane:

This letter is a review of the statement of operations for the twelve months ending December XX, XXXX, for XYZ Shopping Center. The statement of operations is prepared on the cash basis of accounting without audit and shows quarterly as well as year-to-date information compared to the budgeted information.

FINANCIAL

According to the budget for the twelve months ending December XX, XXXX, the Partnership expected to have revenue after debt service and before shopping center and tenant improvements of $_____. As you can see from the enclosed statement of operations, our net revenue after debt service and before shopping center and tenant improvements was $_____ or $_____ more than budgeted. This positive balance is the result of the following:

*[*** A paragraph or two is written explaining major budget variances as to income and expense categories.***]*

LEASING UPDATE

Enclosed for your review and information are a tenant locator chart, leasing plan and leasing status report for XYZ Shopping Center prepared for the fourth quarter of XXXX.

(continued)

Ms. Jane A. Smith

January XX, XXXX
Page 2

I am happy to report the vacancy at XYZ Shopping Center has decreased from last quarter's
_____ square feet or _____% to _____ square feet or _____% of the center as this past quarter
we have leased space to _____, a Rotisserie Chicken restaurant, in Space A1 (1,118 SF),
_____ in Space L-1A (920 SF), and most importantly _____ in 23,460 sf of Space
U4 (part of the former _____ space).

We are very excited about _____, as this high-end _____ store will enable us to
upgrade the entire tenant mix of the upper level of XYZ over the next several years.

In regards to existing tenants, _____ in Space L5/6/7 is now converted to month-to-
month operating under a license agreement to give us flexibility to control the space. Our other
month-to-month tenants (_____, _____ and _____) are content to remain at
the center on a month-to-month basis. Once we open the _____ store, we will work with
these tenants to sign long-term leases that reflect market rents at the time.

As noted in our earlier letter and reflected in the shopping center expenses mentioned above, we
recently closed on a loan with _____ Bank. These monies will be used for a renovation of
the shopping center and will tie into the opening of the _____ by year end.

ACCOUNTS RECEIVABLE

Our total accounts receivable has again been reduced from last quarter's amount. However, half
of this quarter's amount relates to a former tenant that is no longer operating in the shopping
center. We are pleased to report that our current tenant, _____ in Space B (7,200 sf),
has successfully reduced the rental amount that had been past due. Our accounts receivable
remaining outstanding presently is_____ .

MARKETING AND PROMOTIONS

Enclosed for your information is a copy of a recent newspaper article from the *Washington
Suburbs Times Dispatch* about one of our newest tenants at the shopping center. As you can see
from the article, this tenant has extremely loyal customers in the market who are looking forward
to this store opening in our shopping center.

With regards to our latest promotion at the shopping center, enclosed is a memorandum sent to
all merchants about a minor league baseball game between the Washington Suburbs Cannons
and Maryland Suburbs Hillcats. Also enclosed is a sheet of direct mail merchant coupons, which
were mailed out to homeowners in the neighboring subdivisions in the area.

Ms. Jane A. Smith

January XX, XXXX
Page 3

2011 BUDGET

Enclosed for your review is the budgeted statement of operations (cash basis) for the twelve months ending December XX, XXXX, projecting net revenues after debt service and before shopping center and tenant improvements. Please note that we are including monies that might be needed for future leasing commissions and tenant improvements once the _____ store opens.

At this time we expect to continue in 2011 our regular distribution and look forward to possibly increasing our distributions in 2012.

PARTNERSHIP DISTRIBUTIONS

Enclosed is your Partnership distribution.

Please feel free to call me at any time if you have any questions.

Sincerely,

John Doe

General Partner

XYZ SHOPPING CENTER RETAIL, LLC

By: XYZ SHOPPING CENTER ASSOCIATES LIMITED PARTNERSHIP

Figure 12.5 Limited Liability Company Sample Agreement, Table of Contents

LIMITED LIABILITY COMPANY AGREEMENT
OF
CAMERON CHASE HOLDINGS, LLC

TABLE OF CONTENTS

Exhibit A   Members; Percentages
Exhibit B   Allocation of Profit and Loss
Exhibit C   Property Management and Leasing Agreement

Figure 12.6 Sample Property Management and Leasing Agreement

PROPERTY MANAGEMENT AND LEASING AGREEMENT
Table of Contents

Standard Nonanchor Retail Lease

A lease agreement is a document between a tenant and a landlord outlining each other's obligations and responsibilities. In retail properties, the lease is as important as any other form of real estate. It is a legal and binding contract between the landlord or owner and the tenant.

A typical retail lease contains basic lease provisions, such as information about the tenant and shopping center, permitted use of the lease premises, rental fees including minimum, percentage and extra rent for reimbursing the landlord's cost to maintain the center, insure the center and pay property taxes. Lease provisions also cover many other areas that are important to a landlord and tenant, such as assignment, defaults, mortgagee's approval and holding over. Figure 12.7, pages 361–362, depicts a standard TRC lease table of contents between the landlord and small shop tenant.

Construction, Operating and Reciprocal Easement Agreement (COREA)

When more than one entity, such as department store or supermarket anchors (Walmart or Giant Food supermarket, for example), and you as the shopping center landlord own adjacent properties, and the various properties are integrated within the shopping center, an agreement is needed to establish the responsibilities of the various owners. This agreement is called a construction, operations and reciprocal easement agreement (COREA).

The agreement may or may not include construction, although it usually includes elements of operation. When construction is a part of the agreement, the document is commonly known as a COREA. However, many professionals simply call this agreement a reciprocal easement agreement (REA), whether or not construction and operations are a part of the agreement. Therefore, the name is interchangeable, but technically, COREA is not the correct term when the REA excludes any elements of operation or construction, such as an agreement to allow vehicular access between two retail properties.

In a community center, curb cuts between adjacent shopping centers' parking lots for motorists to go from one center to the other, without having to exit into the roads, are the most common in REA language. However, stores, restaurants and gasoline stations located in outparcels as well

Figure 12.7 Sample Nonanchor Lease

TABLE OF CONTENTS
TO
SHOPPING CENTER LEASE

C:\Users\sfa\AppData\Local\Microsoft\Windows\Temporary Internet Files\Content. Outlook\RZOGKPDH\Rappaport Base Lease 2010.doc

(continued)

as those that are adjoining the center and anchors often appear to be a part of the center, but are not owned by your partnership. These types of businesses are also frequently found in REAs for community centers.

When the developer leases to a major retailer, an REA is not necessary because the lease provides for each party's responsibilities regarding construction and operation of the store and the shopping center. Without an REA, the developer, the anchor retailer or the other adjacent property owner could build whatever they wish and create disturbances to the others at any time. Any property owner could prevent the other party from using its parcel for parking or access.

The REA contract benefits all parties by outlining each party's rights and obligations. All parties to the agreement, such as the developer and multiple retailers, should sign the REA. It may also include more property owners that want to jointly develop and operate their adjacent properties.

The REA between a developer and one or more retailers typically deals

Figure 12.8 Sample Construction Operating Reciprocal Easement Agreement (COREA)

CONSTRUCTION OPERATING RECIPROCAL EASEMENT AGREEMENT (COREA)
Table of Contents

Parties

Preliminary Statement

Definitions

Article 1—Grant of Easements

Article 2—Construction Obligations

Article 3—Maintenance and Operations

Article 4—Covenants and Restrictions

Article 5—Casualty and Eminent Domain and Insurance

Article 6—Terms

Article 7—Default/Remedies

Article 8—Effect of Instrument

Article 9—Notices

Article 10—Miscellaneous

with operation and maintenance of common areas; easements (on a non-exclusive basis) and curb cuts for access, parking, encroachments, utilities, construction and architectural compatibility, building insurance, use, recapture rights and rights of first offer, land covenants and protection for the lenders. See Figure 12.8 above.

Some REAs will include an operating covenant stating that each party must stay open for a number of years. REAs might include operating hours when one or more anchor retailer is open for business.

The REA functions somewhat like a lease, but will not contain all the provisions found in a lease. It is, nevertheless, the most heavily negotiated document between the developer and anchor retailers that own their parcels adjacent to and seemingly a part of the developer's property.

To ensure the success of all parties to the COREA, the agreement is intended to ensure that the developer's property and major retailers operate their properties as one integrated shopping center.

Retail Real Estate Investing

The Business of Retail Property

WHETHER YOU ARE considering starting your own retail development company, investing in retail real estate partnerships or already involved in the business and simply want to learn more, I hope I have given you a more detailed overview of the operation I run.

Developing retail takes courage, skills, knowledge and hard work. It is not easy money, but the rewards are significant both in terms of financial payback as well as career satisfaction.

There is no *one way* to do it. No *one size* fits all. The methods I have outlined in this book are my own. Some are standard in the business. Others, I have tweaked over time to fit my model and style. This model has worked for me and has handsomely rewarded my investment partners, my employees and my tenants, who profit from operating stores in my shopping centers.

If you are setting up your own operation, you may want to set it up to suit your needs, skills and type of operation you think will work best for you.

I recognize that not everybody wants to own real estate. Not everybody can be a developer, because the risk you take is why you are getting the returns you get—if you get them at all.

On numerous occasions, I have received satisfaction when one of my students says to me, "Here's a brochure I've put together . . . I purchased this property . . . I created this . . . I put this deal together. . . ." Hopefully, after reading this book, you will one day say the same thing to me.

Nonetheless, as with every learning situation, you have to do your own homework. The retail landscape is changing constantly. To succeed in it you have to be prepared to change with it. Time does not stand still, not even for a day.

What worked yesterday may not work tomorrow. If you do not have a taste for risk or tolerate change easily, maybe this is not the business for you. At least, maybe you are better served by working for someone else who has the stomach for high risks, thirst for rewards and patience to with-

Here at my desk in my McLean, Virginia, headquarters, where I still work seven days a week.

PHOTO: R. E. MILIAN

stand the time horizon that is inherent in the direct ownership of commercial real estate.

So what makes a good investment? Of course, all real estate textbooks would tell you that the property fundamentals and market fundamentals must be right. That alone does not ensure success. Sound management and expertise play a vital role. Then you must invest in making the property the most it can be while allowing the appropriate holding period to see the asset appreciate in value.

For me, there are other key factors:

1. It must be within 50 miles of downtown Washington, D.C., as this is *my market* where I know every planned major road, track every retail projection in every city, county and town in the market and know the demographics and growth in every submarket.
2. It must be retail, not residential, not office, not industrial; that is where my expertise lies.
3. It must be the type of retail that I feel comfortable with, primarily grocery-anchored shopping centers; not enclosed malls, not off-price or outlet, not unanchored lifestyle.
4. It must have good location, good visibility and good accessibility to the road network.
5. It must need new capital infusion to revitalize it and have leases with short enough terms or expansion possibilities where NOI can be increased with the proper capital investment.

It is not unusual for a grocery-anchored community center that is purchased at an attractive price, then renovated, retenanted and expanded, to appreciate to two or three times of the value when acquired, given a holding period of five to 10 years or more.

Likewise, these projects often offer cumulative noncompounded rates of returns averaging higher than 12 percent per year, at least when cash flow stabilizes after a redevelopment. From acquisition to disposition, the annualized investment returns could be even greater when considering the appreciation of the asset realized upon the sale as compared to the initial invested capital.

However, all retail properties are different and offer distinct opportunities based on their own unique situation. As such, one cannot guarantee that your retail real estate investments are going to be as lucrative as some of the examples I depicted here. For me, this business has been very rewarding, and I enjoy devoting a vast amount of my life to it.

In my career, the highs have been higher than the lows have been lower—and the 2008–2010 period was one of the low times. No matter how low things get, I believe the glass is always half full. A better day will come, and I will get by the difficult times of real estate down cycles with even more success than I had before such difficult times. I have lived my whole life with the absolute stress of a developer and I do not regret one minute of it.

I have chosen making deals as a way of life. I try to find a property. I put up the deposit. I might have a 30-day engineering study and due diligence and a deadline to close in 30 days. I am running around trying to raise the money all the time. I may be putting an investment book together even though I may not have this property under contract. Yet I am relentlessly doing all this work in search of the next deal to present to my investors.

However, investors need something tangible in order to part with their hard-earned money. I have not raised money from my investors, even after 25 years, without them seeing the deal and being able to feel comfortable with that particular deal before they will give me any money. They know I am not buying and selling; I am buying and keeping.

Some of my investors suggested I put together a small equity fund comprising "friends and family" that would give me the same returns as I have achieved in the past but more flexibility and financial strength. While I have never done such a thing, it is a provoking thought as I project into the future. It might be the next progression in my career. I guess I can write more about this if we have a second edition to this book, but for now, I will stick to what I know best.

I have been working seven days a week since I was 20. I tell my students at the ICSC University of Shopping Centers that I like to devote my waking hours to three important things in my life besides exercising.

First, and most important, is my family—nothing is more important to me than my family. Next is my business. This is not a 40-hour-a-week job. If I am not traveling, I will be in my office every day of the week including half a day on Saturdays and an hour or two on Sundays. Fortunately, my office is four miles from my house. This quiet time helps to keep me focused on my work, and I am always connected by BlackBerry.

The final third of my time is devoted to the International Council of Shopping Centers. This keeps me linked to the broader retail industry and the people in it. I have met some of my best friends through my involvement in ICSC. I have held almost every volunteer position that ICSC has to offer, from teaching to serving as chairman of this great organization's board of trustees. I am constantly sharing knowledge and learning from my peers.

It is an enormous commitment of my time and resources to travel and take part in ICSC activities, but it is rewarding for me to feel I am giving back to an industry that has been so good to me, to my employees and my family.

This brings me to the final third of my waking hours—my family. I like to spend a third of my hours—perhaps my most valuable time—with my family, most notably my wife, my five lovely daughters and my grandchildren.

Here welcoming Donald Trump to the ICSC New York Idea Exchange and Deal Making in December 2001 while serving as ICSC Eastern divisional vice president.

My daughters are 34, 31, 19, 12 and 6. My two oldest daughters have worked for me but are now both married and involved more with family than business, and I could not be happier for them.

Personal and professional time often seems to converge, but the family life helps to balance the stress of my work life. This third portion of my life dedicated to my family makes the other two thirds even more worthwhile.

Glossary

administration fee [ACCOUNTING] The cost of administering the common area of a shopping center; a standard addition to the overall cost of common area maintenance (CAM), sometimes set between 15 and 20 percent of tenant CAM contribution but may vary due to negotiation between landlord and tenant.

ALTA survey [GENERAL] A survey that is prepared to meet the standards of the American Land Title Association (ALTA) for the title company and the lender. This ALTA survey defines the land and location data needed for issuing title and mortgage insurance. This includes size, location and dimensions of the physical property and its improvements.

amortization [FINANCE/ACCOUNTING] **1:** Gradually paying off a debt by periodic installments of principal and interest, generally in equal payments at regular intervals over a specific period. **2:** The accounting deduction of capital expenses in the operating statement over a specific period of time, typically over the life of the asset or as allowed by law and generally accepted accounting principles (GAAP).

anchor parcel [DEVELOPMENT] A parcel of land occupied by a shopping center anchor store (a major store, usually part of a chain), including the building area and associated parking areas. It may be occupied pursuant to a ground lease or may be owned by the anchor store.

anchor store [RETAIL] A major department store, grocery store or other large chain store in a shopping center having substantial economic strength and occupying substantial square footage. The stores and other uses that occupy the largest spaces in a center and serve as the primary traffic generators. Anchors in a shopping center sometimes own their own land and cooperate with the shopping center owner through a reciprocal easement agreement (REA).

anchor tenant [GENERAL/LEASING] **1:** A tenant with sufficient new worth to enable financing for a project and attract other tenants to the project. **2:** A large retailer that attracts customers to its store as well the shopping center, which benefits other tenants.

appreciation [FINANCE] The increase in value of a property.

ARGUS Software [FINANCE/ACCOUNTING] A company that produces financial software for the commercial real estate industry; formerly known as Realm Business Solutions. The company's products perform valuation and projections and are frequently referred to as ARGUS runs and ARGUS projections. The most widely used product is ARGUS Valuation-DCF, a discounted cash flow (DCF) financial analysis program to forecast cash flows and value for real estate properties.

asset value [FINANCE] The relative worth of a shopping center, typically based on the net operating income (NOI) that the center generates divided by a negotiated capitalization rate. For example: $10,000,000 NOI / .09 cap rate = $111,111,111 in value.

back end [FINANCE/LEGAL] The management or development company, or the developer or managing partner.

back-end promote [FINANCE/LEGAL] The share of excess cash flow that is paid as an incentive to the managing partner/developer for increasing the value of the asset and maximizing return on investment for all equity investors after any agreed-to preferred return is distributed to the investors. Also known as *carried interest.*

bad-boy behavior [FINANCE/LEGAL] A violation or demonstration of lack of ethical practices as specified in loan documents that results in full-recourse liability to the borrower and the guarantor in a loan that provides for no personal guarantees except under bad-boy behavior occurrences, which are specified in nonrecourse carve-outs. Among them is complying with lender disclosures, maintaining a fiduciary role and proper management of the property.

base rent [ACCOUNTING/LEASING] See *minimum rent.*

capitalization (cap) rate [FINANCE] A rate of return used to derive the capital value of an income stream. The ratio of income to price, determined by such factors as the market and the quality of a property, and used along with the NOI to determine value. When two of three values are known (annual net operating income, cap rate, property value estimate), the calculations are: 1. value = NOI / cap rate; 2. NOI = value x cap rate; 3. cap rate = NOI / value. The formula is annual net operating income / value = capitalization rate. See *net operating income.*

carried interest [FINANCE] The portion of proceeds from a real estate transaction or upon refinancing that goes to the managing partner/developer after financial goals are met and the remaining proceeds are distributed to the managing partner's remaining equity investors. Typically, a partnership must return the capital given to it by limited partners plus any preferential rate of return before the managing partner can share in the excess of the targeted proceeds. Also known as *back-end promote.*

cash flow [ACCOUNTING] Sometimes referred to as funds from operations. The amount of remaining income after all payments have been made for operating and capital expenses, and mortgage principal and interest; it is a way of recognizing the timing of receipts and payments. See *funds from operations.*

CMBS [FINANCE] Commercial mortgage-backed securities. Securities collateralized by loans on commercial real estate. Yield on the combined loans is passed through to the investors, less a service charge by the issuing organization, spreading risks over many loans.

community center [GENERAL] A shopping center that typically offers a wider range of apparel and other soft goods than a smaller neighborhood center. Among the more common anchors are supermarkets, drugstores and discount department stores. Community center tenants often include value-oriented, big-box, category-dominant retailers selling such items as apparel, home improvement/furnishings, toys, electronics or sporting goods. The center is usually configured in a straight line as a strip, "L" shape or "U" shape. Of the nine most common center types, community centers encompass the widest range of formats. For example, certain centers that are anchored by a large discount department store often have a discount focus. Others with a high percentage of square footage allocated to off-price retailers can be termed off-price centers. These centers range between 100,000 and 350,000 square feet of gross leasable area encompassing 10 to 40 acres and the primary trade area is between 3 and 6 miles.

competitive advantage [MARKETING] A benefit—feature, location or concept—that will distinguish a shopping center in the mind of the consumer. A competitive advantage may be real or perceived.

compounded [FINANCE/ACCOUNTING] Generating earnings from previous earnings.

compounded interest [FINANCE/ACCOUNTING] When interest earned during a given period is added to the principal and included in the next period's interest calculation. This can be calculated monthly, quarterly, semiannually or annually.

compounded return [FINANCE/ACCOUNTING] The rate of return over a period of time expressed as a percentage, which represents the cumulative effect of a series of gains (or losses) on the capital invested. Compounding can be calculated annually, semiannually or more frequently, and each method would result in different returns for the investor group and the back-end promote. For example, compounding quarterly would result in more money going to the equity and less money to the developer as back-end promote.

construction management [CONSTRUCTION] A form of contracting. The construction manager acts as an agent for the developer or owner, taking no risk or financial responsibility for the outcome of the project, which is different from the responsibilities of a general contractor.

construction manager [CONSTRUCTION] One who supervises, coordinates and administers the work on behalf of the developer. However, all contracts are executed directly between the various trade contractors and the developer, with the construction manager signing as an agent of the owner. The construction manager might hire a general contractor or enter into multiple prime contracts with a variety of trade contractors. In either case, if there is a loss or cost overrun, the dispute is between the developer and the trade contractors, not between the developer and the construction manager.

COREA [DEVELOPMENT] A construction, operations and reciprocal easement agreement among the owners of two or more parcels of adjacent properties for the purpose of working cooperatively from the time of construction through the on-going operations phase. See also *REA.*.

cumulative unpaid return [FINANCE] **1:** The amount of the preferred return that is not distributed because of insufficient cash flow, and thus is accumulated and due until such time as it is paid, before the cash flow is shared with the back-end interest. **2:** The aggregate amount that an investment has gained (or lost) over time, expressed as a percentage.

curb cut [DEVELOPMENT] An opening on the sidewalk or planter curbs to allow motor vehicles to pass from street to parking lot or from the parking lot in one property to another property.

debt service coverage ratio (DSCR) [FINANCE] **1:** The ratio used by lenders in determining how much to lend on a retail property based on the lender's expectations that the property will generate sufficient revenue to pay its debt obligations, allowing for a margin of error. The lender typically prefers a DSCR ratio of 1.0 or greater. **2:** From a developer's point of view, the amount of cash flow available to meet annual interest and principal payments on debt after deducting other operating expenses and setting aside a reserve for future needed funds. The formula is $500,000 in net operating income / $110,000 in annual debt service = 4.55 in DSCR. See *net operating income*.

deed of trust [FINANCE/LEGAL] The legal document of a shopping center mortgage that gives the lender priority rights to foreclose and sell the property if the borrower defaults on repayment terms.

demographic study [RESEARCH] A study of socioeconomic facts—such as gender, annual household income, age and education—pertaining to individuals residing in a shopping center's trade area, used by developers to optimize tenant mix.

distressed buyer [FINANCE] A buyer of distressed property. See *distressed shopping center.*

distressed seller [FINANCE] A seller of distressed property. See *distressed shopping center.*

distressed shopping center [FINANCE/GENERAL] **1:** A shopping center that produces insufficient funds from operations to cover its debt service. **2:** A shopping center with a mortgage debt that reaches maturity and no lender is willing to refinance the existing debt regardless of debt coverage. **3:** An otherwise successful shopping center whose value has decreased because of growing vacancies, declining net operating income and rising cap rates, and holds a debt that is higher than the current market value of the property.

due diligence [GENERAL] A process involving research and analysis of a company or shopping center that a buyer conducts in preparation to purchase the asset. This process includes obtaining information about the financial, legal, physical plant and other material information that can substantiate the value of the acquisition.

equity [FINANCE/LEGAL] The net value of a property, obtained by subtracting from its total value all liens and other charges against it. The term is frequently applied to the value of the owner's (as opposed to the lender's) interest in the property after deducting all claims and liens. The owner's interest in an income-producing property after all obligations are met; analogous to the difference between the value of the shopping center asset and the balance of the debt.

estoppel certificate [LEGAL] A status report that confirms a lease's effectiveness and terms, as well as the absence of claims against it. These are general obligations under the lease and may be required if the center is seeking financing or is being sold.

foreclosure [FINANCE/LEGAL] The process by which the holder of a mortgage seizes the assets of a property owner who has defaulted in making timely interest and/or principal payments as stipulated in the mortgage contract. Usually, the security interest a lender obtains from a borrower in a mortgage includes the property itself, which the lender tries to repossess in foreclosure.

front end [FINANCE/LEGAL] The investment group. See also *back end.*

front-end interest [FINANCE/ACCOUNTING] The portion of cash flow that is paid out to the equity investors, after all fees, expenses, loan payments and working reserves are deducted from revenues, but before any bonus or promote is paid to the developer/managing partner.

funds from operations (FFO) [FINANCE] A measurement favored by real estate investment trusts (REITs) that approximates the cash-generating power of a company. It appears in an operating statement below the net operating income (NOI). FFO is intended to highlight the amount of cash generated by a company's real estate portfolio relative to its total operating cash flow. It consists of net income, excluding gains (or losses) from debt restructuring and sales of property, plus depreciation and amortization after adjustments for unconsolidated partnerships and joint ventures.

GAAP [ACCOUNTING] (U.S.) An acronym for generally accepted accounting principles; an authoritative set of rules, adopted by the accounting profession, that dictates the way a business reports its financial condition and performance.

generally accepted accounting principles [ACCOUNTING] See *GAAP.*

GLA [GENERAL] See *gross leasable area.*

grocery-anchored center [GENERAL] An open-air neighborhood center or community center, frequently ranging between 100,000 and 150,000 square feet of gross leasable area (GLA), where the main tenant is a grocery store and other tenants tend to be convenience- or service-oriented.

gross leasable area (GLA) [GENERAL] **1:** Normally the total area on which a shopping center leases to tenants or is available for lease. The GLA includes all selling space as well as storage and other miscellaneous space. **2:** The square footage of a shopping center that can generate income by being leased to tenants. This figure does not include the area occupied by department stores or anchor users if such anchors own their own site and the area is not leased from the shopping center. **3:** The measurement used to define how much space a tenant has leased and has available to in a center. Leasable area is typically determined by measuring the distance between the middle walls of a space and the distance between the front outside wall to back outside wall. **4:** The total floor area designed for tenant occupancy and exclusive use, including basements, mezzanines and upper floors. It is measured from the center line of joint partitions and from outside wall faces.

institutional investor [FINANCE/GENERAL] An investment institution such as an investment bank, insurance company, retirement or pension fund, endowment fund, hedge fund or mutual fund that pools large sums of money from many sources to invest on behalf of their investment clients.

interest rate [FINANCE] The return stipulated by a lender when making a loan. For real estate loans, interest rates are usually fixed, which means they are a set rate that does not change over the life of the loan. Some loans are floating rate, which means the interest rate is based on some relationship to a benchmark such as the prime rate, the preferred lending rate set by U.S. commercial banks relative to the federal funds rate (U.S.) or Libor (the London Interbank Offering Rate).

internal rate of return (IRR) [FINANCE] A discount rate at which the present value (PV) of projected cash flow exactly equals the initial investment. This discounted cash flow technique is used to determine the single effective rate of return that equates capital outlays and cash flows to a present value of zero.

inventory turnover [RETAIL] A ratio measuring the adequacy and efficiency of the inventory balance, calculated by dividing the annual volume of goods sold by the amount of the monthly average inventory ($1,000,000 in annual retail sales / $250,000 in monthly average inventory at retail = four turns a year). Also known as *stock turn*.

keystone markup [RETAIL] A 50 percent markup (expressed as a percentage of the selling price at full retail). Also, a markup that is double the retailer's cost.

lease plan [LEASING] A detailed plan showing the size and configuration of each space located within the shopping center. Each space is typically numbered for quick identification. Not to be confused with leasing plan and leasing merchandising plan, which relate to the landlord's tenant mix strategy.

Libor [FINANCE] London Interbank Offered Rate. A daily reference rate based on the interest rates at which many worldwide banks borrow unsecured funds from other banks in the London wholesale money market. Loans pegged to Libor rates provide the basis for some of the world's most liquid and active interest-rate markets. Also known as LIBOR. Libor rate cannot be adjusted to control inflation by action of the U.S. Federal Reserve Board's Federal Open Market Committee in the way the federal funds rate is controlled.

lifestyle center [GENERAL] Most often located near affluent residential neighborhoods; this center type caters to the retail needs and "lifestyle" pursuits of consumers in its trading area. It has an open-air configuration and typically includes at least 50,000 square feet of retail space occupied by upscale national chain specialty stores. Other elements, such as restaurants, entertainment venues, and design amenities such as fountains and backyard furniture conducive to relaxation and casual browsing, help make the lifestyle center serve as a multipurpose leisure-time destination, These centers may or may not be anchored by one or more conventional or fashion specialty department stores. Lifestyle centers typically range between 150,000 and 500,000 square feet of gross leasable area encompassing 10 to 40 acres, and the primary trade area is 8 to 12 miles.

limited liability corporation (LLC) [LEGAL/FINANCE] (U.S.) A business that is a combination of a corporation and a partnership, receiving protection from personal liabilities beyond the initial investment. The LLC is popular among real estate investors because of its inherent flexibility to combine a single level of taxation with limited liability. Internal Revenue Service (IRS) provisions allow LLCs to choose whether to be taxed as partnerships with pass-through taxation or as corporations.

loan-to-cost ratio (LTC) [FINANCE] A ratio used to compare the amount of the loan used to finance a project to the cost to build the project (including land acquisition, construction materials, construction labor, professional fees, permits and predevelopment entitlement costs).

loan-to-value (LTV) ratio [FINANCE] **1:** Expressed as a formula, the loan amount divided by the property value. **2:** A ratio used at any point in time to determine the outstanding loan balance as a percentage of the property's current value.

management company [GENERAL] The firm that organizes, manages and administers a shopping center or a group of shopping centers. Functions include providing or subcontracting maintenance services, communicating with tenants and collecting rent.

management fee [ACCOUNTING/GENERAL] The fee charged to the ownership entity by the fee manager or the management company in managing a property for typical management services such as rent collection, administration, common area maintenance (CAM) and tenant relations activities. The fee can be a flat fee or a percentage of gross receipts. Not to be confused with administrative fee. See *administrative fee.*

managing partner [LEGAL] The equity partner responsible to the equity group for managing the active day-to-day operations of the asset and requirements of the legal entity, such as legal filings and filing tax returns. The developer is usually the managing partner and may take risk by personally guaranteeing debt. Also known as the general partner and sponsor. In a limited partnership, one of the partners will be the general partner who assumes unlimited liability and other partners, who will have limited liability.

market rent [LEASING/FINANCE] **1:** Properly, a gross rental amount based on sales potential of various types of retailers that together can do the optimum business in a particular center if it were properly leased by merchandise categories, and as compared to the total occupancy cost each retailer is able to pay and still make a profit. **2:** The rate at which retail space would be leased if offered in a current competitive market based on similar sales and performance; sometimes used interchangeably with *budgeted rent* or *appraisal rent.* This is other than what is necessary to produce a desired return on investment or to cover development costs.

market research [RESEARCH] **1:** The initial and ongoing studies needed to make development, leasing and marketing decisions. **2:** A survey conducted for the developer before commitment to build (feasibility study market research) and on a recurring basis (ongoing market research) for marketing and leasing purposes. **3:** Studies and reports that define demographics and psychographics of the market or the customer profile. Shopper intercept, telephone and Web-based surveys, focus group interviews and examination of secondary data such as census information are examples of market research.

market value [FINANCE] The expected selling price of a shopping center if a reasonable time is allowed to find a purchaser and if both seller and prospective buyer are fully informed and willing to enter into a fair transaction. Connotes what a property is actually worth, and is typically defined in nondistressed income producing properties by dividing the anticipated net operating income for the first full year following the transaction by the market capitalization rate.

marketing fund [ACCOUNTING/MARKETING] A lease-required charge as additional rent that is paid by the tenant to the landlord for the purpose of marketing the center.

merchant builder [DEVELOPMENT] A developer whose primary motive is to build and rent a property, and then try to sell it immediately for a profit. Many of these developers seek short-term revenue gains and cost reductions to inflate NOI and obtain the optimum sale price when disposing of their assets.

minimum rent [ACCOUNTING/LEASING/GENERAL] The base rent a tenant pays; often expressed as an amount per square foot per year. Similar to additional rent, which typically includes recoveries such as common area maintenance, real estate taxes and insurance, this portion of rent does not fluctuate depending on the tenant's sales performance. See *percentage rent.* The specific amount paid by a tenant annually for the amount of square footage leased. The basic rent that a tenant will pay the landlord each year in twelve equal, consecutive installments based on an amount of rent per square foot; also called *base rent* and *fixed minimum rent.*

net operating income (NOI) [FINANCE/ACCOUNTING] The income after deducting from gross income the operating expenses (including property taxes, insurance, utilities, management fees, heating and cooling expenses, repairs and maintenance, general and administrative), but before deducting principal and interest expense, corporate taxes and depreciation.

noncompounded interest [FINANCE/ACCOUNTING] A situation in which there is no payment of interest on past accrued interest.

nonrecourse carve-outs [FINANCE/LEGAL] A loan provision usually found in permanent financing of income-producing real estate in which the general partner is not required to sign a personal guarantee to repay the debt in case the ownership entity is unable to pay the monthly debt service or unable to pay back the loan in full when it is due. Most nonrecourse loans include exceptions or "carve-outs" within the loan document that result in full-recourse liability to the borrower and the guarantor when certain "bad-boy behaviors" exist. See *bad-boy behavior.*

occupancy cost [ACCOUNTING/LEASING/RETAIL] The sum of a tenant's fixed rent, percentage rent and additional rent. Also called *tenancy cost, total rent* and *gross rent.*

occupancy cost ratio [ACCOUNTING/LEASING/RETAIL] A comparison of a retailer's annual occupancy costs (including base and percentage rent, real estate taxes, common area maintenance [CAM], building insurance and marketing/promotion fund) to its annual sales volume, expressed as a percentage of occupancy costs to sales. Also known as *gross rent as a percentage of sales.*

open-air center [GENERAL] One or more rows of stores and/or service providers managed as a unit, with on-site parking usually located in front of the stores with common areas that are not enclosed. Open canopies may connect the storefronts, but an open-air center does not have enclosed walkways linking the stores. The most common variations of this configuration are linear, L-shaped, U-shaped, Z-shaped or cluster. The linear form is often used in neighborhood and community centers. The cluster form and its variations lend themselves to other center types such as the lifestyle center, in which the physical layout stresses the unusual character of the center. Historically, the open-air configuration has been referred to as a "strip center," even though the strip center got its name from the linear form, where stores sit side-by-side in a long and narrow row.

operating expenses [FINANCE/ACCOUNTING] **1:** Building maintenance and repair; advertising and promotion; real estate taxes; insurance; general administrative expenses of the shopping center, most of which are billed to the tenants. **2:** Monies needed to operate a business, as distinct from outlays to finance the business.

pari passu (pro rata) [LEGAL/FINANCE] In which one share of equity has the same rights and privileges as another share of equity.

parking ratio [DEVELOPMENT] The number of automobile parking spaces made available per 1,000 square feet of gross leasable area (GLA) or total retail area including nonleased anchors. In parts of the world where total retail area is measured in meters, it is the number of parking spaces made available per 100 square meters of total retail area. This ratio is the standard comparison used to indicate the relationship between the number of parking spaces and the GLA.

percentage rent [ACCOUNTING/LEASING/GENERAL] **1:** A percentage of the tenant's total annual sales paid in addition to fixed minimum rent. This additional rent is normally paid after a predetermined sales level has been achieved. The percentage factor is then applied to all sales over the agreed sales threshold (break point). Developers in shopping centers customarily charge minimum rent plus a percentage rent when sales exceed a certain volume. Percentage rent is a function of sales activity. A tenant's sales during a lease year are multiplied by the percentage rent rate(s); any excess over the minimum rent is percentage rent. Extra rent paid to a landlord if a tenant's sales figures exceed a prearranged figure. The percentage rent attributed to sales that exceed the break point (overage sales) is also called *overage rent.* **2:** The payment by a tenant as rent of a specified percentage of the gross income from sales transacted within the premises. Some rents are structured exclusively as percentage rent without minimum rent or break point provisions.

power center [GENERAL] A center dominated by mostly large anchors, including discount department stores, off-price stores, warehouse clubs or "category killers," i.e., stores that offer a vast selection in related merchandise categories at very competitive retail prices. The center typically consists of several anchors, some of which may be freestanding (unconnected), and only a minimum amount of small specialty tenants. These centers range between 250,000 and 600,000 square feet in gross leasable area (GLA) encompassing 10 to 50 acres, and the primary trade area is between 5 and 10 miles.

preferred return (pref) [FINANCE] The prearranged percentage of investment (i.e., 8 percent) that gets paid to investor partners before the back-end interest gets a share.

principal amortization [FINANCE] The process of paying down the principal debt borrowed on a commercial loan through regular payments, which decreases the borrower's debt while increasing the borrower's equity in the asset.

private placement [LEGAL/FINANCE] The sale of securities or interest in a property to a small group of investors (generally 35 or fewer) that is exempt from U.S. Securities and Exchange Commission (SEC) registration requirements. The investors execute an investment letter stating that the securities are being purchased for investment without a view toward distribution. A private (non-public) placement, also known as an initial private offering, involves the issuance and sale of equity ownership in a shopping center to an investor to procure financing and raise capital.

private placement memorandum (PPM) [LEGAL/FINANCE] A detailed document resembling a prospectus whereby the primary purpose is to give the developer the opportunity to present all potential risks to the prospective investor. The PPM typically outlines the terms of the investment and resembles a business plan, allowing a company the ability to raise capital through the sale of equity or debt. It must comply with the SEC's Regulation D.

pro forma [FINANCE] The multiyear projection of annual income and expenses for a new or redeveloped center. A pro forma can include various scenarios of development to compare financial impact of developments, including types of anchors, scope of work and timing.

pro rata [FINANCE] **1:** In proportion to, i.e., when costs, proceeds or profits are divided among participants according to ownership or some other factor. A percentage share allotment. [ACCOUNTING] **2:** A proportionate share of payments usually derived by dividing the tenant's square footage (nominator) by the gross leasable area (denominator) to determine the multiplier, i.e., CAM.

promote [FINANCE] **1:** The developer's share, bonus or incentive payment. Also known as back-end interest, back-end promote and carried interest. [GENERAL] **2:** Elevating an employee's position in an organization. [MARKETING] **3:** Publicizing or advertising a shopping center or retail store.

REA [development] See *reciprocal easement agreement* and *COREA.*

reciprocal easement agreement (REA) [DEVELOPMENT] An agreement among the owners of two or more parcels of property granting one another reciprocal rights to the use of their respective parcels for such things as parking, access and signage. In most shopping centers, the anchor stores have significant input and control over the rights and obligations granted or restricted under an REA, which could include items ranging from the use of land to development and design controls, such as permitted parking ratios. An REA in place may be recorded in the public land records. Curb cuts are typical easement agreements in small centers where adjacent property owners permit vehicular traffic to cross between their respective properties.

REIT [FINANCE/LEGAL] An acronym for a real estate investment trust. A form of ownership of shopping centers and other properties that complies with tax pass-through requirements in various countries. A business trust or corporation that combines the capital of many investors to acquire or provide financing for real estate. Under U.S. law, a corporation that qualifies for REIT status is not required to pay corporate income tax if it distributes 90 percent of its taxable income to shareholders. The law was intended to allow small investors to acquire and hold real estate as an investment. However, a private REIT can also function under the REIT status providing its limited shareholders with pass-through taxation benefits.

return after preferred return [FINANCE] If cash flow exceeds the preferred return, the remaining cash flow is often distributed to the back end. See *preferred return.*

sales per square foot [ACCOUNTING/LEASING/RESEARCH] Total annual sales divided by the total number of square feet of leasable area.

securitization [FINANCE] The process of converting an illiquid asset, i.e., a mortgage loan, into a tradable form, such as commercial mortgage-backed securities (CMBS), to distribute risk by aggregating assets in a pool, then issuing new securities backed by the assets and their cash flows. Investors purchase these securities and share the risk and reward from those assets.

specialty store [RETAIL/LEASING] A store that carries a limited number of merchandise categories and provides a high level of service. Not to be confused with "specialty leasing" and "specialty retailing," which connote short-term occupancy.

strip center [GENERAL] A shopping center that consists of an attached row of at least three stores, managed as a coherent retail entity with on-site parking in front of the stores. Gross leasable area for the center must be at least 10,000 square feet. Open canopies may connect the storefronts, but a strip center does not have enclosed walkways or malls linking the stores. These centers may be configured in a straight line or have an "L" or "U" shape. Typically, these centers have a straight line of stores with parking in front and a service lane in the rear. The anchor store, commonly a supermarket in small strip centers, is placed either at one end or in the center of the strip. A strip center is usually a small neighborhood center, and the terms have come to be used interchangeably, although a strip may also be a large center.

sweat equity [GENERAL] A developer's equity position in a property without contributing cash to the equity; derived exclusively from the efforts a developer employs to increase the value of the property as agreed to by the developer's equity partners.

title insurance [INSURANCE/RISK MANAGEMENT] Insurance purchased by the purchaser of a property that protects the purchaser and the lender against any losses incurred due to any defects in the title as a result of improper title search, such as unreported liens.

underwriting [FINANCE] An investment banking firm acting as underwriter sells securities from the issuing corporation to the public. A group of firms may form a syndicate to pool the risk and assure successful distribution of the issue. There are two types of underwriting arrangements: best efforts and firm commitment. With best efforts, the underwriters have the option to buy and authority to sell securities or, if unsuccessful, may cancel the issue and forgo any fees. This arrangement is more common with speculative securities and with new companies. With a firm commitment, the underwriters purchase outright the securities being offered by the issuer.

vanilla box [LEASING/CONSTRUCTION] A space for lease that is partially completed by the landlord based on negotiations between tenant and landlord. Although every landlord's definition is different, a vanilla box normally means heating, ventilation and air-conditioning (HVAC), walls, floors, stockroom wall, basic electrical work, basic plumbing work, rear door and storefront.

waterfall return [FINANCE] An instance in which the incentive sharing agreement is calculated based on the returns that are paid out to the equity investors. This arrangement is not generally set up for individual investor deals, but occasionally for institutional deals where the return is compounded and is calculated as an internal rate of return. The bonus to the developer becomes greater based on his performance.

zoning [DEVELOPMENT] Government regulations that control land use for the common health, safety, community standards and welfare of the populace.

zoning variance [DEVELOPMENT] Special permission for adaptive reuse of a building that is not permitted under zoning regulations and requires application for a change in zoning, which typically involves a public process for approval.

About the Author

Gary D. Rappaport is President and Chief Executive Officer of The Rappaport Companies, a retail real estate company he founded in 1984. The Rappaport Companies provides leasing, tenant representation, management and development services for approximately 13 million square feet, one million of which is planned development in 2012 and 2013.

The Rappaport Companies' portfolio includes more than 45 shopping centers and ground-floor retail in some 100 mixed-use properties, both residential and office, located primarily throughout the mid-Atlantic region. Mr. Rappaport is principal partner for approximately 5 million square feet of the shopping centers managed by The Rappaport Companies.

Mr. Rappaport began his career in real estate as president of Par Construction Corporation, a home-building company responsible for the construction of several hundred single-family homes and townhouses. Later, he was president and chief operating officer of Combined Properties, a shopping center development, management and leasing company headquartered in Washington, D.C.

A former chairman of ICSC, Mr. Rappaport is the only chairman to date to earn all four ICSC designations, Certified Shopping Center Manager (CSM), Certified Marketing Director (CMD), Certified Leasing Specialist (CLS) and Certified Development, Design and Construction Professional (CDP).

He is a member of the ICSC Board of Trustees and serves on ICSC's Audit, Nominating, Government Relations, Long Range Planning and PAC committees.

Mr. Rappaport currently serves on the Washington, D.C., Economic Partnership board, and was named to the 2008 Power 50 most influential people in Washington commercial real estate by Real Estate Bisnow.

He is a prior dean and a perennial instructor at the ICSC University of Shopping Centers and a past Entrepreneur in Residence at the Wharton School of the University of Pennsylvania. Mr. Rappaport continues to lobby for ICSC at the state and federal government levels on many issues important to the shopping center industry.